AF607994

CONSEQUENTIAL ART

Comics Culture in Contemporary Spain

Consequential Art

Comics Culture in Contemporary Spain

Edited by
SAMUEL AMAGO AND MATTHEW J. MARR

UNIVERSITY OF TORONTO PRESS
Toronto Buffalo London

Toronto Buffalo London
utorontopress.com

ISBN 978-1-4875-0503-5

Toronto Iberic

Library and Archives Canada Cataloguing in Publication

Title: Consequential art : comics culture in contemporary Spain / edited by Samuel Amago and Matthew J. Marr.
Names: Amago, Samuel, 1974–, editor. | Marr, Matthew J., editor.
Series: Toronto Iberic.
Description: Series statement: Toronto Iberic | Includes bibliographical references and index.
Identifiers: Canadiana 20190084073 | ISBN 9781487505035 (hardcover)
Subjects: LCSH: Comic books, strips, etc. – Spain – History and criticism. | LCSH: Comic books, strips, etc. – Social aspects – Spain.
Classification: LCC PN6775 .C66 2019 | DDC 741.5/946 – dc23

This book has been published with the assistance of the University of North Carolina at Chapel Hill, the Pennsylvania State University, and the University of Virginia.

University of Toronto Press acknowledges the financial assistance to its publishing program of the Canada Council for the Arts and the Ontario Arts Council, an agency of the Government of Ontario.

Canada Council for the Arts
Conseil des Arts du Canada

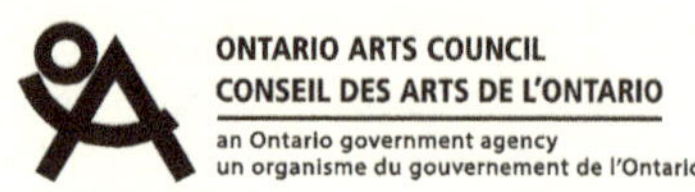

Funded by the Government of Canada
Financé par le gouvernement du Canada

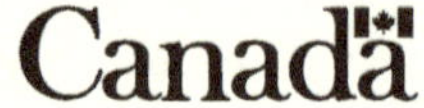

Contents

Figures

Acknowledgments

The idea for this book on contemporary Spanish comics came at a 2015 conference banquet. Now that it has finally come together, the editors wish to extend their thanks to the individuals and institutions that have made its publication possible. We are grateful, first and foremost, to the authors whose insightful and timely scholarship form the core of the book, just as we are sincerely indebted to the talented ensemble of comics practitioners whose creative work has provided occasion for a project of this kind. Anonymous peer readers offered thorough and thoughtful suggestions for improving each of the volume's constituent parts at several crucial points along the way. People have strong feelings about comics. We hope that our efforts as editors will honour the expectations that our readers bring to the book.

The professionalism of the editorial staff at the University of Toronto Press Iberic Series – especially editors Robert Davidson and Frederick A. de Armas and acquisitions editor Mark Thompson – made the sundry phases of the publication process a joyful experience. Carolyn Zapf's copy editing on a referentially rich manuscript was remarkable. We would like to recognize the able work of Neil Anderson in translating original drafts of chapters 3 and 4 from the Spanish, Barbara Amago for her nimble skill in preparing the index, and – last but not least – Ana Galvañ for creating the original illustration featured on the cover. Research funding from the University of North Carolina at Chapel Hill, the Pennsylvania State University, and the University of Virginia were crucial to making this volume a reality.

This book is dedicated to our students.

CONSEQUENTIAL ART

Comics Culture in Contemporary Spain

1 Comics in Contemporary Spain

SAMUEL AMAGO AND MATTHEW J. MARR

For me, drawing pictures is a way of thinking.

José Domingo, "Spanish Fever"

El cómic tiene ya un pasado importante, pero lo mejor aún está por hacerse. Es un medio que tiene aún más potencialidad que Historia.

[Comics already have an important past, but the best lies yet ahead. It is a medium that still has more potentiality than history.][1]

Antonio Altarribia (qtd. in Rucabado)

Within the ever-growing body of work on graphic narrative, critical attention to comics' mixed word-image form is matched – as a matter of quantity – perhaps only by commentary on its mixed reception as a cultural product. Indeed, as recently as 2015, Christopher Pizzino notes in an article published in *PMLA*, for example, that while the graphic novel has "gained a level of respectability in the United States" (912), it has nevertheless struggled with a lingering image problem: a prestige deficit indebted to a history of marginalization against which it continues to toil, even within the seemingly liberal bounds of today's field of cultural production and criticism. Santiago García has described comics' historically marginal position vis-à-vis the literary world along similar lines, referring to the form's "destierro a los arrabales de la cultura" [exile to the outskirts of culture], a fate which only begins to experience something akin to reversal thanks to the creative energy of international underground comics producers in the 1960s (*La novela gráfica* 30). In the European context, comics studies as a theory-driven field of academic enquiry has its origins in the same decade, primarily by virtue of scholarship (by the visible likes of Umberto Eco and Roland Barthes, among others) that "found inspiration in literary studies, film theory, and semiotics" (Heer and Worcester xiv). During these same years in Spain, groundbreaking publications by scholars including Román Gubern, Luis Gasca, Terenci Moix, and Antonio Lara – often historical and/or semiotic in their approaches – also contributed to a nascent moment for the field in Spanish academic circles, though it is most clearly over approximately the past quarter century, both in Spain and abroad, that comics studies as a discipline has etched its mark most definitively in the humanities. Even so, in July 2012, the satirical newspaper *The Onion* lampooned the nagging unshakeability of graphic narrative's lowbrow legacy in a mock column featuring the headline "Comics Not Just for Kids Anymore, Reports 85,000th Mainstream News Story." Ironically, this same headline (with its own sardonic nod to what is, as just suggested, a much retold tale even in scholarly work) has in the intervening years continued to surface regularly as a popular re-post on social media, its perpetual bite the product of what to many observers is a poorly kept secret: namely, contemporary graphic narrative's patent sophistication and relevance as a cultural product.

Yet, while the notion of comics as lowbrow juvenilia may be a risible proposition to those in the know, the success of the medium's march on the fortress of intellectual acceptability remains an uneven affair in other quarters, as if it were a kind of distant echo of comedy and the comedians' own classical exclusion from the solemn space of Aristotle's polis. Indeed, as comics scholar Thierry Groensteen has observed, comics' historical kinship "with humor, caricature, and satire" – modes which tend to "belittle, instead of glorifying" – has rendered much graphic narrative at odds with longstanding Western artistic ideals of "harmony and of the sublime" ("Why" 10): just one among several crimes of association to be counted on its rap sheet.[2] But contemporary comics need not be comical, of course, and worldwide – including in Spain – the form's narrative-visual reflections have quite clearly come to supersede the stuff of child's play, unmistakably assuaging renowned comics author and critic Will Eisner's concern some thirty years ago that "unless more comics addressed subjects of greater moment they could not, as a genre, hope for serious intellectual review" (xi).

The nuanced nomenclature employed in referring to the medium can be signalled, for starters, as a telltale sign of contemporary culture's movement towards the brand of thoughtful recognition referenced by Eisner. Specialized critics and informed readers alike now widely refer to "graphic narrative" or the "graphic novel," and in Spain, as Sánchez-Albornoz underscores, even "[e]l nombre consagrado de cómic, que sustituye al veterano de tebeo, ha perdido su connotación jocosa, fantasiosa e infantil para abordar gráficamente y sin desenfado [relatos imaginados y] acontecimientos reales" [the now-established label "comic," which replaces the longstanding "tebeo," has lost its playful, fanciful, and childish connotation; in turn it has engaged, graphically and without affectation, imagined stories and real events] (5).[3] Santiago García, for his part, has called such cultural products "tebeos *de autor*" [*auteurist* comics] (*La novela gráfica* 23), while at least one noted American practitioner of the ninth art, Daniel Clowes, describes his own work as "comic-strip novel[s]" (qtd. in García, *La novela gráfica* 23–4). Reflecting an intensified sensitivity to the formal and historical particularities of the form, multitudinous lexical variations of this sort have trickled into circulation. Art Spiegelman, avowedly loath to the highbrow connotations of a term like "graphic novel," endorses the label "comix" – a neologism that calls to mind, for one, the contemporary form's genealogical ties to the small press ethos of much underground (and mature audience) production of the 1960s and 1970s (Freedman 30). "Comix" also self-evidently invokes the inseparable word-image "mix" whose dynamism, according to most critical definitions, lies at the heart of what makes the art form distinctive. Eisner's landmark 1985 book opts, for its part, to foreground "sequential art" as essential to understanding the medium, while Scott McCloud later built on this perspective in his own, inimitably drawn, 1993 analytical graphic narrative on the genre, *Understanding Comics: The Invisible Art* – a book whose own definition of comics is extremely precise: "juxtaposed pictorial and other images in deliberate sequence, intended to convey information and/or to produce an aesthetic response in the viewer" (9). Other thoughtful attempts to characterize the form and its variations abound (Freedman, for instance, lists "long form cartooning, picture novel ... long-range pictorial reading" [30]), though few have fallen into lasting lexical circulation. In Spain, "tebeo" (from the weekly Spanish comic book magazine published under the name TBO) has tended to denote a more popular shorter-form comics magazine, while "cómic" and "historieta" [comic strip] function today as the most broadly used academic terms de rigueur.

This fate notwithstanding, like their more efficacious counterparts, such terms reflect "a series of [critical] assumptions about ambition, seriousness, and quality" (Freedman 30): labels often issued (in the face of – or in other cases, as with Spiegelman, in honour of – a legacy of comics' unpretentious origins and its associated monikers, such as "funnies" or "toons") within a body of now veritably canonical, and primarily anglophone, scholarship written by well-known comics authors who straddle a kind of professional border in their work as critics (Freedman 29).[4] But whereas the borders of comics studies as a field have, in recent years, broadened to include an academic, and often interdisciplinary, range of voices from beyond this circle of key practitioner-critics (that is, the likes of Eisner, McCloud, Spiegelman, or, in Spain, Santiago García), a parallel expansion has been surprisingly much less in evidence with respect to the geopolitical (and linguistic) borders that bear on what comics work is placed under the scholarly lens, in what academic venues, and from what theoretical angles, particularly within the North American academy. Despite regular calls within comics studies for scholarship with a more international focus, global anglophone and (in Europe) francophone spheres of influence continue to attract the lion's share of commentary in the field – perhaps with the exception of Japanese manga and, to a much lesser degree, growing interest in certain Latin American developments in the medium. As this volume seeks to demonstrate, however, contemporary Spain – home to a vibrant, diverse, socially invested, and longstanding comics culture – stands out as a space of production deserving of much closer and sustained attention. The authors whose chapters compose this book take up the overarching charge of exploring how contemporary Spanish-language graphic narrative in Spain has confronted questions of cultural legitimacy through its own serious engagement with an array of themes, forms, and approaches: a collective undertaking that, while certainly in step with transnational trends, is most keenly surveyed in a framework carefully attuned to local, regional, and national dimensions particular to the late twentieth and early twenty-first century Spanish milieu.[5]

We are not suggesting that comics have not received serious attention in Spain or that Spanish comics have not already made a mark internationally. *Consequential Art: Comics Culture in Contemporary Spain* naturally builds on analytical work and an array of projects authored by a number of individual and institutional forerunners, both in the field of comics studies and in the culture industry at large. In Spain, *El discurso del cómic* [Comics Discourse] (1988; expanded edition, 2011) by Luis Gasca and Román Gubern is one of the first comprehensive studies of the form and continues to be a reference point for the academic study of comics. Teresa Vilarós weaves the work of comics and *historietista* artists such as Carlos Giménez, Gallardo, Javier Mariscal, and others into her cultural critique of the Spanish Transition, noting that "la ilustración del momento cotidiano en forma de historietas fue una de las grandes explosiones culturales de la posdictadura" [illustrating ordinary times in the comics form was one of the great cultural explosions of the post-dictatorship] (198). Analysing production from the mid-1980s in the Partido Socialista Obrero

Español [Spanish Socialist Workers' Party; PSOE]–financed magazine *Madriz* [a playful transcription of "Madrid"], which included work by Ana Juan, Ana Miralles, and Asun Balzola, Gema Pérez-Sánchez has shown how this publication's "veiled queer plots" and "new representations of women" subversively defy charges of latent traditionalism that have been levied at Madrid's officially sanctioned culture of the period, thus providing a "safe space" in Spanish comics (162, 144) apart from the gendered constraints of the capitalist comics market, whose forces, she proposes, extended at the time even to the stylings of ostensibly more radical venues such as the Barcelona-based *El Víbora* [The Viper] (181–2).

Other recent publications by Spanish comics scholars including Santiago García, Pedro Pérez del Solar, Sergio García Sánchez, Rubén Varillas, Ana Merino, and Enrique Bordes have brought into focus a broad vision of the history of the form in Spain, thereby lending it a meaningful form of "consecration" (Bourdieu 51), as well as a foundation for further critical study, especially with respect to currents and trends in the contemporary moment.[6] The International Comic Arts Forum has featured Spanish comics authors and artists, such as Max and Pere Joan in 2009 and Miguelanxo Prado in 2004. Luis Alberto de Cuenca, director of the Biblioteca Nacional de España from 1996 to 2000, worked to incorporate comics into the archives of that institution, and in 1997 he organized the exposition "Tebeos: Los primeros 100 años" [Comics: The First 100 Years]. Antonio Bonet Correa, in his foreword to Enrique Bordes's book on comics and narrative architecture, points to the various ways that the Museo Nacional del Prado has made meaningful gestures towards the form, recalling that Miguel Falomir, the adjunct director of Conservation and Research at the Prado, has observed that the comics form "tiene mucho que decir y que cuenta con el mismo rango que la pintura, la arquitectura o la escultura" [has a lot to say and reaches the same level as painting, architecture, or sculpture] (12). Bordes later curated a 2019 exposition at the Biblioteca Nacional, titled "¡Beatos, Mecachis y Percebes! Miles de años de tebeos en la Biblioteca Nacional" [The Blessed, the Damned, the Imbeciles! Thousands of Years of Comics at the National Library].[7]

In his preface to Santiago García's *La novela gráfica* [On the Graphic Novel] (2010), the late Juan Antonio Ramírez lamented how "el cómic ha venido siendo considerado hasta fechas muy recientes como un subproducto artístico y literario dirigido a un público 'infantil'" [comics have been understood, until recent times, as an artistic and literary subproduct aimed at a "child-like" audience] (12). This situation remains, even though graphic narrative has enjoyed a groundswell of creative investment through the oeuvre of comics *auteurs* who have sought to "asaltar la fortaleza de la respetabilidad cultural" [storm the fortress of cultural respectability] (12). As Pérez del Solar has observed (drawing in part, as he remarks, on work by Juan Sasturain), comics' hybridic melding of graphic and narrative elements, its historical association with a popular "uneducated" readership, its link to industrialized mass culture, its celebratory absorption of genre forms (science fiction, adventure, humour), and its distributional ties to the popular press have all contributed to the tension with avowedly "high culture" that has characterized the critical reception of comics from their very beginnings (18–20).

In her book *El cómic hispánico* [Hispanic Comics], Merino elaborates on how comics' function as a "factor cultural capaz de representar la modernidad masiva y popular del siglo XX" [cultural element capable of representing the massive popular modernity of the twentieth century] (11):

> Los comics son un tipo de relato gráfico que legitima un saber no desde una dimensión política o filosófica propiamente dicha, sino desde una dimensión ideológica de representación masiva y popular. (11)
>
> [Comics are a type of graphic story that authenticates a type of knowledge not from a political or philosophical dimension per se, but rather, from an ideological dimension of mass popular representation.]

Although Merino opines that the golden age of Spanish comics passed with the dictatorship (145, 270) and that the form is now "sufriendo una serie de transformaciones que denotan su adaptación a una nueva época" [undergoing a series of transformations that denote its adaptation to a new time] (271), Sarah D. Harris and Enrique del Rey Cabero, writing in 2015, are guardedly optimistic about the future of comics in present-day Spain. Harris asserts that "the high quality and broad range of Spanish comics from the past fifteen-odd years suggest that the authors and artists themselves are rising to meet increased expectations" (Harris and Del Rey Cabero). Meanwhile, summer university courses, regional and national conferences, and academics dispersed throughout the Peninsula (and abroad) have gone a long way towards paving a path for comics into the realm of academic and cultural recognition and prestige.

As a multimodal medium, comics as an object of study demands critical methodologies of a correspondingly hybrid nature, namely vis-à-vis the blending of narratological and visual studies approaches.

In the context of his analysis of other mixed-media art – what he calls "image/texts" – W.J.T. Mitchell has described how such forms require a doubled attention to interpenetrating matters of verbal expression *and* pictorial representation:

> The relative positioning of visual and verbal representation ... in these mixed media is ... never simply a formal issue or a question to be settled by "scientific" semiotics. The relative value, location, and the very *identity* of "the verbal" and "the visual" is exactly what is in question. (90)

Comics theorists have thought through the spatial interplay of the sequential and the simultaneous that the form embodies on the page; as Sousanis asserts, "[c]omics hold sequential and simultaneous modes in electric tension" (63). David Lewis describes the "double orientation" that image-text works require of the reader (68–75), and Edward Tufte argues that by holding the visual and the textual together on the page, the reader may escape the "flatlands" of information exchange (12). In Sousanis's words, "[d]rawing is a way of seeing and thus, a way of knowing" (78). Indeed, related notions of cognitive "processes of meaning making" figure prominently in recent work by Karin Kukkonen, whose approach to the medium by way of a pragmatics-based "theory of mind" (7) challenges a more established line of semiotic scholarship that has sought to see in the structures of comics a regulated system of signs (as with works by Eco and Groensteen, particularly in the latter's 2007 book, *The System of Comics*, first published in French in 1999). Kukkonen, for her part, proposes instead that the form's workings appeal at core to our faculties of inference, to the human propensity to posit "mental models" (50). This appeal is in evidence, for example, in comics' ability to induce – through the intricacies of design, illustration, and textual intervention – "alternative gaze paths" that guide the eye across, up, down, around, or back over the page again (36).

As Konstantinou notes, some of the best recent scholarship on comics has addressed its verbal/visual interplay while also excavating the form's historical interaction with other art forms and tendencies. He points to works such as Bart Beaty's *Comics Versus Art* (University of Toronto Press, 2012), Scott Bukatman's *The Poetics of Slumberland* (University of California Press, 2012), and Hillary Chute's *Disaster Drawn* (Harvard University Press, 2016) as contributing to that project in the North American context. Nick Sousanis's *Unflattening* (Harvard University Press, 2015) takes comics into new territory, deploying the form to explore how human perception and cognition functions.

Working against the "flatness" of traditional academic scholarship, Sousanis fuses words and images in a way that aims to trigger new ways of thinking "across" text and image. Reflecting a similar spirit, the 4 June 2017 *New York Times* Sunday magazine supplement was published as a comics-only issue, featuring New York stories, in which the editor's letter to readers promises "every single page drawn by cartoonists – even the crossword!" (Gauld 6); moreover, in December 2017, the *New York Times Book Review* featured a front-page essay by Manohla Dargis on new comics criticism.

As a cultural product, then, comics have merited considerable critical attention internationally; dissertations have been written (some, like Sousanis's, written and drawn entirely in comics), scholarly books published, and Spain's main arbiters of cultural distinction – the press, cultural commerce, and cultural institutions – have devoted noteworthy space to promoting the pleasures and power of graphic narrative to an ever-expanding and knowledgeable readership. In the previously mentioned foreword, Bonet Correa asserts that the growing number of studies, books, and exhibitions published and organized by theorists, historians, and art critics "son una muestra palmaria de la importancia del cómic en la mentalidad y el arte de nuestro tiempo" [are a clear sign of the importance of comics in the mentality and art of our times] (10). Even if the Spanish academy has not yet entirely lent its imprimatur to the form, Spain's culture industry has enthusiastically made space for comics. Madrid's flagship FNAC store in Callao Plaza, the book section of the monumental El Corte Inglés on the Paseo de la Castellana, and La Central in Madrid all have substantial sections devoted to the "Cómic de Autor," sites where customers may browse national and international titles published by commercial and independent comics publishers.

A key sector of vitality for contemporary material book culture, small bookshops specializing in comics, such as Madrid Cómics (Calle Silva 17), Elektra Cómic (Calle San Bernardo 20), Metrópolis (Calle Luna 11), Librería La Sombra (Calle San Pedro 20), and Arte 9 (Calle de la Cruz 37 and Calle del Dr Esquerdo 6), have resisted the otherwise generalized closings of mom-and-pop bookshops specializing in more traditional print-based media. In Barcelona, stores such as Norma Comics (Passeig de Sant Joan 9), Freaks (Carrer d'Alí Bei 10), Gigamesh (Carrer de Bailèn 8), Continuarà Comics (Via Laietana 29), and Antifaz Comic (Carrer Gran de Gràcia 239) reflect the city's deep fondness for comics and graphic art, which takes to the streets perhaps most conspicuously at the yearly Salón del Cómic and GRAF conventions. In the País Vasco, the Komikigunea archive opened in October 2014 as a centre established by the Biblioteca de Koldo Mitxelena Kulturunea to preserve the history of Basque comics art. The archive began, notably, in 2004 with Luis Gasca's personal collection. Its collections currently encompass "cómic, pulp, fanzine, obra gráfica original, cine, estudios sobre el cómic" [comics, pulp fiction, original graphic work, film, studies on comics] (Chávarri). That same year, the Ayuntamiento de Bilbao promoted the first festival devoted to comics featuring text written in Euskera, an event titled "Parrapean – Días de comics." The festival's first edition promoted comics not only in Euskera, but also in Galician (Ruiz Jiménez).

Spanish comics, comics criticism, and comics history have also found a home online. Sites including *Tebeosfera.com* and *Guiadelcomic.es* provide fans, aficionados, and critics detailed information on everything from publishing houses and biographies of comics professionals to series histories and market data, while avant-garde, experimental, and "cómics de autor" series are published regularly at *Tiktokcomics.com*. Satirical print-based graphic venues such as the Barcelona-based weekly *El Jueves* [Thursday] – a fixture of national comics culture since 1977 – and a post-2014 splinter publication, *Orgullo y Satisfacción* [Pride and Satisfaction], have moved increasingly to the internet, although, like other periodical publications in the digital era, they have struggled with funding.[8]

Titles from the catalogue of American comics powerhouses Marvel and DC are reliably found in bookshops and kiosks throughout Spain, although these mainstay commercial publishers face strong competition from the continued publication of traditional popular titles by eminent Spanish comics authors such as Ibáñez and Jan (Juan López Fernández), among others.[9] Astiberri, Dibbuks, Norma Editorial, Sinsentido, Salamandra Graphic, La Cúpula, Caramba, and other medium-sized comics publishers specializing in "cómics de autor" produced by Iberian and international creators boast robust book lists, while avant-garde outlets such as Apa-Apa, Fosfatina, and Fulgencio Pimentel are promoting initiatives in the space of alternative comics whose effect has been to blur the boundaries between narrative, graphic art, printmaking, and painting. Ana Galvañ's cover art for this volume gestures towards independent Spanish comics' uncharted avant-garde future.

In 2016, the US-based publisher Fantagraphics, which promotes itself as a "Publisher of the World's Greatest Cartoonists," released an English-language anthology of work by the "New Spanish Cartoonists," a re-edition of *Panorama. La novela gráfica española* hoy [Panorama. The Spanish Graphic Novel], coordinated by Santiago García and published by Astiberri in 2013 (see figure 1.1). Aimed at North American readers and composed of stories by KIM, Paco Roca, Miguel Gallardo,

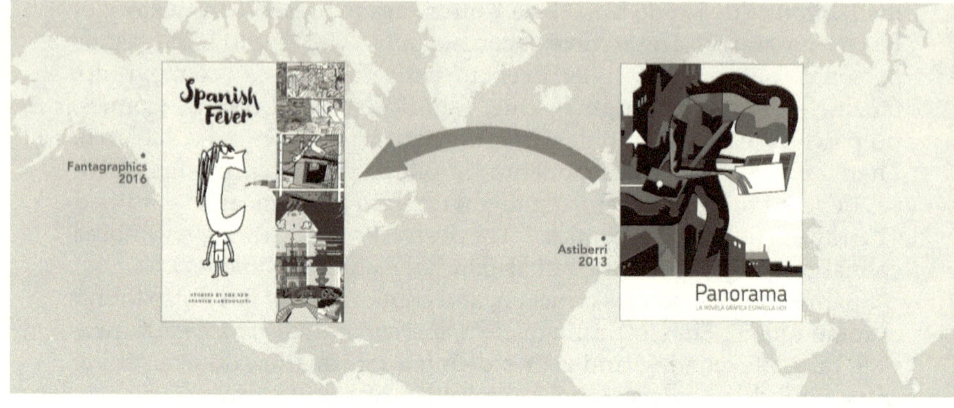

Figure 1.1. "Mañana comienza la gira por EE.UU. de varios de los autores de 'Panorama'" [Tomorrow various authors of the "Panorama" begin their US tour] (Astiberri).

David Rubín, José Domingo, and Miguel Ángel Martín, the anthology also incorporates work by several "newcomers," such as Ana Galvañ, Álvaro Ortiz, and Sergi Puyol (García, *Spanish Fever*). The edition and the tour that accompanied it were organized by García, funded in part by Spain's Ministry of Culture, and promoted in the United States by Spain Arts & Culture.[10] A graphic tweeted by Astiberri Ediciones in advance of the authors' tour promoting this project visualizes the close geographical and economic ties that Spanish *historietistas* have always enjoyed with the North American market (Astiberri). Indeed, many comics artists have begun their careers by first inking panels for the more extensive and developed US industry while moonlighting in the production of "cómics de autor" in their home territories.[11] Max (Francesc Capdevila), for example, one of the founders of *El Víbora* and a key player in underground and alternative comics production in the 1990s, has published work in the United States as both writer and artist. Likewise, North American indie comics authors have found successful representation with Spanish presses. For their part, the Londoner Michael DeForge and the Monctonian Jesse Jacobs have written and inked work in Canada that has been translated and reprinted by the Barcelona-based comics publisher Dehavilland. Future scholarly work on international comics production might explore how these kinds of transatlantic arrangements have impacted independent comics aesthetics, transformed readership patterns, and inspired new narratives of postnational belonging.

Arguably responding to the form's manifest cachet among contemporary readers, certain more established – and traditionally staid – publishers in Spain have increasingly incorporated comics into their catalogues. In a 2016 interview, Max observes that "[s]e están publicando más cómics que nunca" [more comics are being published than ever] (Mercé and Sánchez). Even in the "serious" realm of professional historiography, the comics form has been adopted to explain the origins, ramifications, and legacies of the Spanish Civil War. Paul Preston, for instance, oversaw the graphic narrative adaptation of his *La Guerra Civil española* [The Spanish Civil War] (2006), now featuring artwork by José Pablo García. Published by Debate in 2016, the book was reviewed – alongside other more traditional history book formats – by the eminent historian Julián Casanova in *El País*'s weekly supplement, *Babelia*. In his 18 July 2016 piece, Casanova lauds the García adaptation of Preston's classic work of Spanish history for its "prosa accesible" [accessible prose] and "la garantía de una investigación rigurosa y profesional" [the guarantee of rigorous and professional research] that it offers readers of all stripes (10). An earlier edition of *Babelia* (27 March 2015) also devoted substantial attention to historical comics in Spain (Constenla, "De la Guerra Civil"), while the 3 February 2007 issue of *Babelia* – largely dedicated to the graphic novel – featured a provocative cover story describing how literature as a field of cultural production has been ceding some ground to graphic forms (Pons).

That Paul Preston should lend his backing to a graphic novel adaptation of his *La Guerra Civil española* in 2016 is not just an example of the flexibility of comics as a vehicle for the transmission of historical knowledge, but also an illustration of the evolving cultural prestige of the form. As Casanova notes in his aforementioned review,

> combatir la ignorancia, las manipulaciones, los usos políticos de esa historia desde el presente no es una tarea fácil. Tampoco lo es captar nuevos lectores, atraer la atención de jóvenes estudiantes para los que la historia no es más que una pesada colección de fechas y nombres. (10)
>
> [to combat the ignorance, the manipulations, the political uses of that history from the present is not an easy task. Nor is gaining new readers, attracting the attention of young students for whom history is no more than a tiresome collection of dates and names.]

The vigorous production of historical comics in Spain exemplifies how the country's culture industry has recognized the ways in which well-documented and responsibly rendered comics have the potential to bring historical awareness to a generation of Spaniards who may have grown weary of more traditional approaches. In her conversation with Del Rey Cabero, Sarah D. Harris points out, in fact, that half of the total winners of the Premio Nacional del Cómic [National Comics Prize] to date have been on historical themes.[12]

Similarly, claims-making and consciousness-raising recently stand out as a hallmark of the form's emerging creators vis-à-vis the who, what, where, when, and why of the economic crisis – questions addressed by graphic novelists working throughout the country. *Barcelona. Los vagabundos de la chatarra* [Barcelona: The Scrap Metal Vagabonds], for example, is a 2015 collaborative work created by the artist Sagar Forniés and the writer Jorge Carrión. Carrión compares his text to the Baltimore-centred US television drama, *The Wire* (2002–8), specifically in relation to its "entretejido argumental" [interweaving of plots], which he employs in order to reveal and critique the human impact of the economic crisis and housing precarity in the city of Barcelona (Constenla, "Noticias"). Describing the book as one of the first examples of "cómic periodístico" [journalistic comics] made in Spain, Constenla designates it an example of "periodismo ilustrado" [enlightened journalism] ("Noticias"). *Aquí vivió: Historia de un desahucio* [Here They Lived: The Story of an Eviction] (2016), drawn by Cristina Bueno with a script by Isaac Rosa, offers a more personalized reflection on how the country's economic crisis has impacted its most vulnerable populations. Steven Torres and Christine Martínez have both focused recent essays on the socially and politically committed graphic works written and drawn by Miguel Brieva, texts that convey "una fuerte crítica a la sociedad de consumo y al neoliberalismo en general" [a strong critique of consumer society and of neoliberalism in general] (Torres 49) and work to imagine an affirmative politics based on "contemporary redefinitions of community, activism and knowledge production" (Martínez 191).[13]

Clearly, comics have come into their own as a consequential art form with manifold cultural and epistemological functions. As Konstantinou notes, "[i]f an earlier generation of scholars passionately argued that academics should study comics, scholars now arriving on the scene are asking how best to do so." Thierry Smolderen, one of the foundational figures of comics theory and interpretation, points out that the form has been constantly redefined through "contact with society, with its media, its images and its technologies" (qtd. in Groensteen, *Comics* 3). This volume charts several trends in graphic narrative in Spain, foregrounding throughout how mainstream and independent practitioners of the form have engaged with questions of cultural legitimacy, historiography, and sociopolitical representation from the 1990s to the present. Spanish comics have broached an array of national concerns, from the economy and the housing crisis, to disability, history, memory, and the environment. While a more complete panorama of Spain's comics production might include references to the ample production of genre fare authored and inked by the likes of El Torres, Lolita Aldea, Sandra Molina, Víctor Santos, or David Rubín, this book focuses on the intersection of comics production and contemporary Spanish politics and culture.

Christine M. Martínez's essay on the Forniés and Carrión collaboration, *Los vagabundos de la chatarra*, and Matthew J. Marr's essay on Aleix Saló in this volume demonstrate how the comics form is not incompatible with serious cultural critique and theory. What is noteworthy with respect to Forniés and Carrión is how they deploy some of the approaches, language, and methodologies popularized by Joe Sacco in his graphic journalism in order to critique the logics of urban design and the politics of precarity. For its part, Saló's intermedial intervention is arrayed in order to critique the making of Spain's clumsy national fall into protracted economic crisis. That Saló's online book trailer should make it – via YouTube – into the Moncloa Palace, where José Luis Rodríguez Zapatero and his vice-presidents Alfredo Pérez Rubalcaba and Elena Salgado (not to mention Cristóbal Montoro, the economic advisor for the Partido Popular [People's Party; PP],) viewed and commented on it, constitutes a noteworthy juxtaposition for Mariano Rajoy's later inability to explain the origins of the crisis cogently (Casqueiro).

Comics have enjoyed increasing visibility in curricula, conference programs, and publication trends within the university systems of North America and the United Kingdom, and the graphic novel's fortunes in Spanish institutions of learning have been only slightly less robust. Bordes writes, most recently, that "el cómic ha madurado tanto en contenidos como en audiencia, y ha conseguido atraer a un abanico de autores y lectores de un espectro social cada vez más amplio" [comics have matured greatly in both content and audience, and they have managed to attract an array of authors and readers from an increasingly broad social spectrum] (19). Comics have long enjoyed a vigorous editorial production and readership in Spain, where, indeed, their cultural impact has been substantial and meaningful in ways that merit scholarly attention among Hispanist scholars and students. In a 2004 essay, Anne Magnussen analysed the emerging role of underground comics in Spanish society during the late 1970s and early 1980s, which were "marginal and anti-authoritarian" (101). Following in that line, Pérez del Solar's *Imágenes del desencanto: Nueva historieta española 1980–1986*

[Images of (the) Disenchantment: New Spanish Comics, 1980–1986] (2013) outlines the crucial roles that mainstream and countercultural *historietas* played within the political and cultural contexts of Spain's transition to democracy. And Ana Merino has described how José Escobar Saliente, Manuel Vázquez Gallego, Francisco Ibáñez, and other artists associated with the Bruguera school have always engaged with current events in their work ("The Cultural Dimensions").[14] In that same essay, Merino notes that the collected works of Ibáñez, for instance, are "pedagogically useful" since they allow "students to discuss a range of cultural issues and historical events," from the World Cup to national general elections (276). But encouraging recent developments in the anglophone academy, such as the Modern Language Association (MLA) publication *Teaching the Graphic Novel* (2009) and *The Routledge Companion to Comics* (2016), are of somewhat limited utility to scholars and students working in Spanish cultural studies, since Spain merits only a half chapter in each volume (Tabachnick; Bramlett et al.). Merino's essay in *Teaching the Graphic Novel* argues for the importance of comics produced in Spanish-language contexts in Iberia and the Americas as windows onto local culture, while Simone Castaldi's essay in *The Routledge Companion to Comics* similarly injects an overview of Spanish *tebeos* into a longer history of comics in Spain and Italy.[15]

The present volume aims to expand critical scholarship on Spanish comics emerging from the concrete historical, cultural, and political contexts of Spain since the end of the 1980s. It opens in Chapter 2 with Samuel Amago's essay "Drawing (on) Spanish History," which analyses how comics in Spain have reflexively employed "amphibious thinking" (Sousanis 53) in order to consider those issues of historical memory that, since the end of the twentieth century, have continued unabated in Spain. Amago elaborates specifically on how contemporary Castilian-language *historieta* creators have tacked towards a more serious engagement with the intricacies of representing historical knowledge through meta-comics approaches to representation. Across a broad range of historiographic comics, there is – in addition to a process-oriented narrative structure and mise-en-page of archival materials – a sustained attention to the affective links that make intergenerational communication possible. The texts Amago examines function in terms of what Marianne Hirsch has called "postmemory," a space of transmission in which narrators at a generation's remove attempt to work through traumatic family histories (4–6) – here, through the graphic-verbal medium of comics.

As Amago elaborates in Chapter 2, the bulk of Spanish historical graphic narrative has sought to recover and visualize forgotten or untold stories from the Spanish Civil War and dictatorship from a leftist perspective, responding to the continuing cultural need of the descendants of the victims of Francoist repression to know and represent their past. Chapter 3, by Pedro Pérez del Solar, an authority on Transition-era comics, explores the remarkably countertrend features of Felipe Hernández Cava and Federico del Barrio's *Las memorias de Amorós* [The Memoirs of Amorós]. The thoughtfully historiographic scope of this series of comics albums – published between 1988 and 1993, though set in the Primo de Rivera years (1923–30) and the Second Republic (1931–9) – resists dominant norms for Spanish comics of the eighties and nineties. *Las memorias* narrates the adventures of a fictitious journalist who investigates a series of feuilleton-worthy mysteries; later, returning to Spain after a long exile, this same character struggles as an elderly man to recover his past, a process carried out by way of his exploration of memories intertwined with the mysteries he once investigated. *Las memorias de Amorós* thus fashions a critical memory of the conflictive first decades of the twentieth century. In Pérez del Solar's view, this work constitutes a confrontational project in the context of the 1980s and 1990s, when much of the Spanish comics industry had veered towards pornography and hyper-violence in order to stay afloat commercially. Combining its historiographic impulse with an embrace of popular genres that eschew sexploitation and violence, *Las memorias* bucks contemporary norms, moreover, with its stylized graphics, "modern" lines, and designs that were distinctive of *Madriz* – an emblematic magazine of the Movida Madrileña, which counted Cava and Del Barrio among its creative staff.

In Chapter 4, Xavier Dapena reflects on the uses and politics of memory and the historical imagination in the graphic medium. Both the Hernández Cava and del Barrio texts interweave narrative forms – the memoir, a father's testimonial diary, and metafictional engagements – with popular genres such as the crime thriller in order to explore the ways in which history and genre forms of the past inhabit the present. Drawing on theoretical interventions concerning history and memory by Vázquez Montalbán, Beatriz Sarlo, Dominick LaCapra, and Jacques Rancière, Dapena approaches these comics from three vantage points. First, he inscribes these graphic novels within national debates on collective memory, showing how they respond to the democratization of access to historical knowledge. Second, he explores how these comics engage with a representational economy of signs in which testimony functions to draw attention to subaltern historical positions: an approach that highlights the ways in which these novels' protagonists become mechanisms for collective enunciation from the margins. Dapena concludes by describing some of the problems inherent in the intergenerational transmission of memory, which Rancière and Fernández-Savater call "ficción política" [political fiction] and Gutiérrez calls "hebras de paz de vida" [living strands of peace].

In the volume's fifth chapter, Matthew J. Marr analyses Catalan cartoonist Aleix Saló's *Españistán: De la burbuja inmobilaria a la crisis* [Spainistan: From the Real-Estate Bubble to the Crisis] (May 2011) as an online animated video short whose bold spirit is manifest not only in its humorously irreverent critique of Spanish economic policy, but also in the distinctive intermediality of its form. Among the most viewed online videos in Spain since its upload to YouTube by Saló just ten days after the start of the 15-M protests, the short was originally conceptualized as a "book trailer" companion piece to the artist-author's 144-page graphic novel, *Españistán: Este país se va a la mierda* [Spainistan: This Country Is Going to Shit] (March 2011). Whereas the graphic novel presents a parodic adventure tale revolving around an individual character who haplessly stumbles through a landscape of bureaucracies in a quest to annul his mortgage, the animated video short offers a macro-narrative that more broadly explores the making of Spain's clumsy national fall into economic crisis. Fuelled by the distributional dynamism of the internet, this sardonic, yet lucidly pedagogical, satire on the complexities of Spain's economic disaster garnered unprecedented public attention in short order. The animated video, at first a subsidiary paratext, swiftly eclipsed its source-text graphic novel in Spain's popular consciousness, arguably becoming a definitive shorthand narrative of the Spanish economic crisis for millions of viewers. Its unusual impact in turn built a home for Saló's graphic narrative across various media. The popularity of *Españistán* as a free online video spurred e-book and kiosk-form re-releases of the original graphic novel. Unexpectedly, in times of austerity and rampant piracy, these publications have become bestsellers, and Saló's distributional model is being applied, as a consequence, to his subsequent comics-based works. Marr explores the role of intermediality in the *Españistán* phenomenon, focusing on how this satirical project launches an important mode of public pedagogy: one that challenges the values of neoliberalism through its own parody of media convergence in miniature, which here resonates with comics' own operational proclivity, at a micro level, for hybrid, simultaneous forms.

Informed by a rich tradition of socially invested graphic journalism, Jorge Carrión's non-fiction graphic novel, *Los vagabundos de la chatarra* (2016), grapples with both global crises of environmental abuse and local struggles surrounding social inequity, immigration, and housing in post-crisis Barcelona. Much in the tradition of Joe Sacco (self-referential and embedded), *Los vagabundos* details the artist's incursion into the struggles of scrap merchants and squatters for housing and humane working conditions. In Chapter 6, Christine M. Martínez explores *Los vagabundos* as an engaged piece of social journalism, emphasizing how comics as a fundamentally urban genre employs motifs of strolling and street life to communicate these struggles in complex manners that are representative of the respective communities covered: namely, by foregrounding issues of urban ecology, public space, and community responsibility. The urban nature of comics also allows for a valuable re-articulation of common environmentalist narratives of contamination and crisis, often dependent upon binary divisions of nature/human or idealized conceptions of "purity," as issues of inextricable social and local import. Through comics as journalism and urban genre, *Los vagabundos* re-embeds global catastrophes of resource depletion and waste accumulation into local networks of power and urban experience, particularly as perceived by the city's most disenfranchised. This treatment of environmental issues as fundamentally social issues, related to the need to imagine and value urban communities no longer determined by the mechanisms of big business and consumer society, is something that Carrión shares with contemporary social movements in Spain. Martínez's essay explores how Carrión, through the comics form, is able to contribute to these debates.

Spanish comics authors have increasingly inflected the graphic novel in ways that also foreground diverse experiences of cognitive and physical personhood in the contemporary moment. In Chapter 7, Emily DiFilippo presents a study of the 2011 graphic novel *Alicia en un mundo real* [Alice in a Real World], created by well-known lesbian author Isabel Franc and artist Susanna Martín. Its queer heroine, Alicia, is diagnosed with breast cancer and undergoes treatment that includes a unilateral mastectomy. Like the original Alice in Lewis Carroll's 1865 novel *Alice in Wonderland,* Franc and Martín's Alicia finds herself on an absurd journey that shatters her accustomed reality. DiFilippo's reading begins by considering cancer as an experience of disability, as it obstructs conformity to cultural imperatives of work, productivity, and independence. Drawings of the protagonist's hectic, pre-cancer life in the workplace contrast with images of the debilitating – and sometimes shocking – effects of illness and medical intervention on the body. These panels are interspersed with portraits of the protagonist as superhero(ine), responding to the crisis of cancer with a resolute pursuit of happiness that questions neoliberal, ableist, and heteronormative promises of the good life. While much of the cultural discourse that surrounds breast cancer interpellates the patient as a woman, the effects of the disease and its treatment, including hair loss and mastectomy, bring female embodiment under attack. Franc and Martín's graphic novel, both through its portrayal of a host of queer characters and its protagonist's resistance against norms of gender and sexuality, presents a flexible concept of gender that transcends the binary model. Alicia's story serves to validate a variety of diverse breast cancer experiences, particularly those that lie outside the realm of the conventional and the normative.

In Chapter 8, Eduardo Ledesma examines Rosana Antolí's neo-surrealist graphic novel *Pareidolia* (2014), a self-referential work that places readers within the delirious subjectivity of a woman's unravelling consciousness during her experience of schizophrenia. Rendered in a restrained black and white palette, the novel depicts her delusions by relying on a phenomenon known as "pareidolia": the human tendency – acute in those who suffer from cognitive disorders such as dementia, stroke, and schizophrenia – to see anthropomorphic patterns within random shapes. Antolí's unnamed protagonist experiences visual and auditory pareidolia as coffee stains, wall cracks, and rumpled clothing that morph into pop icons with whom she dialogues, philosophizes, and even dances. These figures include the late glam-rocker David Bowie (a master of transformation), alternative musician Jarvis Cocker (a kind of neo-surrealist), Alan Watts (a popular author who wrote about Zen Buddhism for American audiences), and Joseph Beuys's dead hare (a reference to Beuys's best-known neo-surrealist performance, *How to Explain Pictures to a Dead Hare* [1965]). Steeped in music culture, Buddhist existentialism, and artistic referentiality, *Pareidolia*'s neo-surrealist journey seeks to destabilize the primacy of the rational as it explores existential topics. Here, cognitive disability and delusion are not presented as impairment, but rather as a hallucinatory escape from the straightjacket of reality. Echoing the Surrealists, Dadaists, and later artists such as the shamanistic Beuys himself, *Pareidolia* presents Western logic as a "rotting corpse" that demands (its own) destruction. Through its deployment of intertextuality, the novel facilitates a critique of the contemporary moment in Spain in a project that proposes both the irrational and the adoption of collective values as potential solutions for the socioeconomic crisis.

The common thread connecting both the primary texts and their accompanying critical evaluations in this book is a sustained concern with an evolving Spanish social reality and its hand-drawn/verbal representation in varied comics forms. From memory and history (Amago, Pérez del Solar, and Dapena) to the politics of economic precarity after 15-M (Marr and Martínez), and from the body and personal space to mental geography (DiFilippo and Ledesma), the essays collected here account for some of the ways in which Spanish-language comics in Spain have deployed the image-text connection, an aesthetics of reflexivity, geographical imagination, intermediality, and alternative ways of seeing to interrogate some of the most consequential cultural issues that country has faced since 1990. In this regard, the book takes up Thierry Groensteen's call for comics scholarship that would expand, progress, or open up new approaches to, and perspectives on, this ever-evolving form (*Comics* 4–5), not only by "contrasting different traditions of comics production worldwide" (4), but also by following new avenues of formal, thematic, methodological, and theoretical enquiry.

For a variety of reasons, Spain's vibrant commercial comics scene of the 1940s, '50s, '60s, and early '70s fell into a period of protracted decline after experiencing a kind of brief resurgence at the outset of the 1980s. As Pedro Pérez del Solar underscores in his essay within this volume, the turning of the page from the decade of the 1980s to the 1990s did not leave much space for optimism in the world of Spanish comics. Benoît Mitaine calls the 1990s the "década de crisis para el cómic español" [decade of crisis for Spanish comics] (150). Until the initial years of the new century, many, if not most, Spanish *historietistas* with serious creative ambitions to ink, publish, and market their own personal narratives and perspectives would be forced to work abroad or, in more than a few instances, to toil in a diminished space of Iberian obscurity. Although the situation is improving, the vice-president of the Asociación de Autores del Cómic de España [Association of Spanish Comics Authors], Julio Martínez (who also draws comics under the name Mart), underscores the historical brain drain of Spanish comics authors who have had to work for the French-Belgian publishers in the hopes of perhaps having their work translated and re-released in Spain: "Es eso que se llama fuga de cerebros. Muchos dibujantes se van fuera porque aquí no hay forma de vivir de esto. Aquí sobrevives con trabajitos que te van saliendo" [It's what they call brain drain. Many illustrators leave Spain because there is no way to make a living here. You only survive here with small jobs that come up] (González). In introductory remarks delivered at the *Spanish Fever* panel during the 2016 Small Press Expo held in Bethesda, Maryland, Santiago García went so far as to say that for *historietistas* the decade of the 1990s was, in fact, a virtual desert – barring the inspiring exception of Francesc Capdevila, known as Max, whose work stood out for many at the time as a shining beacon in an otherwise inhospitable cultural milieu (Domingo et al.). Clearly, a sea change occurred around 2000, when independent long-form comics – mostly produced by underground, alternative, and indie artists and authors like Robert Crumb, Art Spiegelman, Jaime, Gilbert and Mario Hernández, Daniel Clowes, Joe Sacco, Marjane Satrapi, and others – began to be published and distributed more widely across Spain. An increasingly dynamic market for graphic narrative soon inspired the country's Ministry of Culture to fund the Premio Nacional del Cómic [National Comics Prize], whose 20,000-euro prize has been awarded since 2007 to the best Spanish *historieta* published in Spain over the course of the preceding year. Fittingly, Max was the recipient of the first award. We have also mentioned earlier the efforts of Luis Alberto de Cuenca, director of the Biblioteca Nacional, who recognized early on the importance of comics within Spain's contemporary cultural life.

Fast forward to Bethesda, Maryland, in September 2016: emerging cartoonists Ana Galvañ, José Domingo, David Rubín, and Javier Olivares – featured as special international guests at the Small Press Expo (a mainstay event of the US independent comics scene) – collectively shared their homegrown graphic work with an enthusiastic, predominantly anglophone, crowd of indie comics–lovers as part of a weeklong promotional tour of the Fantagraphics release of *Spanish Fever: Stories by the New Spanish Cartoonists*. The event marked how far contemporary Spanish graphic narrative had come through the underground: panel by panel, occasionally drifting into the gutter, splashing its image onto the page in something other than a straight line to cultural prestige – or, at the very least, to a "prevalent feeling ... that we are living in a creatively golden age for [Spanish] comics" (García, *Spanish Fever* xiii).

NOTES

1 All translations in this chapter are by the authors unless otherwise indicated.

2 Groensteen's essay highlights three additional ways in which comics can be said to deviate from Western artistic ideals. The first of these involves graphic narrative's hybridized word-image form, which "goes against the 'ideology of purity' that has dominated the West's approach to aesthetics since Lessing" ("Why" 9). Another "sin" stems from comics' supposed "lack of narrative ambition," the perception of which has commonly led to associations with various modes of "paraliterature," such as "adventure stories, historical novels, fantasy and science-fiction, detective novels, erotica, and so on" (9). From a historical perspective, comics' traditional "relationship with childhood" constitutes yet another aspect of the genre that has complicated its accreditation by official culture (10–11).

3 In Spain, the generic term "tebeo" has long been used to describe comics. The word originates with the popular comic book series, *TBO: Seminario*

Festivo Infantil [Children's Fun Weekly], which was first published by the Barcelona publisher Editorial Buigas in 1917 ("TBO").

4 The border-like character of comics studies as a field – a byproduct of the form's own dimension of formal hybridity – is duly noted by Freedman. As an object of study, "[t]he medium of comics not only challenges the border between high art and popular culture and between word and image; it also confounds the distinction between academic and amateur and challenges the separation of disciplines in the academy, since the study of comics involves art, semiotics, literature, culture and history and blurs the borders of each of these categories" (29).

5 Following Labanyi in *Constructing Identity in Contemporary Spain*, we have sought to curate a collection of essays that acknowledges some of the discontinuities in cultural history while keeping in mind that "the complexity of cultural processes which play multiple functions and cannot be separated into tidy categories" (13).

6 Santiago García's book *La novela gráfica* is a well-documented global history of the graphic novel, with a few pages devoted to Spanish production. It expands helpfully beyond the exclusively anglophone focus of Román Gubern's semiological study, *El lenguaje de los comics* [Comics Language] (1972), and Javier Coma's *Los comics. Un arte del siglo XX* [Comics: A Twentieth-Century Art] (1978). Terenci Moix's *Los "comics": Arte para el consumo y formas "pop"* ["Comics": Consumer Art and "Pop" Forms] (1968) was one of the first books on comics to include a section on autochthonous forms (89–202), although its utility today is somewhat limited by its thematic approach. Ana Merino's useful Cátedra monograph, *El cómic hispánico* [Hispanic Comics], situates Spanish comics within the broader context of Hispanic graphic narrative. Pedro Pérez del Solar's book, *Imágenes del desencanto* [Images of (the) Disenchantment], is perhaps the most complete monograph on Spanish comics, though its scope is delimited by a chronology spanning the years 1980–6. Focusing on roughly the same era, Gema Pérez-Sánchez devotes a chapter of her groundbreaking book, *Queer Transitions in Contemporary Spanish Culture*, to analysing how the serially produced, government-subsidized comic *Madriz* explored new graphic representations of gender and sexuality during the transition to democracy.

7 Drawing materials from the Biblioteca Nacional's deep catalogue, the exposition's title is inspired by the centuries-long history of Spanish graphic storytelling. The "Beatos" [monks and lay religious] of the title refer to the pre-history of comics in the form of illuminated religious manuscripts. "Mecachis," which translates roughly to "shoot," is a vernacular expression that appears throughout the popular Spanish comics of the twentieth century; in the late nineteenth century, the artist Eduardo Sáenz Hermúa used the term as a pen name. "Percebes" translates literally to "barnacles,"

but Spanish comics readers would recognize the connection to the foundational series authored by Francisco Ibañez, *13, Rue del Percebe.*

8 Although largely outside the scope of this volume, online and e-book formats of Spanish sequential narrative and graphic novels stand out as important topics for future scholarly work. *Orgullo y Satisfacción* [Pride and Satisfaction] published its last issue in December 2017 ("El cierre").

9 In 2014, 18.2 per cent of comics published in Spain were reportedly of national origin, while 45.3 per cent were American, 16.7 per cent Japanese, 14.3 per cent French, and 5.5 per cent from other countries or nationally unidentifiable ("Cómic en España").

10 Spain Arts & Culture has also promoted Spanish comics artists at the Toronto Comic Arts Festival.

11 At the first day of the 2016 Small Press Expo, for example, José Domingo joined his compatriots Ana Galvañ, David Rubín, Javier Olivares, and Santiago García for an event sponsored by Fantagraphics to promote the *Spanish Fever* anthology, while on Sunday he promoted, alone, his English-language work *Pablo & Jane and the Hot Air Contraption* (2015), published by Flying Eye Books, an imprint of the alternative comics publisher Nobrow.

12 As this volume entered production, Ian Gibson and Quique Palomo had just completed their comics biography of Federico García Lorca's life and death.

13 The third chapter of Benjamin Fraser's *Disability Studies and Spanish Culture: Films, Novels, the Comic and the Public Exhibition* (2013) examines socially invested Spanish comics production in recent years from another important angle, namely in its case study of Miguel Gallardo's *María y yo* [María and Me] (2007): a graphic novel in which the author-artist foregrounds day-to-day life with his autistic daughter, María (a figure he calls his co-author).

14 Merino and Tullis describe other Bruguera-school titles such as Josep Escobar's *Carpanta* and Francisco Ibáñez's *13, Rue del Percebe* as "examples of mid-century titles that explore the hardships and social problems and tensions of the postwar years" (212). They insist, however, that Carlos Giménez's *Paracuellos* marks the moment in which Spanish comics reached full expressive maturity (213).

15 *The Cambridge Companion to the Graphic Novel,* released in 2017, makes allusion to Franco-era Spanish comics production in one line of Dan Mazur and Alexander Danner's chapter titled "The International Graphic Novel" (61).

WORKS CITED

Astiberri Ediciones (Astiberri). "Mañana comienza la gira por EE.UU. de varios de los autores de 'Panorama' y @mandorlablog." *Twitter,* 14 Sept. 2016, 7:25 a.m.

Beaty, Bart. *Comics Versus Art*. U of Toronto P, 2012.

Bonet Correa, Antonio. Prólogo. *Cómic, arquitectura narrativa*, by Enrique Bordes, Cátedra, 2017, 9–12.

Bordes, Enrique. *Cómic, arquitectura narrativa*. Cátedra, 2017.

Bourdieu, Pierre. *The Field of Cultural Production: Essays on Art and Literature*. Edited by Randal Johnson, Columbia UP, 1993.

Bramlett, Frank, Roy T. Cook, and Aaron Meskin, editors. *The Routledge Companion to Comics*. Routledge, 2016.

Bukatman, Scott. *The Poetics of Slumberland: Animated Spirits and the Animating Spirit*. U of California P, 2012.

Casanova, Julián. "La guerra española en el reñidero de Europa." *El País, Babelia*, 18 July 2016, elpais.com/cultura/2016/07/12/babelia/1468324071_273300.html.

Casqueiro, Javier. "La fábula de Españistán." *El País*, 28 June 2011, elpais.com/politica/2011/06/28/actualidad/1309289471_668657.html.

Castaldi, Simone. "A Brief History of Comics in Italy and Spain." *The Routledge Companion to Comics*, edited by Frank Bramlett, Roy T. Cook & Aaron Meskin, Routledge, 2016, 79–87.

Chávarri, Inés P. "La casa del cómic." *El País*, 9 Oct. 2014, elpais.com/ccaa/2014/10/09/paisvasco/1412864167_726681.html.

Chute, Hillary. *Disaster Drawn. Visual Witness, Comics, and Documentary Form*. Harvard UP, 2016.

"El cierre de *Orgullo y Satisfacción*." *Orgullo y Satisfacción*, 17 Feb. 2017, www.orgulloysatisfaccion.com/cerramos/. Accessed 17 Feb. 2017.

Coma, Javier. *Los comics. Un arte del siglo* XX. Guadarrama, 1978.

"Cómic en España en 2014: Checklist y cifras." *Guia del Cómic.es*, 10 Sept. 2016, guiadelcomic.es/editoriales/2014/2014-cifras.htm.

"Comics Not Just for Kids Anymore, Reports 85,000th Mainstream News Story." *The Onion*, 10 July 2012, www.theonion.com/article/comics-not-just-for-kids-anymore-reports-85000th-m-28727.

Constenla, Tereixa. "De la Guerra Civil a la Transición, en viñetas." *El País, Babelia*, 27 March 2015, elpais.com/cultura/2015/03/27/babelia/1427465324_662105.html.

– "Noticias dibujadas desde la chatarra." *El País*, 24 Jul. 2014, elpais.com/cultura/2014/07/23/actualidad/1406127195_363648.html.

Dargis, Manohla. "The Hand of the Comics Artist." *New York Times*, 11 December 2017, www.nytimes.com/2017/12/11/books/review/why-comics-chute-slugfest-tucker.html.

DeForge, Michael. *Lose*. Dehavilland, 2015.

Domingo, José. *Pablo & Jane and the Hot Air Contraption*. Flying Eye Books, 2015.

Domingo, José, Santiago García, Javier Olivares, Ana Galvañ, and David Rubín. "Spanish Fever: Stories by the New Spanish Cartoonists." Small Press Expo 2016, Bethesda, MD, 17 Sept. 2016. Address.

Eisner, Will. *Comics and Sequential Art: Principles and Practices from the Legendary Cartoonist*. 1985. W.W. Norton, 2008.

Fraser, Benjamin. *Disability Studies and Spanish Culture: Films, Novels, the Comic and the Public Exhibition*. Liverpool UP, 2013.

Freedman, Ariela. "Comics, Graphic Novel, Graphic Narrative: A Review." *Literature Compass* 8.1 (2011): 28–46. doi.org/10.1111/j.1741-4113.2010.00764.x.

García, Santiago. *La novela gráfica*. Astiberri, 2010.

–, editor. *Panorama. La novela gráfica española hoy*. Astiberri, 2013.

–, editor. *Spanish Fever: Stories by the New Spanish Cartoonists*. Fantagraphics, 2016.

García Sánchez, Sergio. *Sinfonía gráfica: Variaciones en las unidades estructurales y narrativas del cómic*. Glénat, 2000.

Gasca, Luis. *Los comics en España*. Editorial Lumen, 1969.

– *Los héroes de papel*. Editorial Taber, 1969.

– *Mujeres fantásticas*. Editorial Taber, 1969.

Gasca, Luis, and Román Gubern. *El discurso del cómic*. Cátedra, 1988.

Gauld, Tom. "Editor's Letter." *New York Stories*, Spec. issue of *New York Times Magazine*, 4 June 2017, 6.

Gibson, Ian, and Quique Palomo. *Vida y muerte de Federico García Lorca*. Ediciones B, 2018.

González, Lucía. "El cómic sale del 'gueto.'" *El Mundo*, 9 Dec. 2009, www.elmundo.es/elmundo/2009/12/09/cultura/1260359570.html.

Groensteen, Thierry. *Comics and Narration*. Translated by Ann Miller, UP of Mississippi, 2013.

– *The System of Comics*. Translated by Bart Beaty and Nick Nguyen, UP of Mississippi, 2007.

– "Why Are Comics Still in Search of Cultural Legitimization?" Translated by Shirley Smolderen. *A Comics Studies Reader*, edited by Jeet Heer and Kent Worcester, UP of Mississippi, 2009.

Gubern, Román. *El lenguaje de los comics*. Ediciones Península, 1972.

Harris, Sarah D., and Enrique del Rey Cabero. "The Spanish Civil War in Comics: A Conversation on Spanish Comics, Remembrance, and Trauma. Part 1." *Comics Forum*, 27 April 2015, comicsforum.org/2015/04/27/the-spanish-civil-war-in-comics-a-conversation-on-spanish-comics-remembrance-and-trauma-by-sarah-d-harris-and-enrique-del-rey-cabero-part-1.

Heer, Jeet, and Kent Worcester. Introduction. *A Comics Studies Reader*, edited by Jeet Heer and Kent Worcester, UP of Mississippi, 2009, xi–xv.

Hirsch, Marianne. *The Generation of Postmemory: Writing and Visual Culture After the Holocaust*. Columbia UP, 2012.

Jacobs, Jesse. *Safari Honeymoon*. Dehavilland, 2016.

Konstantinou, Lee. "Comics Studies Comes of Age." *Chronicle of Higher Education*, 19 Feb. 2017, www.chronicle.com/article/Comics-Studies-Comes-of-Age/239213. Accessed 24 Feb. 2017.

Kukkonen, Karin. *Contemporary Comics Storytelling*. U of Nebraska P, 2013.

Labanyi, Jo, editor. *Constructing Identity in Contemporary Spain: Theoretical Debates and Cultural Practice*. Oxford UP, 2002.

Lara, Antonio. *El apasionante mundo del tebeo*. Cuadernos para el Diálogo, 1968.

Lewis, David. *Reading Contemporary Picturebooks: Picturing Text*. Taylor and Francis, 2012.

Magnussen, Anne. "Spanish Underground Comics and Society." *Reading the Popular in Contemporary Spanish Texts*, edited by Shelley Godsland and Nickianne Moody, U of Delaware P, 2004, 100–20.

Martínez, Christine. "The Affirmative Politics of Degrowth: Miguel Brieva's Graphic Narrative *Memorias de la Tierra*." *Journal of Spanish Cultural Studies* 18.2 (2017): 191–212. doi.org/10.1080/14636204.2017.1308631.

Mazur, Dan, and Alexander Danner. "The International Graphic Novel." *The Cambridge Companion to the Graphic Novel*, edited by Stephen E. Tabachnick, Cambridge UP, 2017, 58–79.

McCloud, Scott. *Understanding Comics: The Invisible Art*. HarperCollins, 1994.

Mercé, Joel, and Ana Sánchez. "Max: 'Se están publicando más cómics que nunca.'" *El Periódico*, 29 April 2016, www.elperiodico.com/es/noticias/dominical/max-comic-entrevista-salon-5093949.

Merino, Ana. *El cómic hispánico*. Cátedra, 2003.

– "The Cultural Dimensions of the Hispanic World Seen through Its Graphic Novels." Translated by Derek Petry and Elizabeth Polli. *Teaching the Graphic Novel*, edited by Stephen E. Tabachnick, Modern Language Association of America, 2003, 271–80.

Merino, Ana, and Brittany Tullis. "The Sequential Art of Memory: The Testimonial Struggle of Comics in Spain." *Memory and Its Discontents: Spanish Culture in the Early Twenty-First Century*, edited by Luis Martín-Estudillo and Nicholas Spadaccini, *Hispanic Issues On Line* 11 (Fall 2012): 211–25. cla.stg.umn.edu/sites/cla.umn.edu/files/hiol_11_11_merino_the_sequential_art_of_memory.pdf.

Mitaine, Benoît. "Memorias dibujadas: La representación de la Guerra Civil y del franquismo en el cómic español. El caso de *Un largo silencio*." *Memoria y testimonio. Representaciones memorísticas en la España contemporánea*, edited by Georges Tyras and Juan Vila, Editorial Verbum, 2012, 148–70.

Mitchell, W.J.T. *Picture Theory: Essays on Verbal and Visual Representation*. U of Chicago P, 1994.

Moix, Terenci. *Los "comics": Arte para el consumo y formas "pop."* Libres de Sinera, 1968.

Pérez del Solar, Pedro. *Imágenes del desencanto: Nueva historieta española 1980–1986*. Iberoamericana/Vervuert, 2013.

Pérez-Sánchez, Gema. *Queer Transitions in Contemporary Spanish Culture, from Franco to La Movida*. SUNY Press, 2007.

Pizzino, Christopher. "The Doctor versus the Dagger: Comics Reading and Cultural Memory." *PMLA* 130.3 (2015): 631–47. doi.org/10.1632/pmla.2015.130.3.631.

Pons, Álvaro. "Reportaje: Literatura dibujada. Un tebeo escondido." *El País, Babelia*, 3 Feb. 2007, elpais.com/diario/2007/02/03/babelia/1170463150_850215.html.

Preston, Paul. *La Guerra Civil española*. Debate, 2016.

Ramírez, Juan Antonio. "La novela gráfica y el arte adulto." Prefacio. *La novela gráfica*, by Santiago García, Astiberri, 2010, 11–13.

Rosa, Isaac, and Cristina Bueno. *Aquí vivió: Historia de un desahucio*. Primera edición. Nube de Tinta, Penguin Random House Grupo, 2016.

Rucabado, Beatriz. "El cómic tiene una capacidad de contar historias que la gente a veces ignora." *El Mundo*, 17 Nov. 2010, www.elmundo.es/elmundo/2010/11/16/paisvasco/1289928204.html.

Ruiz Jiménez, Eneko. "El cómic también habla euskera." *El País*, 26 Nov. 2014, elpais.com/ccaa/2014/11/26/paisvasco/1417001622_758538.html.

Sánchez-Albornoz, Nicolás. Prólogo. *Paseo de los canadienses*, by Carlos Guijarro, Edicions de Ponent, 2015.

Sousanis, Nick. *Unflattening*. Harvard UP, 2015.

Tabachnick, Stephen E., editor. *Teaching the Graphic Novel*. Modern Language Association of America, 2009.

"TBO." *Tebeosfera, Cultura Gráfica*. Tebeosfera.com. www.tebeosfera.com/publicaciones/tbo_1917_suarez_buigas_tbo.html.

Torres, Steven. "Extrañamiento y subversión de la imagen en *Dinero* de Miguel Brieva." *Arizona Journal of Hispanic Cultural Studies* 16 (2012): 49–65. doi.org/10.1353/hcs.2012.0016.

Tufte, Edward R. *Envisioning Information*. Graphics Press, 2013.

Varillas, Rubén. *La arquitectura de las viñetas: Texto y discurso en el cómic*. Viaje a Bizancio Ediciones, 2009.

Vilarós, Teresa. *El mono del desencanto: Una crítica cultural de la transición española (1973–93)*. Siglo XXI, 1998.

PART ONE

Comics and Historical Memory

2 Drawing (on) Spanish History

SAMUEL AMAGO

El cómic tiene una enorme capacidad de rescatar el pasado, de volver a hacerlo presente, pero también tiene un gran poder de evocación simbólica.

[Comics have an enormous capacity to rescue the past, to make it present again, but they also have a tremendous power of symbolic evocation.][1]

Antonio Altarribia (qtd. in Rucabado)

While the turn of the twenty-first century began with global prophecies of disaster, chaos, and an altogether uncertain future after Y2K, the new millennium in Spain brought with it an emerging cultural consensus that the country's violent past – which had either been forgotten or purposefully ignored – needed to be revisited.[2] By the end of the 1990s, the question of historical memory had become a virtual obsession: following the exhumation of thirteen victims of the Francoist repression from a mass grave in the Leonese city of Priaranza del Bierzo, Emilio Silva and Santiago Macias founded the Asociación para la Recuperación de la Memoria Histórica [Association for the Recovery of Historical Memory] in 2000; the magistrate Baltazár Garzón began his ultimately unsuccessful attempts to bring perpetrators to justice; and José Luis Zapatero's government passed the Ley de la Memoria Histórica seven years later. Although this wave of memorialization in Spain was not immune to critiques emerging from both sides of the political spectrum, it is nonetheless important to remember that the twenty-first century began with a memory fever that would become one of the country's most visible and noteworthy cultural phenomena. Aguilar and Payne, among many others, have described how this process shed new light on some of "the hidden truths and exposed the skeletal framework of brutal, extralegal, and illegitimate violence" (91) that allowed Francoism to function. Yet, even as some political elites and significant blocks of the state's judicial apparatus sought to reinforce Spain's pact of silence and frustrate further investigation, memorialization, or remembrance, the country's democratic consensus gradually gave way to a more contentious coexistence that has allowed for "political participation, contestation, and expression in practice" for victims' families (Aguilar and Payne 91). But there is still a lot of work to be done.[3]

From the working through of traumatic personal memories to the discovery and preservation of family history, comics in Spain have deployed an array of self-conscious formal strategies to understand some of the ways that the country's authoritarian past still reverberates through its cultural present. Alongside other art forms – photography, fiction, documentary and fiction film, theatre, poetry – comics have taken up the call to contribute to the project of building and expanding the vernacular archive of historical memory of Francoist repression in Spain. New generations of comics artists working with historical material have employed the intimacy and cognitive engagement of the form to further worry, reveal, and uncover untold histories of wartime and post-war Spain.

Notwithstanding important contributions of earlier graphic novelists such as Carlos Giménez (*Paracuellos*, 1976–2003), Felipe Hernández Cava, and others (see the chapters by Pedro Pérez del Solar and Xavier Dapena in this volume), in what follows I elaborate on how contemporary Castilian-language *historieta* authors have tacked towards a more serious engagement with the intricacies of representing historical knowledge through reflexive approaches to hand-drawn representation.[4] As Hillary Chute has noted, the formal grammar of comics – "constantly enacted through the point of view of its most basic syntactical element, drawn frames" (*Disaster* 208) – lends itself to self-reflexivity. It is the structural layering of text and image arranged spatially on the page that allows comics to appeal to the reader in ways that transcend mere reading. As other commentators such as Will Eisner and Scott McCloud have described, reader participation in the construction of cause and effect, time and temporality is crucial to achieving the effect of intimacy because the reader must use his or her imagination to fill in the gaps between frames: "the reader's deliberate, voluntary closure is comics' primary means of simulating time and motion" (McCloud 69). In McCloud's words, "closure in comics fosters an intimacy surpassed only by the written word" (69).

What is noteworthy about recent Spanish historical comics is not only their process-oriented narrative structure, their mise-en-page of archival investigation, or their foregrounding of testimony and witnessing, but also the sustained attention they devote to visualizing the emotional, affective links that make intergenerational communication possible. Sensitively rendered drawings of human beings in distress form the aesthetic core of contemporary Spanish "postmemory" comics. As Groensteen remarks, the key adjectives associated with the comics form – "utterable, describable, interpretable and, ultimately, appreciable" (3) – are precisely what draw the reader into the making of meaning. In this line, historical comics in Spain create a relationship of nearness between comics creators, historical witnesses, and contemporary readers. This nearness or intimacy is a key strategy through which narrators at a generation's remove attempt to work through their national, personal, and familial histories through the graphic-verbal medium of comics.[5]

Spanish historical comics have sought to recover and visualize forgotten or untold stories from the Spanish Civil War and dictatorship from a leftist perspective, responding to the continuing cultural need of the descendants of the victims of Francoist repression to know their past. The aesthetic structures of these historical works, however, are wide ranging; each cartoonist brings to bear a recognizable hand and visual style, from Jorge García and Fidel Martínez's expressionistic *Cuerda de presas* [The Chain Gang] (2005) to Carlos Guijarro's more realist *Paseo de los canadienses* [The Canadian Promenade] (2015). The García-Martínez collaboration, for example, is composed of interrelated vignettes – the "chain" evoked in the title – centring on the lives and experiences of women held in Franco's prisons, including Ventas in Madrid and Les Corts in Barcelona. The black and white work is composed of a series of illustrated testimonies that sketch out an atmosphere of generalized repression and post-war atrocity. Fidel Martínez's drawings particularize the experiences of imprisoned women in a way that creates an ethical link in a chain connecting illustrator, witness, and reader.[6]

In introductory comments published in the 2005 edition of *Cuerda de presas*, the distinguished comics scriptwriter Felipe Hernández Cava describes the book as "la parte apagada del patrimonio de nuestra memoria" [the extinguished part of our remembered legacy] and "una reflexión moral sobre nuestros ayeres" [a moral reflection on our yesterdays] (García and Martínez 6, 7). He also makes the case more broadly for the role that comics have had in making Spanish history known to a popular readership in Spain. Hernández Cava insists that if poetry can be written after Auschwitz, certainly there can be poetry after a dictatorship whose "heridas no pueden cerrarse con mentiras o medias verdades" [wounds cannot be healed with lies or half-truths] (García and Martínez 7). Citing some of the most important Spanish historical *historietas*, Hernández Cava argues that comics play a crucial role in recovering historical memory:

> Necesitamos un patrimonio iconográfico que no sea fácilmente intercambiable y confundible, y que se sustente por sí mismo a contrapié de lo que los revisionistas nos quieren decir sobre aquellos tiempos. Los niños de Paracuellos de Carlos Giménez, los apuntes sobre la guerra de su padre de Miguel Gallardo, o las presas de Jorge García y Fidel Martínez, por ejemplo, son imágenes hechas a prueba de olvido y de incredulidad. El lenguaje de la historieta, afortunadamente, no se ha paralizado ante un horror que los que lo vivieron no se merecen que olvidemos. (García and Martínez 7)
>
> [We need an iconographic patrimony that will not be easily interchangeable or mistakable, and that will be self-sustaining even against what the revisionists would have us believe about those times. Carlos Giménez's *Paracuellos* children, the wartime diaries of Miguel Gallardo's father, or the prisoners recreated by Jorge García and Fidel Martínez, for example, are images that exist as proof against incredulity and oblivion. The language of comics, fortunately, has not been paralyzed by the horrors that those who lived them do not deserve to have forgotten.]

Each story included in *Cuerda de presas* responds to Hernández Cava's call for an aesthetic form that is both specific to historical reality (monstrative) but also aesthetically distinctive (graphiative).[7] Fidel Martínez's extremely stylized pictures create the sense that these women's experiences somehow exceed more straightforward representational modes. Their testimonies – elaborated in black and white – are drawn in a style that evokes early twentieth century expressionist wood cuts. (In this regard, Martínez's drawings fall in line with the shift away from realism in historical comics that Pérez del Solar describes in Chapter 3 of this volume.) The expressive power of *Cuerda de presas* flows from Martínez's limited palette and anti-realist form.[8] The demonic, macabre faces of the women's torturers provide a ghoulish visual counterpoint to the anguished images of the prisoners who remember their experiences in the present. In this way, the book's panels represent iconic structures of traumatic feeling. The uniformity of the book's arrangement of panels on the page (with minimal geometric or spatial variation) represents visually the sense of entrapment voiced by the women protagonists and narrators. There are no bleeds, splash pages, or double spreads, no colours or images that might suggest freedom, dynamism, or flow. The gutters form grids reminiscent of the windows of a prison cell, and the human faces and figures appearing within them are static. There is a formal tension in *Cuerda de presas* between containment of content within the rigid organization of panels and the immensity of a trauma too great to express. The relentlessly regular geometric patterning of the pages is a spatial counterbalance to the emotional excess expressed within them.

In keeping with the reflexive thrust of so many contemporary historical works, Martínez makes certain in *Cuerda de presas* to "produce the scene of testimony" (Chute, *Disaster* 206). As each survivor recounts her horrific experiences, Martínez bears witness, drawing himself into some of the panels. A sketch of a tape recorder, for example, appears interspersed with the images of a woman's memories of being tortured (García and Martínez 30–1), so that the present time of remembering is inflected with the pain that comes with remembering past traumas. This is part of the album's presentation of "a continuous movement between past and present" that draws attention "to the relationship between the two time periods" (Magnussen 63). The capacity of comics to represent past and present on the same page in alternating panels renders graphically the way Doña Carmen inhabits the past simultaneously in the time of remembering. If, as Douglas Wolk proposes, "cartooning can be read as a metaphor for the subjectivity of perception" (qtd. in Groensteen 85), the power of *Cuerda de presas* lies in the way in which Martínez's drawings allow the reader to see and sense a subjective perception of violence and trauma. That is, he not only pictures the remembered thing, time, and place, but also the moment of remembering and recording.

As Antonius Robben has noted in another context, "traumatic experience is ultimately incomprehensible because the violent event is so psychologically overwhelming and disorienting that it can never be grasped, remembered or understood in full" (265). The page layout and breakdown of images in *Cuerda de presas* function to braid together temporal and subjective points of view. Those perspectives are arranged in an expressionistic assemblage that demonstrates the emotional impact that the remembrance of traumatic memories can have. If traumatic experience escapes verbal language's potential to represent it, the drawn image allows the reader to perceive a double-coded form of memory, wherein past and present exist simultaneously. The drama of the comics testimony is achieved, in large part, by the way in which the comics creator may place him or herself in the place of witnessing, at once drawing and inhabiting the page in a doubled act of apprehension (Chute,

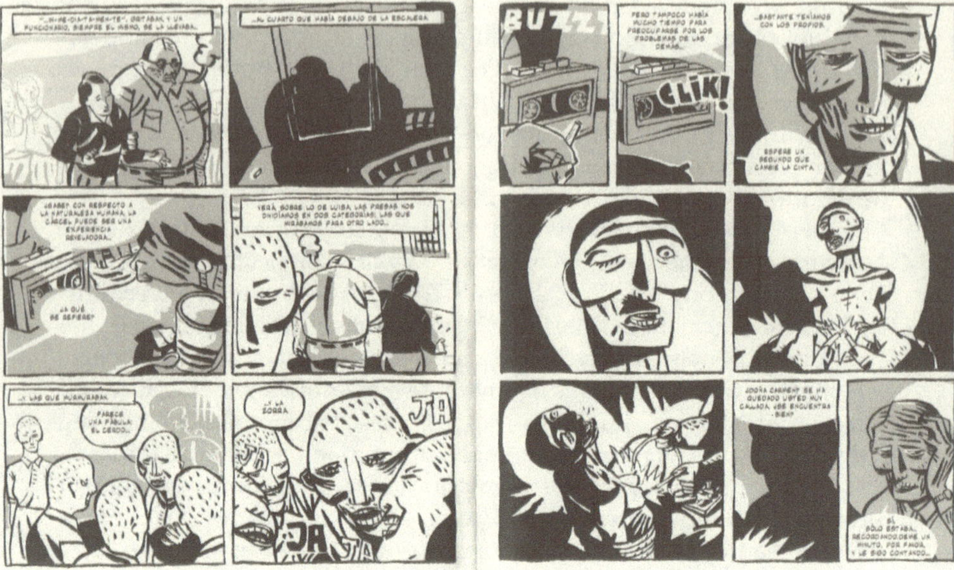

Figure 2.1. Past and present, technology and testimony in García and Martínez's *Cuerda de presas* (30–1).

Disaster 212). The skeletal, macabre figures and faces drawn by Martínez suggest that these witnesses and victims of traumas view the past still through the distorted lens of traumatic memory. To his credit, Martínez does not posit himself as a heroic representative or surrogate for the women. Rather, he remains in the shadows and allows the witness's memories to emerge onto the page (García and Martínez 32, 35).

While Martínez's drawings call attention to the horrors of traumatic memory, García's script makes explicit the modes of testimonial reporting by which the authors collected their narratives. A journalist appearing within the text, who has just heard Doña Carmen's story about an abused companion named Luisa – a fellow prisoner whose hair was left intact at the request of male guards who took her repeatedly to "el cuarto bajo la escalera" [the room under the stairs] – vows that he must render the story "con frialdad" [with cold objectivity] (García and Martínez 35). What is noteworthy about these pages, shown in figure 2.1, is the way that the unnamed author/journalist is drawn into the testimonies he is hearing; he situates himself within the text, appearing alongside the women whose stories he is conveying visually. In this regard, the work might be profitably compared to the comics

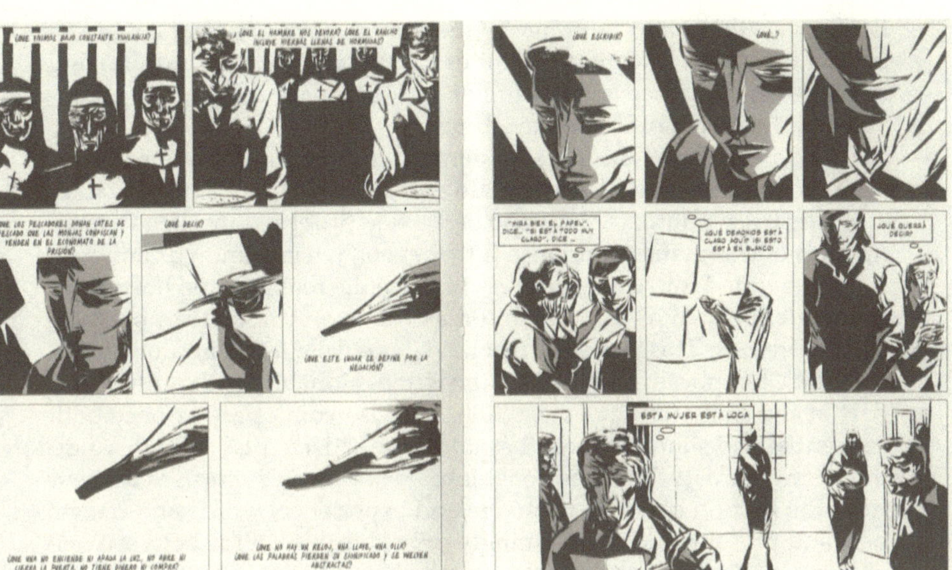

Figure 2.2. Representing traumatic memory in García and Martínez's *Cuerda de presas* (94–5).

analysed by Dapena in this volume, which aim to draw attention to marginal subjects and to construct a "genealogy of indignation."

Other outrages committed against Spanish women during the post-war period are represented elsewhere in *Cuerda de presas*: one vignette is devoted to the children who were taken from the imprisoned women (García and Martínez 39–45); another conveys the final memories of an old woman named Doña Elena who cannot forget "el traslado" [the transfer] by train whereby she was moved from city to city, the heat and excrement and lack of water (47–52) – this train journey is what was known as "salir de expedición" [going on an expedition] (54). The work concludes with a prisoner wondering how she could possibly begin to express her experience with words: "¿Qué decir?" [What to say?] (94), "¿Qué escribir?" [What to write?] (95); the volume's final blank pages suggest visually the danger of the erasure of memory and, ultimately, the difficulty of representing trauma through language or image (95). This difficulty is thematized in the text through Martínez's drawings: an extreme close-up of a gnarled pencil poised above a blank page, for example, places the reader in the moment of expression, a potentially ongoing emergence of narrative (figure 2.2). The blank page holds everything and nothing: "¿Qué querrá decir?" [What could she be saying?] (95). How might a pair of young men writing and drawing in the 2010s do justice to the traumatic testimony of these most vulnerable and forgotten of Franco's victims?

Drawing on Cathy Caruth's influential work on trauma and memory, Robben suggests that "there are always unknowns and unknowables at the heart of trauma," since one of the key problems implicit in testimonials of traumatic experience is that even "what is known cannot be fully integrated into consciousness because the reality is too horrible to acknowledge" (265). Yet, past traumas can exert a relentless pressure on the present. This pressure is what Chute calls the "simultaneity of traumatic temporality," by which the witness inhabits both present and past at the same time (*Disaster* 206). Because comics are at once both sequential and simultaneous, they allow the artist to play with this temporal simultaneity. The emotional impact of *Cuerda de presas* is derived from the friction between language and experience, words and image, past and present, and the seemingly unbridgeable divide between one person's subjectivity and another's.

An array of Spanish comics has explored the ever-changing relationships between generations and the problematic transmission of memory and discourse among and between interpretive communities in Spain since the dictatorship. *Un largo silencio* [A Long Silence] (2012) is a unique graphic diary written by a father – Francisco Gallardo Sarmiento – which was illustrated and published by his son, Miguel Gallardo, after his death. Like later historical *tebeos* such as Paco Roca's *Los surcos del azar* [Furrows of Fate] (2013) and Jaime Martín's *Las guerras silenciosas* [The Silent Wars] (2014), *Un largo silencio*'s written text aims to bring the memories and experiences of an older generation of Spaniards to the attention of a younger one.[9] The book is concerned principally with the ethics of giving voice to the father Francisco. On the opening page, Miguel Gallardo promises to relinquish his own power to speak in order to allow his father's voice to come through: "así voy a intentar contarla, dándole a mi padre una voz ... una voz que cuenta una parte de la historia cada vez más olvidada, pero que los que la vivieron la recordarán para siempre" [that's how I'm going to try to tell it, giving my dad a voice ... a voice that will tell part of a history that is gradually being forgotten, but that those who lived it will remember forever] (Gallardo and Gallardo 7). Thus, he transforms an otherwise unexceptional Spanish paterfamilias into a subject worthy of historical protagonism.[10] In this way, *Un largo silencio* conflates "the concepts of personal, generational, and national history" (Merino and Tullis 220) by repositioning "the Republican soldier not just as a victim, but as a national hero" (219). The work is also noteworthy for the way in which it scales heroism to the context of the nuclear family.

The expanded re-release of *Un largo silencio* (portions of it first appeared in print in 1995) is a hybrid narrative composed of images, occasional sequential graphic episodes, and Francisco's written testimonies. Francisco's diary, typeset in blue typewriter font, is illustrated by Miguel's sketches. Black and white nine-panel grids appear intermittently to illustrate first-hand experiences described in the diary. The effect of this alternation between the verbal narrative of Francisco's diary and Miguel's graphic sequences is to slow the development of Francisco's life story, allowing emblematic episodes to unfold in a more deliberate way.

Throughout *Un largo silencio,* the personal is interwoven with the political, the social, and the historical. Francisco's memories are punctuated with drawings depicting important events and artefacts: a freehand adaptation of the 16 April 1931 cover of *La Vanguardia* depicting the proclamation of the Spanish Republic (Gallardo and Gallardo 19); the exciting first days of the Republic (25–7); the Phalangists' aerial bombings of Madrid (29–31); an anecdote in which Francisco saved a wealthy Barcelonan from serving in the Líster Brigade (40) only to find, after the war, that the new Francoist class system had made their continued friendship impossible (41); Francisco's experiences in a French concentration camp and, upon his return to Spain, in a Barcelona prison (51–3); and so on. This interweaving of the personal and the national/historical is made possible by comics' spatial juxtaposition of frames and text. Images and stories of family life are interspersed with more well-known images of national happenings, so that the larger contours of historical events are scaled to the personal, the domestic, the familiar. The book concludes at the moment when Francisco meets his wife, which suggests – perhaps problematically – that the formation of the nuclear family signals the end of historical time and the beginning of a temporality organized around family events. A facsimile reproduction of a photo of Francisco's wife (figure 2.3) marks the end of his memoire.

Un largo silencio is a male bildungsroman that narrates Francisco Gallardo's coming of age in Franco's Spain. Its aspiration to serious historiography is buttressed by an appendix, titled "Álbum de fotos," containing facsimile reproductions of Francisco's photos, documents, and letters (63–72).

Although their narratives are scaled to the more intimate sphere of the home, the father-as-hero discourse appearing in many historical comics may be linked to a Spanish political present that was constructed largely without the benefit of heroes who, in other national contexts,

A continuación me dijo que no le había ocurrido una cosa igual en todos los años que llevaba examinando.
Me preguntó qué había hecho cuando la guerra, le dije que había sido Capitán de Artillería de la República y que venía de un campo de concentración. Me contestó: "Siento mucho que usted no pueda ingresar en esta empresa, a pesar del buen examen que ha hecho. Para poder ingresar hay que ser de Falange, excombatiente, excautivo o hijo de alguna persona que fuera fusilada por los rojos". Como se ve, los que tuvieron la mala suerte de caer en la zona republicana no tenían derecho nada más que a morirse de hambre, tanto ellos como sus familias.
Le enseñé el documento de mi puesta en libertad, en el cual, como ya he dicho anteriormente, se me clasificaba como "adicto al glorioso movimiento nacional". "Esto cambia las cosas, me dijo aquel señor, ahora puede usted ingresar en la empresa". Algún tiempo después pude comprobar que era una gran persona y fuimos muy buenos amigos.
Ingresé como técnico ensayador en el laboratorio eléctrico de la empresa, sito en la calle Mata, y allí empezó una nueva etapa de mi vida.
Me busqué una pensión en la calle Diputación, al lado de donde vivía la familia que conocía. No tenía amigos y me lo pasaba bastante aburrido. De vez en cuando iba a visitar a esta familia y un día la sirvienta de la casa me dijo: "¿Y tú no tienes novia?". Le dije que no y entonces me citó un día para presentarme a una chica cuya familia era de mi mismo pueblo, Linares.
Acudí a la cita y encontré a una chica preciosa de dieciocho años (yo tenía treinta y dos). Entonces ocurrió el suceso más feliz de mi vida y que la cambió por completo: conocí a la que había de ser mi MUJER.

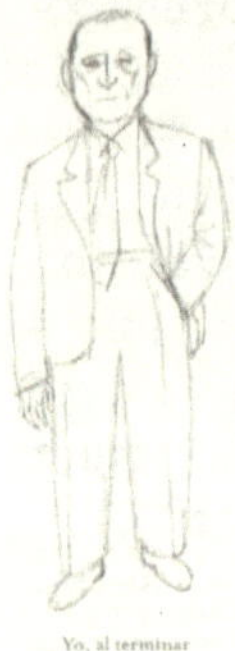
Yo, al terminar la guerra

62

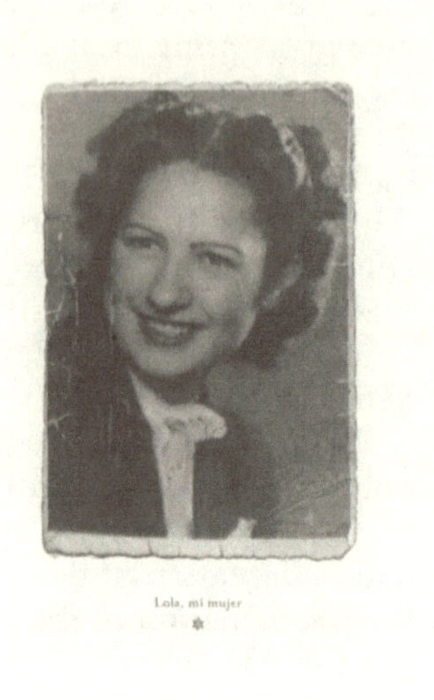
Lola, mi mujer

63

Figure 2.3. Family history in Gallardo and Gallardo's *Un largo silencio* (62–3).

worked as foundational figures. Antonio Gómez López-Quiñones has analysed how historical Spanish fiction has accordingly sought to establish, retroactively, a tradition and a history within which Spanish democracy and its inhabitants might find some kind of ideological satisfaction (*La guerra* 119). Discourses of heroism in democratic Spain, writes Gómez, have offered novelists and filmmakers an opportunity to call for justice for those who in 1936 were on the side of the Republic (*La guerra* 123), while also establishing ideological continuity between the Second Republic and the democratic present.

Following in this line, contemporary historical comics have similarly sought to visualize and establish new modes of heroism scaled to the family. In a graphic prologue to the book composed of several nine-panel pages (figure 2.4), Miguel Gallardo submits that his father was indeed a hero, but perhaps not a traditional one:

> Mi padre fue un héroe. No de esos que salen en las películas ... ni uno de novela barata como las que guardaba en el segundo cajón de su mesa, en

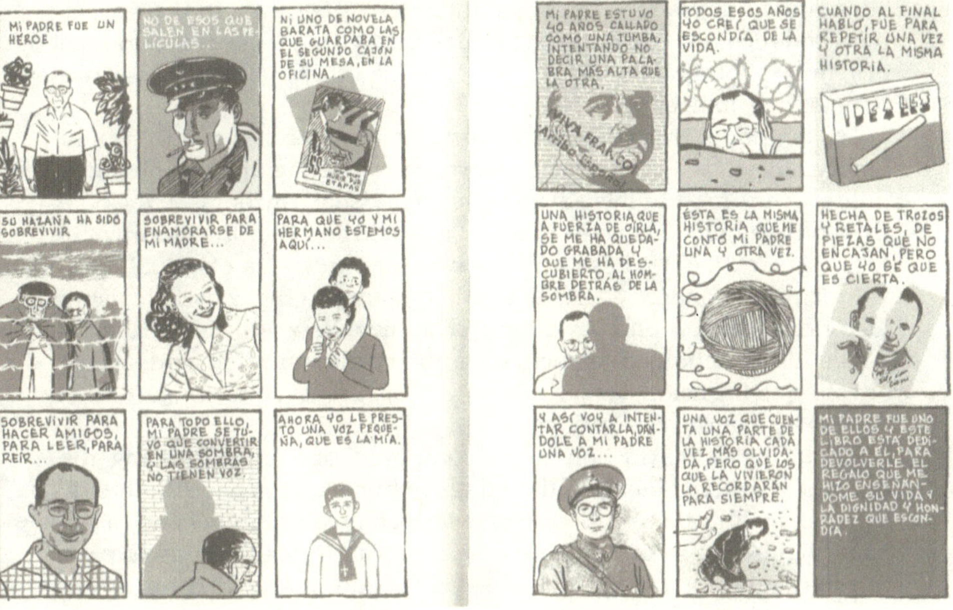

Figure 2.4. Hero-creation in Gallardo and Gallardo's *Un largo silencio* (6–7).

> la oficina ... su hazaña ha sido sobrevivir. Sobrevivir para enamorarse de mi madre para que yo y mi hermano estemos aquí ... sobrevivir para hacer amigos, para leer, para reír ... para todo ello, mi padre se tuvo que convertir en una sombra, y las sombras no tienen voz. Ahora yo le presto una voz pequeña, que es la mía. (6)
>
> [My father was a hero. Not like you see in the movies ... and not like you would read in the dime-store novels that he would keep in the second drawer of his desk at the office ... [H]is great accomplishment was to survive. To survive in order to fall in love with my mother so that my brother and I could be here ... to survive in order to make friends, to read, to laugh ... to achieve all that my father had to transform himself into a shadow, and shadows don't have a voice. But now I am giving him a small voice. That voice is mine.]

The testimonial value of Francisco Gallardo's life story is complemented by the drawn panels which work to stimulate the reader's sense of the passing of time as events transpire in the background. In keeping with the personal-historical dynamics outlined earlier, the alternating images flow back and forth across decades. In their aspect ratio and thematic content, Miguel Gallardo's drawings are reminiscent of family photographs or snapshots, while others reference historical happenings, images, events.

The temporal structure of *Un largo silencio* is organized mainly around family milestones – a marriage, a fortuitous meeting, the completion of military service – but there are also several visual "anchors" in the book that connect national events to their "adapted" hand-drawn form in the text (32, 68; 59, 67). These hand-drawn reproductions of visual archival materials connect Gallardo's father's story to the actually existing historical record. A photographic and archival appendix, including facsimile reproductions of Francisco's military identification card, a letter attesting to his character written by a parish priest, and so on (63–72), creates a powerful realist effect.

While the Gallardo volume is composed of interpenetrating discourses of historical realism (based on archival legitimacy or authenticity) and an ethical obligation to recover personal testimony and family history, it is important to emphasize that Miguel Gallardo takes pains to foreground his own role as interpreter and intermediary of his father's memories. His father's voice can be read – the typewriter font and first-person narration suggest a direct transcription of his recorded testimony – but the photos and drawn graphic elements remind the reader that there is a temporal distance between the living of history and the telling of it; the son authorizes and organizes the father's narrative, inscribing it within a national and familial historical narrative. As in *Cuerda de presas*, it is this play between the sequential and the simultaneous that gives the work its evocative power. If Francisco's life story is somehow more direct or "unfiltered," the drawn elements of the book point to the authorizing and editorial roles played by his son Miguel. For example, there is a panel in which a speech bubble appears atop a photo of a younger Francisco, and the older man's thumb appears holding the image: "Mira ... Esta foto me la hizo Ángel el mismo día que pasó lo que te explico, igual unas horas antes" [Look. Angel took this picture of me on the same day that what I'm telling you about occurred, maybe a few hours beforehand] (32; figure 2.5).[11]

This use of reproductions of real historical material (the facsimile reproduction of the photo appearing in this drawn page can be seen in figure 2.6) is a significant technique appearing in several of the historical comics analysed in this chapter. These gestures towards the archival record function at once to reinforce their narrators' claims to truth, while also rendering visible the materials from which history is made.[12]

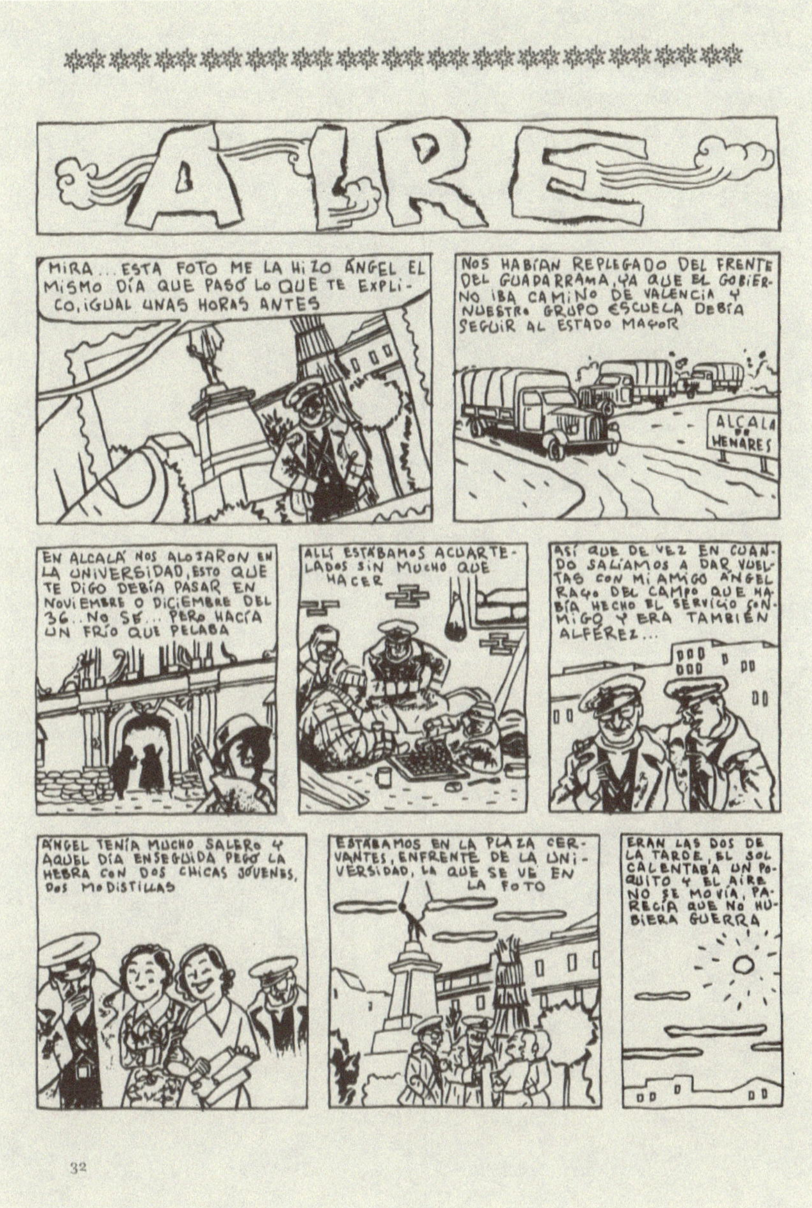

Figure 2.5. Drawing the archive into the personal narrative in Gallardo and Gallardo's *Un largo silencio* (32).

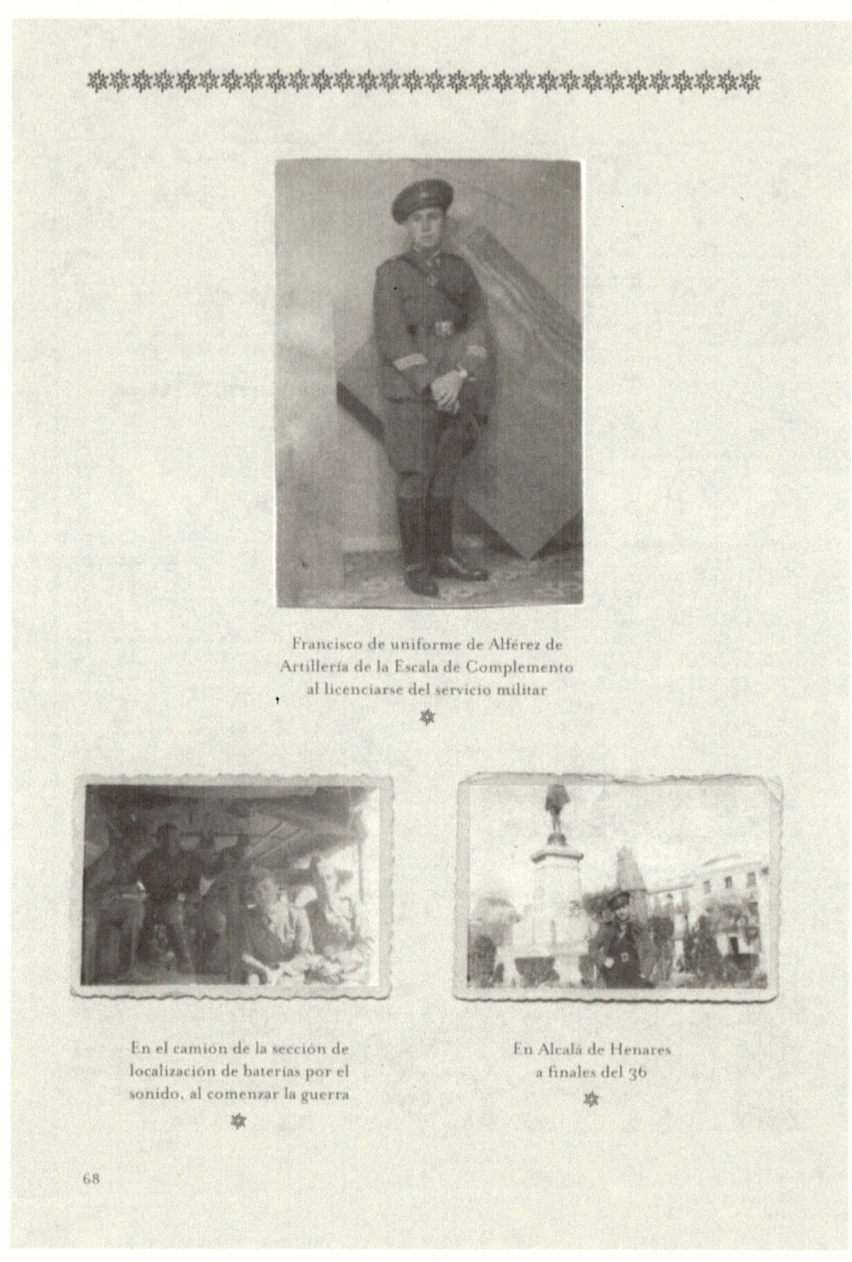

Figure 2.6. Facsimile archival images in Gallardo and Gallardo's *Un largo silencio* (68).

Comics have the capacity to bear witness, presenting visual evidence through drawn marks on a page. In a slightly more realist register, Paco Roca's *Los surcos del azar* [Furrows of Fate] (2013) is also engaged in the political project of recovering Republican heroes for Spanish democracy. The book details the efforts of a comics journalist, not unlike Paco Roca himself, who travels to France to interview a Spanish veteran of Spain's Civil War and World War II. Having lived many years in exile, the man, Miguel Ruiz, grudgingly shares his story of fighting fascism in France under General Leclerc following the defeat of the Spanish Republic. The book tells two stories: Miguel's experiences fighting fascism in Southern Europe and the story of how Roca recovers and represents Miguel's memories through an engaged process of interviewing, researching, and drawing. Throughout *Los surcos del azar* Roca collapses – through overlapping panels picturing past and present – the affective and chronological distance between the generation of the Spanish Civil War's survivors and their grandchildren.

As Antonio Altarribia asserts in the first epigraph to this chapter, comics allow readers to recover and visualize the past, to make it present, to draw it nearer. But the graphic form also has the power to evoke things symbolically. *Los surcos del azar*, the best comic book produced in Spain in 2013 by Pons's account, has since been reprinted several times. Roca deploys alternating panels in colour (past) and black and white (present). Harris proposes that this colour scheme works to bring "vibrancy to the past events," while also inverting the reader's expectation of a typical cinematic flashback. The past, in other words, is drawn on the page much more vibrantly than the present (Harris and Del Rey Cabero).

If Roca is to be criticized, it is perhaps because the thematic content and narrative development of *Los surcos del azar* is so similar to Javier Cercas's novel *Soldados de Salamina* (2001) and its film adaptation, directed by David Trueba in 2003.[13] Both the Cercas novel and Trueba film explored – through a self-reflexive lens – the intricacies of recovering the historical memories of survivors who had either died, been forgotten, or had no interest in delving into their own painful past.[14] Like Cercas, Roca focuses his historical narrative on the life and wartime exploits of a Republican soldier exiled in France and with whom the narrator shares an imagined familiar link. And, again, like Cercas and Trueba, Roca deploys the figure of Antonio Machado as a way to infuse his tale with pathos while staking a claim to cultural distinction. The poet is drawn into Roca's account of the exiles' road to Southern France where Machado perished (figure 2.7).

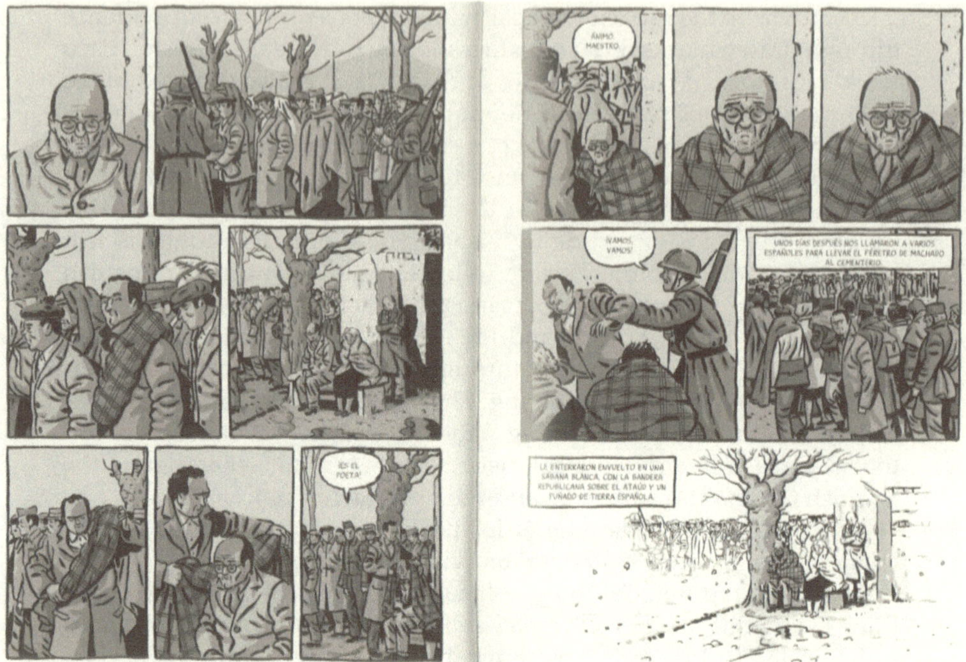

Figure 2.7. Antonio Machado on the road to France in Roca's *Los surcos del azar* (62–3).

In an essay on the Trueba adaptation of *Soldados de Salamina*, Andrew Anderson has described how the film's use of a well-known image of Antonio Machado is actually a "conventional and even rather hackneyed starting-point, as it is a much reproduced picture of Machado who is, alongside Lorca and Miguel Hernández, one of the Second Republic's most cited and recognizable figures" (158).[15] Roca uses the images of Antonio Machado with similar ends, while also harvesting a Machado poem for use in the book's epigraph and title. Roca uses Machado to suffuse his text with a similar kind of nostalgic, male-centred structure of feeling.

Although it is arguably derivative, *Los surcos del azar* nonetheless deserves mention for the way that it links Roca's long-time interest in social issues – especially in terms of how contemporary Spanish society treats its older citizens, as in his earlier *Arrugas* [Wrinkles] – to his corollary project to uncover some of the forgotten intimate histories and memories of that generation, seen in *La casa* [The House] and *El invierno del dibujante* [The Cartoonist's Winter]. In formal terms, *Los*

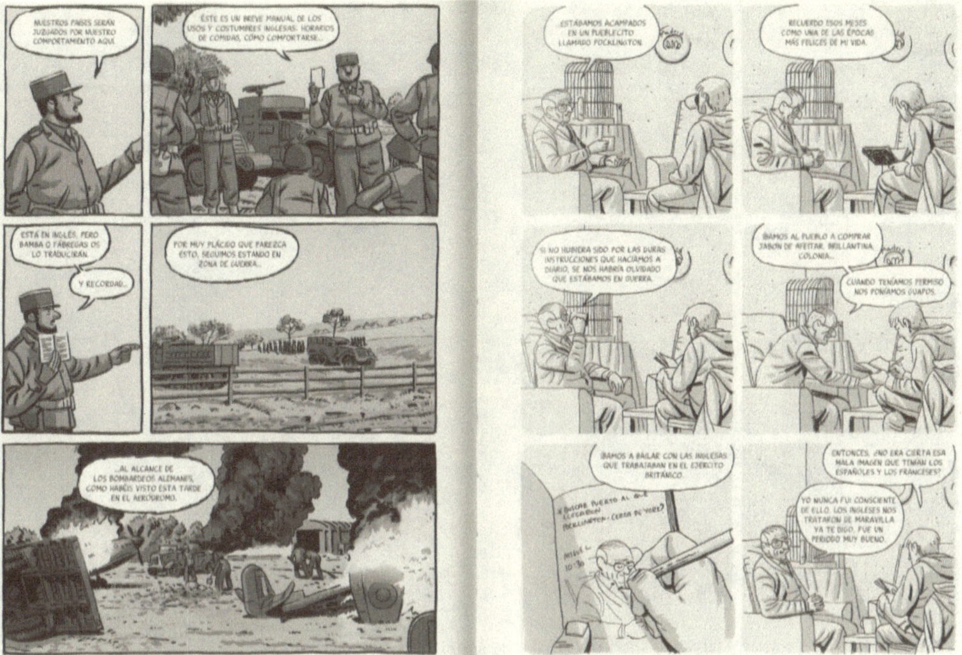

Figure 2.8. Reflexivity and memory in Roca's *Los surcos del azar* (168–9).

surcos del azar is not as innovative or visually adventurous as other Spanish historical comics analysed in this chapter. Roca's panelling hews to three- and four-row organizational schemes, with only a handful of two-thirds page panels interspersed through the text (*Los surcos* 12, 160, 173, 186, 268, 270–1, 272).[16] This rigid spatial arrangement of smaller panels arranged on the page emphasizes Roca's interest in the microhistories that can be gleaned from personal experiences of history and memory. The emotional closeness of his story of male friendship combines with self-reflexivity in order to situate the graphic novelist as a testimonial writer, historiographer, and champion of the recovery of historical memory (figure 2.8) in a postmodern society all too prepared to sever its ties to the past.

In terms of aesthetics and narrative structure, Jaime Martín's *Las guerras silenciosas* (2014), originally published in France in 2013, offers perhaps a more innovative account of a father's coming of age. The book begins with a cartoonist struggling with writer's block who decides to draw the story of his father's experiences during Spain's last colonial war in the

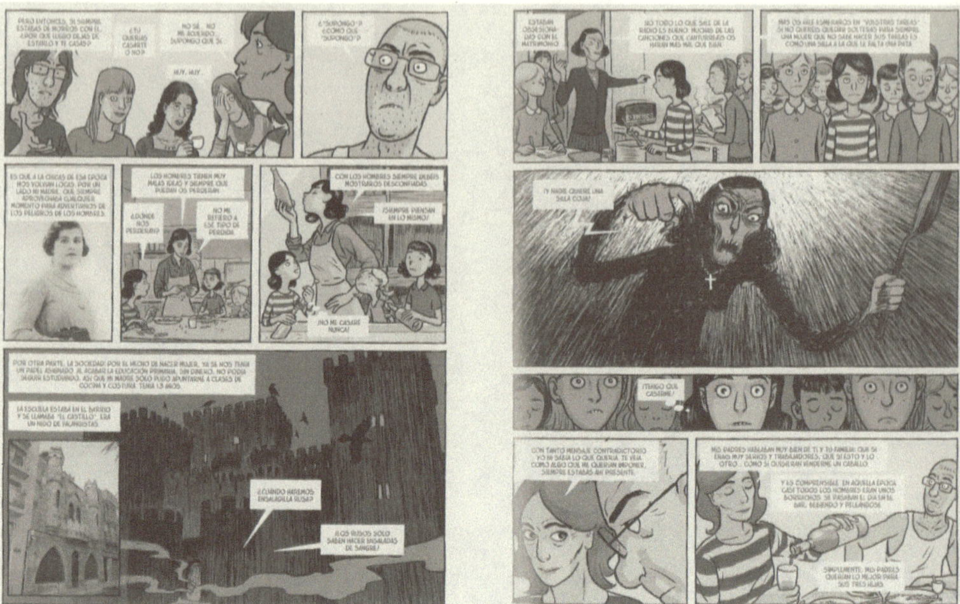

Figure 2.9. Family history and memory in Martín's *Las guerras silenciosas* (26–7).

Western Sahara, known as "La guerra silenciosa." Like the other comics analysed in this chapter, Martín's account of his father's time in "la mili" [the military] in the early 1970s is imbedded within a broader family story of how the narrator's parents met and fell in love, offering a kind of visual version of Carmen Martín Gaite's *Usos amorosos de la posguerra española* [Love Customs of the Spanish Post-War Period]. Martín's mother contributes a mostly complementary perspective on love customs and their courtship during the Franco dictatorship (figure 2.9).

In *Las guerras silenciosas*, the protagonist – a comics artist resembling Martín himself (figure 2.10) – travels to his parents' house in the country for a paella lunch where his father tells a few stories about his time doing military service in the Western Sahara. As the narrator builds his story around his father's memories, his mother approvingly describes the project as "un tebeo histórico" [a historical comic book] (100). The ensuing narrative weaves together the young novelist's attempts to put his father's life experiences on the page, alongside graphic visualizations of his father's actual experiences. The narrator/protagonist constantly weighs alternative modes of telling his tale: "Soy demasiado clásico. Me resulta extraño desordenar el relato" [I'm too classical. I can't jumble up the story] (101). The resulting comic book is as much about Martín's own

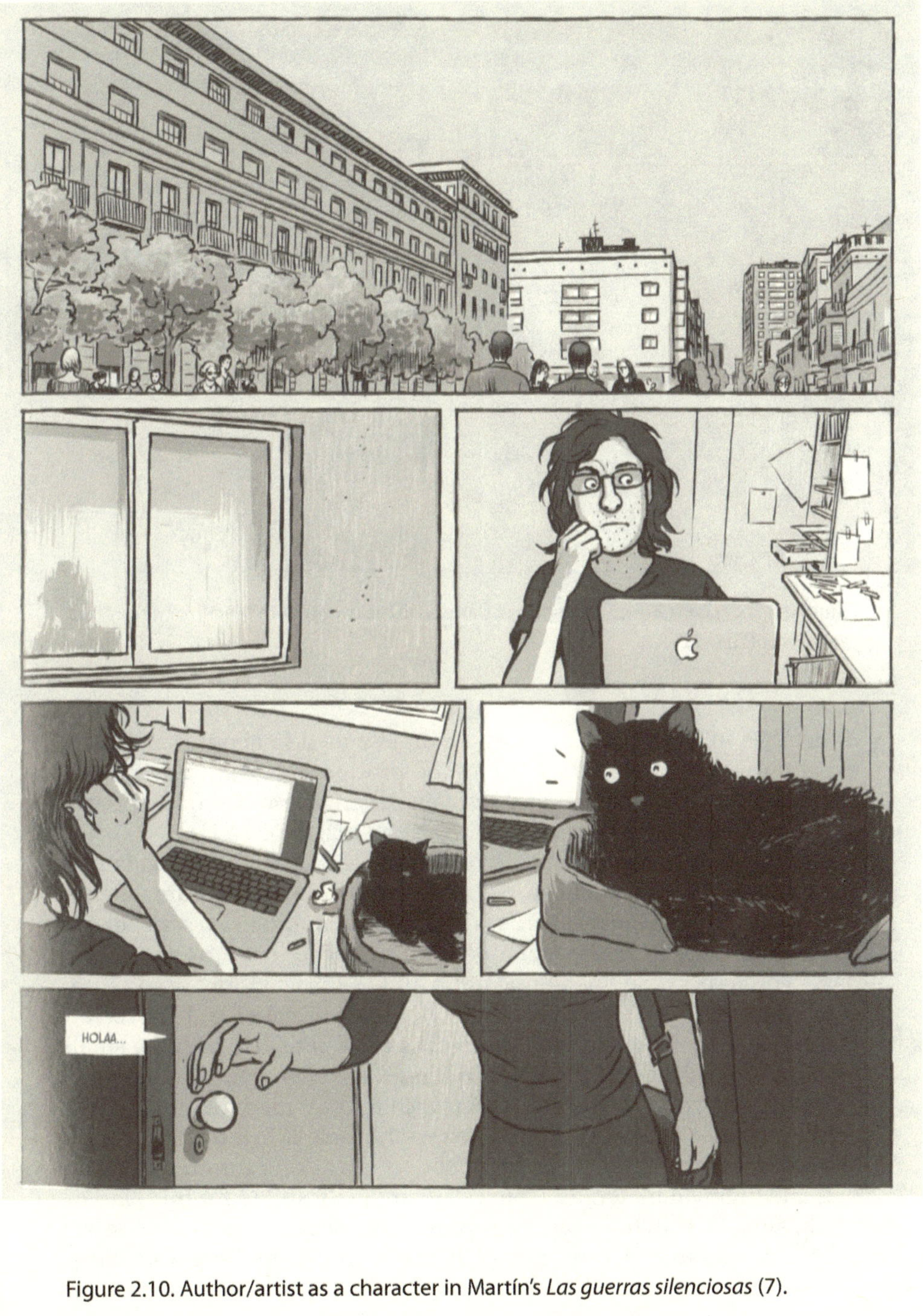

Figure 2.10. Author/artist as a character in Martín's *Las guerras silenciosas* (7).

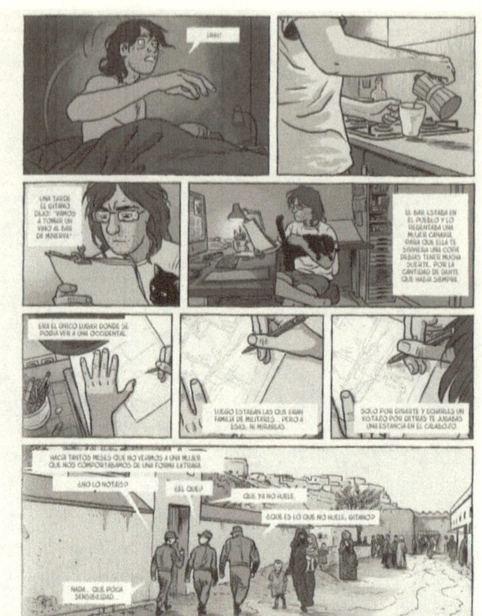

Figure 2.11. Captain America inspires Spanish historiography in Martín's *Las guerras silenciosas* (102–3).

difficulties in rendering the story accurately as it is about his father's experiences in North Africa (103). The process is leavened with self-reflexive humour: an imaginary Captain America, for example, appears at one point to offer his help to the narrator (102; figure 2.11).

The narrator discusses his interpretation of the past with his father, asking why he always told stories as if it were a fun adventure when it was really a miserable mess. His father responds, "Pues lo escribí en un papel y me guardé la porquería para mí. ¡Y luego uno aprende a quedarse con lo poco de bueno que hubo allí! ¡Y lo transforma y lo estira, como un chicle!" [Well, I wrote it all on a piece of paper and I saved all the garbage for me. And later one learns to be satisfied with the small amount of positive stuff that was in there! And then you take the positive stuff and you transform it and stretch it like a piece of gum!] (152).

Like Miguel Gallardo, Martín draws himself into his comic book about his father. On the page, he can be seen working through testimonies and archival materials. Comics are uniquely suited for this kind of work, since the archive can be rendered visually alongside the interpretive narrative structures forged by the historian/investigator/artist. The panels in figure 2.12, for example, depict a telephone conversation

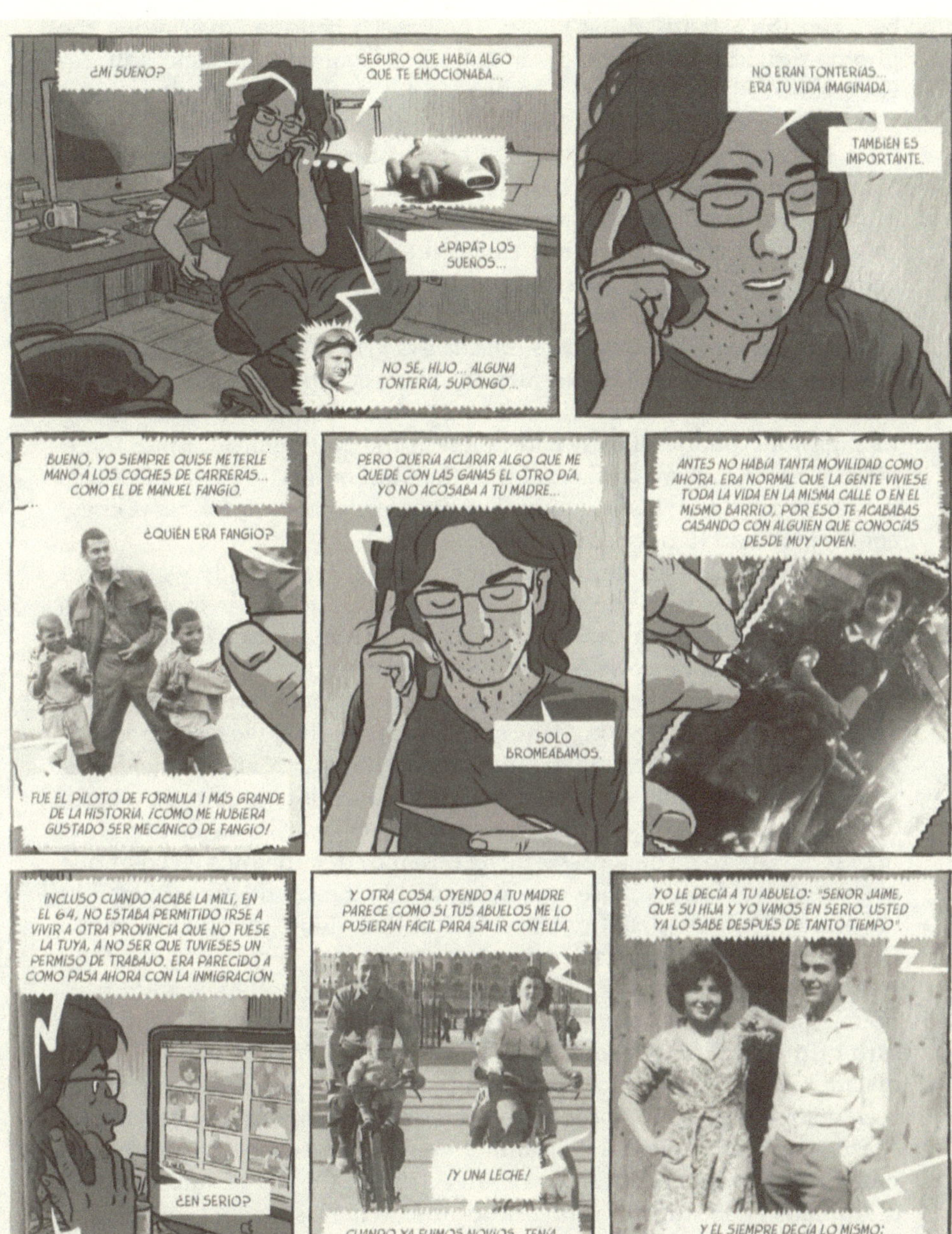

Figure 2.12. Getting the story straight in Martín's *Las guerras silenciosas* (59).

between the artist and his father. The speech balloons overlaying the photos provide what Smolderen calls a "visual sound track" (qtd. in Groensteen 3), as the artist attempts to fill in the gaps in his father's story. The inclusion of photographic reproductions within the comic book text moors his father's story to the historical record. This gesture towards realism is buttressed by a closing section titled "Extras," which provides further facsimile reproductions of photos from his father's archive, including military draft cards, the printed text of the "jura de bandera," [swearing of allegiance to the flag], historical photos of Ifni, camps, streets, and military vehicles.

Carlos Guijarro's *Paseo de los canadienses* [The Canadian Promenade] (2015) relates a lesser-known atrocity that occurred in February 1937, when German and Italian aviation bombarded the refugees fleeing Málaga for Almería after it had fallen to the Nationalists. In an interview, Carlos Guijarro explained that the motivation for his project was the fact that so few Malagueños – or Spaniards for that matter – knew about what had happened (Jiménez).

Also known as "La desbandá" [the escape], the episode was one of the greatest massacres of civilians (between five and fifteen thousand) to occur during the Spanish Civil War. Unsurprisingly, the event was denied during the Franco years and then forgotten during the democratic period ("Masacre"; Bollero). Guijarro's book opens with a full-page splash that draws attention to the chromatic tones that we tend to associate with historical memory, so often rendered in black and white. Hand lettering contextualizes the images: "En nuestro imaginario, la Guerra Civil sucedió en blanco y negro: Kappa, Centelles, Gerda Taro, por no hablar del Guernica de Picasso, no recordamos documentos en color que nos acerquen el suceso" [In our imagination, the Civil War occurred in black and white: Kappa, Centelles, Gerda Taro, not to mention Picasso's *Guernica*. We don't want to remember documents in colour when they draw the event closer.] (7). The book's second page offers several panoramic panels depicting the full-colour historical present. Thus, with a turn of the page, the reader may see the formal links between a more distant historical time and a present time in which young people can be seen enjoying the same beaches on holiday. The apparently ahistorical coastal space is overlaid with traumatic national memory: the bright colours of swimwear, beers, and coloured tablecloths detail sunny scenes of Andalusian leisure in the precise location where, seventy years before, Italian military air forces strafed Spanish civilian refugees.

Like the other artists and scriptwriters appearing in the comics detailed previously, Guijarro makes a place for himself in his text, where he appears as a slightly fictionalized man whom his friends call "Charli."

On holiday in Málaga, an impromptu walk in the hills above the beach leads Charli and his friends to the "Paseo de los canadienses," a maritime esplanade where an older gentleman relates briefly the story of the "carretera de la muerte" [highway of death]. As the narrative develops, the artist's investigations lead him to a meeting with Macarena, one of the few remaining witnesses of the atrocities that had occurred on the road to Almería. Although Guijarro replicates the chromatic trope common in historiographic comics – whereby the remembered past is rendered in a limited palette (22) – he does take the liberty of including some flourishes of red ink where blood is spilled. Guijarro also draws attention to the comics format through a staged dialogue with Macarena, who expresses doubt about how a "tebeo" might represent her experience adequately (figure 2.13).

The main contribution of *Paseo de los canadienses* is didactic, since it illustrates how German and Italian aviation aided Spanish Nationalist naval power in an unprecedented early attack on refugees fleeing the city, where they killed between five and fifteen thousand civilians. Guijarro concludes the book with some written observations on the importance of recovering historical memory in Spain. The author reflexively inserts his own text into the broader social and political context of memory and history in Spain, noting that "bajo el pretexto de no reabrir viejas heridas se ha pretendido pasar página arrancándola del libro" [under the pretext of not opening old wounds, they have tried to turn the page by tearing it from the book] (117). The narrator continues his reverie when he and his companions join Macarena at the site of the historical trauma: "mientras, de solapado, se reescribe la historia, se dulcifica y se banaliza. Y no, no se puede banalizar el franquismo. Venimos de sus horrores y su rastro todavía se deja sentir" [while history is being rewritten secretly it is also sweetened and banalized. But no! You cannot banalize Francoism. We are descended from its horrors and its trace can still be felt] (117).

Guijarro had never before worked in comics. He notes in an interview that he chose the graphic form because it would allow him to reach a broader public unaccustomed to consuming history in a conventional sense (Jiménez). In discussing his story of the "carretera de la muerte," Guijarro remarks that memory is the most powerful instrument that victims have to battle injustice (Jiménez). Like Roca, Martín, and Gallardo, Guijarro incorporates historical footnotes (25) and an appendix of "fuentes bibliográficas, gráficas y audiovisuales," which includes works written by eyewitnesses in the 1930s, more recent historical sources, published testimonies by survivors, documentary films, and novels (119–20). Footnotes appearing in the gutters also denote specific vignettes that reproduce more directly historical documents

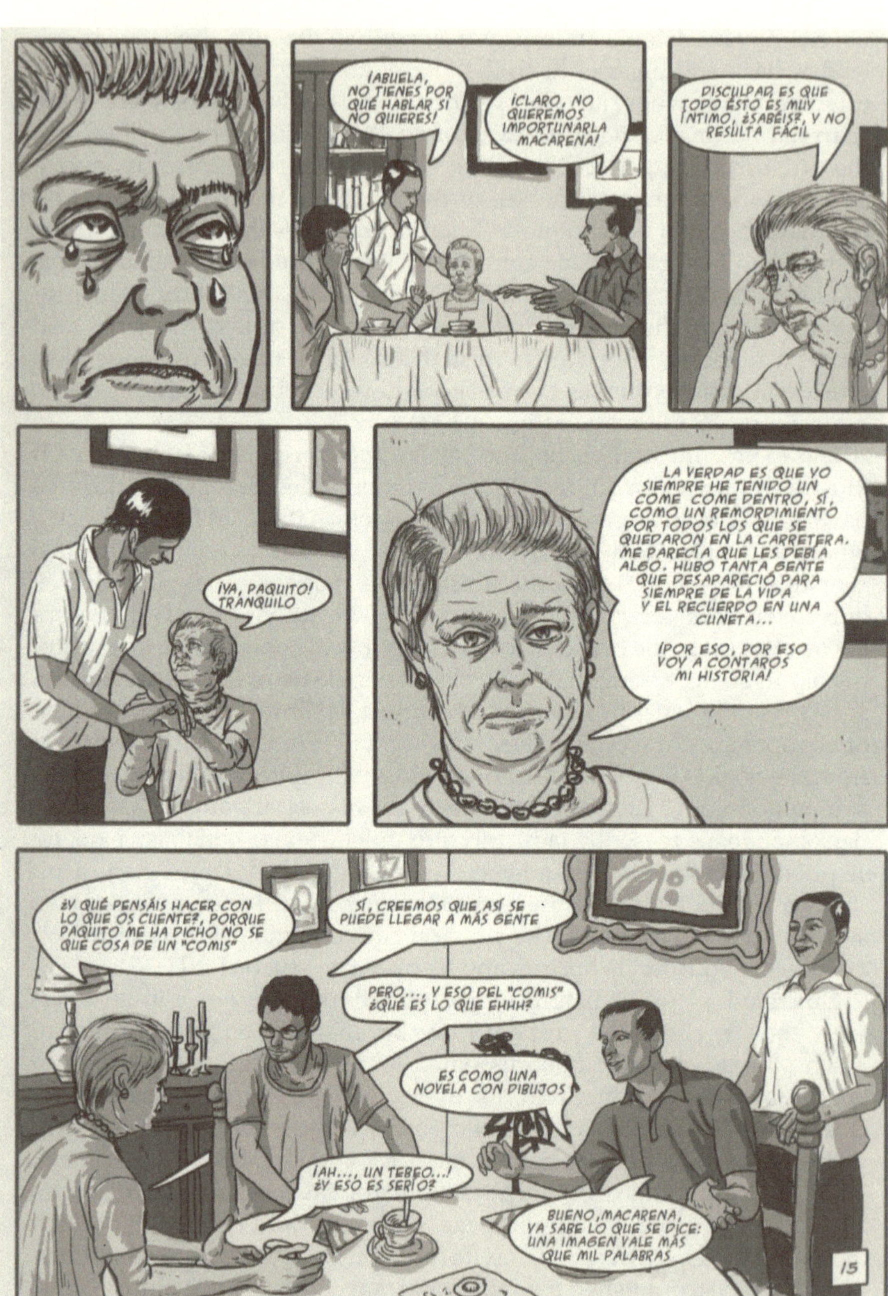

Figure 2.13. Visualizing emotion in Guijarro's *Paseo de los canadienses* (15).

and photographs; photographs taken by the Canadian Hazen Sise, who accompanied Norman Bethune during his time in Andalucía as an ambulance driver for the Red Cross, appear in this form (15, 113). Spanish historical comics rely on a similar aesthetic by which comics artists render, adapt, or transform archival photographic images in ink (Martín, *Las guerras* 103, 159; Martel and Santolaya; García and Martínez 63; Gallardo and Gallardo 32, 68 and 59, 67). The historical and linguistic footnote also appears in the García and Martínez volume (back cover, "cuerda de presas" from the DRAE [Dictionary of the Spanish Royal Academy], "junta de casado" [spouses' meeting] 21, "las posteriores" [the rearguard] 34, "salir de expedición" 54, Pilar Primo de Rivera 66, and Gallardo 31). Guijarro includes direct quotation from Peter Chalmers-Mitchell and Arthur Koestler, well-known Northern European witnesses to the Spanish Civil War who went on to author books about their experiences (Guijarro 51), and, in a testimonial piece about life in post-war Spain, a brief overview of Vallejo-Nájera's discredited scientific views on the "red gene" (83; a quote from Vallejo-Nájera is also found in García and Martínez 39).

Guijarro carefully links his story to the historical record, signals and footnotes his archival sources, and insists that his main aim is to make his images "lo más contenidos posible" [the most restrained as possible] (Jiménez). It is thus noteworthy that throughout the text he also draws attention to the emotional structures of feeling that historical remembrance has for its witnesses. Guijarro is perhaps the least formally accomplished of those graphic novelists working with historical material, yet the emotional charge of his images is remarkable. Throughout his book, he takes pains to draw the tears flowing from the eyes of people as they recount their experiences (Guijarro 39, 63, 65, 73, 80, 89, 90, 96, 116). Only the family history narrated in Jaime Martín's most recent work, *Jamás tendré 20 años* [I Will Never Be 20 Years Old] (published in Spanish in 2017), which begins with a prologue in which his grandmother weeps as she remembers the violence of the post-war years, is more emphatic in its lachrymose visuality. In figure 2.14, four sequential vertical panels focus ever more closely on the tears flowing from a woman's eyes.

These images reveal the strong emotions that are still attached to temporally distant traumas, and they show the depth of feeling that oral testimonies can evoke. As Luisa Elena Delgado, Pura Fernández, and Jo Labanyi note, emotions also have "a social and socializing function," since they bring together "emotional communities" through the performance of emotion (4). The formal grammar of comics is uniquely suited to doing this kind of work through its inherent reflexivity. Yet, Guijarro is clearly in tune with the emotional power of testimonial

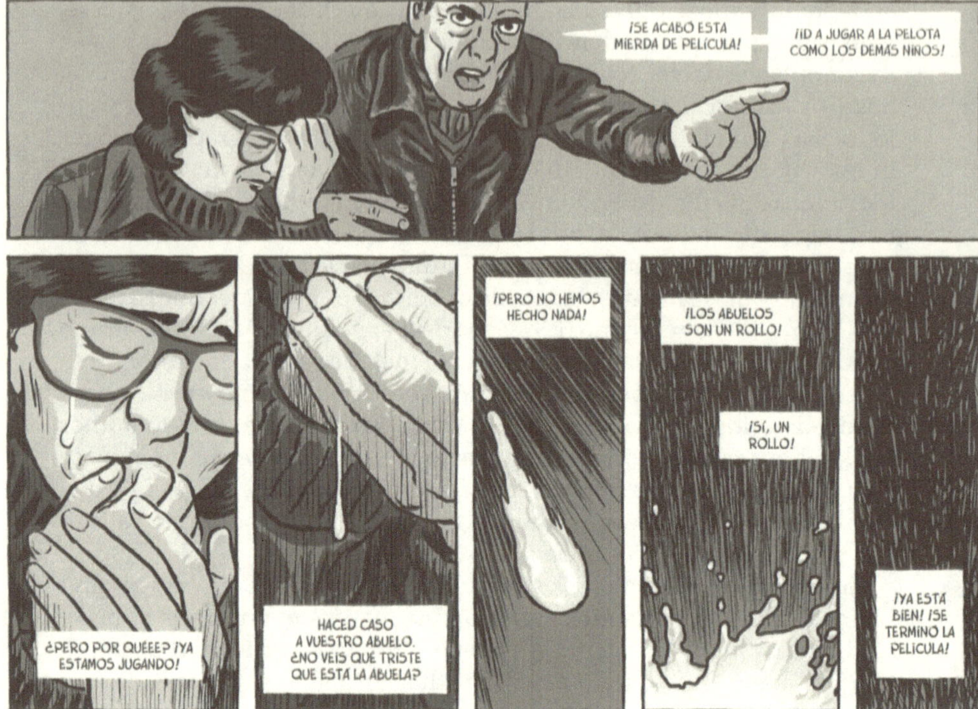

Figure 2.14. Memory, tears, emotion in Martín's *Jamás tendré 20 años* (8).

memory, and he works purposefully to draw tears onto the faces of his interlocutors. Fittingly, the last image of Guijarro's text pictures a full-page splash of the artist at his drafting table, titling his work: *Paseo de los canadienses*. Thus, the conclusion of the work is also its beginning. The author/artist, who begins his narrative sunbathing on the beach, draws himself, in the end, committing himself to bringing a silenced and forgotten historical event to the public's awareness. By placing himself onto the page, drawn with his own hand – literally leaving traces of his hand in the text – he represents a form of solidarity with the historical victims of Francoist violence.

The emergence of personal and family memories within the heart of historiographical discourse in Spain is part of a process we might describe as the democratization of history and memory on the Peninsula. In an essay on the evolving contours of historical discourse and the concomitant rise of memory and subjectivity within its epistemological structures, Beatriz Sarlo has remarked on how oral histories and testimony can function to empower the people who tell personal stories about their private, public, affective, and political lives. Oral history and testimony thus work to preserve memory and repair damaged identities (22). This "personalization" of a Spanish national history, focalized through individual's subjectivities, has not been without its critics. The historian Antonio Cazorla-Sánchez has argued for what he calls a more "balanced" approach to memory that would resist what he sees as a dangerous prominence of victimhood discourses in the historical realm (not just in Spain, but also in the United States [47–8], Germany [49], and Israel [45–6]) by victims who "may or may not have been killers themselves" (49). Accordingly, Cazorla-Sánchez outlines what he sees as some of the risks inherent in the shift from more institutional or professional practices of history towards the individual ones that have taken centre stage in Spain, and what these might mean for the field of history generally. Although he clearly takes pains to temper his own account, Cazorla-Sánchez's essay critiques the prominence of emotion to the articulation of personal memory in the field of history. But in discounting emotion, the author fails to consider its cultural functions in the present. On the one hand, part of the emotional intensity of memory discourses in Spain and elsewhere derives from the perceived need of the "generación de los nietos" [grandchildren's generation] to preserve the individual memories of survivors who are disappearing every day. This desire to record family history is linked to the silence that, for good or for bad, kept many personal accounts unexpressed publicly after the death of the dictator.

Memory, along with the personal and public emotions it evokes, can function as a complementary discourse to the soberer institutional discourses emerging from university faculties of history. One suspects that critics of memory and emotion such as Cazorla-Sánchez are uncomfortable with new methodologies that have shaped new directions for Iberian area studies. Cultural studies of history, memory, emotion, and testimony, such as the volume edited by Delgado, Fernández, and Labanyi, have shown how emotion is not just "a topic of exhibition and display" or "a controlled, intellectually light, emotionally loaded excursion" aimed at uncritical cultural consumers, as Cazorla-Sánchez (40, 41) would have us believe. Emotion is also part of the lesson to be learnt about the architectures of lived present-day experience.

Why have memory, emotion, and the melodramatic mode risen to prominence in the spectacular structures of contemporary Iberian cultural production? Josep Català has engaged with these questions, via Hannah Arendt, in terms of what he has called "el apogeo de lo íntimo" [the rise of intimacy] (29–39), whereby the private realm has been progressively spectacularized in and by global visual cultures. Juli Highfill notes that the "complex affective content" of early twentieth century cultural production has become "ever more acute today as thinkers ponder the complexities of media experience in the digital age" (136). And Delgado, Fernández, and Labanyi have outlined how culturally specific forms of emotional expression and experience have always gone hand in hand with the production and interpretation of thought and knowledge (1–20).[17]

What we can see operating in contemporary Spanish historical comics is how artists, scriptwriters, and amateur historians have sought to make audible and visible precisely those quotidian, domestic, and familiar perspectives on history that have tended to be left out of the academic historical record. Across the comics analysed in this chapter, Spanish *historietistas* have drawn themselves into their own stories, where they become engaged participants in the crucial task of recovering historical memory, bearing witness to trauma, and drawing remembrance into the panels of the present. Armed with notebooks, tape players, photographs, pens, and archival materials, contemporary Spanish comics creators personalize national history, making perceptible the smaller scale stories that have not yet been heard or seen.

In one way or another, all these historical comics deploy two conventions that have tended to dominate contemporary independent comics internationally: the autobiographical and the historical. Their creators demonstrate an ethical concern with giving voice to the silenced victims of the systematized abuses of the Franco dictatorship. First-person narrators, graphic novelists, sons, daughters, and grandchildren appear and disappear on the page to elicit and listen to the testimonies and historical memories of the aged characters with whom they come into contact. These comics evince a compelling interest not only in memorializing the last surviving witnesses of the Spanish Civil War and, increasingly, of the post-war period, but also in explaining the present through the emotional experiences of older people's memories of the past. These comics tell the stories of how youthful protagonists get over their self-centred obliviousness and acquire a new historical epistephilia. They look beyond the contemporary Spanish present by uncovering and seeking to comprehend historical episodes previously unknown to them. In this regard, following Marianne Hirsch, these works of postmemory reveal the "*structure* of inter- and trans-generational transmission of traumatic knowledge and experience" (106).

If, as Robert Musil has said, "nothing is as invisible as monuments" (qtd. in Linden 162), these historical comics strive not only to make the past visible again, but also to make it felt again by a generation far removed from the look and feel of Spain's violent history. Melding personal and collective memory, history, and testimony, Spanish graphic histories aim to permeate the present with images and consciousness of the past as monuments to history's forgotten protagonists. From the copious tears flowing from the illustrated faces of the characters of *Paseo de los canadienses* to Paco Roca's moving reflections on time, ageing, and the intergenerational transfer of memory, graphic novelists in Spain have worked purposefully to signal the crucial interdependence of narratological agency and historical and political commitment. *Historietistas* entangled in the Spanish present – with its crises, its politics of forgetting, its multimedial cacophony – have in turn sought to imbue a hyperconnected neoliberal present with significance through the urgent creation of historical comics on topics that have not yet found hospitable places in that present. In these works, meaning comes through principled engagement with people and their stories. Testimonies, dialogue, tears, connections: they are the look and feel of Castilian-language historiographic comics in Spain.

NOTES

1 All translations from the Spanish are my own.

2 The Y2K bug was a generalized fear that the shift of the calendar to 1 January 2000 might wreak havoc on computing systems designed for a two-digit year marker.

3 The bibliography on the recovery of historical memory in Spain is ample and growing. See Jerez-Farrán and Amago. Magnussen proposes that the renewed interest in memory in Spain may be part of a broader "more general European *memory culture*" that has emerged to provide "coherence, identity and a sense of security in a world in which identities and belonging are not a given" (60).

4 Carlos Giménez is, according to Vilarós, one of post-Franco Spain's most interesting comics producers and "uno de los poquísimos que explícitamente se ha dedicado a explorar la enterrada historia reciente española" [one of the very few who have dedicated themselves to exploring explicitly the buried recent history of Spain] (Vilarós 161).

5 Seeking to explain the rise of interest in memory over the last thirty years in Spain, Ofelia Ferrán argues that self-reflexivity in what she calls "meta-memory texts" functions "as a model for a culture of countermemory, using Foucault's term for a practice of remembrance that recovers historical perspectives marginalized by official versions of the past" (15). According to Ferrán's account, Spanish memory texts "are part of a larger cultural dynamic by means of which Spanish society is still trying to work through its repressive and traumatic history" by drawing attention to the

ways in which "literature and narrative are crucial elements of that enterprise" (15). Contemporary Spanish historical comics have employed similar formal strategies in contributing to this work.

6 In her introduction to an essay on the Spanish Civil War in comics, Sarah Harris notes that because comics are "an inherently fragmentary medium (in that they narrate through sequential art), they can be especially powerful in narrating traumatic memories" (Harris and Del Rey Cabero). The fragmentation inherent to the grammar of comics form is one of the ways that it heightens reader participation, as the reader makes connections between times and places across the gutters between frames. Thierry Groensteen argues that all comics trigger "the active participation of the reader in the construction of meaning and in the assessment of the work" (3). The gutter especially requires connective leaps of imagination, logic, causality, and temporality. In this way, comics are especially well suited for rendering the dynamics of historiography.

7 By drawing attention to the seams and conventions of their own artifice, visual/textual narratives may not only reject the transparency of conventional history but also render both textualization and visualization conspicuous. This effect is related to the two operations that Thierry Groensteen identifies – via Philippe Marion – as constitutive parts of graphic enunciation: the monstrative and graphiative (Groensteen 85). In other words, all graphic expression will at once call attention to reality – gesture towards the real – while also bearing the traces of its status as visual or graphic thing. As hand-drawn images, comics call reflexive attention to themselves (graphiation) while also pointing to other things (monstration).

8 Anne Magnussen argues that the text works to undermine narrative coherence through visual fragmentation and disequilibrium. The resulting plural vision of *Cuerda de presas* thus functions to "create an opening for the questioning of dominant memories and for the constructing of new ones, starting up alternative sense-making processes and leading to new memories and new ways of understanding the past" (77).

9 Unlike *Cuerda de presas*, these subsequent works centre on the experiences of men and are drawn and narrated by men. The gendered logics of historical comics production in Spain is a topic worth exploring. Although in other realms of auteurist comics there has been a notable "feminization of the comics profession" (Groensteen 5), Laura Martel's script and Antonia Santolaya's illustration in their *Winnipeg: El barco de Neruda* (2014) is one of the few Spanish historical comics authored by women. In Spain, women have had a stronger presence in avant-garde and independent comics; Conxita Herrero, Roberta Vázquez, Cristina Daura, Teresa Ferreiro, Begoña García-Alén, and Ana Galvañ are producing some of the most innovative and visually appealing comics and graphic art in Spain. Their

"post-graphic novel" work is characterized by panel experimentation, play with narrative structure, simultaneous action, painterly innovation, wordless comics, and whimsical panel design. In her important book on the queer cultures of the Spanish Transition, Gema Pérez-Sánchez devotes substantial space to an earlier generation of talented women comic book artists such as Ana Juan, Ana Miralles, and Asun Balzola (162–71). These women's work, published in *Madriz*, expanded "the traditional form of the comic book to include feminist narratives and radically new aesthetic proposals" (162).

10 The ensuing narrative is the father's coming of age, from his childhood through his military service; the same narrative is also the subject of Martín's *Las guerras silenciosas*, in which an otherwise unremarkable Spanish father is elevated by his narrating son to the status of historical actor and minor hero.

11 Miguel Gallardo has clearly done some historical research; another vignette that takes place during the post-war years contains a sketch of a "Brave" poster claiming, "Los rojos no usaban sombrero" [The reds didn't wear hats] (Gallardo and Gallardo 41). While it is unlikely that a Madrid hat manufacturer would post advertisements such as this one on the streets of Barcelona, the novelist's aim for authenticity is noteworthy.

12 In his chapter included in this volume, Dapena illustrates how historical graphic narratives such as *Un largo silencio* represent memories of resistance – or what Ofelia Ferrán has described, in Foucauldian terms, as "countermemory" (15) – that aim to recover the silenced histories and memories of the defeated. These graphic works, often narrated from the democratic present looking back, attempt to recover forgotten or silenced historical accounts.

13 Along with many of the historical details, Roca also borrowed visual and graphic images from Alberto Marquardt's 2010 documentary *La Nueve, los olvidados de la victoria*.

14 Cercas's novel *Soldados de Salamina* has sold more than one million copies. By the time *Los surcos del azar* was being drawn, *Soldados de Salamina* would have been in its fourteenth printing.

15 Anderson painstakingly charts the many uses of archival images of the past – filtered through the characters' subjectivities – in order to illustrate how people's "need to reach out into the past, explore it, interact with it, and seek to understand it is forcefully conveyed in the many juxtapositions that result from the interpolations and framings" (164) that give form to the text. Anderson has noted the "to-and-fro movement" and colour palette shifts that characterize the Trueba version of *Soldados de Salamina* (153) and analysed the way in which it offers a "finely nuanced" representation of how the Spanish Civil War is felt in the present (165).

16 Even Miguel's ostensibly heroic participation in the liberation of Paris is not given a splash page; the event occupies a half-page panel framed on the top and bottom by narrower panels depicting other perspectives on the event (Roca, *Los surcos* 285).

17 Despite Delgado et al.'s stated aim to "draw on a wide range of sources" (3), curiously the editors neglect the contributions that graphic novels, comics, *tebeos*, and *historietas* have made to the cultures of emotion in Spain.

WORKS CITED

Aguilar, Paloma, and Leigh A. Payne. *Revealing New Truths about Spain's Violent Past: Perpetrators' Confessions and Victim Exhumations.* Palgrave Macmillan, 2016.

Anderson, Andrew A. "Picture in Picture: Interpolation and Framing, Past and Present in David Trueba's *Soldados de Salamina.*" *Hispanic Research Journal* 17.2 (2016): 152–67. doi.org/10.1080/14682737.2016.1140509.

Bollero, David. "La Desbandá, la mayor tragedia de la Guerra Civil, encerrada políticamente." *Público*, 6 Feb. 2016, www.publico.es/politica/desbanda-mayor-tragedia-guerra-civil.html.

Català, Josep. *Pasión y conocimiento: El nuevo realismo melodramático.* Cátedra, 2009.

Cazorla-Sánchez, Antonio. "From Anti-Fascism to Humanism: The Spanish Civil War as a Crisis of Memory." *Memory and Cultural History of the Spanish Civil War*, edited by Aurora G. Morcillo, Brill, 2014, 21–50.

Cercas, Javier. *Soldados de Salamina.* Tusquets, 2001.

Chute, Hillary. *Disaster Drawn. Visual Witness, Comics, and Documentary Form.* Harvard UP, 2016.

Delgado, Luisa Elena, Pura Fernández, and Jo Labanyi, editors. *Engaging the Emotions in Spanish Culture and History.* Vanderbilt UP, 2016.

Eisner, Will. *Comics and Sequential Art: Principles and Practices from the Legendary Cartoonist.* W.W. Norton, 2008.

Ferrán, Ofelia. *Working through Memory: Writing and Remembrance in Contemporary Spanish Narrative.* Bucknell UP, 2007.

Gallardo Sarmiento, Francisco, and Miguel Gallardo. *Un largo silencio.* Astiberri, 2012.

García, Jorge, and Fidel Martínez. *Cuerda de presas.* Astiberri, 2005.

Giménez, Carlos. *Todo Paracuellos.* De Bolsillo, 2007.

Gómez López-Quiñones, Antonio. *La guerra persistente: Memoria, violencia y utopía: Representaciones contemporáneas de la Guerra Civil española.* Iberoamericana, 2006.

Groensteen, Thierry. *Comics and Narration.* Translated by Ann Miller, U of Mississippi P, 2013.

Guijarro, Carlos. *Paseo de los canadienses*. Edicions de Ponent, 2015.
Harris, Sarah D., and Enrique del Rey Cabero. "The Spanish Civil War in Comics: A Conversation on Spanish Comics, Remembrance, and Trauma. Part 2." *Comics Forum*, 27 April 2015, comicsforum.org/2015/04/27/the-spanish-civil-war-in-comics-a-conversation-on-spanish-comics-remembrance-and-trauma-by-sarah-d-harris-and-enrique-del-rey-cabero-part-1.
Highfill, Juli. "A Sentient Landscape: Cinematic Experience in 1920s Spain." *Engaging the Emotions in Spanish Culture and History*, edited by Luisa Elena Delgado, Pura Fernández, and Jo Labanyi, Vanderbilt UP, 2016, 120–40.
Hirsch, Marianne. "The Generation of Postmemory." *Poetics Today* 29.1 (2008): 103–28. doi.org/10.1215/03335372-2007-019.
Jerez-Farrán, Carlos, and Samuel Amago. *Unearthing Franco's Legacy: Mass Graves and the Recovery of Historical Memory in Spain*. U of Notre Dame P, 2010.
Jiménez, Jesús. "'Paseo de los canadienses,' la dramática huida de Málaga a Almería llega al cómic." *RTVE*, 25 Feb. 2015, www.rtve.es/noticias/20150225/paseo-canadienses-dramatica-huida-malaga-almeria-llega-comic/1104480.shtml.
Linden, Diana L. "Monumental Acts: American Public Sculpture and the Representation of Race, Gender, and Class." *Radical History Review* 81 (2001): 162–9.
Magnussen, Anne. "The New Spanish Memory Comics: The Example of *Cuerda de presas*." *European Comic Art* 7.1 (2014): 56–84. doi.org/10.3167/eca.2014.070104.
Martel, Laura, and Antonia Santolaya. *Winnipeg: El barco de Neruda*. Editorial Grupo5, 2014.
Martín, Jaime. *Las guerras silenciosas*. Norma Editorial, 2014.
– *Jamás tendré 20 años*. Norma Editorial, 2018.
Martín Gaite, Carmen. *Usos amorosos de la posguerra española*. Anagrama, 1994.
"Masacre en la carretera." *El País*, 11 February 2012, elpais.com/ccaa/2012/02/10/andalucia/1328898809_855627.html.
McCloud, Scott. *Understanding Comics: The Invisible Art*. Harper Perennial, 1994.
Merino, Ana, and Brittany Tullis. "The Sequential Art of Memory: The Testimonial Struggle of Comics in Spain." *Memory and Its Discontents: Spanish Culture in the Early Twenty-First Century*, edited by Luis Martín-Estudillo and Nicholas Spadaccini, *Hispanic Issues On Line* 11 (Fall 2012): 211–25. cla.stg.umn.edu/sites/cla.umn.edu/files/hiol_11_11_merino_the_sequential_art_of_memory.pdf.
Pérez-Sánchez, Gema. *Queer Transitions in Contemporary Spanish Culture, from Franco to La Movida*. SUNY Press, 2007.
Pons, Álvaro. "Mejor cómic del año, según los lectores de EL PAÍS: 'Los surcos del azar,' de Paco Roca." *El País*, 17 December 2013, elpais.com/cultura/2013/12/17/actualidad/1387288446_136765.html.

Robben, Antonius. "Memory Politics among Perpetrators and Bereaved Relatives about Spain's Mass Graves." *Unearthing Franco's Legacy: Mass Graves and the Recovery of Historical Memory in Spain*, edited by Carlos Jerez-Farrán and Samuel Amago, U of Notre Dame P, 2010, 264–78.

Roca, Paco. *Arrugas*. Astiberri, 2009.

– *La casa*. Astiberri, 2015.

– *El invierno del dibujante*. Astiberri, 2010.

– *Los surcos del azar*. Astiberri, 2013.

Rucabado, Beatriz. "El cómic tiene una capacidad de contar historias que la gente a veces ignora." *El Mundo*, 17 Nov. 2010, www.elmundo.es/elmundo/2010/11/16/paisvasco/1289928204.html.

Sarlo, Beatriz. *Tiempo pasado: Cultura de la memoria y giro subjetivo. Una discusión*. Siglo Veintiuno Editores Argentina, 2005.

Vilarós, Teresa. *El mono del desencanto: Una crítica cultural de la transición española (1973–93)*. Siglo XXI, 1998.

3 Comics, History, and Memory in the '90s: *Las memorias de Amorós*

PEDRO PÉREZ DEL SOLAR

The early 1990s was a time of scarce optimism in the field of Spanish comics. In a few short years, the publishing boom of the early 1980s had gone bust, and the few national magazines that remained in the market survived with weak sales numbers.[1] In the meantime, the market was inundated by Manga and superhero comics, material that was imported, attractive, and less costly than locally produced work. Some of the most visible magazines, like *El Víbora*, stayed in business by shifting their content (and their covers especially) towards porn and extreme violence. Faced with this situation, some authors and editors refused to give in, continuing in their commitment (tenaciously, with little hope for commercial success) to comics that were not circumscribed thematically or stylistically.[2]

One such case was the magazine *Medios revueltos* (1988–9), which followed in the wake of *Madriz* (1984–7) and championed comics that were open to new themes and to narrative and visual experimentation. The series *Las memorias de Amorós* [The Memoirs of Amorós] shares close ties to these publications. The author of the series, Felipe Hernández Cava, was the creative driver and artistic director of both magazines, while its illustrator, Federico del Barrio, was one of their most representative and original artists. In those years, during which comics were "un medio más proclive a mantener en un estado de aletargamiento el pensamiento de sus lectores que a generar la reflexión" [a medium more likely to keep readers in a state of intellectual lethargy than to stimulate reflection] (Hernández Cava, 37), *Las memorias de Amorós* set itself apart by going against prevailing currents. The series represented a move towards comics that were denser, both graphically and thematically, while maintaining their ability to entertain and at the same time offering a fluid reading experience – comics, in short, that demonstrated the full potential of the medium.[3]

Las memorias de Amorós narrates the adventures of the journalist Ángel Amorós and is composed of four volumes: *Firmado: Mister Foo* [Signed: Mr Foo], *La luz de un siglo muerto* [The Light of a Dead Century], *Las alas calmas* [The Quiet Wings], and *Ars profética*, published in 1993.[4] The stories take place in 1927, 1928, 1929, and 1934, respectively; that is, three during Primo de Rivera's dictatorship and one during the Spanish Second Republic.[5] In these books, the everyday conflicts of the period are rendered, by means of brilliant artwork and a careful combination of narrative genres, in an unidealized fashion.

In this chapter I concentrate on a fundamental aspect of *Las memorias de Amorós*: its work of reflecting on historical memory. As memoir and as "period" adventure stories, these narrations involve the recollection of the past and are anchored in real historical events that serve as context for the adventures. In addition, Spanish history functions in these works as a key for resolving mysteries that can only be accessed through historical memory, which in turn is explicitly problematized throughout the series. This thematics is announced from the opening epigraph which – like in a game – is shared by all the volumes and contains the title of each (emphasis mine):

> Y el *siglo murió* apenas sin luz ni *ars profética* que pudiera guiarles en el futuro. Ya jamás volará el albatros con la majestad de sus *alas calmas. Firmado*: *Mister Foo.*
>
> [And the century died without light or ars prophetica to guide them in the future. The albatross, with the calm majesty of its wings, shall never fly again. Signed: Mister Foo.]

The first sentence is significant when we take into account the year of publication; it indicates that the twentieth century is dying, leaving no guide for the future, no *ars prophetica*, no memory.[6] *Las memorias de Amorós*, which takes shape as a reflection on historical memory – and an invitation to such reflection – opens a new path for Spanish comics.

Memoir

For a project that offers a reflection on memory, it is perhaps not surprising that the authors should choose the genre of memoir which, as I have noted, immediately invokes the act of remembering.

> Por lo general, los críticos ven en las memorias un texto histórico más fidedigno y una buena fuente de información, dado que supondrían un carácter más objetivo y una mirada más cifrada en el contexto histórico que en la vivencia personal. Muchas de ellas se restringen, además, a un período determinado (uno, diez años) y se centran en un episodio particular (un viaje o una guerra, por ejemplo). (Amaro Castro 9)
>
> [Critics generally see memoirs [as opposed to autobiography] as more reliable as historical texts and as good sources of information, given that the genre is supposedly more objective, based more in the historical context than in personal experience. Moreover, many memoirs are limited to a specific period (a year, ten years) and focus on a particular episode (a voyage or a war, for example).]

This passage is part of a discussion on the topic of "memoir versus autobiography," not a conclusion; for all intents and purposes, however, one can say that such a description can be readily applied to *Las memorias de Amorós*: each volume narrates a specific episode and takes place within a clearly delimited period. Further, the genre of memoir requires a doubling of the person who remembers, as narrative voice in the present and as protagonist in the past. The past is thus always anchored to the present by that voice.

The past is that of the young journalist Amorós, "[con] veinte años y un brillante porvenir como periodista" [twenty years old and with a brilliant career ahead of him] (MF 11). There is a certain irony in these words, pronounced by the old man, his journalism career having been ruined by the Nationalists' victory in the Spanish Civil War. He has only the present, the here and now of the series, in which he relates his memories to a young interviewer. Just as in literary memoir, the main narrative voice of these stories stands at a distance from the character of his younger self and evaluates his stories in light of his later experiences in the war and in exile. Unlike literary memoir, comics allow us to see this scene, to visualize Amorós holding forth and the interviewer taking notes and asking questions. The comic book format also allows the images to appear not only in sequence but in parallel; it offers the possibility, for example, of contrasting the Amorós of the past with the Amorós of the present, presenting them simultaneously on the page. In this sense, we cannot strictly talk about a narrator (the old man) opposed to a character (the young reporter), because in the comic strip both are characters by necessity. The old Amorós, the memoirist, is more than a narrator.[7] He is a presence, someone who is still there:

fragile, with his glasses and his nearly bald pate, surrounded by books; a person who exists in the present and gives his testimony of the past; in other words, a mediator between the past and the present. The aged Amorós is a man trying to remember. Significantly, *Firmado: Mister Foo* begins with the following dialogue: [Interviewer:] "¿Y recuerda por qué cerraron 'La Voz' en esa ocasión?" [And do you remember why they shut down *La Voz* that time?]; [Amorós:] "Pues, no ... la memoria empieza a jugarme malas pasadas" [Well, no ... my memory is starting to play tricks on me"] (11); while *Las alas calmas* begins with the sentence "Ángel Amorós jamás olvidará." [Ángel Amorós will never forget.] (9). The version of the past that we read in these books should be seen in this way, altered by the passage of time, existing in the tension between Amorós's personal processes of remembering and forgetting. As the aged Amorós comments, "Primero he sido inmaduro ... más tarde anarquista ... y hoy soy simplemente escéptico" [First I was immature ... later an anarchist ... and now I'm just sceptical] (AC 20). It is from this position that he tells the story of his past.

The young interviewer represents an audience who belong to another generation, who want to know, just like the ideal hypothetical reader of this series. She takes note of his memories, asks questions, and must, at times, pick up the narrative thread when the narrator loses it.[8] This relationship, then, symbolizes the idea that these memoirs are meant to be a bridge between the past, the present, and, in a certain sense, the future (figure 3.1).

The fact that these memoires are fictitious does not make them false. Inventing a memoirist is one way of creating continuity between the past that is being retold and the present from which this memoirist is remembering it. Whether false or not, memoir is a genre with a unique ability to bring the past into the present. *Las memorias de Amorós* presents something that might have been, something that comes into being in the laboratory of fiction. It also presents a plausible protagonist: a survivor, someone whose intense experience of the 1920s and 1930s he now recalls.

This protagonist, while fictional, is constructed to be representative of his times, and his profession allows the work to become a homage to an entire generation. As stated in the introductory text that accompanies each of volumes, in *Las memorias de Amorós*

> hay un tributo a una generación atrapada por la Historia y que supo estar a la altura de unos elevados ideales ... hombres y mujeres que nacieron marcados por el desastre colonial del 98 y terminaron en la guerra civil

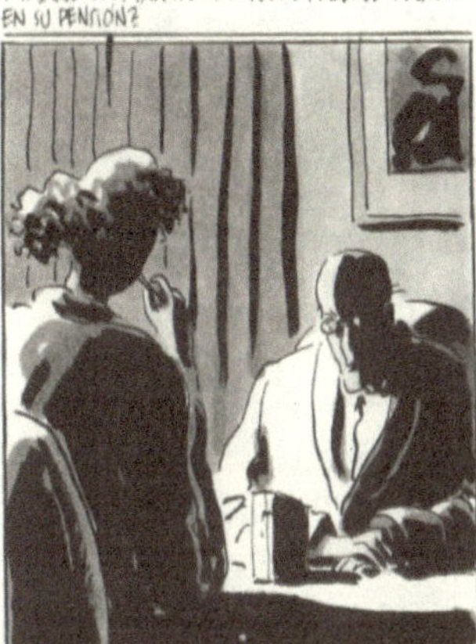

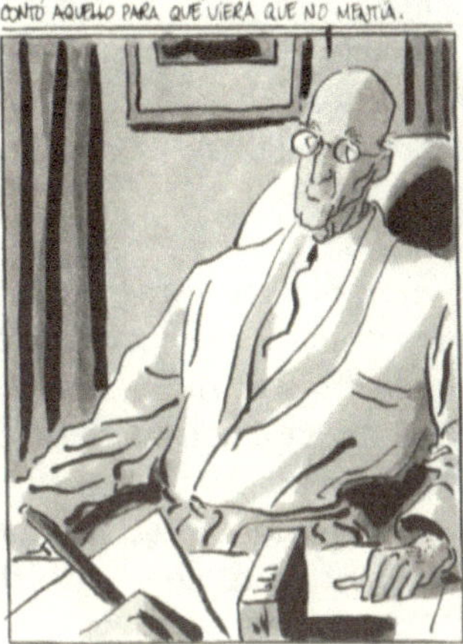

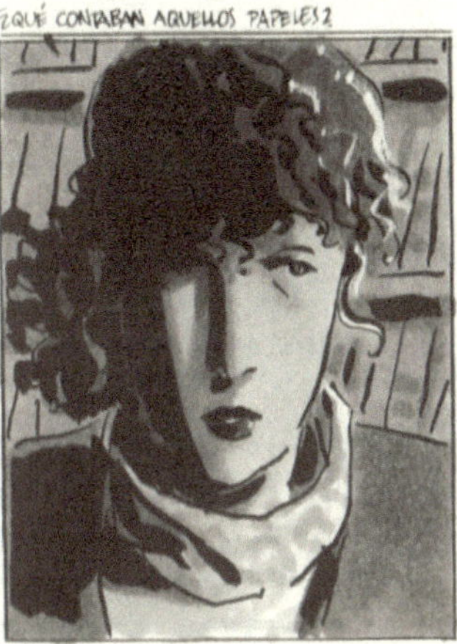

Figure 3.1. Amorós and the young interviewer in Hernández Cava and Del Barrio's *Firmado: Mister Foo* (50).

> y en el exilio. Talantes forjados en la adversidad y que dieron muestras de unas inquietudes éticas y de una curiosidad intelectual fuera de lo común. (MF 6)
>
> [there is a tribute here to a generation trapped by history, one that managed to live up to some high ideals ... men and women who were born into the colonial disaster of 1898 and who ended up in the Civil War or in exile. People whose character was forged in adversity and who demonstrated both a concern for ethics and an unusual degree of intellectual curiosity.]

We should imagine Amorós as one of these subjects, someone who has survived and is now able to recount his adventures. As the journalist Eduardo Haro Tecglen writes in his prologue to *Firmado: Mister Foo*:

> Este periodista que se llama Ángel Amorós, este reportero que empezó en "La Voz," pudo trabajar en la ficción con Eduardo de Guzmán en "Castilla libre"; y en sus viñetas le he visto en las guerras, en los cercos, en las entrañas sangrientas y humeantes de la sociedad a las que bajaron los reporteros como Eduardo, como Ángel de Guzmán. O en las que estuvieron otros, como Ramón J. Sender o como Arturo Barea. (6)

> [This journalist by the name of Ángel Amorós, this reporter who began at La Voz, who worked with Eduardo de Guzmán as an author of fiction on Castilla libre; in his strips I have seen him in wars, in sieges, in the steaming, bloody innards of society that reporters like Eduardo, like Ángel de Guzmán, descended into, where others, like Ramón J. Sender and Arturo Barea have also been.]

Just as in non-fiction memoir, these memoirs take care in constructing their temporal "being there." The present of the aged Amorós is always the semi-darkness of his library, from which he tells his story. Telltale signs of the 1990s are not found there, except in the clothing and hairstyle of the interviewer. For his part, the young Amorós inhabits a Madrid of the 1920s and 1930s, and the mise-en-scène must be believable; the comic must be replete with the identifying signs of those years.

Las memorias de Amorós is clearly well researched, but the research does not stifle the flow of the storytelling or unnecessarily distance the story from the present. There is a careful use of verbal expressions from the era, as well as specific information regarding popular personages, songs, billboards, notable events, and well-known businesses. Along with these elements, there is abundant mention of the everyday political life of the period. In *Firmado: Mister Foo*, for example, the FAI [Iberian Anarchist Federation] routinely falls under police suspicion (12), and there is reference to the parapolice organization Somatén (20). In *La luz de un siglo muerto*, the war in Morocco is mentioned, as is the use of the *ley de fugas* – the law which legitimized the shooting of detainees trying to escape[9] – against workplace agitators and Amorós's exile in Mexico after the war (51), while the context of *Ars profética* is Spain's growing political polarization and the public visibility of the Falange. These details frequently appear against a backdrop of recognizable sites in Madrid.

Amorós's memories are accessed through these scenarios, nuances of language, references to half-forgotten characters, and so on.[10] Possibly obscured though the facts may be, our ability to read these comics is unimpeded; instead, any lack of clarity only serves to invite the curious reader to dig deeper. All the work dedicated to context is fundamental to the construction of these stories.

Popular Genres

Las memorias de Amorós is constructed through a crossing of genres. While the general framework is that of memoir, there is an air of adventure with its concomitant risks, movements from place to place, and unexpected events. These are adventures that move freely between the hard-boiled detective genre and the more cerebral genres of mystery and tales of enigma, with numerous forays into melodrama or *folletín*. The reflection on memory rests upon these genres and styles.

The *folletín*, more than a genre per se, is a way of working with and presenting various popular genres, and was originally defined by its format: *folletines* were serialized stories published in mass-market magazines and newspapers, and generally ended with a cliffhanger and a "to be continued," features that have defined everything from the serialized novels of the nineteenth century to the soap operas of today, from multi-film franchises to adventure comics. With time, the *folletín* came to be characterized by the traits common to most of the material published in the format, most notably narrative replete with sensationalism, cliché, and stereotypes.[11] This type of excess is what is generally adduced when something is defined as "*folletinesco.*" In this sense, love stories as well as tales of adventure, terror, mystery, and the like might just as easily be "*folletinescos*" as not. Another characteristic of this kind of publication is that the *folletín* "agita, denuncia contradicciones atroces en la sociedad, pero en el mismo movimiento trata de resolverlas 'sin mover al lector'; la solución responderá a lo que él espera y le devolverá la paz" [stirs things up, it denounces society's atrocious contradictions, but at the same time tries to resolve these contradictions "without changing the reader"; the ending will correspond to what the reader expects and will restore his peace of mind] (Martín Barbero 188). The solace offered by the *folletín* and its at once excessive and familiar character are determining factors for the popularity of this form.

In *Las memorias*, many of the characters fit the stereotypes forged in the *folletín*; their deployment is a kind of narrative shorthand, given that their physiognomy amounts to a declaration of their personality. We might mention Guillermo Jaratá (AP), with his undeniably villainous appearance: shaved head, "demonic" pointed beard (figure 3.2); the swaggering "Patillitas" (AC), a morphine dealer; the corpulent wholesaler of necklaces; the Barón of Carvía, who bears the stereotype of the elegant delinquent – monocle, thin moustache with upturned ends; the brutal faces of the Falangists (AP); Inspector Caparrós, his body as desiccated as his personality; or Concha, the lady in charge of the opium den (figure 3.3), a movie or comic book villainess with her cigarette in hand and menacing eyebrows, outfitted with a toque, a close-fitting leopard print chinesque dress, and a pearl necklace (AC).

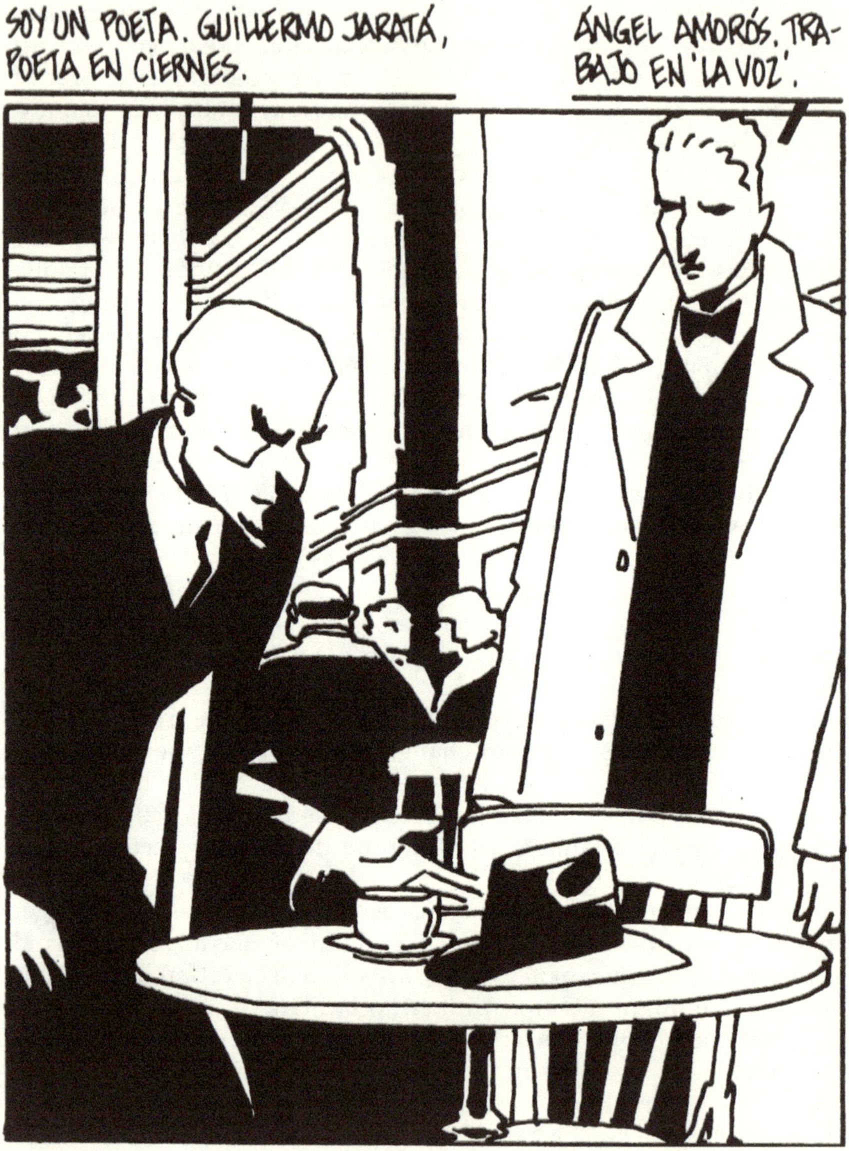

Figure 3.2. Guillermo Jaratá and Amorós in Hernández Cava and Del Barrio's *Ars profética* (11).

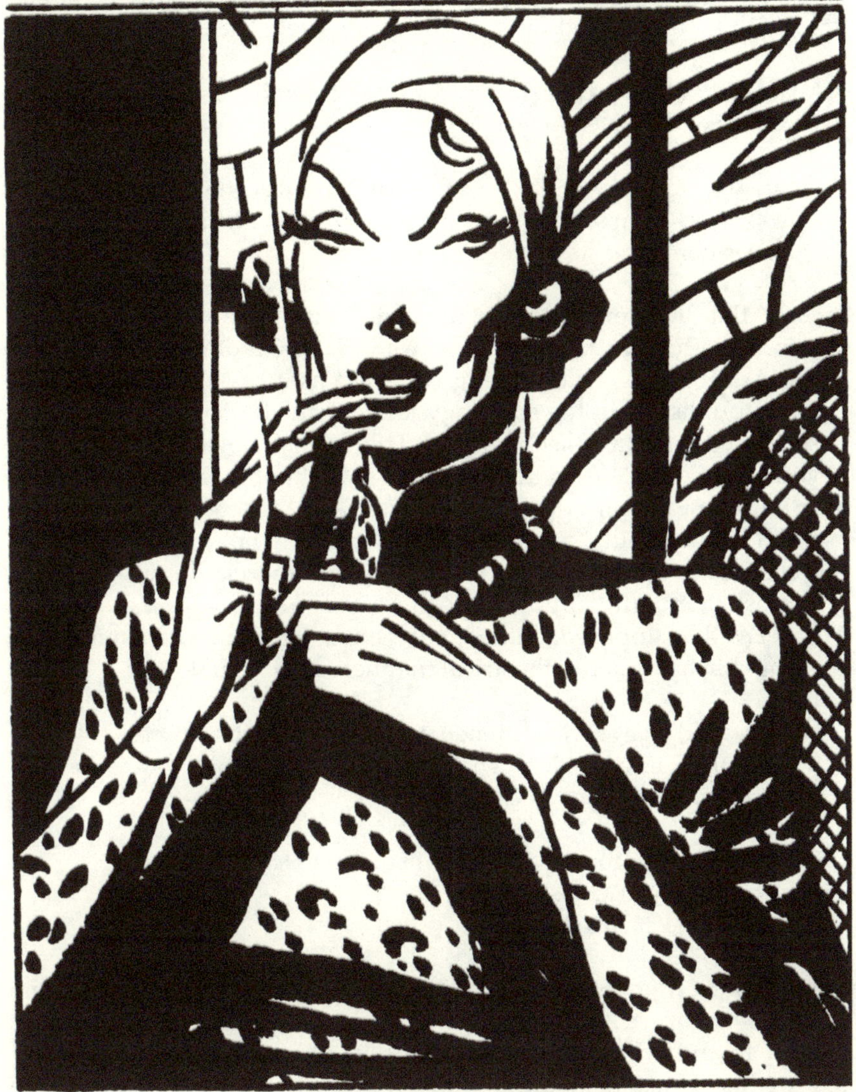

Figure 3.3. Concha, the lady in charge of the opium den, in Hernández Cava and Del Barrio's *Las alas calmas* (47).

The volume where references to the *folletín* are most abundant is *Firmado: Mister Foo*, beginning with the name of the eponymous character, which is commented upon in the comic itself:

> [AMORÓS:] ¿Y Mister Foo? ¿Le dice algo ese nombre?
> [MAYER:] Solo que suena a folletín y yo, por no leer, ni cosas de esas leo. (29)
>
> [(AMORÓS:) And Mister Foo? Does that name mean anything to you?
> (MAYER:) Just that it sounds like something from a *folletín* and I, not being a reader, don't read such things.]

In fact, the "mysterious oriental villain" is a type of character that abounds in the adventure comics from Flash Gordon to Roberto Alcázar. Additionally, before being collected as a book, *Firmado: Mister Foo* was published in the sociology and urban studies magazine *Alfoz* in serialized form (as *folletines* were). This format, however, does not go beyond the first stories, and that which at first appears exotic is merely a scrim, like the opium den in *Las alas calmas*, where the orientalized "señora" is, in reality, a nurse named Concha who, instead of giving her customers opium, has them smoke "una mezcla de tabaco inglés y nueces" [a mixture of English tobacco and walnuts] (47). In *Firmado: Mister Foo* the supposed Chinese characters are Filipino; Mister Foo is presented in a markedly theatrical manner, even in dialogue:

> [MISTER FOO:] Bienvenido al mundo de los sueños, señor Amorós.
> [AMORÓS:] ¿Es usted ... Mister Foo?
> [MISTER FOO:] Soy su sombra. (36)
>
> [(MISTER FOO:) Welcome to the world of dreams, Señor Amorós.
> (AMORÓS:) Are you ... Mister Foo?
> (MISTER FOO:) I am his shadow.]

Mister Foo is, literally and figuratively, a shadow projected on a screen; he is only an apparition, someone who plays the role of a non-existent villain. In the end, everything points to the person truly responsible for his crimes as being a Spanish police detective.[12] That is, the "oriental" villain, who represents that which is exotic and radically other, turns out to be not foreign but rather endogenous to the body of Spanish society.

The resolution – if only symbolic – of fantasies and social contradictions that is typical of the *folletín* is also left unfulfilled here; *Las memorias de Amorós* does not offer relief from the discomfort provoked by the history it presents. In this sense, *Las memorias* bears a resemblance to North American crime fiction, especially the *género negro* or "hard-boiled" genre, which, like the *folletín*, is an inexpensive, popular, and widely distributed form filled with its own stereotypes and clichés, and which does not resolve social contradictions but rather illuminates them, thus providing a check against the potential excesses endemic to the *folletín*.[13] *Las memorias* exhibits some of the basic characteristics of the *género negro* where, as Ricardo Piglia writes:

> No parece haber otro criterio de verdad que la experiencia: el investigador se lanza, ciegamente, al encuentro de los hechos, se deja llevar por los acontecimientos y su investigación produce fatalmente nuevos crímenes; una cadena de acontecimientos cuyo efecto es el descubrimiento, el desciframiento. (*Crítica* 115)
>
> [There seems to be no criterion for truth other than that of experience: the detective throws himself blindly into searching for the facts, he is carried away by events, and his investigation leads fatally to new crimes; a chain of events whose effect is discovery, decipherment.]

Amorós moves through the story leaving death in his wake: a Filipino seller of necklaces, "*el patillitas*," "*la argentina*," "*el pintao*." The criminals are not captured, and sometimes not even identified.[14] Del Barrio, for his part, offers up a graphic style that incorporates the conventions of hard-boiled and detective comics, for example, in his use of stark contrasts between black and white (figure 3.4).

But *Las memorias de Amorós* makes liberal use of the conventions of the hard-boiled *serie negra* without being bound to it. Amorós, for example, does not demonstrate the cynicism that taints most hard-boiled protagonists. Çommissioner Olmedilla characterizes him thus: "Amorós, sigue siendo un ingenuo ... y los ingenuos tienen siempre una debilidad: el idealismo" [Amorós, you are still naïve ... and the naïve always have a weakness: idealism] (MF 56). Even Amorós's physical appearance escapes the standards of the genre. He is very stylized, especially in the last two volumes: stretched out, quite thin and tall, recognizable by his silhouette alone (figure 3.5), in the style of Del Barrio's characters in *Madriz* and *Medios revueltos*, like León Doderlin, for example.

As I have mentioned, Amorós is the incarnation of a very specific type of detective, the "curious reporter" who wants to know so that others can know. By moving freely between *folletín*, mystery, and police fiction,

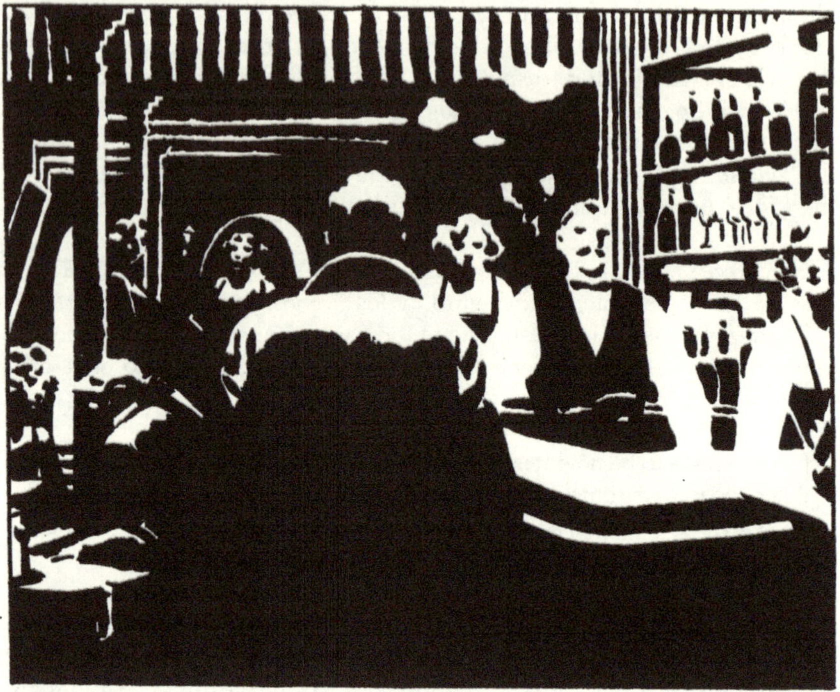

Figure 3.4. Contrasts between black and white in Doña Toda's bar in Hernández Cava and Del Barrio's *Las alas calmas* (13).

Las memorias de Amorós delivers an effective combination of fluid storytelling and suspense, demonstrating a will to create an accessible comic capable of reaching a wide audience and with a recognizable "flavour."

As mysteries, three of the volumes that compose *Las memorias de Amorós* function as "fábulas sobre la historia" [historical fables]. Like fables, *Firmado: Mister Foo, Las alas calmas,* and *Ars profética* are exemplary tales created to spur reflection, in this case, on history and memory. In these plot lines centred on solving a mystery, the keys to the solution are in history itself: the treaty of Westphalia, the war in the Philippines, the war in Morocco, the Primo de Rivera dictatorship, and the emergence of Spanish fascism. This structure gives the history of Spain enormous weight and makes it relevant in the present of both the young and the aged Amorós.

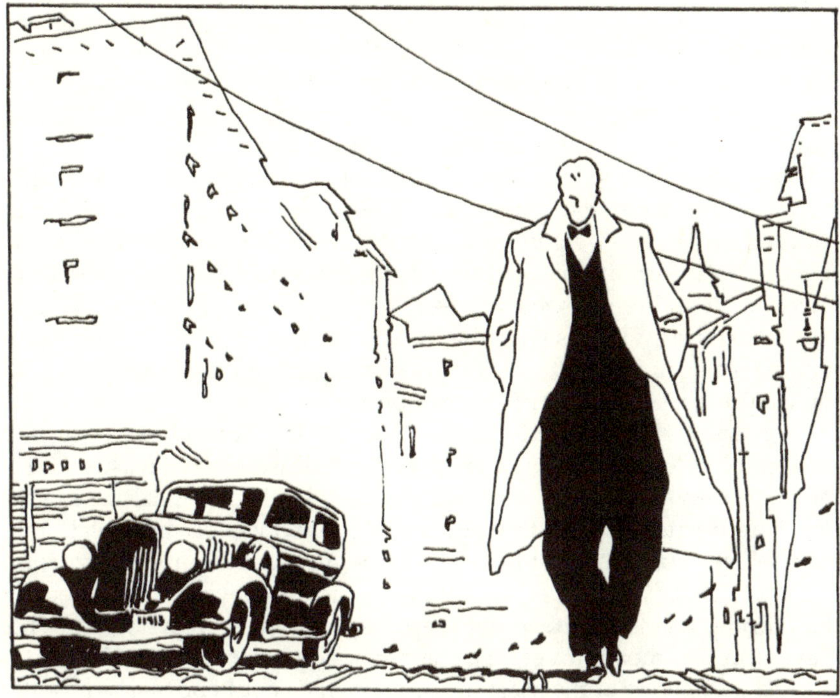

Figure 3.5. Ángel Amorós in Hernández Cava and Del Barrio's *Ars profética* (21).

Historical Fables

As I have stated, by including contextual references and utilizing well-established popular genres, *Firmado: Mister Foo*, *Las alas calmas*, and *Ars profética* make the history of Spain into one of their narrative axes, although each book employs different strategies to do so. In the first book, *Firmado: Mister Foo*, there is a series of murders that have in common the signature "Mister Foo" written in blood on the wall. When Mister Foo brings Amorós before him, Spanish history comes to occupy centre stage in the story. Although the crimes are blamed on a war between "oriental" mafias, the villain's explanation is different: Foo claims the violence dates back to the revolution in the Philippines (1896–8) and the brutally repressive Spanish response directed by General Polavieja, which included celebrated writer José Rizal's execution by firing squad.

When Amorós remarks that he is unaware of this history, Mister Foo responds, "El problema de ustedes los españoles es que no solo desconocen esa historia sino la historia en general" [The problem with you Spaniards is not just your ignorance of that history but of history in general] (36), and he suggests to Amorós that some Filipinos are still in search of vengeance, which has so far resulted in the aforementioned crimes, several explosions, and a death threat to the dictator.

Even though the story of what happened in the Philippines is real, it turns out that there is another part to Mister Foo's tale, later revealed to Amorós by a young Argentine anarchist: in the years of the Philippine revolution, information about the conflict was manipulated in order to attack Spanish Freemasons, who – it was said – supported the Tagalog revolutionaries.[15] In this way, the conspiracy theory regarding an internal/external threat to the nation was strengthened, external given the internationalist character of Freemasonry.[16]

Eventually, Amorós understands that "Mister Foo no existe, es una ilusión" [Mister Foo does not exist, he is an illusion] (49); Mister Foo is merely an invention that serves to set the wheels of a machine in motion. The journalist learns that he himself is but one piece in an elaborate plan. Mister Foo, whoever he might be, wants him to publish a version of events that would cast the crimes as acts of revenge executed by the Filipino rebels for the violent repression of thirty years before. This "revelation" is meant to set off a chain reaction, the objective of which is to raise the spectre of the Masonic threat, which could be blamed for the country's instability.[17] If there are certain "historical memories" that are also paranoid narratives designed to shore up unstable regimes, Mister Foo's intentions are to bring this story into the present in order to also bring back the ghosts that had become attached to it. One must not forget, as Domínguez-Arribas observes, that Franco would later again raise the spectre of Freemasonry, not only as a justification for the military uprising but also as an explanation for Spain's isolation during the 1940s and 1950s (405–9).

After his conversation with the Argentine anarchist, Amorós begins to suspect that Commissioner Olmedilla, who is in charge of the investigation and stands to gain politically by manipulating the instability of the situation, is behind these machinations. In this book, knowledge of history confers power, for good or for evil; the commissioner manipulates it in his favour in order to preserve his position. Amorós is not able to prove his theory until ten years later, when, at the height of the Civil War, he finds Olmedilla acting as a political commissar (54) and at the same time working as a Nationalist agent in the "quinta columna" [fifth column].[18] The commissioner ends the conversation with nearly the same sentence uttered by the supposed Mister Foo in their encounter: "y el problema de ustedes los españoles es que desconocen la historia" [And the problem with you Spaniards is that you don't know history] (56). By repeating what Mister Foo had said to him privately, Commissioner Olmedilla is confirmed to be the mastermind behind the illusion of Mister Foo (or at least someone with privileged information about him). At the same time, the sentence, directed at Amorós's young interlocutor, is a warning about the lack of historical memory that afflicts the present.

In *Las alas calmas,* Amorós must find his friend and colleague Buendía, after Buendía's wife reveals that he has been addicted to morphine and has escaped from the clinic where he was being treated. This search leads to an investigation into the world of morphine trafficking in Madrid, which, unsurprisingly, is a trade as lucrative as it is sordid. The search is a success in that Amorós manages to find Buendía; it is a failure in that he is unable to return him to his wife alive, and fails to bring about the capture of the drug dealers.

The mystery of Buendía's disappearance begins with his participation in the Battle of Annual in Morocco, specifically the siege of Monte Arruit in 1921, in which Spanish soldiers holding a fort were besieged by the Riffians and massacred after having surrendered. The retelling of this event employs not only a different narrator, Buendía, but also a different graphic style: there is a shift to brushwork and the line quality is much more "expressionist" than that used in Amorós's narration, with drawings often made in white on black. This style is suited to conveying both the testimony of an extreme experience and the fact that this testimony comes from a disturbed narrator, an addict without access to his drug (figure 3.6). In this same book, one of Amorós's nightmares is drawn much more freely, with violent light contrasts rendered in ragged brushstrokes (AC 28–9). This use of different drawing styles to mark levels of narrative and/or the mental states of the narrators prefigures one of the techniques central to the much more ambitious book *El artefacto perverso* [The Perverse Machine], published later by the same authors.

Buendía, a soldier at the fort under siege by the Moroccans, is gravely injured, but manages to leave the fort with a companion who is deserting and is later saved by a Moroccan whom he had previously defended. In this way he is saved from the massacre that followed the siege, and upon his return to Spain manages to invent an excuse for having survived. There, in the hospital, he is given morphine, which allows him to bear the pain of his wounds. Buendía's addiction is a physical and psychological mark of the war, and is his secret.[19] As in *Las alas calmas,* the knowledge of history is indispensable for understanding the unhealed

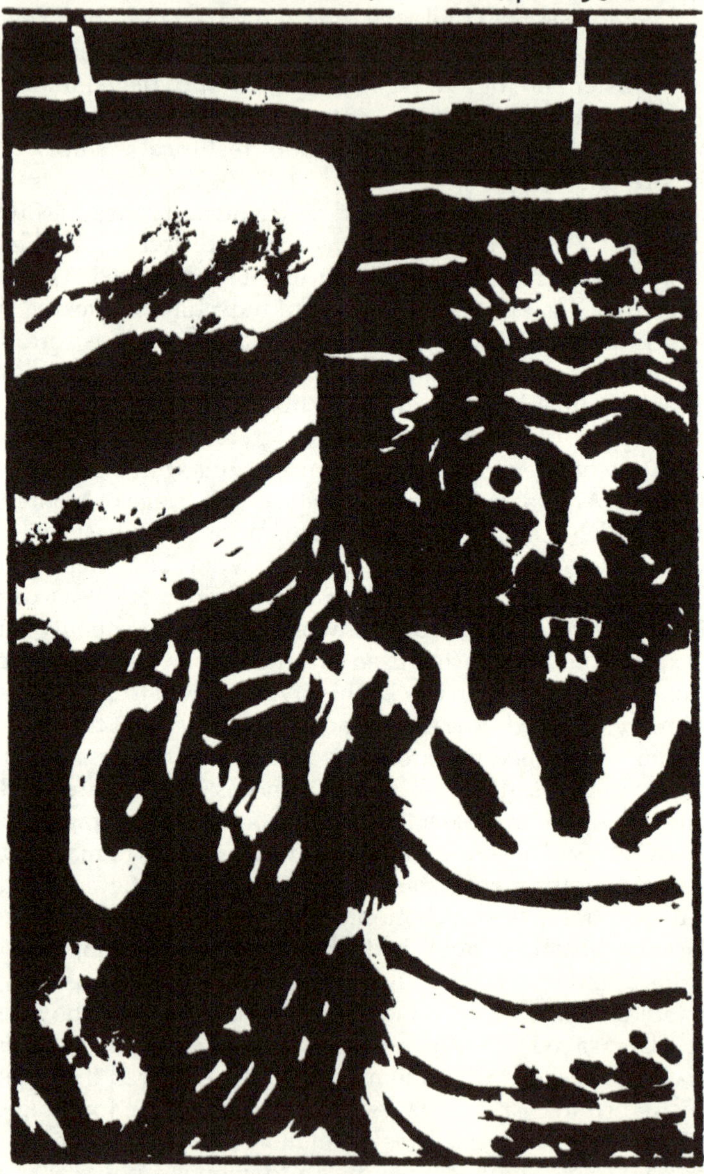

Figure 3.6. Representing extreme experiences from a disturbed narrator's point of view in Hernández Cava and Del Barrio's *Las alas calmas* (43).

wounds and addictions caused by the Moroccan war. It is important to remember that this war was the breeding ground of a group of "tough and uncompromising colonial officers, the so-called Africanistas ... [who] benefited from irregular and vertiginous battlefield promotions" (Preston 46) and will constitute the core of the 1936 coup against the Spanish Republic – including General Francisco Franco, also wounded in Morocco in 1916. Preston offers the following passage on the Africanistas:

> Their opposition to Republican reforms would inaugurate a process whereby the violence of Spain's recent colonial history found a route back into the metropolis. The rigours and horrors of the Moroccan tribal wars between 1909 and 1925 had brutalized them. Morocco had also given them a beleaguered sense that, in their commitment to fighting to defend the colony, they alone were concerned with the fate of the Patria. Long before 1931, this had developed into a deep contempt both for professional politicians and for the pacifist left-wing masses that the Africanistas regarded as obstacles to the successful execution of their patriotic mission. (46)

In short, just as it is necessary to know history in order to understand Buendía's addiction, it is also necessary to know how the Moroccan war marked a whole group of Spanish officers in order to understand later events, especially the Spanish Civil War.

On another note, it is important to mention that *Las alas calmas* is also a commentary on the times in which it was published, when the trafficking and use of heroin, another opiate like morphine, was at its most devastating in Spain.

History plays a central role in solving the mystery in *Ars profética* as well. Amidst the tensions of 1934, the country plagued by political crimes on the right and the left, a string of apparently meaningless murders is committed on the streetcars of Madrid. Amorós suspects a poet that he has just met, who subscribes to an avant-garde poetics including the possibility of violent crime as a poetic act, and who, in front of Amorós, practiced for one of his poems by shooting a dog (11).[20] Just as in *Firmado: Mister Foo*, the solution to the mystery is found in history, in knowledge of the events of the past as well as in a particular interpretation of those events. Amorós discovers that the key to Guillermo Jaratá's serial crimes is to be found in the fact that the numbers of the streetcars correspond to the year of the Peace of Westphalia. In the book *Genio de España* [Genius of Spain] by the fascist avant-garde writer Ernesto Giménez Caballero, found among Jaratá's effects, the author states that that treaty was "el primer 98 de España, el del 15 de mayo de 1648, cuando se firmó aquel primer pacto entre España y Holanda por el cual perdía ya el vertebrado imperio de España sus primeros miembros" [Spain's first 1898, 15 May 1648, when that first pact between Spain and Holland was signed, by which the vertebrate Spanish Empire lost the first of its members] (AP 48). Amorós and Inspector Caparrós have this to say regarding the possible relationship between this date and the crimes:

> [Inspector:] ¿Está insinuando que ese sujeto mata sólo para recordar que España debe ser de nuevo el imperio que fuera un día?
> [Amorós:] Más o menos. Él utiliza sus crímenes como Josué utilizaba las trompetas frente a las almenas de Jericó ... Como un aldabonazo con el que sacarnos del derrotismo y anunciar que hay que volver a resucitar el mundo. (49)
>
> [(Inspector:) Are you insinuating that this person kills simply to remind us that Spain should return to being the empire it once was?
> (Amorós:) More or less. He uses his crimes the way Joshua used trumpets before the walls of Jericho. A wake-up call to draw us out of our defeatism and announce that we must bring the world back to life.]

Jaratá is a kind of Giménez Caballero, but one who is able to put into practice that which, for Giménez, is nothing but pure rhetoric. Indeed, it is in fiction that we are able to contemplate the criminal potential of this rhetoric. In 1932, in *Genio de España*, Giménez Caballero explained his work this way:

> Como para mí esta labor de sentir el sentido de un pueblo no radica en la erudición, ni en la teoría ni en ningún armadijo intelectual e inerte, sino en la Profecía, en la comunión de un alma alerta con el genio callado de su pueblo, sé que mi labor tiene el estremecimiento del trance, de la visión sagrada, de lo religioso. (20–1)
>
> [For me the work of feeling the spirit of a people is not rooted in erudition, nor in theory, nor in any inert intellectual framework, but rather in Prophecy, in the communion between an alert soul and the quiet genius of its people. I know that my work has the shiver of a trance, a holy vision, of religion.]

For Giménez Caballero, the "work of feeling the spirit of a people," "my work," is "Prophecy." If art is prophecy and the artist is a prophet, he "quiso ser el profeta San Juan Bautista que anuncia y prepara la llegada del Redentor" [wanted to be the prophet St John the Baptist, who announces and prepares for the arrival of the Redeemer] (Corella

Lacasa 69). Jaratá makes this position his own, even citing nearly verbatim the Giménez Caballero paragraph just quoted (AP 51). But unlike Giménez Caballero himself, Jaratá is a man of action. His art – his crimes – "la poesía que destruye" [poetry that destroys], indeed turns out to be a prophecy of the years to come. Like John the Baptist, Jaratá is a prophet not of the distant future but rather of what is already there, beginning. The next scene, the procession for Matías Montero, the student slain in a violent show of force by the Falange, seems to confirm this beginning. As Amorós rightly observes, Jaratá "estaba loco, sí, pero en sus palabras había algo más que la carencia de razón" [was crazy, it's true, but in his words there was more than just a lack of reason] (51).

At the beginning of the story, Jaratá – after mocking Falangist ideology in a bar – is faced with a threat from a militant of that group: "¡Se acordará!" [You will remember!] Jaratá answers: "De todo, me acuerdo de todo" [Everything, I remember everything] (10). The fictional Jaratá and the real-life Giménez Caballero recall certain historical events in pursuit of an objective relevant to their own times: that of motivating Spaniards to return the nation to glory. As a reader of the Futurists, Jaratá believes that the path to glory will involve the destruction of the bourgeois order. In this way, the announcement of a new Spain is also an announcement of the violence and destruction that will precede it. Accordingly, in his own criminal activity – which he understands as poetics – Jaratá remembers the past in order to announce the future in all its violence. It is an *Ars prophetica*, like the play on words in the title. As in the case concerning the supposed connections between the Philippine revolution and Freemasonry, here we see that historical memory is ambiguous, always linked to a project, in this case a destructive one.

At the end of the story, during the procession following the death of Matías Montero, the Falangists have their arms raised and oblige the spectators to raise theirs as well; when Amorós refuses, the exchange is the same as Jaratá's from the beginning of the book.[21] An enraged Falangist says to the journalist: "¡Se acordará!" [You will remember!]. Amorós answers: "De todo, me acuerdo de todo" [Everything, I remember everything] (52). The meaning has changed, however. Amorós has understood Jaratá's prophecy, but he opposes it, he does not give in to it in a fatalist manner; he has no intention of allowing a new order to be imposed through violence and threats. These sentences mark Amorós's evolution, the path from "ustedes los españoles desconocen la historia" [you Spaniards don't know history] in the first book to "me acuerdo de todo" [I remember everything]. In this way, memory is established in *Ars profética* as a memory that allows resistance.

Showing (the Glass through which We See) History

To complete this essay, we must attend to certain elements of visual design in *Las memorias de Amorós*. It is clear that the narrative structure of these works relies not only on the liberal deployment of the conventions of popular genres, but also on Del Barrio's stylized drawings, his elaborately composed panels, and his pages in which elements within the individual panels serve to create symmetries and contrasts across panels.[22] For example, in *La luz de un siglo muerto* pages are organized into three strips, each of which is divided into three panels of equal size. Although strips with two panels are also common, one of these panels always occupies twice the space of the other and is organized internally such that some element (a character, a shadow, a tree, a piece of furniture) divides the panel in two, preserving the three-part organization of the strip. On one of the pages, the straight line created by Buendía's overcoat cuts the first panel down the centre; in the fourth panel the car door does the same, and in the fifth panel it is the line of the curb (figure 3.7).

Part of this careful attention to layout involves an effort to keep certain graphic conventions of comic books from interfering with the composition, thus the absence of text or thought bubbles. Dialogue is placed outside of the panels, set in small, sharp letters and distinguishable from the narrator's voice only by the thin lines that point to the character speaking. To this same end, Del Barrio employs a bare minimum of conventional movement lines, instead positioning characters to create an impression of movement (figure 3.8).

In terms of visual design, however, it is Del Barrio's style of illustration that most attracts our attention, a style that is very personal while at the same time drawing from the tradition of comics, illustration, and modern art (figure 3.9). His style breaks with "comic book realism," a representational mode that, according to Reggiani, can be understood as "aquel dibujo que busca realizar transformaciones gráficas coherentes en la representación de las proporciones de la figura humana" [drawings that seek to carry out coherent graphical transformations in the representation of the proportions of the human figure] (134) as opposed to caricatural representation. Comic book realism had dominated historical fiction in comics until that point.

This brand of realism dominates, for example, in the collection "Imágenes de la historia" ["Images of History"] from the Ikusager publishing house, where *Las memorias de Amorós* was also published.[23] The collection opens with the comic book series *Eloy* by Antonio Hernández Palacios, one of first to take on the Spanish Civil War, followed by titles such as *Roncesvalles*, *Simón Bolívar*, and the *El Cid* series, also

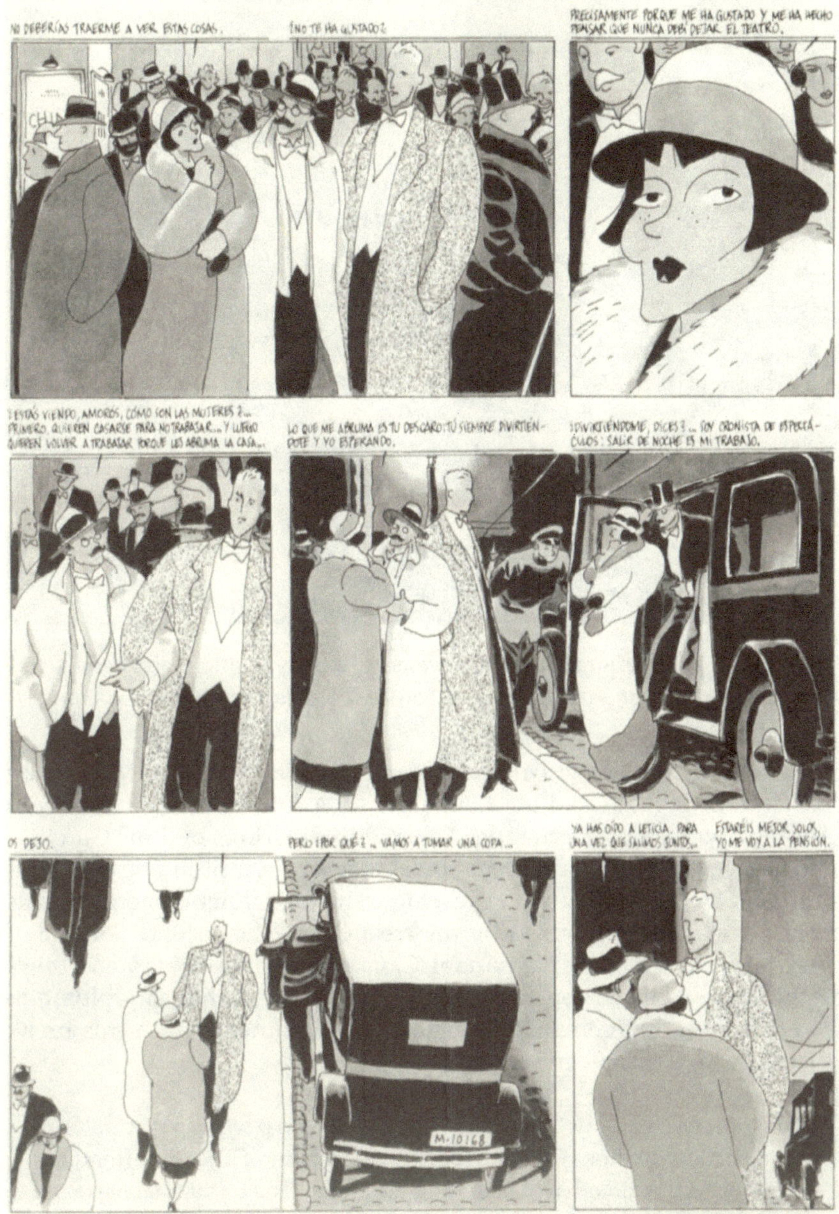

Figure 3.7. Example of page composition in Hernández Cava and Del Barrio's *La luz de un siglo muerto* (20).

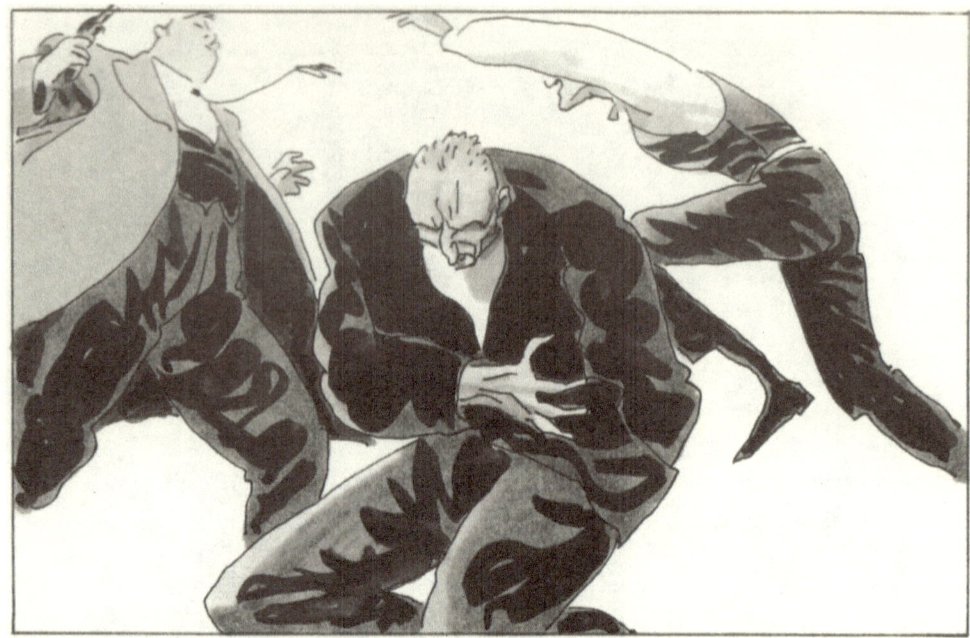

Figure 3.8. Creating an impression of movement by body positions and frame composition in Hernández Cava and Del Barrio's *La luz de un siglo muerto* (43).

by Hernández Palacios; *La batalla de Vitoria* [The Battle of Vitoria] by Hernández Cava, José Luis Salinas, and Adolfo Usero; and *Argelia* [Algeria], written by Hernández Cava with drawings by Luis García.

In fact, in this series *Las memorias de Amorós* is symptomatic of a drastic change in the approach to drawing in historical fiction comics. This change was later confirmed by the freedom of the second volume of *Lope de Aguirre* – also by Hernández Cava and Del Barrio – and *Macandé* by the same scriptwriter and Laura Pérez Vernetti, the last volume in the collection "Imágenes de la historia."[24] Commenting on this break with realism, Groensteen writes:

> By his innovative drawing and design, Del Barrio's work participates in the aesthetic evolution of comics for the past quarter of a century [that] has been toward the direction of liberating the image. The traditional narrative drawing ... is seen to be concurrent with writing that is freer, more pictorial, and more poetic. From Moebius to Alagbé, from Loustal to Barbier, from Baudoin to Vanoli, comics has shown that it can accommodate the illustrative drawing, and it can even completely abandon the linear drawing, at the profit of a play with surfaces and colors, lights and intensities. (163)

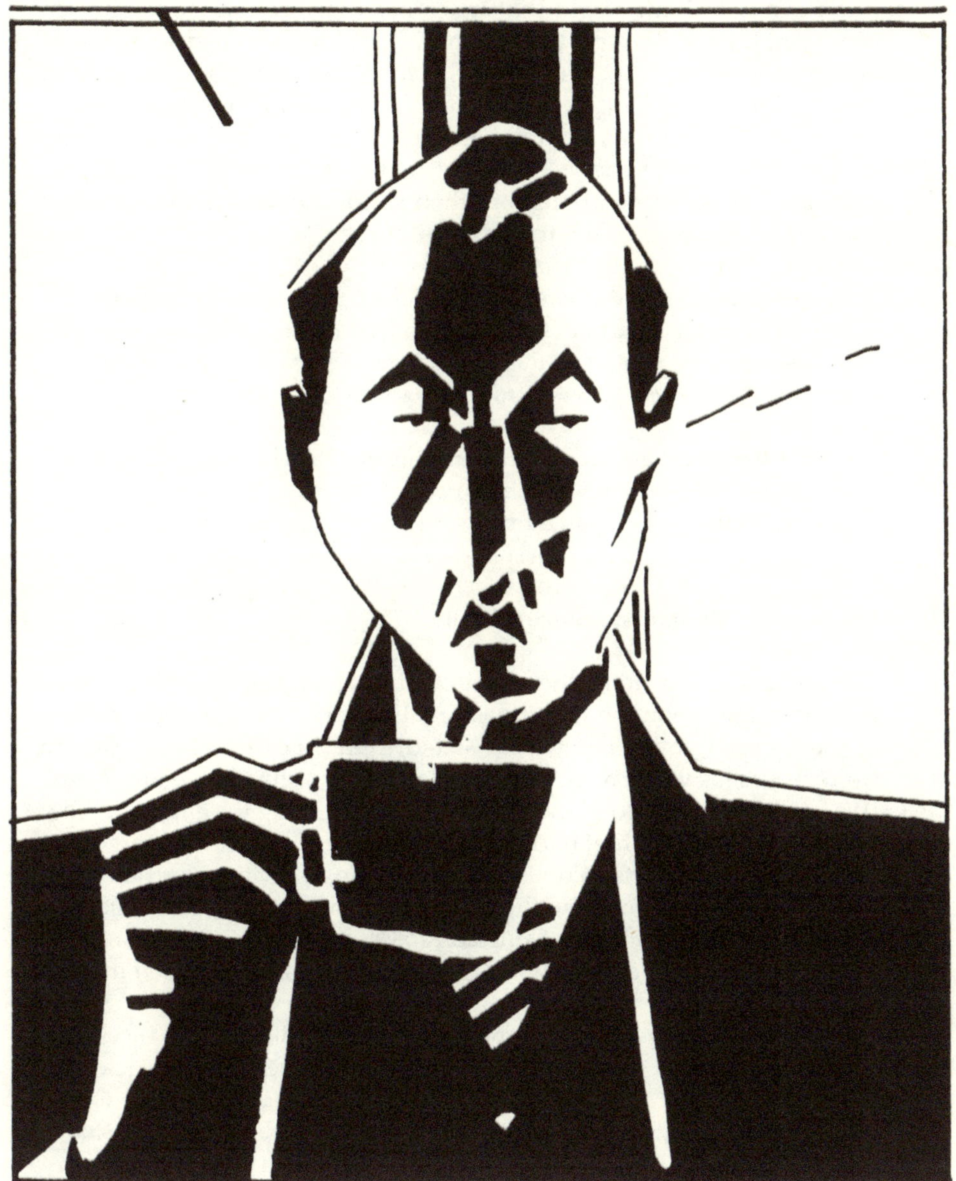

Figure 3.9. Stylized face in backlight in Hernández Cava and Del Barrio's *Ars profética* (37).

In moving away from realism, *Las memorias de Amorós* also moves away from offering "una ilusión de transparencia, de suceso que se produce sin origen ante los ojos del lector" [an illusion of transparency, of an event without origin that takes place before the reader's eyes] (Reggiani 136). Although the graphic style does not lead to a loss of verisimilitude, it does create an obstacle to the reader's experience of psychological proximity to the tale – it makes clear that the narration is mediated through its graphic representation. This technique further strengthens *Las memorias* as a project that exists more to stimulate reflection upon history and memory than to impose predetermined ideas about them. Federico del Barrio himself writes:

> Esta es la labor de todo verdadero trabajo cultural: sacudir la historia ... En este momento, creo que es preciso detenerse (y esto significa, ni más ni menos, oponerse a un ritmo que nos es ajeno), reflexionar y escuchar. No comprendo otro principio de actuación pacifica. (7)
>
> [This is the task of any true cultural activity: to shake up history ... At this moment, I believe that it is necessary to stop (and this means, more or less, resisting a pace imposed from without), to reflect and listen. I cannot understand any other principle of peaceful action.]

Overcoming Obstacles / Blazing Trails

During Spain's transition, the state issued a message of forgetting, rather than reflecting upon the recent past. As Felipe González, then president of the Spanish government, later stated, "Quisimos superar el pasado sin remover los viejos rescoldos, bajo los cuales seguía habiendo fuego" [We tried to move beyond the past without disturbing the embers, below which there was still fire] (González). This pact of silence and forgetting was not limited to acts of omission but was in fact actively promoted.[25] It is relevant to mention here the case of Ludolfo Paramio, an intellectual linked to the party of Felipe González, PSOE [Spanish Socialist Workers' Party], and a critic of comics, who stated in the magazine *Complot!* in 1985:

> Debemos optar, aquí y ahora, por ser el Príncipe Valiente, que envejece feliz en medio del caos de la Edad Oscura, o el abuelito Cebolleta, que martiriza al público con la añoranza de las estúpidas batallas que vivió en su estúpida juventud, batallas que, además, muy bien podrían haber sido sólo imaginarias. (29)
>
> [We must choose, here and now, either to be Prince Valiant, growing old happily amidst the chaos of the Dark Ages, or Grandpa Cebolleta, boring

the audience and pining for the stupid battles he witnessed in his stupid youth, battles which, moreover, might well have been merely imaginary.]

The hegemony of positions such as this one may serve to explain the difficulties *Las memorias de Amorós* experienced in getting published. As Hernández Cava has commented: "De repente a nadie le interesaba ese tipo de historieta, nadie quería publicarnos esto, les atacaba de los nervios cualquier cosa de estas características, 'ya están aquí estos pesados, ya vienen con la Historia'" [Suddenly no one was interested in this kind of comic book, no one wanted to publish it, anything with these characteristics made them nervous, like "look at these pests, here they come with their History"] (García and Pérez).[26] *Las memorias* directly challenged this position by presenting an old man as protagonist, one who relayed the memories of his youth, thereby reclaiming the memory of a whole generation of journalists who came on the scene during the last years of the Primo de Rivera dictatorship, defended the Republic during the Civil War, and were finally dying out as *Las memorias* was being published. *Las memorias* went against the prevailing current of its day by underscoring that historical unmemory was an injustice against "los vencidos de la Guerra Civil y los luchadores antifranquistas" [those defeated in the Civil War and those who fought against Franco], for as Vicenç Navarro states, democracy "ha significado la continuación de su marginación y falta de reconocimiento" [has led to their continued marginalization and lack of social recognition] (Navarro).

Nevertheless, with time, the path that *Las memorias* helped to blaze has been more and more travelled. From our current perspective, we can consider these works as precursors to the proliferation, beginning in the mid-2000s, of comics set in the years between the Second Republic and the post-war period. This growth has been mainly due to two phenomena. The first is the appearance and rise of new publishing venues sustained by the "graphic novel" format, with houses like De Ponent y Astiberri willing to take on innovative graphic and narrative projects. The second is the boom in novels and films about the Spanish Civil War that began around the turn of the new century.[27] Among these comics, we must mention *Cuerda de presas* [The Chain Gang] (2005) by Jorge García and Fidel Martínez; the anthology *Nuestra Guerra Civil* [Our Civil War] (2006) by authors representing various generations; *36–39, malos tiempos* [36–39, Bad Times] (2007–8) by Carlos Giménez; the controversial series *Nuevas hazañas bélicas* [New War Feats] (2011–12) by Hernan Migoya; the very humorous *La vida es un tango y te piso bailando* [Life Is a Tango and I Step on Your Toes While We Dance It] (2015) by Ramón Boldú; *Paseo de los canadienses* [The Canadian Promenade] (2015) by Carlos Guijarro; *Dr Uriel* (2017) by Sento; and *Jamás tendré 20 años* [I Will Never Be 20 Years Old] (2017) by Jaime Martín.

The technique of creating a protagonist who narrates from the perspective of old age, thus uniting the present with a (pre- or post-)wartime past, was also employed around the same time as *Las memorias de Amorós* by Miguel Ángel Gallardo in *Un largo silencio* [A Long Silence] (1997), in which he combined his father's written memoirs with comic book versions of certain fragments. This technique can also be found in two masterpieces of recent Spanish comics: *Los surcos del azar* [Furrows of Fate] (2013) by Paco Roca, a work of fiction about an elderly Spanish emigré from the times of the war; and *El arte de volar* [The Art of Flying] (2009) by Antonio Altarriba and Kim, a comic book adaptation of Altarriba's father's memoirs. Without suggesting a direct relationship between these works and *Las memorias de Amorós*, they all take part, each in its way, in a reflection on memory and history, which makes them stand out from the majority of historical comics centred around remembering a past that is still close at hand.

For his part, in much of his work Felipe Hernández Cava has continued to interrogate the problematic crossings between history and memory. Some examples include the indispensable books *Soy mi sueño* [I Am My Dream] (2008), with drawings by Pablo Auladell; *Las serpientes ciegas* [Blind Snakes] (2008); *Hágase el caos* [Let There Be Chaos] (2011, 2012), and *Las oscuras manos del olvido* [The Dark Hands of Oblivion] (2014), with drawings by Bartolomé Seguí.

Just like these books, *Las memorias de Amorós* does not limit itself to being a "period piece" like so many others; instead, it underlines that knowing history allows one to understand – not to heal – the wounds and addictions, metaphorical and otherwise, of a whole generation. *Las memorias* shows that historical memory, although it can be a source of resistance to abuses of power and to intolerance, tends always to be biased by its connection to some project or position. In this sense, knowing history also allows one to be alert to when, why, and to what ends historical memory is being manipulated.[28]

NOTES

1 After a number of years during which the defence of comics as an art form had gained traction within mainstream cultural institutions, many comic book artists left the field in order to work as illustrators or painters, while new authors without any public visibility were getting experience in the field by producing semi-clandestine self-published fanzines, with all the freedom and financial precariousness that that entails.

2 This chapter was translated from the Spanish by Neil Anderson.

3 The introductory text that accompanies each volume of *Las memorias* has this to say on the matter: "En estos cuatro volúmenes se encontrarán misterios y peripecias rocambolescas, aventuras y amores construidos siguiendo las pautas de los mejores relatos" [In these four volumes you will find mysteries and tall tales, stories of love and adventure constructed in imitation of the best stories ever told].

4 In the quotes I will refer to these works using their initials: *Firmado: Mister Foo* (MF), *La luz de un siglo muerto* (LSM), *Las alas calmas* (AC) and *Ars profética* (AP). *Firmado: Mister Foo* was previously published by *Medios revueltos* in 1988.

5 Hernández Cava and del Barrio's next project, *El artefacto perverso* (serialized in 1994 and published as a book in 1996), is very much connected to *Las memorias de Amorós.* The book is set in Madrid in the 1940s during the worst of the post-war period. Although it has different protagonists (the main one being a Republican school teacher who has become an illustrator of comic books), Amorós does appear briefly in the concentration camp for Spanish exiles in Argelès, France. *El artefacto perverso* and *Las memorias de Amorós* bracket the years of the Spanish Civil War, which is the invisible axis around which these stories turn. This gap, however, was not intentional. Hernández Cava mentions a failed project in a 1995 interview for *Tebeósfera*: a comic book about the Civil War, also created with Del Barrio, called *La tierra a la cintura.*

6 Obviously, *Ars profética* combines the notion of *prophecy* with that of *Ars poetica*, which means "the art of poetry." It was used for the first time to describe the *Epistle to the Pisos* by the poet Horace (65–8 BCE), a work that, among other things, gives advice to young poets on the subject of poetry.

7 The only places in which we find an external narrator are located in the texts that open two of the volumes, with a third-person narrator who speaks about Amorós:

> Ángel Amorós jamás olvidará el mes de diciembre de 1929, porque fue por entonces cuando el joven cronista de sucesos del periódico "La Voz" descubrió que en la capital también había sus infiernos ... aunque algunos los llamasen paraísos. (AC 9)
>
> [Ángel Amorós will never forget the month of December, 1929, because it was then that the young reporter for *La Voz* discovered that the capital had its own hellholes, although some people called them paradise.]
>
> Fue como si 1934 hubiera traído consigo la violencia a las calles de Madrid. Grupos de izquierdas y derechas dirimían sus diferencias a tiros, y Ángel Amorós iba a encontrarse en el mismo centro de aquel torbellino. (AP 9)

[It was as if 1934 had brought with it the violence that filled the streets of Madrid. Groups on the left and the right settled their differences with gunfire, and Ángel Amorós would find himself at the very centre of that maelstrom.]

We can imagine that this technique is meant to allow into the story a narrative voice whose tone is, unlike that of Amorós, clearly melodramatic.

8 The interviewer is indispensable in keeping Amorós on track when he gets lost in his thoughts (MF 27) or when the pain of remembering stops him, for example, when he remembers Lola Negri (LSM 49) or the killing of the Argentine woman (MF 56).

9 See Casanova, 98.

10 At times, the aged Amorós has to "translate" some of his references for the interviewer; in *Ars profética*, for example, he places the action "en un bar de la Plaza Fermín Galán, la misma que usted conoce como Plaza de Ópera" [in a bar in Plaza Fermín Galán, the same one you know as Plaza de Ópera] (10). The reference is significant: Fermín Galán was considered a martyr for the Republic and the Plaza de Isabel II (commonly known as Plaza de Ópera) was given his name during the Republican period. Indeed, the name emphasizes that the action of this book, unlike that of the earlier volumes, takes place during the Republic. Amorós's comment further draws attention to his distance from the present, as well as to his efforts to bring a forgotten past closer to hand and bring it to life, even in its minor details.

11 The *folletín* shares this sensationalism with crime journalism. In *Las alas calmas* Amorós remembers a specific case:

[AMORÓS:] "Por esos días toda España se conmovió con el crimen de Ricardito, un homosexual que despedazó a su señorito y amante."
[ENTREVISTADORA:] "Conozco la historia, Ricardo Franco hizo una excelente adaptación en la serie de televisión *La huella del crimen*." (12)

[(AMORÓS:)"In those days all of Spain was in an uproar over the case of Ricardito, a homosexual who chopped up the body of his young boss (and lover)."
(INTERVIEWER:) "I know the story, Ricardo Franco did an excellent adaptation for the television series *La huella del crimen* (The Footprint of the Crime)."]

Here, in passing, we see the potential of television drama, which keeps the memory of this crime alive. It is worthwhile to mention that each episode of the television series opened with the sentence, "La historia de un país es también la historia de sus crímenes, de aquellos crímenes que dejaron huella" [The history of a country is also the history of its crimes, of those crimes that left their mark].

12 As a provocation, Amorós wears a stereotypical "Chinese" costume in a *Círculo de bellas artes* carnival, some scenes after his meeting with Mister Foo (MF 32).

13 It should be mentioned that Eduardo de Guzmán, one of the journalists who inspired *Las memorias* and a victim of retaliation during Franco's rule, wrote police novels under the pseudonyms Edward Goodman, Eddie Thorny, Richard Jackson, Anthony Lancaster, and Charles G. Brown. It is interesting to imagine Amorós as an Eduardo de Guzmán who remembers his past by layering it over one of the narrative genres that he knows best.

14 In *Las alas calmas,* the organizers of the morphine trafficking ring are not captured, nor does it become clear who they are. In *La luz de un siglo muerto,* those trafficking in weapons and art forgeries end up killing each other. In *Ars profética,* the serial killer, Jaratá, calmly commits suicide after announcing his intentions over the telephone. As regards Mister Foo, who is apparently responsible for a series of crimes, he is first believed to be Chinese, later Filipino, and in the end, everything points to his being none other than the police officer in charge of the case, although his guilt is never conclusively proven.

15 The Tagalogs "combatían sobre todo contra la colonización religiosa y se les acusó de ser masones" [were largely fighting against religious colonization and were accused of being Freemasons] (MF 51); this notion was used to bring about the closure of the Masonic lodge in Madrid "de la que se dijo que era cómplice de los rebeldes" [which they claimed was complicit with the rebels].

> El tema colonial fue uno de los preferidos del catolicismo y de los profesionales de la antimasonería para convencer a la opinión pública de que la masonería había impulsado la independencia de las colonias españolas. Era una historia en la que los masones eran convertidos en traidores a España por haber vendido las colonias y desgajar el territorio patrio para satisfacer las ambiciones de poderosos centros internacionales situados siempre en el extranjero y que habían puesto sus codiciosos ojos en España. (Sánchez Ferré 81)

> [The colonies were a favourite topic within Catholicism and among those who dedicated themselves professionally to opposing the Masons. The goal was to convince public opinion that Masonic activity was responsible for promoting independence movements among the Spanish colonies. It was a story in which the Masons became traitors to Spain for having sold off the colonies and broken apart the empire in

order to satisfy the ambitions of powerful international centres, always located abroad, that had placed their greedy eyes on Spain.]

16 As Manuel de Paz-Sánchez states, the greatest likelihood regarding these threats is that

> como había sucedido en los casos de Cuba y Filipinas, ciertos sectores de la opinión más conservadora y alienada del país creyesen que, en última instancia, los culpables de los errores propios siempre tenían que ser otros, preferiblemente tan misteriosos, nebulosos y crípticos como los masones, imposibles por tanto de identificar fácilmente y, en cualquier caso, válidos como minoría singular para desatar sobre ellos, como había sucedido en la Edad Media, las iras o las culpas del descontento popular y político por los errores o las maldades de los verdaderos culpables. (758)
>
> [as had happened in the cases of Cuba and the Philippines, the most conservative sectors of public opinion and those most alienated from the country believed, as a last resort, that their own errors had to be the fault of others, preferably someone as mysterious, nebulous, and cryptic as the Masons, who were thus impossible to easily identify and were, in any case, a suitable minority upon which to unleash, as had happened in the Middle Ages, the rage and the blame for popular discontent over the mistakes or evils of those who were truly to blame.]

17 Amorós says: "Supón que una vez publicada mi información sale a relucir esta historia otra vez / otra vez el peligro de los masones intentando subvertir el orden de España / otra vez el peligro de los conjurados para exorcizar los fantasmas de un pueblo en tensión" [Suppose that once my information is published this story comes to light again / once again, the danger of the Masons trying to undermine order in Spain / once again, the danger of the conjurations meant to exorcise the ghosts of a country in conflict] (MF 51).

18 Gabriel Jackson mentions that, during the Civil War, the government of Largo Caballero created "a corps of political commissars, modeled on that of the Red Army during the Russian Revolution. The commissars were supposed to serve the dual function of orienting the political consciousness of the troops and checking on the loyalty of professional officers. In fact, they also had considerable influence over promotions and the distribution of supplies. In the hands of a single, disciplined party, they would obviously constitute a hierarchy of their own parallel to the military command under the War Minister. Caballero had named Alvarez del Vayo to head the war commissariat, and the latter appointed mostly Communists

to these key posts, doubtless counting on the expected evolution of the Prime Minister toward closer collaboration with the Party"(363).

19 As he is dying of a morphine overdose in a Madrid sewer, many years after the Moroccan war, Buendía says, "yo no quiero morir en este fuerte" [I don't want to die in this fort] (AC 52).

20 The call to violence, especially as a radical anti-bourgeoisie posture, was not uncommon in avant-garde manifestos. Early on, Marinetti's 1909 *Futurist Manifesto* stated:

> 7. There is no longer any beauty except the struggle. Any work of art that lacks a sense of aggression can never be a masterpiece. Poetry must be thought of as a violent assault upon the forces of the unknown with the intention of making them prostrate themselves at the feet of mankind.
>
> ...
>
> 9. We wish to glorify war – the sole cleanser of the world – militarism, patriotism, the destructive act of the libertarian, beautiful ideas worth dying for, and scorn for women. (Danchev 58–9)

Twenty years later, in 1930, André Breton wrote in the *Second Surrealist Manifesto*:

> One can understand why Surrealism was not afraid to make for itself a tenet of total revolt, complete insubordination, of sabotage according to rule, and why it still expects nothing save from violence. The simplest Surrealist act consists of dashing down into the street, pistol in hand, and firing blindly, as fast as you can pull the trigger, into the crowd. Anyone who, at least once in his life, has not dreamed of thus putting an end to the petty system of debasement and cretinization in effect has a well-defined place in that crowd, with his belly at barrel level. (125; Trans. Seaver and Lane)

21 Here one can see in action one of the key narrative resources of comics: "retroactive determination." By this technique, "the meaning of a panel can be informed and determined by the panel that preceded it much like the one that follows it" (Groensteen 108). As Barbara Postema says, in different terms, "Comics call for a process of retroactive resignification, where one must continually loop back to reconsider meanings and make new meanings as one goes forward in the text" (50).

22 Between *La luz de un siglo muerto* and *Las alas calmas* there is a stylistic shift. Gone are the grays, there is a starker contrast between black and white, the

lines are thicker and more defined, and the drawings more stylized. The composition of the page has changed as well. In *La luz de un siglo muerto* the tendency had been to divide each strip into two panels, one that took up one-third of the length and another that took up the remaining two-thirds. In *Las alas calmas* the tendency is towards strips composed of three panels of varying width.

23 This style also dominates the series *The Spanish Civil War*, published in *Cimoc* magazine during 1986, fifty years after the beginning of the war. It comprises eight episodes, all written by Víctor Mora and with drawings from authors such as Florenci Clavé, Jesús Blasco, Annie Goetzinger, José Ortiz, Víctor de la Fuente, Alfonso Font, Attilio Micheluzzi, and Tha. All the artists were already veterans, and some of them – such as Blasco – even war veterans. This series was compiled in a volume named *1936–1939: Tormenta sobre España* [1936–1939: Storm over Spain] (Glenat, 2008).

24 This graphic innovation was anticipated in *Luis Candelas*, a work by the El Cubri collective (at that time made up of Pedro Arjona and Hernández Cava), an occasional series published in the magazine *Madriz* during the 1980s that was issued as a book in 2001. *Las memorias de Amorós* creates indirect connections with this series by mentioning the film *Luis Candelas o El bandido de Madrid* (1926), directed by Armand Guerra (MF 17); and in the scene in which Lola Negri asks, "¿Conocías esta calle?" [Did you know this street?], to which Amorós replies, "Sí. ¿No es aquí donde cuentan que nació Luis Candelas?" [Yes. Isn't this where they say Luis Candelas was born?] (LSM 35). Similarly, *El artefacto perverso*, Hernández Cava and Del Barrio's next work, creates a link to *Las memorias de Amorós* by briefly presenting Amorós as a character in a camp for Spanish refugees in France.

25 It is important to mention that this position was kept throughout the long period of Felipe González's government, between 1982 and 1996. Not surprisingly, his successor, José María Aznar, of the conservative Partido Popular [People's Party; PP], between 1996 and 2004, preserved the pact of silence. The first calls to memory from the government came during José Luis Rodríguez Zapatero's term (Partido Socialista Obrero Español [Spanish Socialist Workers' Party]; PSOE), between 2004 and 2011.

26 As Michael Matly writes, in the field of comics "después de los diez primeros años relativamente fértiles en obras, se instala una reticencia a abordar el tema de la Guerra Civil que va más allá de los creadores de cómic" [after the first ten relatively fertile years, a certain reticence to tackle the Spanish Civil War settles in, which goes beyond the creators of comics] (105).

27 On one hand, this boom has had the desirable effect of bringing the Spanish Civil War into the present, and we have seen interesting discussions and new points of view on the topic, along with some remarkable works, such as the novels *Soldados de Salamina* (Javier Cercas, 2001), *La voz dormida*

(Dulce Chacón, 2002), and *El lápiz del carpintero* (Manuel Rivas, 1998) or the films *El laberinto del Fauno* (2006) by Mexican director Guillermo del Toro and *Pa negre* (2010) by Agustí Villaronga. On the other hand, as a trend, this boom has engendered a multitude of banal stories (the just-mentioned works being the exception), dashed off quickly in order to take advantage of a trend while it is in season, as every fashion has its date of expiry.

28 In this regard *Las memorias* concords with Muñoz Molina, following Rieff, when he states that

> [e]l antídoto de una memoria histórica dañina o inconveniente no es otra memoria histórica más justiciera. Es la Historia ... El antídoto de las fantasías adánicas o criminales sobre el pasado es el estudio sobrio de la Historia, que no avanza en ninguna dirección favorable y ni siquiera inteligible, y que es demasiado complicada y en general amarga como para ofrecer las simplificaciones consoladoras que alimentan la nostalgia o la movilización. (Muñoz Molina)

> [the antidote to a historical memory that is harmful or problematic is not another historical memory with a greater will to justice. It is History ... The antidote to fantasies about the past – ranging from the criminal to the Edenic – is the sober-minded study of History, which does not advance in a favourable direction, nor even any discernable direction at all, and which is in general too complicated and too sad to be able to offer reassuring simplifications that feed nostalgia or mobilization.]

WORKS CITED

Amaro Castro, Lorena. "Que les perdonen la vida: Autobiografía y memorias en el campo literario chileno." *Revista Chilena de Literatura* 78 (2011): 5–28. doi.org/10.4067/s0718-22952011000100001.

Bretón, André. *Manifestoes of Surrealism.* Translated by Richard Seaver and Helen R. Lane, U of Michigan P, 1969.

Casanova, Julián. *The Spanish Republic and Civil War.* Cambridge UP, 2010.

Corella Lacasa, Miguel. "Ernesto Giménez Caballero, o la estetización de la política." *Res Publica* 6 (2000): 57–70.

Danchev, Alex. *100 Artists' Manifestos.* Penguin, 2011.

Del Barrio, Federico. "La soledad de la quietud." *Madriz* 26 (1986): 5–7.

Domínguez-Arribas, Javier. *El Enemigo Judeo-masónico en la propaganda franquista (1936–1945).* Marcial Pons, Historia, 2009.

García, Jorge, and Álvaro Pérez. "Las memorias de Cava. Entrevista a Felipe Hernández Cava." *Tebeósfera,* 27 May 1995, www.tebeosfera.com/1/Documento/Entrevista/Cava/FelipeH.htm.

Giménez Caballero, Ernesto. *Genio de España*. Jerarquía, 1939.
González, Felipe. "Distintas formas de ajustar cuentas con el pasado." *Clarín*, 3 May 2001, www.clarin.com/opinion/distintas-formas-ajustar-cuentas-pasado_0_S1DxNueAte.html.
Groensteen, Thierry. *The System of Comics*. UP of Mississippi, 2007.
Haro Tecglen, Eduardo. "Las memorias de Amorós." Prólogo. *Firmado: Mister Foo*, by Felipe Hernández Cava and Federico del Barrio, Ikusager, 1993, 6–7.
Hernández Cava, Felipe. "El ojo avisor." *El Ojo Clínico* 2 (1997): 37.
Jackson, Gabriel. *Spanish Republic and the Civil War, 1931–1939*. Princeton UP, 1965
Martín Barbero, Jesús. *De los medios a las mediaciones: Comunicación, cultura y hegemonía*. Gustavo Gili, 2003.
Matly, Michel. "Dibujando la guerra civil. Representación de la guerra civil (1936–1939) en los cómics publicados desde 1976." *Hispania Nova. Revista de Historia Contemporánea* 13 (2015): 99–125. Universidad Carlos III de Madrid, Biblioteca, e-revistas.uc3m.es/index.php/HISPNOV/article/view/2397/1296.
Muñoz Molina, Antonio. "Ida y vuelta: Elogio del olvido." *El País, Suplemento Babelia*, 17 June 2016, elpais.com/cultura/2016/06/14/babelia/1465922683_781498.html.
Navarro, Vicenç. "Los costes de la desmemoria histórica." *El País*, 16 June 2001, elpais.com/diario/2001/06/16/opinion/992642408_850215.html.
Paramio, Ludolfo. "Olvidar los sesenta." *Complot!* 0 (1985): 27–9.
Paz-Sánchez, Manuel de. "Masonería española y emancipación colonial." *Revista de Indias* 66.238 (2006): 737–60. doi.org/10.3989/revindias.2006.i238.338.
Piglia, Ricardo. *Crítica y ficción*. U Nacional del Litoral, 1990.
Postema, Barbara. *Narrative Structure in Comics: Making Sense of Fragments*. Rochester Institute of Technology, 2013.
Preston, Paul. *The Spanish Holocaust: Inquisition and Extermination in Twentieth-Century Spain*. W.W. Norton, 2012.
Reggiani, Federico. "La única verdad es la realidad: Apuntes sobre la noción de historieta realista." *Cultura, Lenguaje y Representación. Revista de Estudios Culturales de la Universitat Jaume I* 10 (2012): 129–37. doi.org/10.6035/clr.2012.10.9.
Rieff, David. *In Praise of Forgetting: Historical Memory and Its Ironies*. Yale UP, 2016.
Sánchez Ferré, Pedro. "Masonería y colonialismo." *Exposición La masonería española, 1728–1939*, edited by José Antonio Ferrer Benimeli, Instituto de Cultura "Juan Gil-Albert" (Diputación Provincial de Alicante), 1989, 81–90.

COMICS CITED

Altarriba, Antonio, and Kim. *El arte de volar*. De Ponent, 2009.
Boldú, Ramón. *La vida es un tango y te piso bailando*. Astiberri, 2015.

Gallardo, Miguel Ángel, and Francisco Gallardo Sarmiento. *Un largo silencio.* De Ponent, 1997.
García, Jorge, and Fidel Martínez. *Cuerda de presas*. Astiberri, 2005.
Giménez, Carlos. *36–39, malos tiempos*. Glenat, 2007–8.
Guijarro, Carlos. *Paseo de los canadienses*. De Ponent, 2015.
Hernández Cava, Felipe, and Pablo Auladell. *Soy mi sueño*. De Ponent, 2008.
Hernández Cava, Felipe, and Federico del Barrio. *Las alas calmas*. Ikusager, 1993.
– *Ars profética*. Ikusager, 1993.
– *El artefacto perverso.* Planeta-DeAgostini, 1996.
– *Firmado: Mister Foo*. Ikusager, 1993.
– *La luz de un siglo muerto*. Ikusager, 1993.
– *Las memorias de Amorós*. Ikusager, 1993. 4 vols.
Hernández Cava, Felipe, Federico del Barrio, and Carlos Saura. *Lope de Aguirre: La conjura*. Ikusager, 1993.
Hernández Cava, Felipe, Luis García, and Adolfo Usero. *Argelia*. Ikusager, 1981.
Hernández Cava, Felipe, and Laura Pérez Vernetti. *Macandé*. Ikusager, 2000.
Hernández Cava, Felipe, José Luis Salinas, and Adolfo Usero. *La batalla de Vitoria.* Ikusager, 1985.
Hernández Cava, Felipe, and Bartolomé Seguí. *Hágase el caos.* vols. 1–2, Norma Editorial, 2011–12.
– *Las oscuras manos del olvido*. Norma Editorial, 2014.
– *Las serpientes ciegas*. BD Banda, 2008.
Hernández Palacios, Antonio. *El Cid*. Ikusager, 1982.
– *Eloy* (Eloy series, 1). Ikusager, 1979.
– *Euzkadi en llamas* (Eloy series, 3). Ikusager, 1981.
– *Gorka Gudari* (Eloy series, 4). Ikusager, 1987.
– *Río Manzanares* (Eloy series, 2). Ikusager, 1980.
– *Roncesvalles*. Ikusager, 1983.
– *Simón Bolívar*. Ikusager, 1987.
Martín, Jaime. *Jamás tendré veinte años*. Norma Editorial, 2017.
Migoya, Hernán, et al. *Nuevas hazañas bélicas*. Glenat, 2011.
Mora, Víctor, et al. *1936–1939: Tormenta sobre España*. Glenat, 2008.
Nuestra Guerra Civil. Ariadna, 2006.
Roca, Paco. *Los surcos del azar*. Astiberri, 2013.
Sento [Vicente Llobell], *Dr Uriel*. Astiberri, 2017.

4 "Shadows Have No Voice": Democratic Memory in Felipe Hernández Cava and Federico del Barrio's *El artefacto perverso* (1996) and Francisco and Miguel Gallardo's *Un largo silencio* (1997)

XAVIER DAPENA

In the mid-1990s, Spain's political crisis and the deterioration of Felipe González's governing Socialist Party (1982–96) was becoming acute.[1] One example of González's "fúnebre éxito" [grim success] (Vázquez Montalbán, "El sillón") can be found in corruption scandals such as the Filesa affair and in state terrorism as adjudicated in the Grupos Antiterroristas de Liberación [Anti-Terrorist Liberation Groups] (GAL) case, which proved government participation in parapolice groups whose purpose was to attack the Basque nationalist terrorist group ETA (Euskadi Ta Askatasuna [Basque Homeland and Freedom]). The resulting electoral loss led to the creation of a government headed by José María Aznar (1996–2004), a period referred to as *La aznaridad* by Vázquez Montalbán. The Aznar government pursued policies that hewed to the emerging neoliberal model – delocalization, privatization, and deregulatory policies – and to the economic acceleration associated with real estate speculation.

In this context of political tension during the second half of the 1990s, with the socialist government's lack of legitimacy, calls for the recovery of the "memory of the defeated" became increasingly common in the public sphere, both in cultural products dealing with the issue and in academic discourse such as that of Paloma Aguilar Fernández and Santos Juliá.[2] In 1996, Aguilar published *Memoria y olvido de la Guerra Civil* [Memory and Amnesia: The Role of the Spanish Civil War in the Transition to Democracy], which brought into play the notion that the Transition was predicated on a supposed "pacto del olvido" [pact of silence] that would forge democratic consensus through the Amnesty Law of 1977.[3] In *Víctimas de la Guerra Civil* [Victims of the Civil War] (1999), Juliá presented an edited volume of essays organized around the victims of the military coup and subsequent war across space and time. Nevertheless, it would still be a number of years before the idea of the recovery of historical memory and its key role in the construction of a democratic citizenry would achieve broad acceptance, thanks to grassroots efforts and to the work of the Asociación para la Recuperación de la Memoria Histórica [Association for the Recovery of Historical Memory], founded by Emilio Silva in 2000. Civil society's calls for transitional justice programs, protections for victims of human rights violations, and remedies for forced disappearances and child theft during Francoism are still relevant today, as made clear by the ongoing complaints against the Spanish state brought by the United Nations High Commission for Human Rights.[4]

During this period, growing interest in memory and the imaginaries of history can also be found in the realm of comics. Beginning around the end of the 1980s, there is a notable decline in the publication of specialty periodicals, which had come to form a "nuevo régimen de la historieta" [new paradigm in comics], one associated with the Transition and characterized by a clear break with the past. Between 1985 and 1996, *Tótem, Rambla, Comix Internacional, Madriz, Cairo, 1984* (later *Zona 84*), and *Cimoc* would all go under, one by one. With the exception of *El Jueves* and *El Víbora,* the predominance of magazines with shared authorship gave way to other formats and formulae, such as the comic book. As Altarriba points out, authors who led the way throughout the 1970s and 1980s did not contribute to the production of comics in the nineties and "fueron abandonando el terreno como consecuencia, fundamentalmente, del cansancio y de la frustración que dejó una época tan agitada" [they left the field as a result, essentially, of being frustrated and worn out by such tumultuous times] ("La historieta" 111).[5]

The graphic narratives examined in this essay belong to the significant repertoire of cultural products that refer to memory as a public, political, and cultural discussion. In this sense, the context in which both are produced – between 1994, when *El artefacto perverso* [The Perverse Machine] is serialized in the journal *Top cómics*, and 1995, when the first pages of *Un largo silencio* [A Long Silence] appear in the journal *No somos los muertos* – points to the growing interest in post-war memory, which had, to a lesser or greater extent, been avoided as the cultural pillars of the Transition were being established. The "graphic novels" studied here follow in the wake of earlier works on the Civil War and Francoist repression that began to appear in the mid-1980s.[6] In the pages that follow, I argue that *El artefacto perverso* and *Un largo silencio* anticipate and are inscribed within the debate over collective national memory. Given the potential for abstraction conferred by their visual styles and their "economía sígnica" [economy of signification], both novels can be read through the lens of "political fiction" (Rancière; Fernández-Savater, "Política literal"), as they portray characters that serve as devices for the collective enunciation of marginalized, subaltern narratives and problematize the present-day transfer of intergenerational memory with concepts such as "hoja de paz de vida" [strands of living peace] (Gutiérrez).[7] Both the work of Hernández Cava and Del Barrio, and that of Francisco and Miguel Gallardo, take part in national debates over memory and are early examples of how comics, by giving voice to marginalized subjects or collectives and promoting the common good, can be used as a site for the expression of outrage and for demanding the democratization of the political sphere, access to the historical imaginary, and historical knowledge.[8] They also question the idea of symbolic authority and historical knowledge's place of enunciation, in the case of *Un largo silencio* by presenting autobiographical portraits with a transgenerational perspective. In short, both works show, with thorough research and documentation, that "to retrieve the past is also to encode it" (Resina 88).

After brief appearances in periodicals, *El artefacto perverso*, with text by Felipe Hernández Cava and drawings by Federico del Barrio, was first compiled and released as a book by Planeta-DeAgostini in 1996, and later reissued by ECC in 2015. *Un largo silencio* was published in 1997 by Edicions de Ponent and reissued in 2012 by Astiberri, the product of a collaboration between Miguel Gallardo and his father Francisco Gallardo Sarmiento that combined the illustrations of the former with the direct narration of the latter's wartime experiences.[9]

For its part, *El artefacto perverso* is an activist comic book, a metafictional tale of the life of Enrique Montero, a cartoonist active during the post–Civil War years but also a former combatant on the Republican side and a teacher targeted for retaliation by the regime. The precarious situation in which he and his wife, Josita, find themselves leads him to try working in the *tebeo* (comic book) industry at the same time as he begins to deal with the tension between his militant antifascist convictions and his desire to live in peace, which he experiences as a betrayal of those convictions (figure 4.1). Two narrative threads are intertwined: one pertaining to the clandestine antifascist resistance groups and the other to Enrique Montero's work on an adventure comic book. In the prologue to *El artefacto perverso*, Vázquez Montalbán affirms that the work positions itself "como instrumento al servicio de esa poética" [as an instrument in service of the poetics] of the Resistance and that it manifests a "nivel extraordinario tanto en lo que se refiere a los códigos específicos del género como a la coherencia del discurso rememorativo y crítico que alienta la historieta" [extraordinary level of achievement

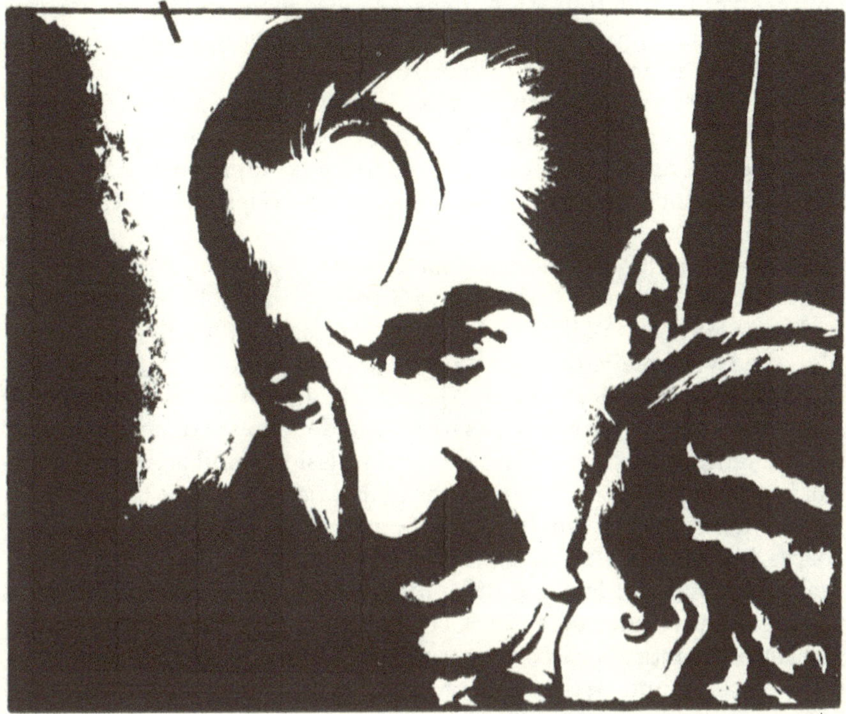

Figure 4.1. Enrique Montero talking with Josita in Hernández Cava and Del Barrio's *El artefacto perverso* (11).

both in terms of the specific codes of the genre and in terms of the coherence of the critical memory discourse that drives the comic book] ("La memoria" 4).

In the first narrative thread, a clandestine resistance group made up of former companions-in-arms from the Fifth Regiment asks for Enrique's help in finding one of their old friends, Matías Bozal, "que sigue la guerra por su cuenta y se da al estraperlo, esencialmente de penicilina, para, dice, conseguir fondos" [who is still fighting the war on his own and is involved in smuggling, mostly penicillin, in order to get money, so he claims] (Alsina 212). The "discurso rememorativo y crítico" [critical memory discourse] of which Vázquez Montalbán speaks is evident not only in the reminiscences of a wartime past that emerge in Enrique Montero's anonymous present, but also serves to question the very morality of the armed struggle against Francoist repression. The second thread, Enrique Montero's own comic book, emphasizes conflicting discourses around memory, as it presents Pedro Guzmán, a parody of the pro-Franco comic book hero Roberto Alcázar, as an archetypical detective who fights crime in a starkly polarized adventure story. Pedro Guzmán fights against his own underworld boss, Belial, who is trying to take over the city with the help of a machine that causes people to forget their past (figure 4.2): the same device that gives the book its title (Hernández Cava and Del Barrio 54).

As Alsina and Pérez del Solar have pointed out, *El artefacto perverso* offers several narrative threads, and its development becomes increasingly complicated as the book moves forward, although in terms of plot, the two threads described here are what hold the story together. Besides being a memory tool, as Alsina and Pérez del Solar have argued, Hernández Cava's project seeks to show a deliberate engagement with key contemporary debates and public discussion about access to historical knowledge. Alsina discusses the global perspective of the "graphic novel" trend and delves into the graphical reconstruction of urban spaces, but also speaks "de la memoria perdida y a menudo intencionalmente borrada" [of lost and often intentionally erased memory] (210). On the other hand, Pérez del Solar considers this graphic narration's subject of memory as a comment about memory and the limits of its transmissions, and, at the same time, posits the unmemory of new generations as the basis of the Transition cultural paradigm and the newly developed democratic discourse of the Spanish state. In this sense, *El artefacto perverso* is presented as part and parcel of a resistant genealogy and the avant-garde of the "New Spanish Memory Comics," to use the label proposed by Anne Magnussen.

Winner of "Best Work by a Spanish Author" and "Best Script" from the 1997 Salón Internacional del Cómic de Barcelona, Hernández Cava's work describes the repressive environment of the "Francoist city." Through Federico del Barrio's use of various styles and graphic techniques, which mix, overlap, and blend with one other (Hernández Cava and Del Barrio 61), the work problematizes both public attempts to manage memory and the past, and the personal dilemmas of this former teacher, who admits that "lo único que quiero es vivir. ¿es eso egoísmo Josita?" [I just want to live. Is that being selfish, Josita?] (see figure 4.1). The versatility of Del Barrio's palette goes beyond what was shown by the same pair, for example, in the story of the fictitious journalist Angel Amorós in *Las memorias de Amorós* [The Memoirs of Amorós] (1993). From the graphic point of view, the

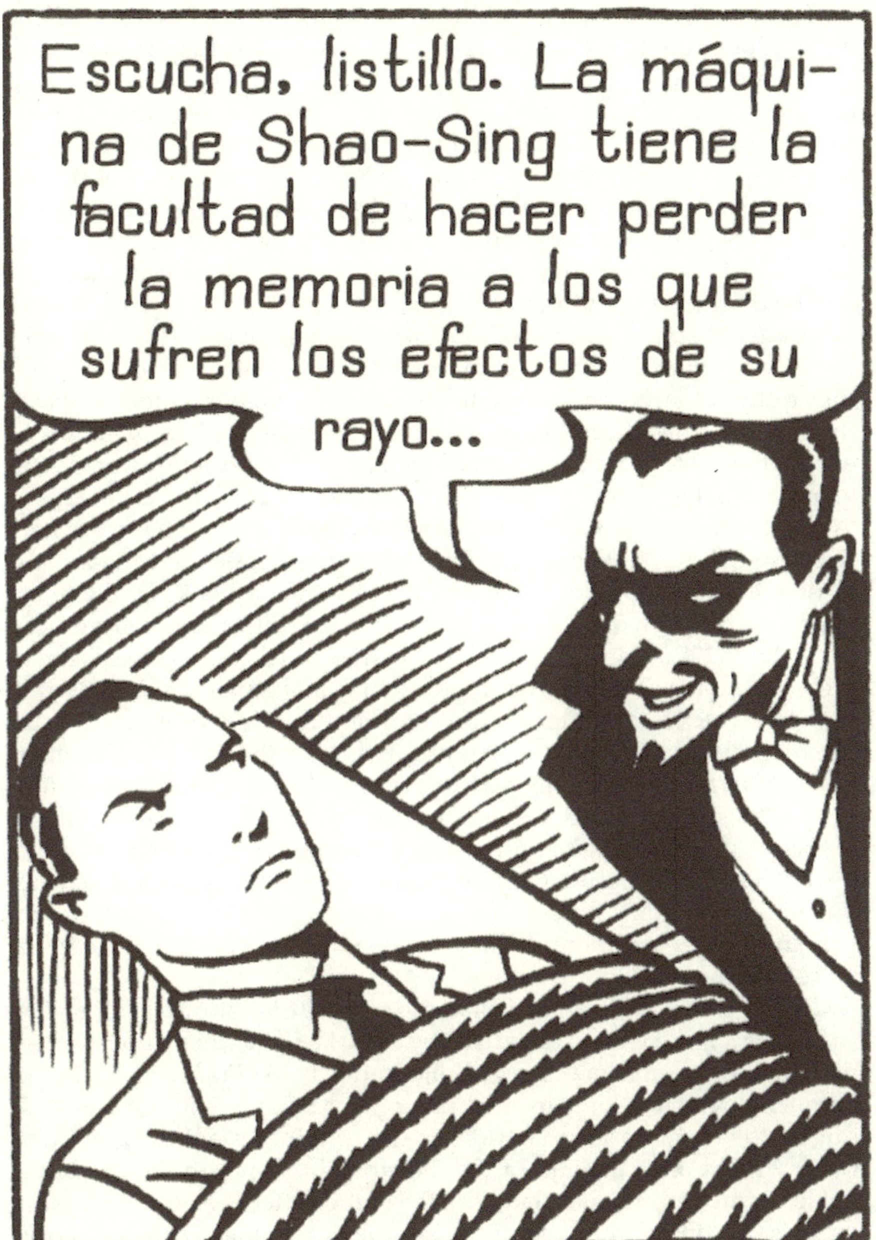

Figure 4.2. Pedro Guzmán is held captive by Belial in the machine of forgetting in Hernández Cava and Del Barrio's *El artefacto perverso* (54).

different threads of the narration in *El artefacto perverso* have a differential plot of the black and white game. While "The City in Danger," the story featuring Pedro Guzmán, presents traces of a more classical cut, the luminosity and the clear distinction of the colours endorses the Manichaeanism of the cartoon. In the foreground, Enrique Montero's story predominates in blacks, also with the intention of representing that hostile and repressive environment. On the other hand, the last chapters progressively dismantle the previous natural page layout and the symbolic repertoire collapses the representation, as will be discussed later in the chapter.

Because of graphic narrative's reliance on image, its proximity to orality, its reproducibility, and its marginality both within academia and the culture at large, this genre tends towards subaltern stories, those that are excluded from hegemonic narratives. Nevertheless, its presence in the context of Spanish memory discourse "sorprende por escasa y por reciente" [is surprisingly sparse and recent] (Ausente 126).[10] While the Spanish Civil War and the Franco dictatorship have become recurring themes in the area of film and literature, Benoît Mitaine has written that, in the realm of comics, scarcely twenty books on the topic appeared between 1977 and 2008 (149). As Eddie Campbell argues, since the 1940s autobiographical and confessional comics have been a growing trend, becoming even more notable in the 1960s and 1970s due to the prevalence of underground comics in the United States (30). In fact, the establishment of the "graphic novel" as the dominant form of graphic narrative is due in part to the role that autobiography plays in the "despegue del cómic alternativo en su viaje hacia la novela gráfica" [initiation of alternative comics' journey towards the graphic novel] (García 234) and the "voluntad de testimonio individual de una vida anónima y la necesidad de dar voz a las sombras" [desire to give individual testimony to anonymous lives, to give the shadows a voice] (Ausente 126).

Comics prove to be a particularly apt format for stories such as *Un largo silencio*, which is characterized by a markedly familiar and testimonial tone that recalls oral storytelling. In this book, Francisco Gallardo Sarmiento tells his life story, including his experiences in the war and during the early post-war period, in the form of an autobiographical diary written after the end of the dictatorship. Through the narrative device of his son, Miguel Gallardo, the author offers his testimony as a "necessary condition of agency" (LaCapra 12). In the Gallardos' story, the need for agency, denied to them during the dictatorship, signifies a break from their traumatic silence. Through his testimony, reproduced and illustrated by his son, Gallardo Sarmiento overcomes the period of latency imposed by the coercive nature of the "Francoist city."

In this sense, *Un largo silencio* is not a conventional graphic novel; rather, it moves towards becoming another kind of artefact, one in which the text, the voice of the father, the son's drawings, and the numerous sketches, photographs, and fragments all lend an air of authenticity to this family album, a vehicle for transmitting family memories. The balanced and classic page layout (3×3 panels) of *Un largo silencio* remains stable throughout the narration. However, except for the long textual fragments, that stability is lost in the moments that Gallardo describes the period of the war. As a result the sequence of figures highlights the predominance of medium frontal shots that brings the figures closer to the photographs and other documents that we can find in the volume (figure 4.3a).

In the original prologue (an illustrated version of which is included in the re-edition), Miguel Gallardo writes that his father had been obliged to "convertir[se] en una sombra durante mucho tiempo y las sombras no tienen voz" [become a shadow for a long time, and shadows have no voice] (5; figure 4.3b). Much like Enrique Montero, in whom Hernández Cava finds a poetics of resistance and survival, Gallardo Sarmiento is an anonymous hero whose greatest feat is survival. Miguel Gallardo writes that his father

> [e]stuvo cuarenta años callado como una tumba, intentando no decir una palabra más alta que otra. Todos esos años yo creí que se escondía de la vida. Cuando al final abrió la boca, fue para repetir una y otra vez la misma historia. Una historia que, a fuerza de oír, se me ha quedado grabada y que me ha descubierto al hombre detrás de la sombra. (5)

> [was quiet as a tomb for forty years, trying never to draw attention to his words. All that time I thought he was hiding from life. When he finally opened his mouth, he told the same story over and over. A story that I have heard so many times that it's etched in my memory, it has revealed to me the man behind the shadow.]

Miguel Gallardo's prologue reflects the traumatic nature of the story, first in the suspension and rupture brought about by the Franco regime and second in its constant repetition (figure 4.3c). As Jo Labanyi argues, silence is not necessarily caused by a traumatic block; it can also be the result of coercion ("Languages of Silence" 28). More than a failure of memory, the tension between coerced silence and Gallardo's act of repetition suggest a purposeful strategy of memory.

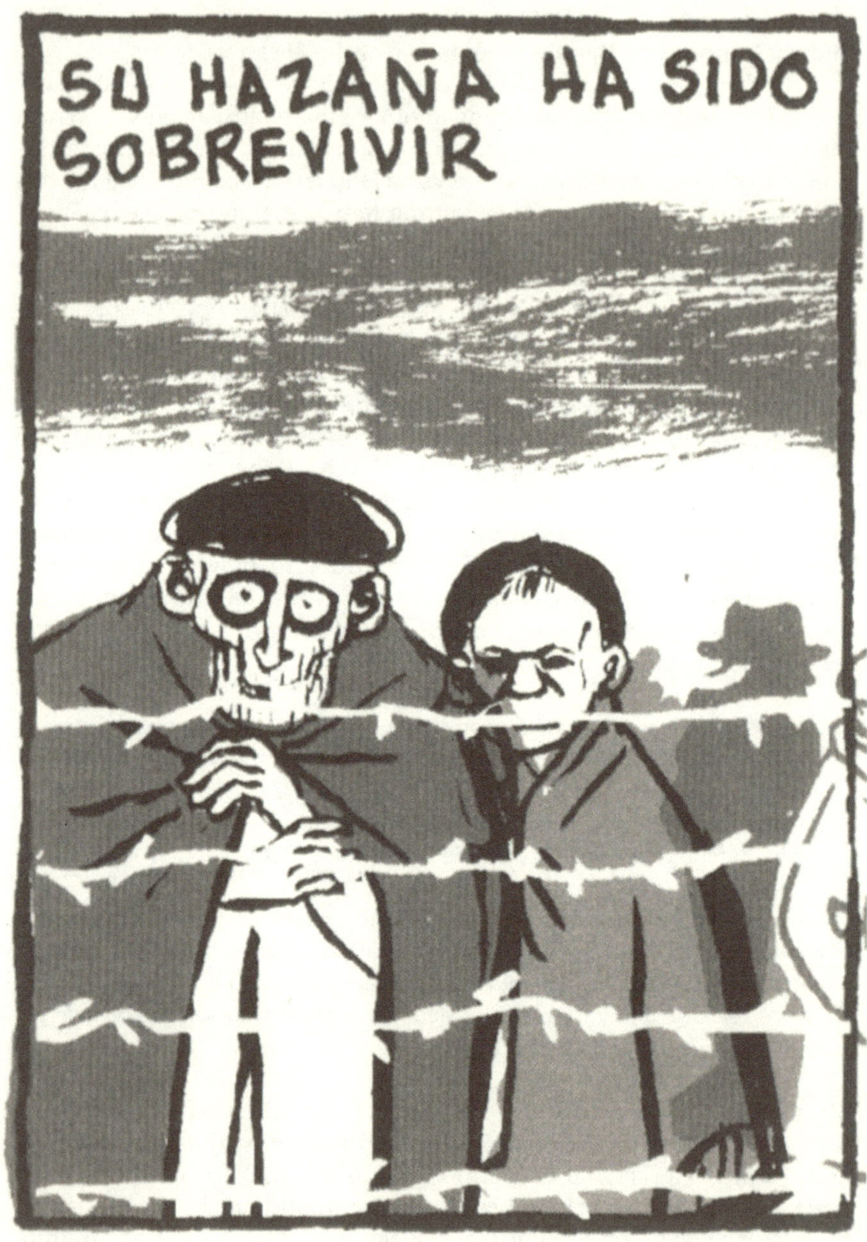

Figure 4.3a. A Franco-era concentration camp in Gallardo and Gallardo's *Un largo silencio* (6).

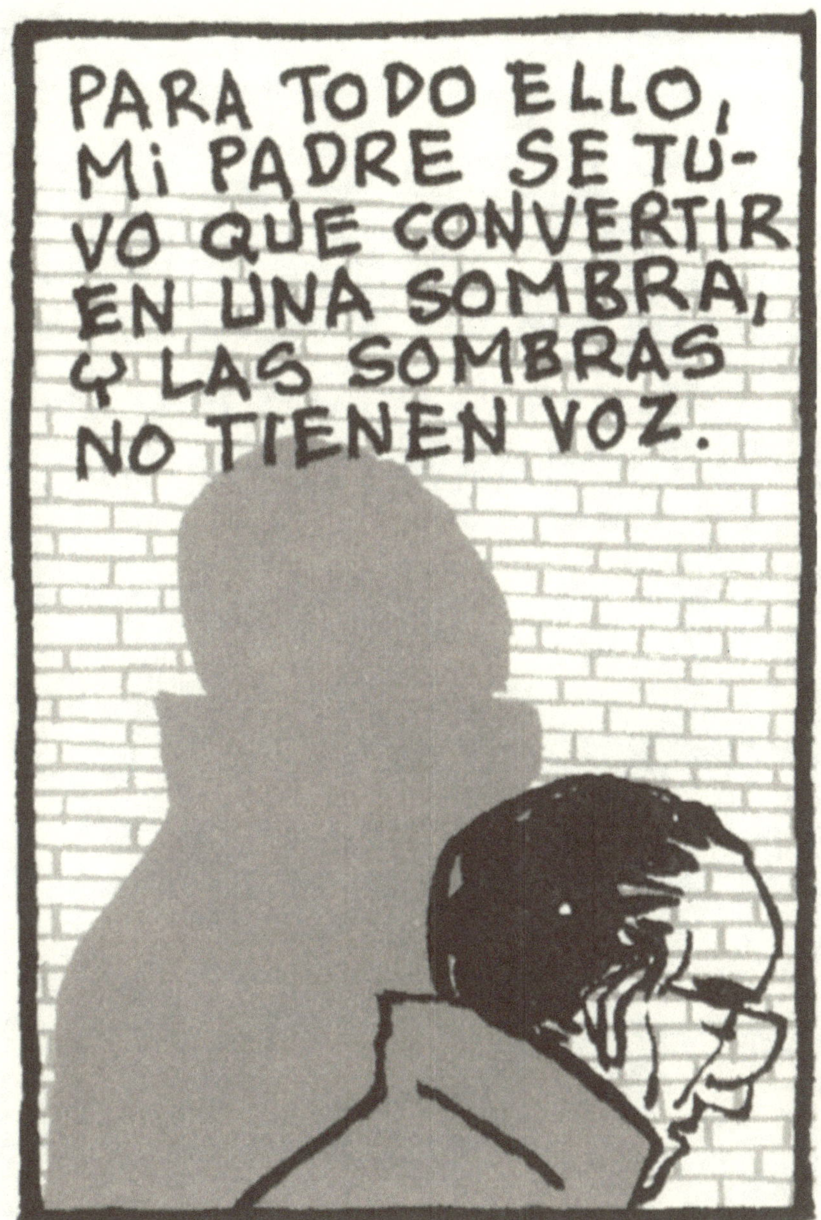

Figure 4.3b. Francisco Gallardo Sarmiento becomes a silent shadow during the dictatorship in Gallardo and Gallardo's *Un largo silencio* (6).

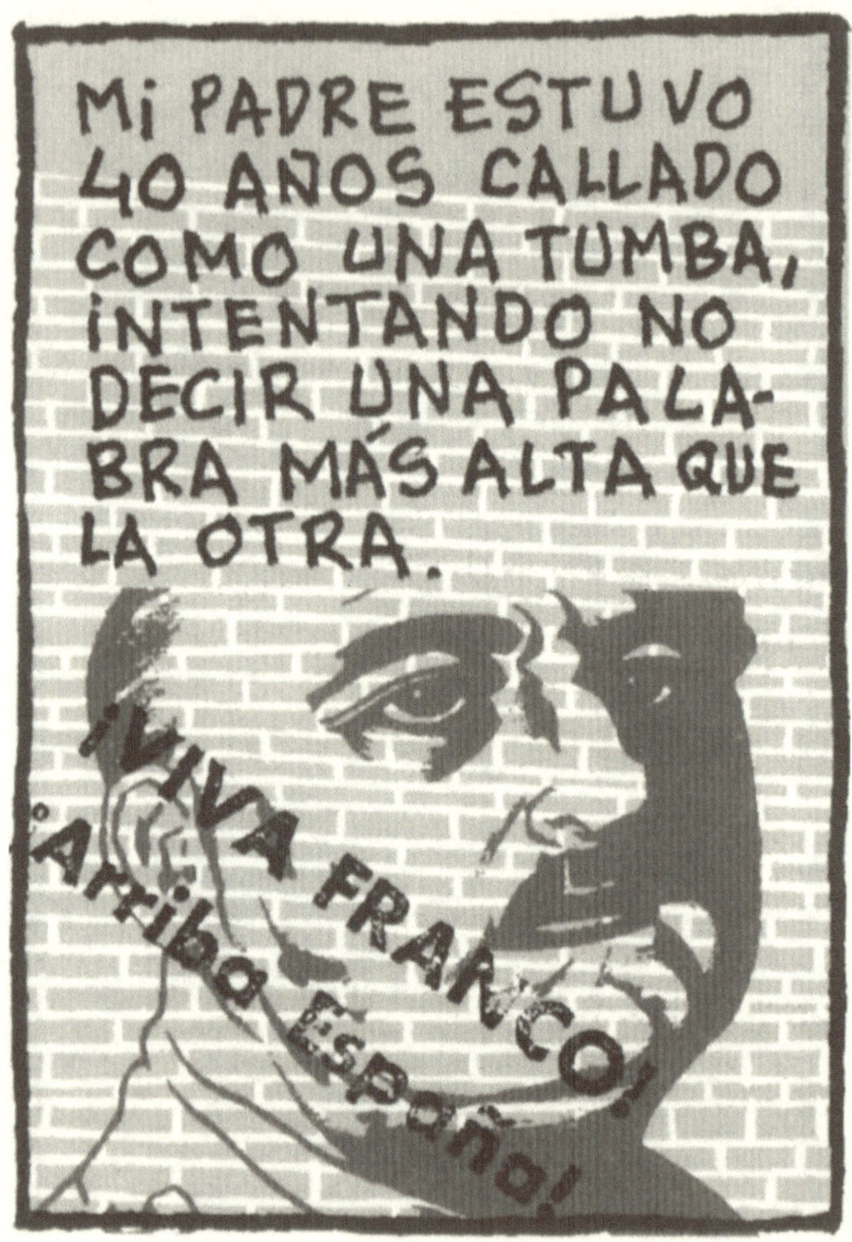

Figure 4.3c. Franco's face in graffiti in Gallardo and Gallardo's *Un largo silencio* (7).

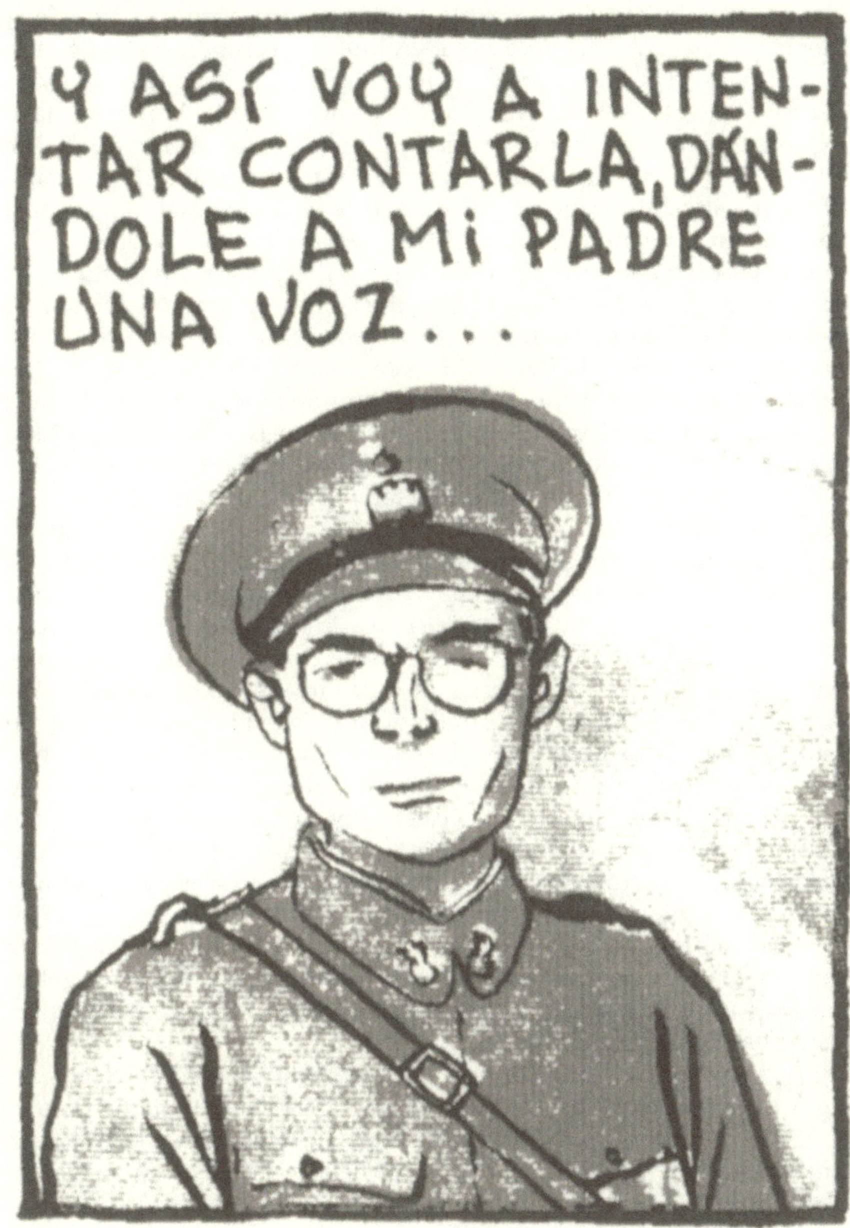

Figure 4.3d. Francisco Gallardo Sarmiento as a Republican soldier in Gallardo and Gallardo's *Un largo silencio* (7).

Additionally, *Un largo silencio* manifests the coordinates of postmemory, based as it is on autobiographical work by artists a generation removed from traumatic events (figure 4.3d), which Marianne Hirsch, as well as Dominick LaCapra and Andreas Huyssen, have explored with respect to Art Spiegelman's *Maus: A Survivor's Tale* (1977–91). The stylized visual grammar of the book and its economy of signification limit the degree of artifice and thus make it an ideal conduit for a memory discourse that gives rise to an "uneasy oscillation between continuity and rupture" (Hirsch 106). Given the commercial and critical success of *Maus*, the work is an important point of reference in terms of the themes that comics can take on, as LaCapra has indicated (179). *Un largo silencio*, for its part, does not present the same degree of complexity in its interrogation of identity and the lack of distinction between fiction and non-fiction (LaCapra 142). Quite the opposite: Gallardo leaves behind any notion of problematizing his father's voice, and the text is characterized by a certain stylistic simplicity – naiveté even – which distances it from Spiegelman's formally and conceptually more sophisticated work. Spiegelman's *Maus* was constructed through a deliberate "distancing move which is transmitted to the reader," with the idea steering clear of sentimentalism (Huyssen 128). In Gallardo's case, however, the son literally takes on his father's unadorned voice in order to *reduce* the sense of distance. Further, Gallardo's illustrations and his bold lines reinforce the father's story, which rarely goes beyond the framework established by the written text. In this sense, Francisco Gallardo's text moves away from the allegorical mode and rejects any pretence of taking on the absolute immeasurability of trauma or the representability of the unrepresentable horror of war. On the contrary, the story is presented as a series of anecdotes, from the declaration of the Second Spanish Republic, to the war story in which Gallardo would become artillery captain, to his later experiences in the concentration camps at Argèles-sur-Mer, el Palacio de Misiones, and the Depósito de Prisioneros de Guerra at Reus (figure 4.4).

El artefacto perverso and *Un largo silencio* are inscribed within contemporary memory debates, particularly those that emphasize the democratizing, contestatory power of memory against the modernizing impulses of the Transition, which was believed to require an "echar al olvido" [casting into oblivion] (Juliá) or the "fábula crítica" [critical fable] of the "pacto del olvido" [pact of forgetting] (Labrador Méndez, "Review" 381). This debate over our ability to remember – be it a matter of individual, collective, or historical memory – and its insertion

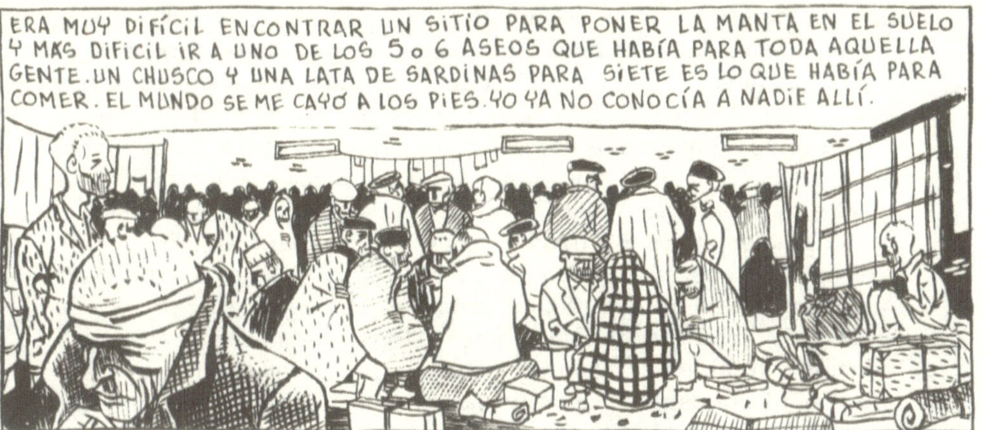

Figure 4.4. Prisoners of war at Reus in Gallardo and Gallardo's *Un largo silencio* (53).

into the public sphere, is still active today, as evidenced by successive periods of interest within academia and in the written press, which the Ley de la Memoria Histórica (Historical Memory Law 52/2007 of 26 December 2007) only served to enliven.[11] It is within the context of the increasing obsolescence of older cultural imaginaries and the initial emergence of the memory debates in public discourse that these works by Hernández Cava and Del Barrio, as well as those by the Gallardos, were produced. For Francisco Espinosa Maestre, this context is characterized by a change in public policy regarding memory, which ranged from what he calls the "suspensión de la memoria" [suspension of memory] that took place between 1982 and 1996 to its "resurgir" [resurgence] thereafter (184). For Labanyi, the memory boom is characterized by an accumulation of testimonies that have become commonplace in the Spanish cultural scene in which economic modernization reverberates ("Languages of Silence"; "Memory"; "Politics of Memory").

In *Tiempo pasado: Cultura de la memoria y giro subjetivo* [Time Past: Memory Culture and the Subjective Turn], Beatriz Sarlo reflects on the epistemological, as opposed to the moral or legal, dimension of these testimonies, and she notes the emergence of both the subject and individual narratives. Faced with this theoretical and ideological turn in memory narratives, Sarlo emphasizes the limits of testimony and the questions it raises, and, at the same time, the "potencial de la primera persona para reconstruir la experiencia y las dudas que el recurso a la primera persona abre en cuanto se coloca allí donde parece moverse con más naturalidad: el de la verdad de esa experiencia" [potential of the first person for the reconstruction of experience and the questions that a move towards the first person raises for everything placed there, where things move more naturally: the potential of the truth of that experience] (163). This shift is marked by a focus on stories of marginal subjects and on what Primo Levi has called "the raw material of indignation" that testimony provides (qtd. in Sarlo 42). The works analysed here question fiction as the repository of memory and testimony. In terms of representation, both the fictional *El artefacto perverso* and the autobiographical *Un largo silencio* resist the Transition's "casting into oblivion," as they question the site of enunciation – in the case of Hernández Cava by means of a deliberately polyphonic narrative style, and in the case of Gallardo by presenting a supposedly univocal objectivity.

At times, the debates over memory in Spain have given rise to disagreements among historians, experts, intellectuals, and memory activists, with obvious dissonances issuing from the editorial and media conglomerates that support them. Heated discussions have been generated over memory politics and policies, the distinction between memory and history, concepts like "historical memory" and "the pact of forgetting," the symbolic authority of historians and experts, and the "power of telling" history. If the iconicity that belongs to the comics genre gives rise to phenomena of remembering, comics are a testament to the movement away from expert discourse and towards citizen discourse, and a reminder of their own ever-problematic marginal site of enunciation. In this discursive conflict, Hernández Cava and Miguel Gallardo problematize the role of voices and point of view as means of questioning and legitimizing stories of memory, accepting the intrinsically collective nature of their construction and their polyphonic multiplicity, at the same time that they call for the democratization of both historical knowledge and the ability to represent it: the "poder contar" [being able/the power to tell] (Faber et al. 478).

Vázquez Montalbán has signalled the "trazos arqueológicos" [archaeological tendencies] of this *total comics*, the "cómic crítico, el que proponía una nueva manera de mirar una historia o el que utilizaba la historia para ofrecer una mirada crítica de la realidad" [comics of critique, which set out a new way of looking at a story, or used the story to offer a critical perspective on reality] ("Dibujar" 2). These comics of critique possess "un código, una gramática pictográfica, una retórica escriptoicónica, un combinado léxico-gráfico, que las dota de originalidad al tiempo que las hace legibles" [a code, a pictographic grammar, a scripto-iconic rhetoric, lexical-graphical blending, that makes them original and, at the same time, legible] (Altarriba, "Sobre" 9). In the works that concern us here, however, we find two problematic areas. The first, as Hafter has pointed out, is that the discourse of *Un largo silencio* is simultaneously a transmission and an appropriation of the past (7); the second, as Pérez del Solar has noted, involves the difficulty, occasioned by the multiplicity of premise and form in each of *El artefacto perverso*'s various narrative threads, of interpreting the novel's discourse on memory (248). In comics, the text is by its nature difficult to attribute to a diegetic or extradiegetic source, as it finds its meaning altered by its distribution in space. This distribution can "ser en sí marco" [be, in itself, a frame] that points to a "suerte de polifonía, debida a la multiplicidad de materiales que se ofrecen con sus articulaciones a la vista" [sort of polyphony, given the multiplicity of materials which are presented with their moving parts exposed] (Reggiani 423). This code depends on the very fact that the voice is indeterminate; the code, organized by the images through which the discourse is created, "pertenece a la cultura industrial, y como tal, construye relatos modernos, aunque su capacidad legitimadora está en tensión con el discurso letrado" [belongs to the culture industry, and as such it constructs modern stories, although its capacity to confer legitimacy exists in tension with learned discourse] (Merino 11).

In *La literatura en la construcción de la ciudad democrática* [Literature in the Construction of the Democratic City] (1998), Vázquez Montalbán has analysed the metaphors of the "ciudad franquista" [Francoist city], the "ciudad socialista" [socialist city], and the "ciudad democrática" [democratic city], which summarize the author's own utopian longings and dystopian fears while at the same time allowing him to study the evolution of these changing metaphors within the historical imaginary. A recurring theme in the author's work, this longing reveals his critical stance towards Spanish democracy. For Vázquez Montalbán, the project of rebuilding the "democratic city" is undergirded by the role of literature and art, whose most essential objective would be "la recuperación de la memoria del vencido y la descripción de la realidad en clave no triunfalista, en busca de un nuevo lenguaje solidario y, por lo tanto, comunicativo y crítico" [the recovery of the memory of the vanquished and the description of reality without recourse to triumphalism, in search of a new language of solidarity and, accordingly, of communication and critique] (*La literatura* 62). This position, upon which the author also remarks in the prologue to *El artefacto perverso*, is affirmed by the words of Hernández Cava which precede the novel. Hernández Cava writes:

> [U]n velo de silencio y olvido cayó sobre los españoles cuando comenzó la tantas veces citada transición política. En aras de un cambio pacífico y no traumático de la dictadura a la democracia, se decidió hacer borrón y cuenta nueva de un pasado no tan lejano, que podía despertar algunas heridas todavía a flor de piel. Y, así las cosas, a los jóvenes se les negó la memoria de lo que fue el régimen franquista y sus antecedentes. (Hernández Cava and Del Barrio 3)

> [A veil of silence and forgetting fell over Spain when the oft-mentioned political transition began. In the interest of a peaceful, non-traumatic shift from dictatorship to democracy, it was decided that there would be a fresh start, leaving behind a not-so-distant past that might reopen wounds that were still raw. And, this being the case, the youth were denied the memory of the Franco regime and of what had come before.]

These words of introduction by Hernández Cava confirm the notion of a "suspensión de la memoria" [suspension of memory], in Espinosa's formulation, echoing also the public call for the recovery of the memory of the defeated that configures the poetics of this critical and communicative device.

The novels by Hernández Cava and Gallardo describe the repressive atmosphere of a *longa noite de pedra* [long night of stone] of the past and future "ciudad franquista" [Francoist city] "para reconstruir una sola ciudad: la de la memoria" [in order to reconstruct a single city: that of memory] (Vázquez Montalbán, "La memoria" 3). Fittingly, Hernández Cava titles the first volume of his Pedro Guzmán series "La ciudad en peligro" [The City in Danger], a city threatened by the perverse anti-memory device (figure 4.5).

Memory or narration that reaches back into the past demands certain kinds of stories, characters, and situations. These works by Hernández Cava and Del Barrio and by the Gallardos take two different approaches; both, however, problematize the kind of story that the past demands, its legitimacy, and its contraposition with lived experience. *Un largo silencio* makes explicit the memory of the everyday and the "transference problem as it involves the reader and the narrator" (LaCapra 153), while *El artefacto perverso* functions in the hermeneutic movement between resistance and survival. The graphic novel "se muestra capaz de restituir la superposición y la contaminación de lo

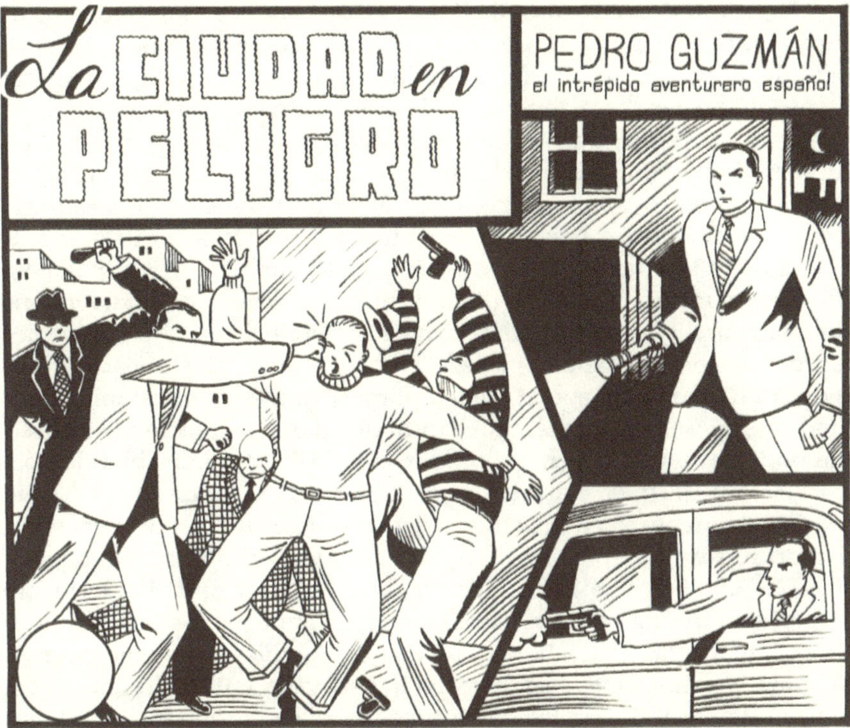

Figure 4.5. Pedro Guzmán fighting with criminals in Hernández Cava and Del Barrio's *El artefacto perverso* (11).

declarado y de lo silenciado en torno a una temática de la reminiscencia que solicita fuertemente la actividad del lector" [is capable of restoring the overlapping and contamination of that which is declared and that which is silenced, both around a thematics of remembering that demands the active participation of the reader] (Alsina 224).

There are several reasons for situating these works within the story of the origins of the 1978 democratic government. First, *El artefacto perverso* problematizes the site of enunciation and gives voice to marginal narratives, which amplifies these comics as "dispositivos de enunciación colectiva" [means for collective emancipation] (Deleuze and Guattari 31). Second, *Un largo silencio* proposes an open and inspiring kind of memory, which, with concepts such as "hebras de paz de vida" [living strands of peace] (Gutiérrez), includes a call for spaces of mutual encounter, as I elaborate further on.

The cultural paradigm of the CT or "Cultura de la Transición" [Culture of the Transition] is based on the concepts of verticality, consensus, and depoliticization (Martínez 17). This hegemonic paradigm does not question the neoliberal logic of the late-Franco regime, which imagined a society marked by individualism and the consumerism of an educated urban middle class (Sánchez León), a "señuelo de la modernidad, como sustitutivo del proyecto de reconstrucción de la ciudad democrática" [dummy modernity, meant to substitute for the project of the reconstruction of the democratic city] (Vázquez Montalbán, *La literatura* 99). Resistance memoirs work to disrupt this logic, favouring interventions in which orality is cast as an instrument of politicization. These stories encourage the emergence of a new "sujeto histórico" [historical subject], which involves a change in the temporality of the historical imaginary and is proposed as an alternative form of historical knowledge focused around the public sphere (Labrador Méndez, "¿Lo llamaban democracia?" 33). Jacques Rancière and Amador Fernández-Savater have analysed the construction of this "sujeto histórico emergente" [emergent historical subject] in fiction (Labrador Méndez, "¿Lo llamaban democracia?" 33). For Fernández-Savater, both politics and literature are articulated through the power of fiction, metaphor, and story. The politics of emancipation is a literary politics or a politics-fiction that invents a name or a collective character to represent those who do not have a voice ("Política" 3). At the same time, it "plays important moral and political roles" by echoing the "locus of belonging and commitment" (LaCapra 142). Fernández-Savater sketches out the conjoined manner in which politics and literature construct shared worlds and populate them with characters and events. These devices, like the established features of a *"literatura menor"* [minor literature], move between the individual and the collective in which politics takes over enunciation (Deleuze and Guattari 31). Just as in comics, where modes of expression intermix, so too do they intermix in the fields of fiction and politics. Following Rancière, this intermixing allows us to explore the presentational modes of individuals, situations, or events that are native to graphic narrative, which are not dissimilar to the modes of presentation that define communities, themes, situations, and actions as political.

Enrique Montero, in *El artefacto perverso*, and Francisco Gallardo, in *Un largo silencio*, are characters constructed as devices of enunciation possessed of the collective potential of the anonymous. They infuse subaltern, marginalized narratives and interpretations, spaces where subjects articulate themselves voicelessly in the shadows. These characters must also be understood as part of the genealogy of the anonymous described by Fernández-Savater ("Cómo se organiza"); their approach to memory is characterized by an epistemological drive in which "escribir historia y escribir historias dependen de un mismo régimen de verdad" [the writing of history and the writing of stories both depend on the same regimen of truth] (Rancière 49). They point, thus, to memory as a common good, as opposed to the externally imposed models of memory that Fernández-Savater has called "la memoria-trinchera y la memoria-fetiche" [memory-as-trench and memory-as-fetish] ("¿Hay que guardarse?").

Gallardo and Hernández Cava move away from anything resembling heroic narrative and focus, respectively, on the faithful translation of the story of personal experience via a multiplicity of voices. Enrique Montero is a representation of the draughtsmen who, as Hernández Cava confirms in his prologue, dedicated themselves to the silent and hidden work of the creation of comic books and were obliged to hide their own pasts. Francisco Sarmiento is the story of a Republican survivor who is allowed to live in exchange for remaining silent about his experiences and taking on a new role in society as an "adicto al glorioso movimiento nacional" [adherent to the glorious national movement] (Gallardo and Gallardo 69). In this sense, these characters transcend their own experience through their testimony and take on the potentiality of collective representation, which Fernández-Savater explores.

On the stage of the "Francoist city," Francisco Gallardo's temporary inability to articulate defeat is based not on a traumatic event but rather on the implicit coercion effected by the Francoist regime. By contrast, *El artefacto perverso* describes the confrontations between subversive groups on one hand and the state's machinery of repression on the other in its explicitly coercive framework, recodifying that defeat through four narrative voices, each with a distinct graphic style, which together serve to question the processes of memory. Enrique Montero's objective is to claim his right to "desmemoria" [unmemory], his right to hand himself over to that "artefacto perverso" [perverse machine] in order to survive in peace. It is this very same longing to survive that constitutes the reason for Francisco Gallardo's silence. Enrique Montero's story stands in contrast to the one he draws for Pedro Guzmán, in which good and evil are well-defined. "Dime, ¿quién es Guzmán? ¿Tú o yo?" [Tell me. Who is Guzmán? You or me?], a shadowy figure aiming a revolver asks himself (figure 4.6), interpellating the reader just as he seems to interpellate the blacklisted teacher (Hernández Cava and Del Barrio 16). Here, the graphic technique "en sí ya es un comentario sobre la memoria, sobre la importancia y los límites de la transmisión de los recuerdos" [is in itself a comment on memory, on the importance and

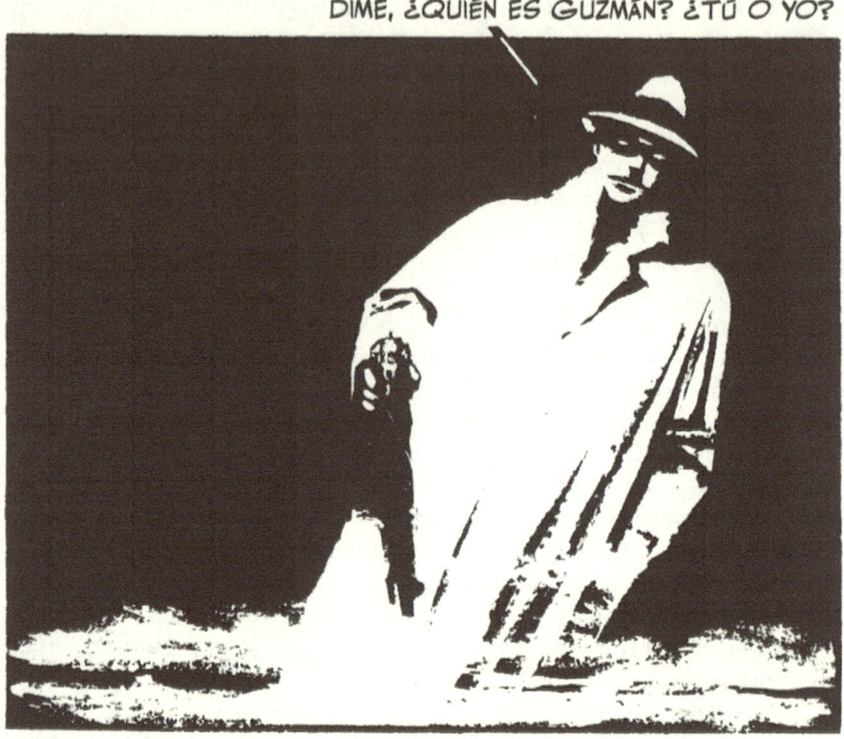

Figure 4.6. A shadow that asks Enrique Montero about his creation in Hernández Cava and Del Barrio's *El artefacto perverso* (16).

the limits of the transmission of memories] as referentiality becomes increasingly irrecoverable (Pérez del Solar 251).

As the reader delves deeper into Enrique's adventures, his search for Bozal, and the ambush in which he finds himself mixed up (and where Bozal is mortally wounded), the contrast increases between the dark, sombre style of the draughtsman's story and the technical simplicity of Pedro Guzmán's *tebeos*. In a desperate attempt, the former teacher takes Bozal to his own home, where he and Josita try to save him. It is at this point where Bozal's deathbed testimony of his experiences in the Argelès concentration camp begins. Bozal, in turn, centres his narration on the story told to him by Jordi, a visionary prisoner who is also bedridden (figure 4.7a). Here Hernández Cava and Del Barrio's comic book takes on its maximum level of cross-contamination as the panels flow one after the other, the faces and graphic styles overlapping. Jordi tells Bozal, who then tells Enrique Montero, the story of

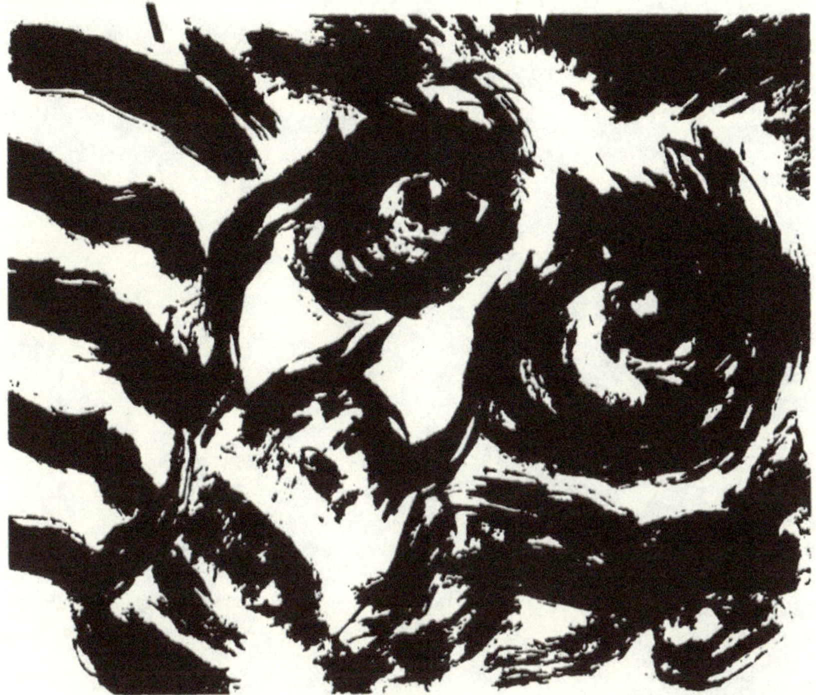

Figure 4.7a. Distorted face of Jordi in Hernández Cava and Del Barrio's *El artefacto perverso* (52).

the train heading to Francoist Spain, transporting paintings from the Museo del Prado (figure 4.7b), and various visual styles are superimposed one upon the other with multiple references to the paintings themselves.

For Alsina, the story Jordi tells Bozal culminates in a panel that becomes the axis of this tale of contamination (222). Enrique struggles to narrate, to live through the telling of stories that ultimately codify the Francoist machinery of unmemory, which encourages the silencing of a traumatic past of defeat and loss (figure 4.7c). In a certain way, after having destroyed the device that causes the loss of memory, Enrique and Pedro Guzmán's survival increases the feeling of defeat that fills the last panel of the comic book, where the outline of Enrique and Josita is backlit against the window. This window, as Alsina suggests, reflects Enrique's situation of limbo, the difficulty inherent in the negotiation between the public and private realms.

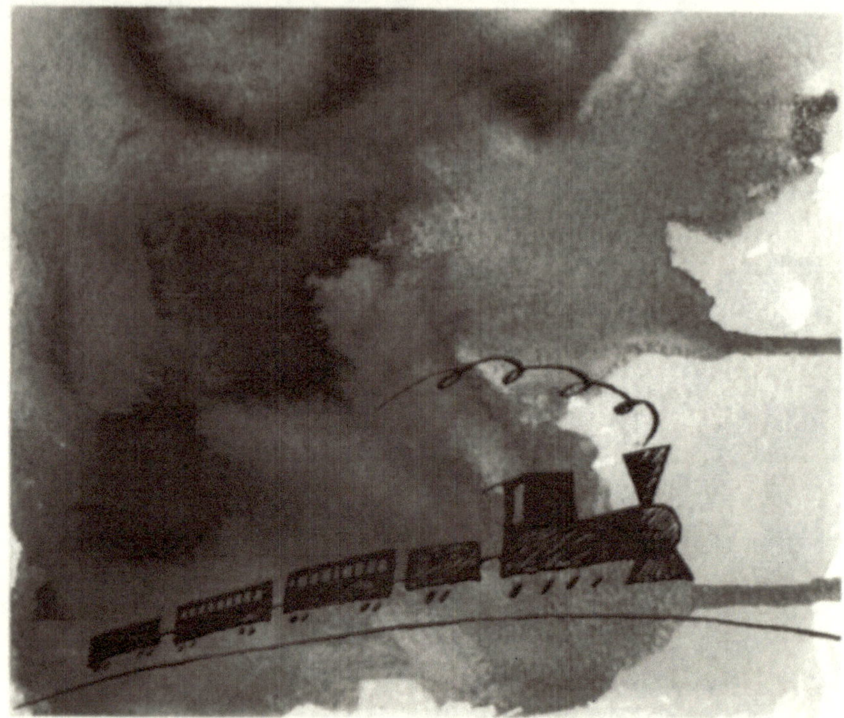

Figure 4.7b. A train heading to Francoist Spain, transporting paintings from the Museo del Prado, in Hernández Cava and Del Barrio's *El artefacto perverso* (44).

If this reading of *El artefacto perverso* is determined by the work's polyphony, the single-voiced character of the Gallardos' *Un largo silencio* can be read through the concept of "hebras de paz" [strands of peace] put forth by Juan Gutiérrez. It translates into a simplified and natural style, far from the time of Makoki, in which the black and white does not predetermine the characters nor predominate the Manichaeism of Enrique Montero's story in *El artefacto perverso*. Among the processes of democratizing knowledge and access to the historical record that have appeared in the new millennium, one of the most notable is the Media Lab Prado working group "Memoria y procomún" [Memory and Common Good], coordinated by philosopher Juan Gutiérrez, founder of the Centre d'Investigacions per la Pau, Gernika Gogoratuz, and member of the international network of people impacted by political violence, in which Sánchez León and Fernández-Savater, among others, also collaborate.[12]

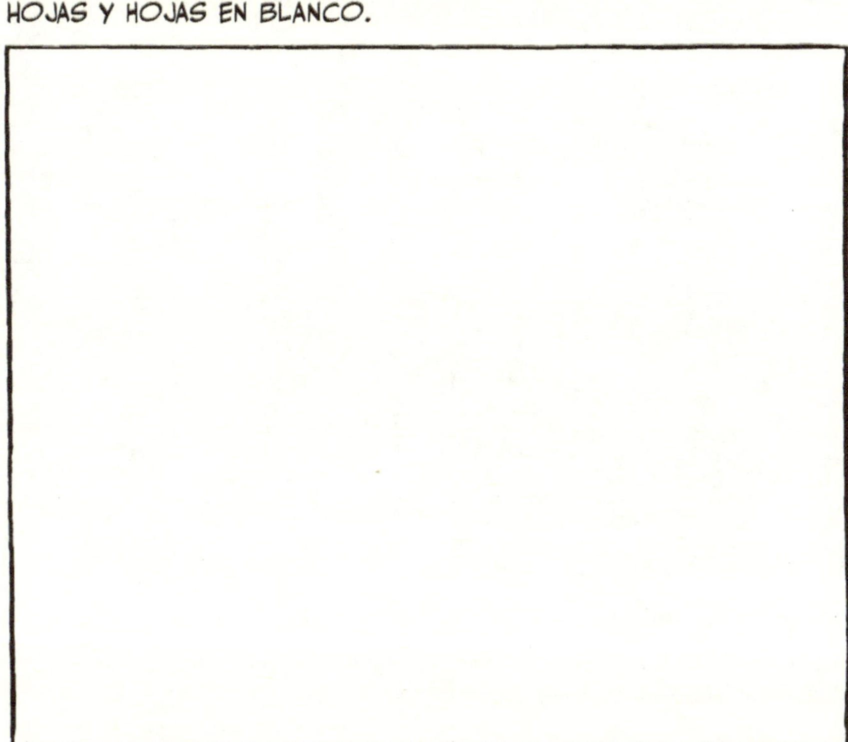

Figure 4.7c. A blank panel codifying the representational impossibility of "unmemory" and the traumatic past in Hernández Cava and Del Barrio's *El artefacto perverso* (52).

Un largo silencio offers an episode that should be framed in terms of these "strands of living peace" that run throughout and structure these stories of memory and, in this case, turn out to be a central concern in the Gallardos' graphic novel. After Francisco Sarmiento's travels through various camps and prisons, in the Depósito de Prisioneros de Guerra de Reus, one of the soldiers calls for him. In the illustration, all of Francisco's fears of being "paseado" [summarily executed] are rekindled, and he even remembers the experience of various Nationalist officials who were assassinated, in that case by Republican soldiers themselves (Gallardo and Gallardo 57–8). Finally, Francisco discovers that his destiny lies elsewhere, as they take him, to his surprise, before the lieutenant in charge of the camp. "Pero¿qué carajo haces tú aquí, Paco?" [What the hell are you doing here, Paco?], asks the officer, startling Francisco (59). The officer turns out to be Ginés Campos Godoy, a

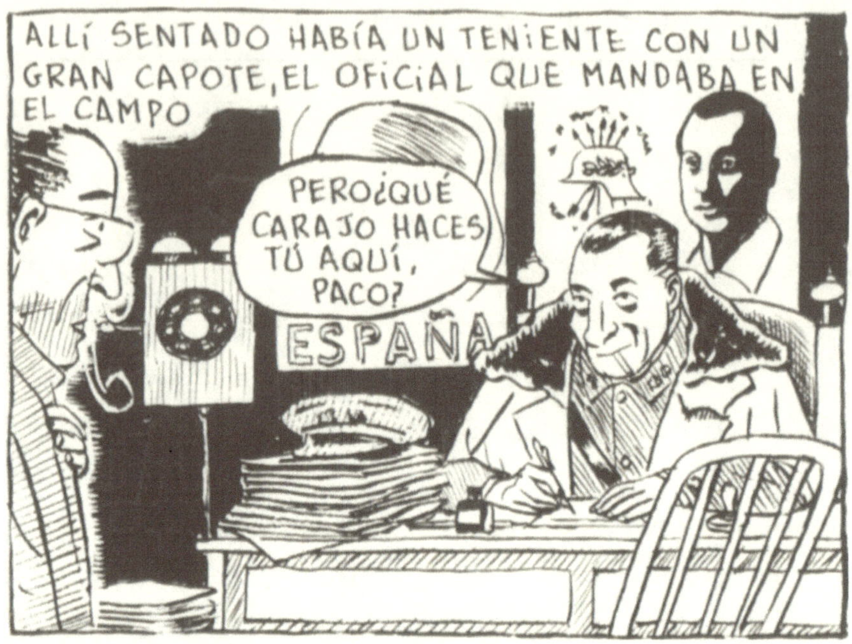

Figure 4.8a. Francisco Gallardo Sarmiento reunites with Ginés Campos Godoy in Gallardo and Gallardo's *Un largo silencio* (59).

classmate from the Escuela Industrial de Linares in Francisco's hometown, with whom he had gone to school for seven years. The subjective shot of the panel (figure 4.8a) facilitates the surprise of the meeting, and the warmth of Ginés's face and smile – which contrasts with the fascist military attire under the iconography of the Falange and the portrait of José Antonio Primo de Rivera and the overall seriousness of the figure of Francisco – stands out as well. As a reflex, Gallardo shows us a photograph to corroborate the common past between the officer and the prisoner (figure 4.8b). The unfurling of events causes the lives of these two friends to become intertwined, linking them in the positive peace of which Gutiérrez writes. This positive peace "tiene que ver con la convivencia en equidad y el engarce de vidas que se ayudan, sostienen, enriquecen y salvan entre sí, motivadas, no por un cálculo de interés personal, sino por la compasión y el afecto hacia otros seres humanos" [has to do with living together in equality and with the joining together of lives that help each other, sustain, enrich, and save each other, motivated not by the calculation of personal interest, but by compassion and fellow-feeling towards other human beings] (Gutiérrez). It is this

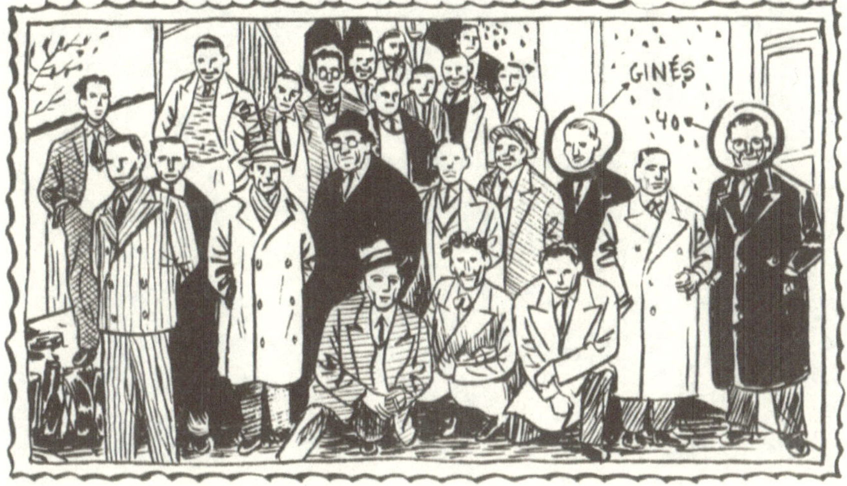

Figure 4.8b. Picture of Escuela Industrial de Linares Group in Gallardo and Gallardo's *Un largo silencio* (59).

fellow-feeling, this linking together, and the subsequent move away from the logic of friend versus enemy and away from a more dogmatic taking of sides, that allows this officer to help Francisco Sarmiento, first by sharing his table and later by making the necessary arrangements to improve Sarmiento's situation at the camp by putting him in charge of logistics and assigning him to teach a course for officers wishing to enter the military academy. With the help of Campos Godoy and coupons purchased from the Falange and the municipal government, Francisco finally obtains his release papers (figure 4.8c), which define him as an "adicto al glorioso movimiento nacional" [adherent to the glorious national movement] and will allow him to work in the future (Gallardo and Gallardo 69). This chance gesture, these "strands of peace," define Francisco Sarmiento's story, for it is here that his tale ends as he begins working as a master electrician with the company Riegos y Fuerzas del Ebro, S. A., where he also meets his future wife.

El artefacto perverso and *Un largo silencio* take part in the "sedimento ético" [ethical sediment] in the collective construction of the past, while also issuing a call for equality in the exercise of citizenship by leaving themselves open to interpretation, to the problematization of their tales

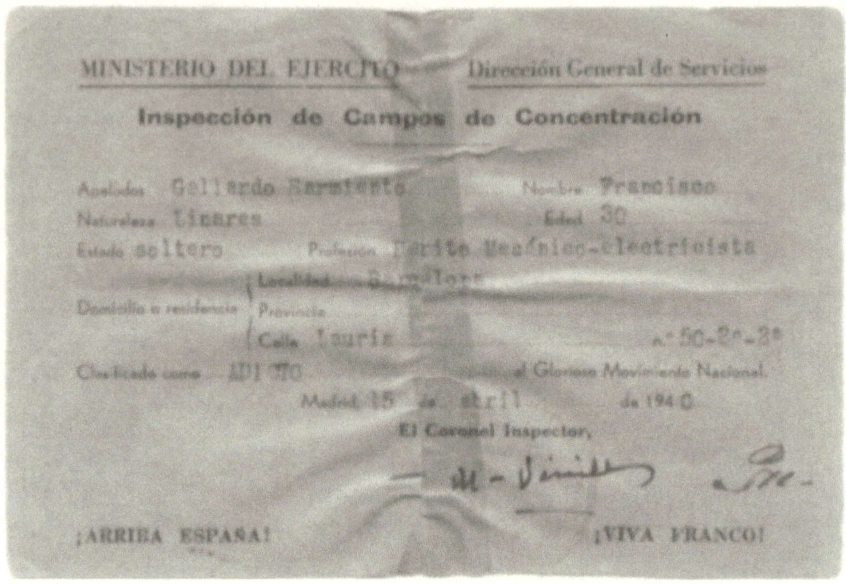

MINISTERIO DEL EJERCITO — Dirección General de Servicios

Inspección de Campos de Concentración

Apellidos Gallardo Sarmiento — Nombre Francisco
Naturaleza Linares — Edad 30
Estado soltero — Profesión Perito Mecánico-Electricista
Domicilio o residencia: Localidad [illegible] / Provincia / Calle Lauria n.° 50-2°-2ª
Clasificado como ADICTO [illegible] al Glorioso Movimiento Nacional.
Madrid 15 de abril de 1940
El Coronel Inspector,

¡ARRIBA ESPAÑA! — ¡VIVA FRANCO!

Figure 4.8c. Francisco Gallardo Sarmiento's release papers in Gallardo and Gallardo's *Un largo silencio* (69).

(Vinyes 25). In spite of their allusion to "memories of the vanquished," in the end these works cannot be defined simply as Republican narratives, given their deliberate move away from closed interpretations and their avoidance of dichotomous or archetypical approaches. These narratives unfold in a medium, the comic book, which until recently has tended to avoid engaging with memory discourse. They also offer themselves as legitimate sources of historical knowledge, and are necessarily connected to the debates over public policy with respect to memory.

In this chapter, I have endeavoured to position these novels within the memory debates, and we have pointed to their connection with the historical roots of the 1978 democracy of consensus and, by extension, with the "calibrado inédito de subjetividades" [new-found calibration of identities] of the climate of indignation following the 2008 crisis (Fernández-Savater "Cómo se organiza"). This context suggests a new paradigm for the configuration of the historical imaginary in the graphic novel through a poetics that prioritizes lived experience, and, further, it makes evident the crisis of the expert class and of symbolic authority in the democratization of historical knowledge. In sum, the ongoing process of democratic emancipation in contemporary Spain finds its precursors in these graphic novels, in these two devices against unmemory.

NOTES

1 This essay was translated from the Spanish by Neil Anderson.
2 Santos Juliá (*Memoria;* 2006) and Paloma Aguilar Fernández ("Cultura"; 2007) have shown that works on the Civil War and the dictatorship have been a constant since the Transition. Although the memorializing character of these works has increased since the mid-eighties, this feature does not serve as "prueba de que no hubo ni silencio ni desconocimiento social" [proof that there wasn't silence or a lack of social knowledge] (Vinyes 32).
3 This work also coincided with Cathy Caruth's classic volume *Unclaimed Experience* and the growth of the "ola omnipresente del trauma" [ever-present wave of trauma], as Huyssen labels it (121).
4 Among its systematic legal actions since 2012, this body has denounced the derogation of the Amnesty Law of 1977 and sought the investigation of forced disappearances. Spokesperson Rupert Colville has declared: "España tiene la obligación según la legislación internacional de investigar las graves violaciones de los derechos humanos que han ocurrido en el pasado, incluidas las cometidas durante el régimen de Franco" [Spain is obligated by international law to investigate the serious violations of human rights that have occurred in the past, including those committed during the Franco regime] (ONU).
5 See also Perez del Solar's essay in this volume.
6 The term "graphic novel" has been controversial since Will Eisner first brought it into use, and has been the source of lively debates. To some extent, the term reflects the desire for legitimacy that has troubled the medium from its beginnings. "Cómic social" [social comics] is another term that situates the form halfway between inherent reproducibility and marketing in conflict with the emergence of authorship. For a deeper look at this issue, Santiago García's 2010 book *La novela gráfica* is illuminating.
7 By "economy of signification," I mean the management of signs, because there are a number of variables in the process by which certain signs are reduced instead of others. This assignment is semiotic due to its "enclosure" in a "vignette" or panel. Thus the iconographic reduction, in other words, the comic's transformation to icon, defines its meaning. For "strands of living peace," see note 12.
8 The operative notion of "historical imaginaries," derived from the realm of the imaginary or the imagination, has had various declensions depending on the area of knowledge (sociology, anthropology, philosophy, psychoanalysis, and history) and the different approaches (Bachelard, Sartre, Lacan, Durand, Castoriadis, Chartier, Le Goff, and so on). From history, which is my anchor point, *imaginary* is a concept coined by the *Annales* school based on the idea of mentality and ideology. Consequently, imaginary registers

as "categoría de representaciones colectivas, ideas-imágenes de la sociedad global y de todo lo que tiene que ver con ella" [a category of collective representations, representations of social reality, ideas-images of the global society and everything that is related to it] (Baczko 8). Following the historian Jacques Le Goff, this network of collective representations (social) would be nourished by artistic and literary works. "Historical imaginaries" are the network of signs, representations, or images that a collective creates to give meaning to its existence in a certain historical context and whose main substrate can be found in literary or artistic works.

9 Felipe Hernández Cava, Federico del Barrio, and Miguel Gallardo each have a long history in the world of comics. As Frattini and Palmer have highlighted, Hernández Cava has been one of the Spanish authors "que más se han aplicado a una búsqueda de la memoria, de la colectiva y de la individual" [who has been most dedicated to the search for memory, both collective and individual] and has done so "desde un medio vilipendiado como el cómic" [working in a vilified medium like comics] (97–8). Felipe Hernández Cava is one of the most important (and prolific) figures in the Spanish comics scene because of his social and ethical commitments and his interest in historical imaginaries. He began writing comics in the early 1970s under the group pseudonym El Cubri. He served as editor of *Madriz* and later of *Medios revueltos*, which shared many of the same authors and content. In 2009, he and co-author Bartolomé Seguí received the Premio Nacional del Cómic [National Comics Prize] for *Las serpientes ciegas*; the two continued their collaboration with *Hágase el caos* (2011) and *Las oscuras manos del olvido* (2014). Federico del Barrio joined the *Madriz* group; his work, with stories by Elisa Galvez, stands out among the comics of the 1980s. Del Barrio and Hernández Cava broke with convention in *Las memorias de Amorós* (1993). Later, the experimentation continued in *Relaciones* (1999) and *Simple* (1999). In 2010 he published *El hombre de arena*, based on a story by E.T.A. Hoffman. Miguel Gallardo got his start in comics in the late 1970s and early 1980s, serving as editor during Makoki's early period. The popularity of his character Makoki, "adalid de la línea chunga" [champion of the crappy line], "oscureció su compleja personalidad de autor gráfico multidisciplinar" [obscured his complex personality as a multidisciplinary graphic artist-author] (Cuadrado 511). As Gallardo himself confirms, talking about *Un largo silencio*, "yo abandoné el cómic en los noventa con el álbum de mi padre como último intento de hacer una historia más personal, a raíz del nacimiento de mi hija y la revolución que supuso en mi vida. También fue una entrada de aire fresco en mi manera de ver el cómic, que se simplificó hasta extremos minimalistas" [I abandoned comics in the nineties with my father's album as the last attempt to make a more personal story, following the birth of my daughter and the

revolution that this entailed in my life. It was also a breath of fresh air in my way of seeing comics, which was simplified to minimalist extremes] ("Entrevista"). This particular revolution ultimately took the form of the prize-winning *María y yo*, published in 2007.

10 The most important exception is Carlos Giménez's *Paracuellos* (1977–2003), an eloquent, politically charged comic that is based on his childhood experiences in a residence run by the Auxilio Social. The re-release of *Todo Paracuellos* in 2007 coincided with the passing of the Historical Memory Law. *Paracuellos* is the "pioneer of the testimonial comic that "vindicates the personal history of memory, which in certain ways confronts objective institutionalized history and, containing contradictory information, seeks to offer other perspectives" (Merino and Tullis, 217). Much as Art Spiegelman's *Maus* had been for the North American (and international) underground comic, Giménez's comics are a point of reference for the Spanish comic, evidencing the growing importance of testimony and memory, and the key role of the witness and the victim.

11 See, for example, Ruíz Torres, Faber, Aguilar Fernández, Loureiro, or Faber et al.

12 Concepts such as "paz positiva" [positive peace], "no violencia" [non-violence], "vida compartida" [shared life], and "engarce de vidas" [linking of lives] have been explored in the various sessions in which the group works to broaden the ways in which memory is discussed and understood. "Hebras de paz de vida" [living strands of peace], one of their most oft-cited concepts, is a compendium of testimonies that are not aligned with a given faction or political persuasion, but which emphasize the communication of their human dimension, especially in those stories that involve breaking ranks and helping the enemy in a dangerous situation, or, as Gutiérrez himself defines it, "actos desinteresados, insumisos a la disciplina del propio grupo, en socorro y ayuda a seres humanos en peligro por ser considerados parte del enemigo o intrusos indeseados" [disinterested acts, unbound to the discipline of one's own group, in help and aid to human beings who, because they are considered enemies or unwanted intruders, find themselves in danger].

WORKS CITED

Aguilar Fernández, Paloma. "Cultura política, consumo cultural y memoria durante la transición." *Tiempo de Transición (1975–1982)*, edited by José Luis Rodriguez Zapatero, Fundación Pablo Iglesias, 2007, 80–116.

– "Los debates sobre la memoria histórica." *Claves de razón práctica* 172 (2007): 64–9.

– *Memoria y olvido de la Guerra Civil española*. Alianza, 1996.

Alsina, Jean. "La narración en *El artefacto perverso* algunas calas en un objeto inagotable." *Historietas, cómics y tebeos españoles*, edited by Viviane Alary, PU du Mirail, 2002, 210–33.

Altarriba, Antonio. "La historieta española de 1960 a 2000." *Historietas, cómics y tebeos españoles*, edited by Vivian Alary, PU du Mirail, 2002, 76–121.

– "Sobre el origen, evolución, límites y otros debates teóricos en torno a la historieta." *Arbor: ciencia, pensamiento y cultura* 187.2 (2011): 9–14. doi.org/10.3989/arbor.2011.2extran2111.

Ausente, Daniel. "La memoria gráfica y las sombras del pasado." *Supercómic: Mutaciones de la novela gráfica contemporánea*, edited by Santiago García, Errata Naturae, 2013, 107–36.

Baczko, Bronislaw. *Los imaginarios sociales: Memorias y esperanzas colectivas*. Nueva Vision, 2005.

Campbell, Eddie. "La autobiografía en el cómic. Una muy breve introducción a un tema muy extenso, visto desde una bicicleta en marcha." *Supercómic Mutaciones de La Novela Gráfica Contemporánea*, edited by Santiago García, Errata Naturae, 2013.

Caruth, Cathy. *Unclaimed Experience: Trauma, Narrative, and History*. Johns Hopkins UP, 1996.

Cuadrado, Jesús. *Atlas español de la cultura popular de la Historieta y su uso, 1873–2000*. Salamanca ed., Sinsentido Fundación Germán Sánchez Ruipérez, 2000.

Deleuze, Gilles, and Félix Guattari. *Kafka, por una literatura menor*. Ediciones Era, 1978.

Espinosa Maestre, Francisco. *Contra el olvido: Historia y memoria de la Guerra Civil*. Crítica, 2006.

Faber, Sebastiaan. "The Debate about Spain's Past and the Crisis of Academic Legitimacy: The Case of Santos Juliá." *Colorado Review of Hispanic Studies* 5 (2007): 165–90.

Faber, Sebastiaan, Pablo Sánchez León, and Jesús Izquierdo Martín. "El poder de contar y el paraíso perdido. Polémicas mediáticas y construcción colectiva de la memoria en España." *Política y Sociedad* 48.3 (2011): 463–80. doi.org/10.5209/rev_poso.2011.v48.n3.36423.

Fernández-Savater, Amador. "¿Cómo se organiza un *clima*?" *Público*, 9 Jan. 2012, blogs.publico.es/fueradelugar/1438/¿como-se-organiza-un-clima.

– "¿Hay que guardarse la memoria en el bolsillo?" *El Diario.es*, 28 Feb. 2014, www.eldiario.es/interferencias/guardarse-memoria-bolsillo_6_233836627.html.

– "Política literal y política literaria (sobre ficciones políticas y 15-M)." *El Diario.es*, 30 Nov. 2012, www.eldiario.es/interferencias/ficcion-politica-15-M_6_71452864.html.

Frattini, Eric, and Oscar Palmer. *Guía básica del cómic*. Nuer Ediciones, 1999.

Gallardo, Miguel. "Entrevista a Miguel Gallardo." By Borja Crespo, *Guia de Cómic.es*, Jan. 2010, www.guiadelcomic.es/miguel-gallardo/entrevista.htm.

Gallardo Sarmiento, Francisco, and Miguel Gallardo. *Un largo silencio*. Astiberri, 2012.

García, Santiago. *La novela gráfica*. Astiberri, 2010.

Gutiérrez, Juan. "Violencia, memoria colectiva y paz positiva: El proyecto hebras de paz de vida." *Público*, 17 Apr. 2016, blogs.publico.es/universidad-del-barrio/2016/04/17/violencia-memoria-colectiva-y-paz-positiva-el-proyecto-hebras-de-paz-viva-por-juan-gutierrez/.

Hafter, Evelyn. "Representaciones del pasado en una novela gráfica sobre la Guerra Civil española: Memorias en conflicto en *Un largo silencio* de F. Gallardo Sarmiento y M.A. Gallardo." *Viñetas Serias: Primer Congreso Internacional de Historietas, Buenos Aires, Argentina, 23–25 Sept. 2010*. www.vinetas-sueltas.com.ar/congreso/mesas.html.

Hernández Cava, Felipe, and Federico del Barrio. *El artefacto perverso*. ECC, 2015.

Hirsch, Marianne. "The Generation of Postmemory." *Poetics Today* 29.1 (2008): 103–28. doi.org/10.1215/03335372-2007-019.

Huyssen, Andreas. *En busca del futuro perdido: Cultura y memoria en tiempos de globalización*. Fondo de Cultura Económica, 2002.

Juliá, Santos. "Echar al olvido." *El País*, 15 Jun. 2002, elpais.com/diario/2002/06/15/espana/1024092029_850215.html.

– *Memoria de la Guerra y del franquismo*. Taurus, 2006.

–, editor. *Victimas de la Guerra Civil*. Temas de Hoy, 1999.

Labanyi, Jo. "The Languages of Silence: Historical Memory, Generational Transmission and Witnessing in Contemporary Spain. *Journal of Romance Studies* 9.3 (2009): 23–35. doi.org/10.3828/jrs.9.3.23.

– "Memory and Modernity in Democratic Spain: The Difficulty of Coming to Terms with the Spanish Civil War. *Poetics Today* 28.1 (2007): 89–116. doi.org/10.1215/03335372-2006-016.

– "The Politics of Memory in Contemporary Spain." *Journal of Spanish Cultural Studies* 9.2 (2008): 119–25. doi.org/10.1080/14636200802283621.

Labrador Méndez, Germán. "¿Lo llamaban democracia? La crítica estética de la política en la transición española y el imaginario de la historia en el 15-M." *Kamchatka* 4 (2014): 11–61. doi.org/10.7203/kam.4.4296.

– "Review of *Unearthing Franco's Legacy: Mass Graves and the Recovery of Historical Memory in Spain*." *Arizona Journal of Hispanic Cultural Studies* 14 (2010): 379–83. doi.org/10.1353/hcs.2011.0380.

LaCapra, Dominick. *History and Memory after Auschwitz*. Cornell UP, 1998.

Le Goff, Jacques. *L'Imaginaire médiéval: Essais*. Gallimard, 1994.

Loureiro, Ángel G. "Pathetic Arguments." *Journal of Spanish Cultural Studies* 9.2 (2008): 225–37. doi.org/10.1080/14636200802283746.

Magnussen, Anne. "The New Spanish Memory Comics: The Example of *Cuerda de presas.*" *European Comic Art* 7.1 (2014): 56–84. doi.org/10.3167/eca.2014.070104.

Martínez, Guillem. *CT o la Cultura de la Transición: Crítica a 35 años de cultura española.* Debolsillo, 2012.

Merino, Ana. *El cómic hispánico.* Cátedra, 2003.

Merino, Ana, and Brittany Tullis. "The Sequential Art of Memory: The Testimonial Struggle of Comics in Spain." *Memory and Its Discontents: Spanish Culture in the Early Twenty-First Century*, edited by Luis Martín-Estudillo and Nicholas Spadaccini, *Hispanic Issues On Line* 11 (Fall 2012): 211–25. cla.stg.umn.edu/sites/cla.umn.edu/files/hiol_11_11_merino_the_sequential_art_of_memory.pdf.

Mitaine, Benoît. "Memorias dibujadas: La representación de la Guerra Civil y del franquismo en el cómic español. El caso de Un largo silencio." *Memoria y testimonio. Representaciones memorísticas en la España contemporánea*, edited by Georges Tyras and Juan Vila, Verbum, 2012. *HAL*, Université de Bourogne, hal-univ-bourgogne.archives-ouvertes.fr/hal-01104380.

L'Organisation des Nations Unies (ONU). "ONU señala que España debe revocar ley de amnistía." *Noticias ONU*, 10 Feb. 2012, news.un.org/es/story/2012/02/1234621.

Pérez del Solar, Pedro. "La perversa máquina del olvido: Cómics y memoria de la posguerra en la España de los 90." *Espacio, Tiempo y Forma. Serie V, Historia Contemporánea* 0.26 (2014): 227–55. doi.org/10.5944/etfv.26.2014.14516.

Rancière, Jacques. *El reparto de lo sensible.* Prometeo Libros, 2014.

Reggiani, Federico. "La historieta como pariente pobre: Sistemas de enunciación y 'Jerarquía de los géneros' (la historieta frente a la literatura y el cine)." *Arbor: ciencia, pensamiento y cultura* 185.2 (2009): 407–26. doi: 10.3989/arbor.2009.anexo21238.

Resina, Joan Ramon. *Disremembering the Dictatorship: The Politics of Memory in the Spanish Transition to Democracy.* Rodopi, 2003.

Ruíz Torres, Pedro. "Los discursos de la memoria histórica en España." *Hispania Nova: Revista de historia contemporánea* 7 (2007). hispanianova.rediris.es/7/dossier/07d001.pdf.

Sánchez León, Pablo. "El ciudadano, el historiador y la democratización del conocimiento del pasado." *El fin de los historiadores: pensar históricamente el siglo XXI*, edited by Pablo Sánchez León and Jesús Izquierdo Martín, Siglo XXI, 2008, 115–51.

Sarlo, Beatriz. *Tiempo pasado: Cultura de la memoria y giro subjetivo: Una discusión.* Siglo Veintiuno Editores Argentina, 2005.

Vázquez Montalbán, Manuel. *La aznaridad por el imperio hacia Dios o por Dios hacia el imperio.* Diario Público, 2009.

– "Dibujar la memoria, dibujar el deseo." Introducción. *Rambla arriba, Rambla abajo,* by Carlos Giménez, Glenat, 2001, 2–4.
– *La literatura en la construcción de la ciudad democrática.* Crítica, 1998.
– "La memoria, esa novela." Prólogo. *El artefacto perverso,* by Felipe Hernández Cava and Federico del Barrio, Planeta-DeAgostini, 1996, 3–4.
– "El sillón de González." *El País,* 5 June 1995, elpais.com/diario/1995/06/06/opinion/802389609_850215.html.
Vinyes, Ricard. "La memoria del estado." *El estado y la memoria: Gobiernos y ciudadanos frente a los traumas de la historia,* edited by Ricard Vinyes, RBA Libros, 2009, 23–66.

PART TWO

Comics and Economic Crisis

5 Building a Home for Crisis Narrative: Intermediality and Comic(s) Pedagogy in Aleix Saló's *Españistán* Project

MATTHEW J. MARR

Catalan satirical cartoonist Aleix Saló's first animated online film short, *Españistán: De la burbuja inmobiliaria a la crisis* [Spainistan: From the Real Estate Bubble to the Crisis] exudes a dissident ethos whose timely inflections served, in the spring of 2011, to engender a kind of generationally iconic status for this six-minute, forty-six-second video: a status that swiftly grew in the days, and even in the immediate hours, following its release on YouTube.[1] The activist spirit of satire in Saló's *Españistán* project – whether considered in regard to the internet short or, indeed, with an eye towards its source-text companion piece, the 144-page, print-form (and later e-book) graphic novel, *Españistán: Este país se va a la mierda* [Spainistan: This Country Is Going to Shit], originally published by Ediciones Glénat in 2011 – is perhaps most intimately recognizable with respect to thematic content and internal stylings.[2] In both the graphic novel and the animated short, the artist-author embarks on a memorably irreverent, though lucid and incisive, comic(s) deconstruction of a series of government policies and consumerist practices that paved Spain's gilded road to the housing bubble and its aftermath in the post–2008 recession: without a doubt, the most seismic period in Spanish history since the late years of Francoism, the subsequent transition to constitutional democracy, and the development of an economy more fully embedded within the structures of global capitalism.

As of the spring of 2011, the socioeconomic and political underpinnings of the economic crisis arguably eluded an emblematic, shorthand narrative encapsulation in Spain's popular consciousness, particularly one emanating from the realm of visual culture. The appearance of Saló's *Españistán* project represents an unexpectedly meaningful and memorable intervention on this front, though its underpinnings have remained largely unexamined in scholarly criticism to date. This chapter will explore this *appearance* itself (in other words, the conditions of publication and dissemination that give rise to the popular success of Saló's take on the Spanish economic crisis), and, specifically, it will examine this phenomenon in relation to the dynamics of intermediality that shape *Españistán*'s distributional organization as a cultural product. Released by way of a hybrid platform composed of several interconnected parts, Saló's online animated video was initially posted online as a sort of subsidiary support act for *Españistán* as a graphic novel, an arrangement contributing to his project's overall suite-like form, whose design nimbly combines diverse media forms to extraordinary effect. Ultimately, these components extend well beyond the animated short and various editions of the graphic novel to ex post facto add-on comics content and text-form commentary posted on Saló's own website, his Facebook page, and his Twitter account, as well as to a heavy campaign of television appearances and radio, newspaper, and online magazine interviews with the artist-author, particularly during the heart of the anti-austerity *indignados* [outraged] movement and related *desahucio* [eviction] protests in the spring and summer of 2011.

By virtue of this gesture towards a kind of media convergence in miniature, Saló's critique of neoliberalism in the recent Spanish context can be seen as emanating – like much subversive satire – from within the very belly of the beast. This is to say that his comics-based satirical enterprise surfaces by way of a content-distribution scheme that could be said to mirror, as if with an ironic wink, certain media strategies whose logic of integration and pervasiveness lies near and dear to the foundations of neoliberal practices at large. In a certain sense, then, Saló's operative mode of bringing the *Españistán* package to the public structurally complements its own discursive content (a critique of neoliberalism): namely, by drawing attention in various ways to its own brand of intermediality, a trend in corporate media and entertainment of the digital era – forces whose profound influence on the ways and means of creating and placing checks on public knowledge (or, to wit, public [ir]rationality) plays no small role in fostering some of the values that led to the culture of financial overextension, which precipitated the economic crisis, globally and in Spain alike. Saló's *Españistán* suite capitalizes on, while at the same time ideologically undermining, a contemporary media landscape beholden to the interests of what Giroux, writing in the North American context, identifies as the contemporary moment's "dominant public pedagogy" (134): in his words, that vast apparatus – extending well beyond schools to "advertising, film, the internet, video games, and the popular press" (137) – whose guiding principle of "market fundamentalism" has seized the "educational force of ... culture" at multiple, interconnected sites of knowledge production and dissemination (6). The concurrent expansion of this apparatus in terms of visibility, not to mention its consolidation vis-à-vis ownership and ideology, has led to what Giroux and others see as a gradual erosion of citizens' "basic conditions for critical agency" (134). This chapter will underscore how Saló's *Españistán* project amounts to a visual-culture intervention that challenges this paradigm. It is a comics-based exercise in public pedagogy that, in keeping with much effectual satire (whether graphic or otherwise), along the way subversively "uses and abuses" certain elements of "the very structures and values it takes to task" (Hutcheon 106).[3]

In the images and text whose mix composes the final page of the introduction to Saló's debut graphic novel, *Hijos de los 80: La Generación Burbuja* [Children of the 80s: The Bubble Generation], first published in Catalan as *Fills dels 80: La Generació Bombolla* in 2009 and re-released in Castilian in 2014, Saló (born in Ripollet, Cataluña, in 1983) unequivocally places a kind of divisive velvet rope between two theatres of contemporary cultural production in crisis-era Spain. On one side of the rope, there stands what he points to as his own craft: that is, as a comics author invested in constructing a humorous graphic narrative chronicling, through the vehicle of satire, his own generation's experience of a seemingly unjust fall from high professional expectations and relative socioeconomic privilege to a space of post-2008 precarity. On the other side of the rope, Saló positions as a point of contrast the work of certain more "radical" (his language) members of this same generation, artists whose own critiques of this period of malaise take the form of what this same page pejoratively ridicules as a "cruel" *cine de autor* [auteurist cinema] (*Hijos* 18). Following the contextual logic of Saló's line of reasoning, such filmmaking suffers from a tone and tenor out of step with what this page of the graphic novel (an unabashed self-endorsement) submits as the more pleasing, and, by association, publicly powerful dimension of contemporary comics culture. If, as his sketch (figure 5.1) communicates to the reader, the notion of achieving revenge against the injustices of a cruel world can be seen as a goal of every generation and its attendant, socially minded artists, then what this segue into the main pages of *Hijos de los 80: La Generación Burbuja* suggests is that certain young "auteurs" of the contemporary Spanish film scene are misdirecting their vengeful energies. Indeed, the mainly pen-and-ink sketch features a self-important film director standing behind and above a cinema audience; this figure laughs haughtily as moviegoers suffer through what one spectator's speech bubble bluntly maligns as nothing less than a "truño de película" [turd of a movie]. The word "Venganza" [Revenge], penned in cursive script, contrasts with

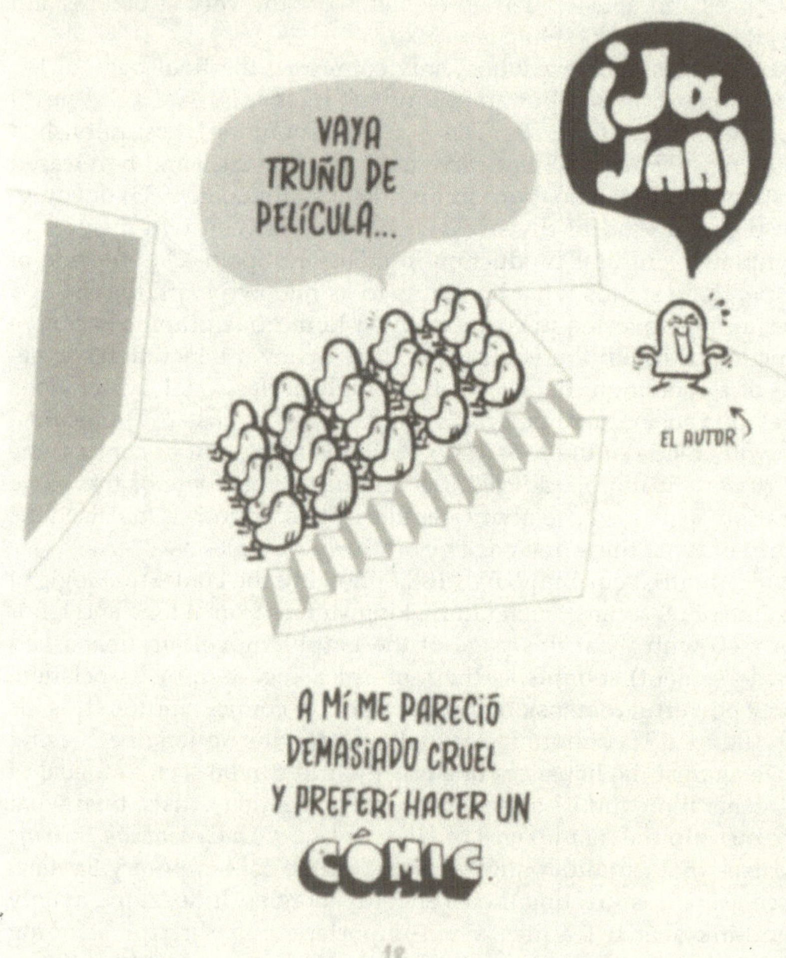

Figure 5.1. Making a case for comics in Saló's *Hijos de los 80: La Generación Burbuja* (18).

the block lettering of the rest of the page, as if to highlight that each generation will be remembered as having crafted its own "signature" response to social challenges. Here, Saló forthrightly promotes comics' suitability to the times as a medium of consequential expression.

In his book *Satire: Spirit and Art*, George A. Test sets out to delineate a working understanding of satire: a concept, much like humour itself, for which academic definitions have often proven elusive. Test convincingly asserts that satire is built in varying proportions of four key components. These include the vital critical forces of *aggression* and *judgement*, both of which function alongside – and never in isolation from – the more conventionally pleasurable elements of *play* and *laughter* (13). In considering the occasionally aggressive, and clearly judgemental, mode of purposeful critique at the heart of a relatively recent cinematic revival in Spanish auteurist documentary, it is fair to say that laughter and the play of humour (as has typically been the case with most documentary in any national context) tend to exist in relatively scarce supply. What is more, it is enticing to suggest that this line of recent auteurist documentary is in fact one and the same with the so-called *"cine de autor"* to which Saló refers in the movie theatre setting depicted on the last page of the introduction to *Hijos de los 80*. It seems likely that Saló as a comics author here alludes, at least in part, to a socially committed slate of Spanish non-fiction films from roughly the first decade of the 2000s – projects often guided by emerging filmmakers who, as Luis Moreno-Caballud has explored in a pair of essays, share a concern with the flux of Spanish cityscapes and communities in the face of gentrification ("Looking" 64; "La imaginación" 548–9). As Saló's own comics and animated shorts likewise foreground, gentrification in the contemporary urban milieu plays a fundamental role in catalysing Spain's more generalized boom-and-bust turmoil.

At the level of style, some of these non-fiction films and documentaries (which I here propose are only obliquely invoked by Saló) reveal a certain degree of influence from the unobtrusive, quiet, or even "lyrical" sensibility of veteran filmmaker José Luis Guerín, a director whose film *En construcción* [Work in Progress] (2001) constitutes a touchstone project in this particular subgenre. At the same time, the intensely engaged, situational, place-inscribed documentaries of a director such as Joaquim Jordà can also be pointed to as a significant source of inspiration for younger filmmakers working in this arena (Moreno-Caballud, "La imaginación" 548). In keeping with these twin sources of influence, then, this recent movement in Spanish non-fiction film (whether carried out under the guidance of individual directors or by collectives) frequently embraces collaborative practices of production that combine the contributions of filmmakers themselves with the actions and speech of "filmed social actors" (Moreno-Caballud, "Looking" 61) – or rather, those very residents of various distressed communities whose neighbourhoods are placed under the documentarian lens. As Moreno-Caballud highlights, films such as Claudio Zulian's *A través del Carmel* [The Shifting City] (2006) and Juan Vicente Córdoba's *Flores de luna* [Night Flowers] (2008) exemplify this tendency, as do films and other filmically inclusive activist projects and experiences organized by collectives including Cine Sin Autor [Cinema Without an Author], whose *Sinfonía Tetuán* [Tetuán Symphony] was produced between 2009 and 2012, and Laboratorio de Trabajadoras [Women Workers' Laboratory], who released the investigatory film *Precarias a la deriva* [Women Adrift in Precarity] as part of a broader socio-filmic initiative in 2004 ("La imaginación" 548).

Even in those instances where an individual director for such films is identified, the aspect of collaborative creation evident in much of this non-fiction film movement effectively destabilizes the unitary notion of an "auteur" – that is, the very figure expressly lampooned in Saló's sketched scene at the movie theatre in *Hijos de los 80* (see figure 5.1). Yet, the aforementioned page from his debut graphic novel should be taken as anything but an incursion into the intricacies of academic debates concerning the viability of the auteur as a cinematic concept. It bears mentioning, too, that the same choice of language ("de autor" [auteurist]) contains an element of comics-specific, self-reflexive humour, given contemporary labels in the marketing of Spanish graphic narrative. As referenced in the introduction to this volume, "cómic de autor" [auteurist comics] is a category often deployed in bookstores and online sales outlets (in addition to its appearance in some critics' work), and Saló evidently seeks to distinguish his own creative style from this prominent trend in comics culture. Indeed, the pared down, almost childlike register of the drawings and script on the page from *Hijos* reproduced in figure 5.1 indicates no less, with Saló's hand-drawn figures in many instances – as we also find throughout much of the *Españistán* suite – resembling the rudimentary form of a literal human thumbnail. And so, the Catalan cartoonist's reference to a *cine de autor* here has the thrust of a playful judgement cast against the force of solemnity as style, or what Bill Nichols has identified as documentary film's flimsy pretence of "kinship" with other power-wielding "discourses of sobriety" within capitalist culture: those *serious* "systems" – such as science, politics, economics, and foreign policy – that "effect change and entail consequences" in our everyday material world (3–6).

Saló's non-fiction work as a comics satirist stands in defiance before a sombre sensibility that scholars such as Matt Labash have seen, in a general sense, as a defining characteristic of the traditionally "low-sugar, high fiber," even "medicinal," mode of much "social-conscience" documentary film (qtd. in Benson and Snee 3). Yet, as Labash maintains, such soberness is a convention resolutely turned onto its head with the "dark," but "devastatingly funny," regimen of "social satire" one finds at the heart of the documentary filmography of American director Michael Moore, a style that emerges most compellingly in 1989 with the release of his feature-length debut, *Roger & Me* (qtd. in Benson and Snee 3). With this analysis in mind, is there a form of connective tissue tying the work of a figure like Saló to Moore? Is it germane to reference high-budget feature-length documentary film in the same breath as Saló's animated short, whose production value is modest? To a large extent, what we find in key critical histories of comics production, such as those by Santiago García (*La novela gráfica*, later translated and published in the United States as *On the Graphic Novel*) or David Carrier (*The Aesthetics of Comics*), is in fact that many academic critics resist positioning graphic narrative in a comparative space adjacent to film or television. Yet, other critics (especially in recent years) have embraced the potential for insight that the analytical compagination of these forms enables, particularly in regard to the genre of documentary, as Nina Mickwitz's *Documentary Comics: Graphic Truth-Telling in a Skeptical Age* (2016) or Jan Baetens's 2017 contribution to *The Cambridge Companion to the Graphic Novel* (a chapter simply titled "Other Non-Fiction") demonstrate. As Baetens proposes in the following passage, the worldwide rise of documentary comics and, subsequently, of graphic journalism can only be understood by considering the contemporary evolution of screen culture:

> Medium change is not only the consequence of an internal makeover ... Given the growing interweaving of media in our "convergence culture," one must also take into account relationships between media, in this case between the graphic novel and non-comics media. The most striking impact on the graphic novel in this regard is undoubtedly represented by the shift from fiction to docu-fiction as well as documentary and non-fiction in film and television, two media whose social hegemony, although challenged today by video-game culture and other forms of digital culture on the internet, are much stronger than that of the graphic novel, which is still a niche product catering to relatively small audiences. One can plausibly suppose that the ubiquity of docu-fiction and non-fiction in Hollywood and in many television production houses has had an influence on the remarkable progress of non-fictional graphic novels.[4] (131)

Notwithstanding the self-evident point that the video module of *Españistán* is a "Flash" animation production, juxtaposing the practices of a mainly (though not always) live-action documentary filmmaker such as Moore to those of a comics practitioner like Aleix Saló is altogether fitting.[5] This connection is true not only with respect to the ways in which both artists, when confronted with social circumstances of disaster, harness the power of dark humour in their respective projects of satirical public pedagogy. Rather, the viability of the comparison also rests on both figures' adept construction of an intermedial platform for their respective forms of sociopolitical critique. With Moore, this practice is most clearly in evidence in his publication of books that complement his films, as well as in his regular media offensives that have served to construct a celebrity persona – one ultimately inseparable, as it were, from the ostensibly selfsame figure of Leftist advocacy who narrates and, in many instances, appears in his films (Benson and Snee 6–7).

Something analogous takes place with Saló after his debut project. Though the introduction to Saló's first long-form work, *Hijos de los 80: La Generación Burbuja*, advances a sense of his relative antipathy to film (or, at the very least, to what he sees as a high-minded incarnation thereof), and while this book's own self-conscious foray into his vision of graphic narrative overtly endorses confidence in the greater potential impact of comics as a socially inflected art form, the artist-author's perspective in his subsequent project, *Españistán*, appears very much open to incorporating the power of certain cinema-based practices. In essence, Saló here moves towards hybridity (already implicit, at a micro level, in the word-image comics form itself), disconnecting the divisive velvet rope that his introduction to *Hijos de los 80* had deliberately placed between contemporary comics and film as fields of production. After all, as suggested from the outset of this chapter, *Españistán: De la burbuja inmobiliaria a la crisis* is – from a certain perspective – an animated documentary film short, and it is one whose humorous satire would seem to counter the comparatively solemn line of live-action, non-fiction (or social documentary) cinema broached by a critic like Moreno-Caballud (figures 5.2a and 5.2b).

An unprecedented internet phenomenon in the Spanish context, Saló's best-known work is this six-minute, forty-six-second online video, whose cultural impact is part and parcel, for one, of the comical irreverence of its equal-opportunity critique of both Spanish governmental economic policy and a societal shift towards rampant consumerism: the latter being a socioeconomic force, which, according to Saló's narrative, took hold in Spain in the 1990s (although, as he responsibly remarks in passing, this tendency has much more longstanding foundations in modern Spanish culture). From a critical standpoint, *Españistán*'s efficacy as a work of public pedagogy and its resultant position in the field of crisis-era Spanish cultural production are of special interest by virtue of the distinctive *intermediality* reflected in this comics-based project's overall distributional apparatus, by which I mean to

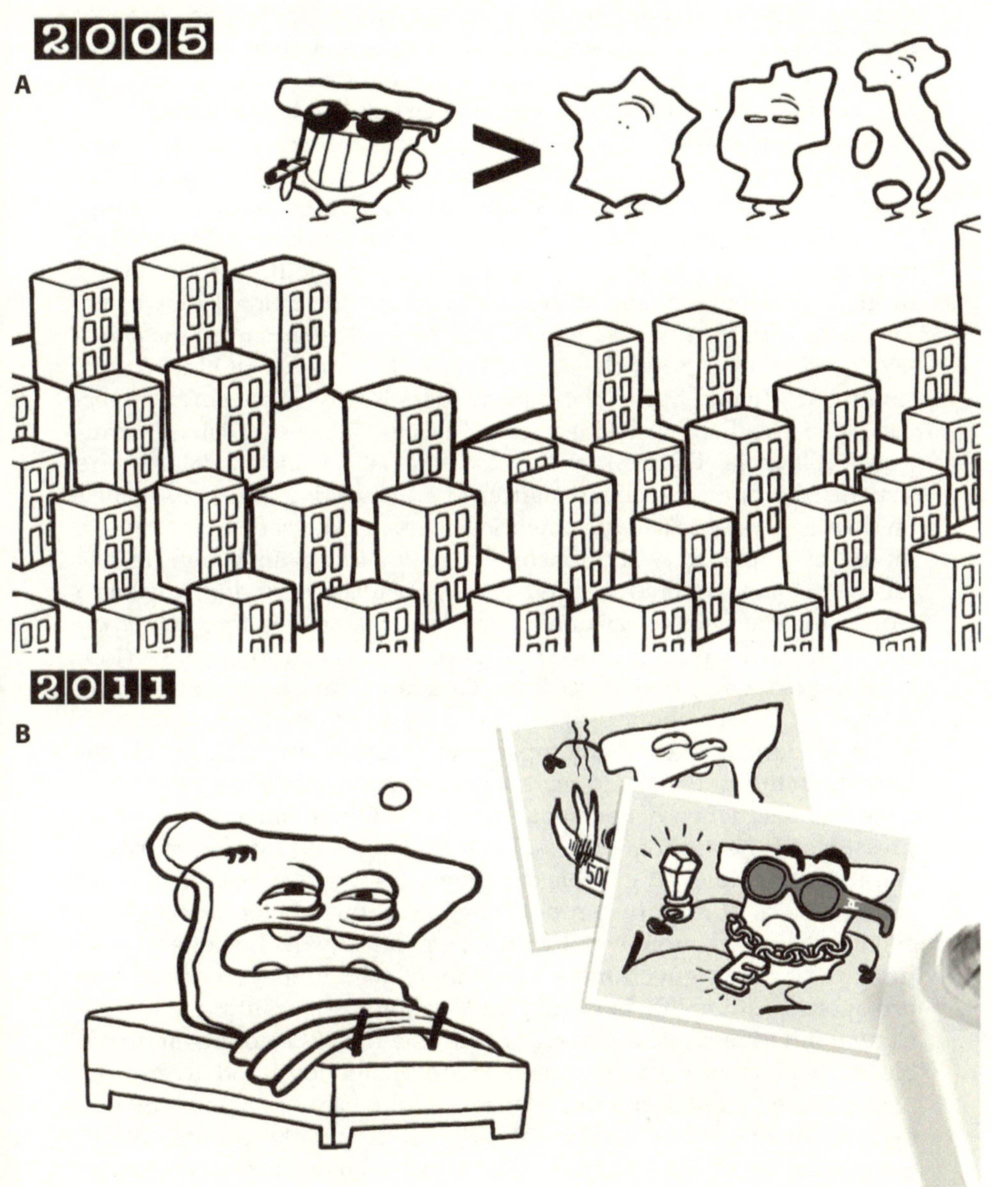

Figures 5.2a. and 5.2b. *Españistán: De la burbuja inmobiliaria a la crisis*. An online animated short (on Spain's consumerist hangover) deployed to promote consumer interest in a graphic novel (Saló, *Españistán* [film]).

refer to Saló's deft integration of online video, paper-form graphic novel, and e-book. Viewed several million times since being uploaded to Saló's personal website on 25 March 2011 – and then, to startlingly viral effect, on the artist-author's YouTube page just ten days after the 15-M protests began in Madrid's Puerta del Sol – the animated short was conceptualized as a promotional companion piece to the 144-page graphic novel *Españistán: Este país se va a la mierda*, whose first hardback edition was published in early March 2011. This second graphic novel by Saló unfolds as a mock-epic quest narrative with ironic nods to a variety of literary, cinematic, and televisual intertexts including *Don Quijote*, *The Lord of the Rings*, *The Wizard of Oz*, *Harry Potter*, and even the *Odyssey*. Its six place-centred chapters ("País de los curritos" [Odd-Jobbers' Country], "Ciudad burocrática" [Bureaucratic City], "Las tierras muertas" [The Deadlands], "Aldea santa" [Holy Village], "Distrito financiero" [Financial District], and "La Moncloa" [Moncloa Palace]) are structured around the circumstances of a blundering anti-hero named Fredo (figure 5.3), a twenty-something character sketched in the impish mould of a Spanish Bart Simpson or *South Park*'s Stan Marsh (in this regard, see note 5). Fredo's hand-drawn form is inflected in ways also akin to the late Catalan cartoonist Ivà's lead character in the *Makinavaja* comic strip, as well as to the stylings of Mexican cartoonists Jis (José Ignacio Solórzano) and Trino (José Trinidad Camacho) – particularly in their *La Jornada* comic strip, *El Santos* (an important reference, too, given the latter project's accompanying animated material on the internet).[6] In this quest, Fredo seeks a pathway towards having his mortgage annulled when his personal finances implode under the extreme pressures of the economic crisis. He is accompanied by a close friend, Samu, an unemployed graphic designer who works part-time in retail clothing sales at Zara (when not blogging about Madonna); both are eventually joined, moreover, by Frida, a politically disillusioned "pija" [preppy or posh] government functionary who, unbeknownst to the protagonist (ultimately her budding love interest), is sitting on a substantial inheritance. Also travelling with the trio is Gandolfo, an irritable barfly pensioner who frequents Fredo's neighbourhood tavern.

Departing from the humble environs of the bar – a business owned by a family of Chinese immigrants who work marathon shifts unfathomable to the novel's Spanish characters – Fredo, Samu, Gandolfo, and eventually Frida together traverse an allegorical country whose vast landscape is littered with fortress-like government bureaucracies and other traditional seats of power, including a parodic version of the Catholic Church. The book's characters haplessly stumble through misadventures with bureaucrats, bankers, and clergy, not to mention encounters with tribes of unfunded university scientists and

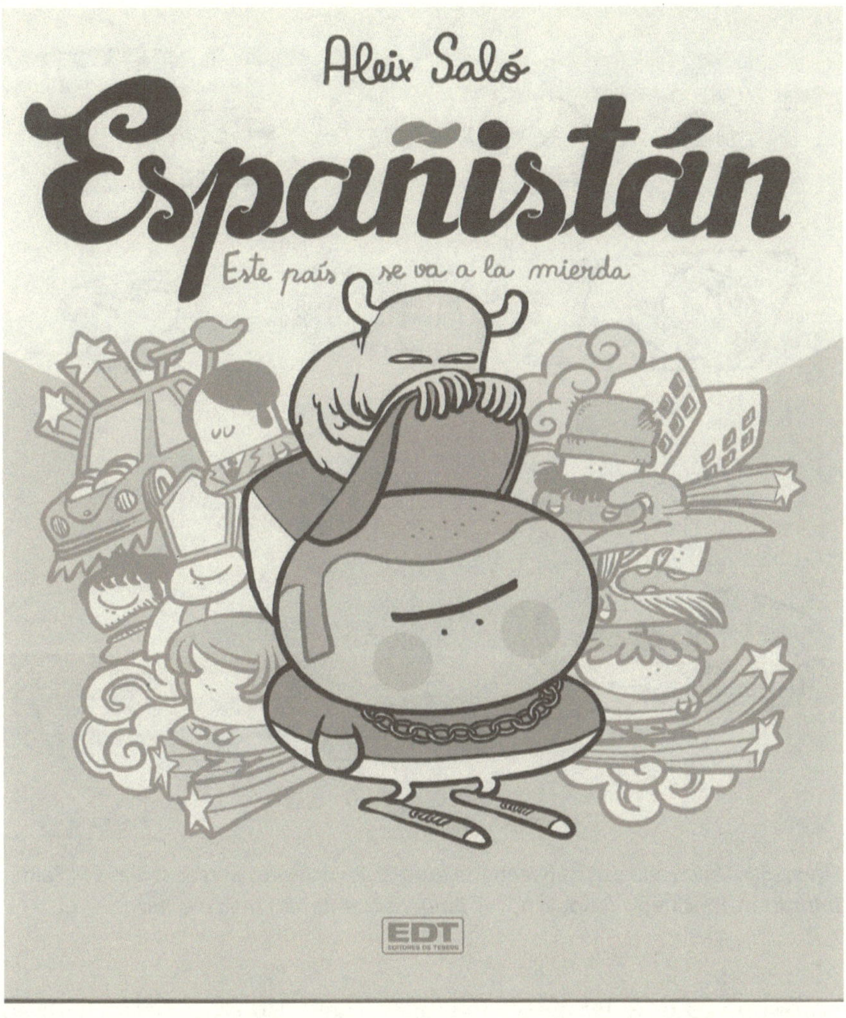

Figure 5.3. *Españistán: Este país se va a la mierda.* "La historia de un cani que, en su empeño por deshacerse de la hipoteca, deberá recorrer el depauperado reino de Españistán para enfrentarse con ... los malandrines, meapilas y soplagaitas que lo pueblan ... un relato plagado de tópicos, tacos y faltas de ortografía, con bien de lobbies, parados, mileuristas, pensionistas, funcionarios, obispos, SGAE, telebasura, sobornos y estilismos poligoneros." [The story of a young, boorish, wannabe high roller who, in his endeavour to get out from under a mortgage, must traverse the impoverished kingdom of Spainistan to confront ... the scoundrels, the self-righteous, and the morons who inhabit it ... a tale chock-full of clichés, curse words, spelling errors, and plenty of political interest groups, unemployed and under-employed people, pensioners, state functionaries, bishops, unionized artists, trash TV, bribes, and tasteless stylings] (Saló, *Españistán: Este país* back cover).

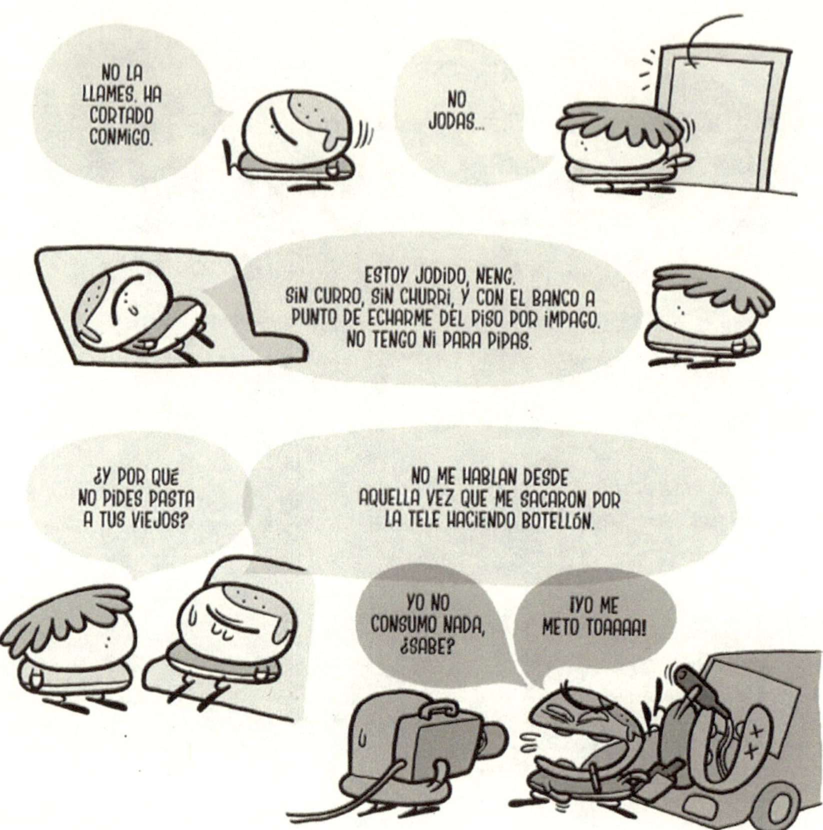

Figure 5.4. Down and out between the gutters. Fredo and Samu as stylized in Saló's print-form, mock-epic graphic novel, *Españistán: Este país se va a la mierda* (16).

philosophers now living off the land. They also cross paths with an angry gang of roving pop stars who demand tribute for the right of passage through their lands; this tribute is to come in the form of unpaid copyright royalties for illegal downloads, products that millennials like the Madonna-obsessed Samu presumably have stolen for years on end and that point, in a self-reflexive sense, to the difficulties of publishing creative work – even comics – in an era of online piracy.

Fredo's quest proves a fruitless campaign (figure 5.4). As his farcical journey comes to its conclusion, he has failed to locate any magical agent capable of removing the crushing burden of his home mortgage. Nevertheless, in an ironic plot twist, he makes amorous inroads with the heiress

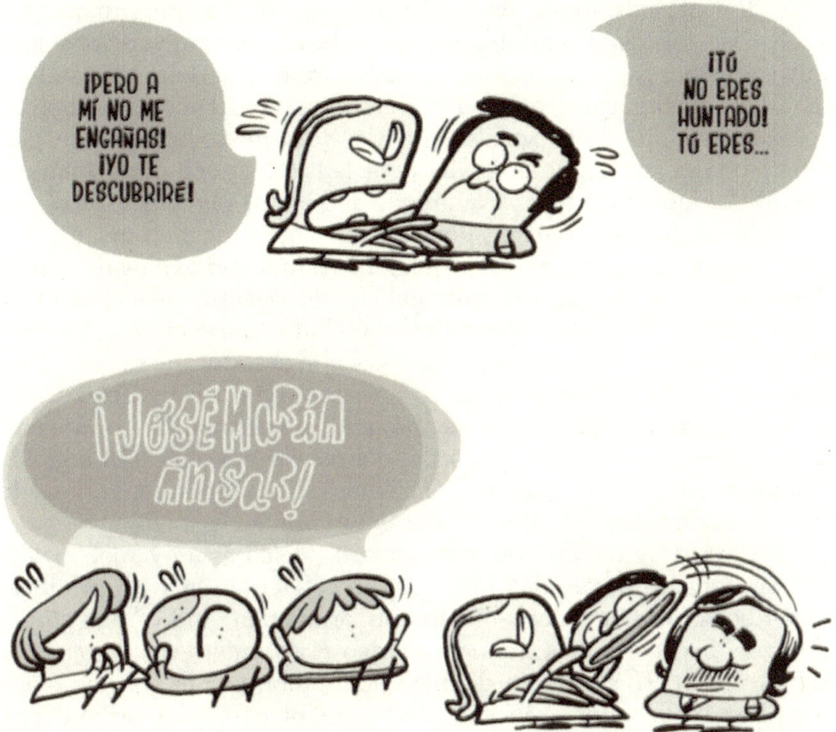

Figure 5.5. Unmasking the ostensible wizard behind the curtain at the end of the gilded road in Saló's *Españistán: Este país se va a la mierda* (123).

Frida: a turn of events portrayed as close enough to a pot of gold. In the end, a kind of narrative circularity carries the humour-laden graphic novel to its concluding punch line(s). Penetrating the executive confines of the Moncloa Palace in one last-ditch effort to locate and confront the alleged powers-that-be responsible for paving Spain's golden-brick road to economic collapse, Fredo and company endeavour to unmask the ostensible wizard behind the curtain.[7] At first, this figure is revealed to be long-time Spanish radio and television presenter Jordi Hurtado (here, Jordi *Huntado*, a pun on "untado" [bribed]), though an additional unmasking reveals this same character to be former conservative president of the government – and, as he is sketched in the animated short, faithful disciple of the "Dios del Neoliberalismo" [God of Neoliberalism] – José María *Ánsar* [Goose], a derisive corruption of the surname Aznar popularly attributed in actual news reports to a George W. Bush gaffe (figure 5.5).

But the gags continue. In a scenario parodying the climax of a *Scooby-Doo* television cartoon mystery, these initial revelations lead only to further unveilings. After several further entertaining disguises are taken off this same enigmatic character ("Rob Esponja" [Sponge-Rob SquarePants], "una gamba al ajillo" [a grilled shrimp with garlic], "Jabba el Hutt"), he is finally revealed to be none other than the friendly Chinese barkeeper from Fredo and Samu's favourite local watering hole: the very starting point of their quest at the outset of the book. Symbolizing, in one sense, the global clout and expansiveness of Chinese finance, this figure smilingly stands in as the mastermind, or the genuine noteholder, behind the hoax that is the economy: namely, China. At the same time, when one takes into account the satire's early commentary on the harsh working conditions endured by Chinese immigrants in Spain and elsewhere abroad, this selfsame face of the barkeeper simultaneously points to the dehumanizing effects of a global capitalism built on the shoulders of alienated and displaced workers. In the end, no one living in *Españistán* can be counted as a winner.

Self-funded by the author-artist himself ("Españistán y Aleix Saló") and brought to the animation format in collaboration with producer Álex Roca of the Barcelona illustration, animation, and design studio Quarantados, the online animated video *Españistán: De la burbuja inmobiliaria a la crisis* is not a distilled adaptation of the graphic novel described earlier, nor is its narrative content based on carbon-copy out-takes of extant material from that book. In an *RTVE* interview from 13 June 2011 uploaded to Saló's YouTube account, the artist-author claims that the video was designed "para completar un poco" [to round out] the character-based story already set forth in the graphic novel, with the two works being planned as "dos caras de la misma moneda" [two sides of the same coin] ("Españistán y Aleix Saló") – an aptly chosen idiom, given its allusion to money. Whereas the graphic novel presents a whimsical micro-narrative revolving around one *nini* [slacker] protagonist's quest to have his mortgage annulled, the online short, for its part, offers a national macro-narrative – one whose contours, while crafted with dark humour, are more akin to the genre of documentary in the sense that this research-driven video broadly and cogently explores Spain's clumsy fall into economic crisis by way of the real estate bubble. While modestly underscoring in the press that his intention was never to "postular[se] como experto en la materia" [present himself as an expert in the field] of economic theory ("no es la liga en que quise jugar" [it's not the league in which I wanted to play]) (Saló, "*Españistán* simplifica"), Saló has acknowledged poring over doctoral theses and scores of newspaper reports ("La Ventana")

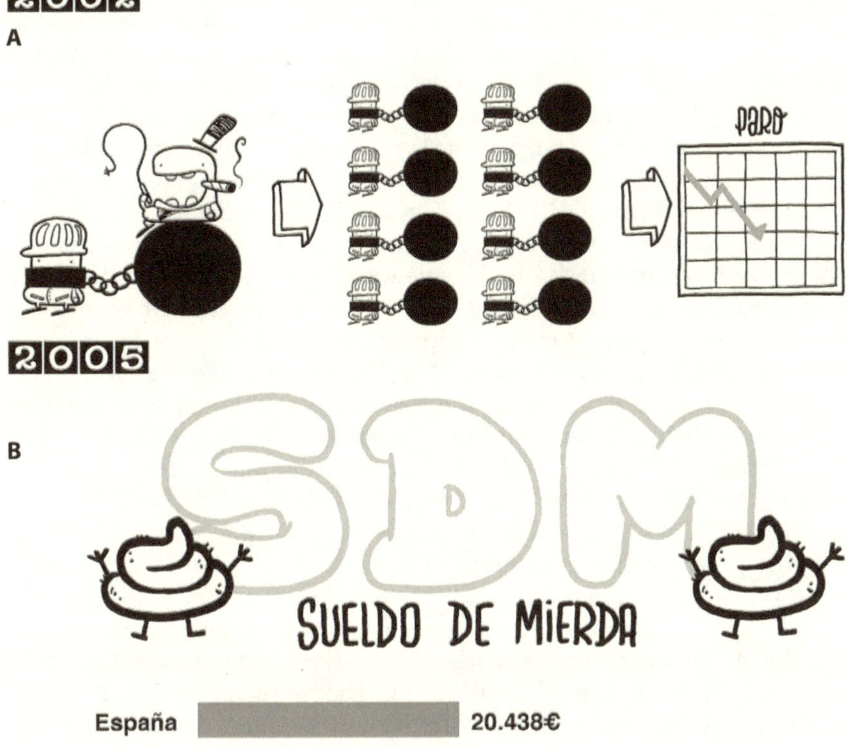

Figures 5.6a. and 5.6b. Charting comic(s) pedagogy in Saló's animated short, *Españistán: De la burbuja inmobiliaria a la crisis.*

while synthesizing his account of the crisis, a narrative he pens, in his words, as a sort of missing link "entre la información que publican los periódicos económicos y el ciudadano medio" [between the information that economic periodicals publish and the average citizen] ("*Españistán* simplifica").

The *Españistán* online short deploys a satirical, yet actively pedagogical, approach to lifting the curtain on the complexities of the Spanish economic crisis (figure 5.6a). Saló here unmistakably aspires to educate, and not simply to critique, at the same time that he entertains (figure 5.6b).[8] Self-identifying first and foremost as a cartoonist – a public role he juxtaposes to the ostensibly less restrictive realm of artistic play inhabited by many comics authors – Saló describes his work as having a deliberate "propósito didáctico" [didactic purpose] with journalistic implications ("Entrevista"). With the decline of newspapers, this mission is ideally suited to the internet, not only because of the forum-like environment facilitated by sites such as YouTube (which fosters immediate dissemination and the possibility of something like dialogue in the comments section), but moreover, quite simply because of the short attention spans of today's viewers and readers. As Saló quips, it is as if satirical cartooning were actually an invention of the internet era ("Entrevista"). With *Españistán: De la burbuja inmobiliaria a la crisis,* however, Saló adds new dimensions to his previously static, silent, and somewhat limited-viewership oeuvre as a single-panel, journalistic, print-form satirical cartoonist working (albeit with reliably less visual realism) in the stripped-down tradition of figures like El Roto (Andrés Rabago García). The *Españistán* video arguably takes a cue from information-intensive projects of graphic satire by the likes of Mexican political cartoonists El Fisgón (Rafael Barajas Durán) and Rius (Eduardo Humberto del Río García), utilizing concrete reference to statistics, data, and the historical record in lieu of the sort of visual and verbal subtlety to which the modern, politically invested Spanish graphic tradition has gravitated at least since Goya's *Caprichos* etchings. While a strain of public pedagogy had certainly been in evidence in Saló's earlier endeavours – whether in *Hijos de los 80,* the *Españistán* graphic novel, or in regular work with outlets like Spain's pre-eminent satirical magazine, *El Jueves,* and his own hometown periodical, *Revista de Ripollet* (Cataluña) – his keen ability to teach and delight is powerfully augmented by animation, by the amusingly droll voiceover track he himself performs and records (punctuated – often at the end of individual Flash-animated "shots" – by cheeky sound effects, or by recurring theme music that spoofs Bobby McFerrin's "Don't Worry, Be Happy"), and by the distributional power of the internet video clip format: a formula that garnered significant public attention for *Españistán: De la burbuja inmobiliaria a la crisis* in short order.

This attention proved especially pronounced as the *indignados* protest movement went into full swing during the second half of May 2011, a moment characterized by an intensification of national debates surrounding the Spanish economic disaster and, in particular, its effects on younger generations of Spaniards. As the fervour of the 15-M movement spread to other corners of the Peninsula, bloggers, journalists, and millions of interested citizens took notice of Saló's video and began to disseminate its online link by way of e-mail, Facebook, and Twitter with marked frequency. In effect, the short became a national social media sensation, attaining uncommonly popular status as a shorthand history of Spain's economic malaise: fame achieved in a period of just days by a video that unfolds in mere minutes. A flurry of articles and interviews in traditional media outlets including *El País*, *El Economista*, *ABC*, *La Vanguardia*, and other publications quickly caught wind of Saló's animated internet short. In their reports, they focused not only on the meta-journalistic story of the swiftness and magnitude of its dissemination, but also issued judgements concerning the value of its distinctive incisiveness as a social-issue documentary on the makings of the crisis in Spain. For instance, in a 12 June 2011 online article, Olga Merino asserted that "[p]uede que ningún sesudo artículo de fondo en la prensa haya explicado el descalabro económico con más claridad que el cortometraje de animación [de Saló]" [it may be that no brainy in-depth article in the press has explained the economic disaster with more clarity than (Saló's) animated film short] (Merino). Its reach as a media phenomenon was remarkably immediate and widespread. Cutting through the muddled arguments of prominent experts on the Spanish economy (at least one of whom, José Luis Ruiz Bartolomé, later took some of Saló's arguments to task in his blog ["Desmontando Españistán"]), through the hot air of disingenuous politicians in the throes of an election campaign, through the chatter of television and radio talking heads, or even through the anxious accounts of citizens commiserating – as Olga Merino noted – in "[todas] las salas de espera ... las barras de los bares ... [y] cualquier sobremesa" [every waiting room ... tavern bar ... (and) everyday after-dinner conversation], Saló's online video reportedly reached three million viewers within fifteen days of its 25 May 2011 posting on YouTube. It went on to be downloaded by another four million visitors to Saló's personal website by October of the same year: the fifth most overall views of any online video in Spain in 2011. Moreover, the project proved itself to be anything but a flash in the pan. It continued to be enormously popular with online viewers well after the initial wave of interest in 2011. Indeed, it reportedly attracted 5.2 million views on Saló's own YouTube account by August 2012, a figure that does not take into account more than one million additional views of other repackaged online copies of the short (including subtitled versions in several other languages), which soon became available on other YouTube users' accounts and various video-sharing websites (Serrano).

This viral success quickly built a home for Saló's non-animated graphic satire in yet another medium. The popularity of *Españistán* as a free online short spurred publisher Glénat – a firm renamed as Editores de Tebeos in 2012 – to issue six reprint editions of the original graphic novel by January of that same year. This move was followed by the publication of a smaller paperback edition designed for sale at kiosks (Serrano). Soon thereafter, an Amazon Kindle e-book was issued by Penguin Random House Group. Unexpectedly, then, in times of economic austerity and rampant piracy (a theme that, as noted earlier, one episode of Saló's own graphic novel lampoons with respect to the recording industry), these for-purchase editions of the graphic novel *Españistán* soon became bestsellers. As early as 8 July 2011, writing in *El País*, Luis Doncel already referred to Saló's book as the "ya archifamoso cómic *Españistán. Este país se va a la mierda*" [already renowned comic book, Spainistan: This Country Is Going to Shit].

As a result, the intermedial platform design that led to this unmitigated success – the release of a graphic novel, followed by a free online animated short, and then an e-book edition, whose appearance is accompanied by various peripheral materials on Saló's website – became the artist-author's operative model for his next two comics-based projects: the sociopolitical satires *Simiocracia: Crónica de la gran resaca económica* [Simiocracy: Chronicle of the Great Economic Hangover] (2012) and *Europesadilla: Alguien se ha comido a la clase media* [Euronightmare: Someone Devoured the Middle Class] (2013). The publication of both comics occurred alongside the distribution of complementary – and complimentary (that is, gratis) – online animated film shorts, videos whose style and content have much more in common with the style and content of *Españistán* (as an online short) than with the latter's source-text graphic novel, *Españistán: Este país se va a la mierda*. But, like this print-form forerunner, both *Simiocracia* and *Europesadilla* went into multiple editions and a follow-up release in the e-book format. Similarly, as with his first project, Saló again created publicity for both projects by making the rounds in a number of press interviews and by allowing approved teaser segments of both books to trickle out to various websites (as with, to cite just one example, several facsimile pages of *Europesadilla*, which were embedded within an online review published on 1 April 2013 in the Spanish edition of *The Huffington Post* [González]). Especially in the case of *Simiocracia*, this model of promotion and distribution again proved highly effective in terms of impact. By the spring of 2012, the e-book version of this third title by Saló already occupied "el número uno en la lista de los más vendidos" [the number-one spot on the bestseller list] (García Mongay).

As an intermedial cultural product, Saló's *Españistán* venture occupies a special site of public pedagogy in the recent Spanish context. It constitutes a kind of "inside job": a phrase I cite not only as an oblique reference to American director Charles H. Ferguson's Oscar-winning documentary on the 2008 collapse of the US financial system, *Inside Job* (2010), but also because of the methodological setup through which

Saló's 2011 project co-opted structural devices of neoliberal market culture: a prime target of his vigorous satire, given its implications in the crescendo of consumerism that drove the housing bubble. The keenest example of this brand of co-optation came, of course, in the form of Saló's promotion of the graphic novel through a free internet video, a move that fuelled his work's visibility among potential comics consumers – a form that, from a critical perspective, begs certain questions with respect to genre. Indeed, throughout this chapter, I have deliberately vacillated in my nomenclature when faced with the matter of how to refer to the animated online incarnation of *Españistán.* After all, is Saló's video genuinely classifiable as an animated "film short"? Perhaps not. Across several journalistic reports, a few scattered references in academic articles, in interviews with the author-artist, on Saló's own website, and within his epilogue to updated editions of the graphic novel *Españistán,* a host of terms are used to describe this complementary online video. These include "corto" [short], "corto de animación" [animated short], "vídeo," "vídeo promocional" [promotional video], "vídeo de animación" [animated video], "cinta" [film], "teaser," "publicidad viral" [viral advertising], and "prólogo" [prologue], among others.

The assortment of labels in itself invites a closer consideration of the function of this particular form, a task which I will now take up by way of moving this discussion towards the chapter's conclusion. In his book *Screen Traffic: Movies, Multiplexes, and Global Culture,* Charles Acland interrogates the limitations of a conception of cinema studies premised on discipline "boundaries" that have been drawn in reference to a "medium" – specifically, film – which is a fundamentally "mutable technological apparatus." As he aptly notes, "a problem ensues when it is apparent that film is not film anymore" (46). Yet, even if we turn to *screen studies* as a more supple and inclusive disciplinary model, scant academic attention has been dedicated to internet videos like Saló's *Españistán,* a cultural product perhaps more descriptively classifiable as a "book trailer." In a 2014 academic article, Grøn notes that the phenomenon of the online book trailer constitutes a "relatively new" and understudied "paratextual genre," which presents a variation on, or "a counterpart to[,] the [promotional] movie trailer" (81) – albeit one that enjoys, as the same critic observes in one of just a handful of scholarly essays on the topic, a "distinctive[ly] intermedial" (91) relationship with its source text. In other words, whereas *movie* trailers have, in Grøn's words, "an isomorphic relation to their source texts, as they share the same" cinematic code (or language), *book* trailers, whether for literary or graphic novels, are expressed through a "representational mode" that necessarily yields "an independent text with its own" audiovisual character and appeal (97–8). Moreover, as Jonathan Gray points out in a 2010 book *Show Sold Separately: Promos, Spoilers, and Other Media Paratexts*, the paratext that originally frames, acts as a gateway to, or simply "extends the horizons of the narrative universe" of a source text can sometimes eclipse the primacy of its antecedent. Indeed, as Gray notes in his largely Hollywood-focused analysis, viewers may very well come to "find that [this] universe is more interesting at its horizons" (46). In such cases, "the paratext either stands in for or [even] becomes a key and 'primary' platform for" the source text itself (176), thus challenging the idea of a "binary" and "forcing us to wonder exactly what is 'primary' or 'the original' and what is 'secondary' or 'peripheral'" (21).[9]

The *Españistán* phenomenon exemplifies this latter scenario. The paratextual video component of the overall project cannot be said, in the end, to exist as subsidiary to the graphic novel by any reasonable measure. In some ways, too, *Españistán* reflects the integrative promotional strategies of many large-scale entertainment products, as if to spite – albeit within the bracketed context of humorous satire – what might be characterized as the work's avowedly "indie" ethos.[10] The online book trailer features opening and closing shots that, for one, show images of the cover of the hardcopy graphic novel. The second-to-last "shot" of this trailer suggests, moreover, that "la historia continúa" [the story continues] in the for-purchase text, while the final image refers viewers directly to Saló's personal website: a space that now primarily features his more recent work (funded, as the author-artist has remarked in interviews with the press, by capital generated from *Españistán*). This more recent work (that is, *Simiocracia, Europesadilla*) refers, in turn, back to *Españistán* through references included in the vehicle of the author's biographical blurb, just as Saló's book-trailer videos for these more recent publications inevitably cluster together in cyberspace on sites like YouTube. Perhaps unsurprisingly, updated editions of the original *Españistán* graphic novel feature an epilogue in which Saló self-professes the rationale for his initiative on the intermedial front: "con el deseo de romper los límites del formato del cómic *y llegar un poco más lejos* ... he realizado un vídeo de animación que completa este relato" [with a desire to break the limits of the comics format *and to go a bit further* ... I have created an animated video that completes this tale] (my emphasis). Notwithstanding the hazards of citing authorial intention, the cultural product generated through said ventures (already multimodal, as the introduction to this volume would suggest, by virtue of its comics [word-image mix] origins) does indeed hybridize its form at a macro, suite-like level. In this way, it can be more than comfortably understood as resonating with contemporary notions of "convergence" as delineated in media studies scholarship:

> There are at least four ways that the expression "convergence" has been deployed and its meaning solidified – as a description of new synergy (a "horizontal" realignment) among media companies and industries, as the multiplication of "platforms" for news and information, as a technological hybridity that has folded the uses of separate media into one another (e.g., watching a television broadcast on a cell phone), and as a new media aesthetic involving the mixing of documentary and non-documentary forms. (Hay and Couldry 473)

The *Españistán* suite arguably takes the form of the book trailer one step further in the direction of what some have envisaged as an intermedial environment in which novels, graphic or otherwise, will incorporate "video into the body of the text" (Irvine qtd. in Voigt 683). The electronic versions of Saló's book-form comics offer a platform that positions readers at a point of close technological access to sites such as YouTube, thus facilitating accessibility to both the online book trailers (or video shorts) and Saló's own YouTube page (which, as of early 2018, remains replete with posted television interviews with the artist-author). It is tempting to suggest, then, that the intermedial platform that houses the *Españistán* project entails a sort of virtual, activist squatters' residence within a setting that scholars like Henry A. Giroux have seen as the "cultural apparatus" that in recent years has been massively "hijacked" (7) by what he calls "new sites of [public] pedagogy" – not brick-and-mortar schools or institutions, but rather, "a distinctive confluence of new digital and media technologies," a landscape wherein "growing concentrations of corporate power, and unparalleled meaning-producing capabilities" (135) have served the interest of "educating young people to define themselves simply through the logic of commodification" (7): specifically, as consumers, rather than citizens (8).

Fittingly, within a number of interviews, Saló has drawn attention to what he views as the problematics of an ingrained consumerist identity, or a logic of commodification, ostensibly common among many of his generation in Spain, a cohort that came of age during the late 1980s through the early 2000s. If, in a move of professional gamesmanship, the author-artist has constructed a kind of parody of a corporate-minded, intermedial model as his "última baza" [last card] (Olga Merino's phrase) in a campaign to find an audience – a tactic deployed in an effort to generate kiosk and comic-book shop sales for his second book – then it is also true, more broadly speaking, that material from this same project provides some of the first stones thrown in the politics of resistance so vital to the crisis-era Spanish civic experience (Pons). Looking beyond the page and screen, *Españistán* is a performance that exists for more than its own commercial or aesthetic sake alone, standing out on the contemporary landscape of non-fiction Spanish comics culture as a significant intervention in the public pedagogy of its time.

NOTES

1 All translations in this chapter are my own.

2 Olga Merino offers an explanation of the *Españistán* title in step with comments made by the artist-author in various interviews. She notes, "El tono sarcástico ya se intuye desde el título: el sufijo *istán* (tierra, en persa) alude a remotas repúblicas en Asia Central, cuyos régimenes se asocian de inmediato con pobreza a ras de suelo y corrupción en las alturas" [We sense the sarcastic tone beginning with the title: the suffix *istan* (land, in Persian) refers to remote republics in central Asia whose political systems we immediately associate with poverty at the bottom and corruption at the top] (Merino). During a 29 June 2011 radio interview on Cadena Ser, Saló underscored that the term had already passed into popular parlance on the internet *well before* his graphic novel and animated short were published. He noted that around the time he began work on *Españistán*, the term was being used by many to draw attention to a widespread perception that Spain was conspicuously no longer the First World economy it had once (erroneously, in his view) believed itself to be ("La Ventana").

3 Here I borrow an apt phrase deployed by Linda Hutcheon in her description of postmodernism as a "contradictory cultural enterprise, one that is heavily implicated in that which it seeks to contest" (106). My inclusion of this quotation is largely for rhetorical purposes, chosen by virtue of Hutcheon's wonderfully pithy language. While this chapter is not invested in a discussion of postmodernism, some allusion to parody (which Hutcheon sees as "a perfect postmodern form," observing how it "incorporates and challenges that which it parodies" [11]) is inevitable in any examination of the tools of contemporary satire.

4 In referencing "convergence culture" in passing, Baetens cites Henry Jenkins's 2006 book of the same name in an endnote. Jenkins's book, not without its scholarly detractors, explores our contemporary, digital-era culture as a space where "new and old media collide, where grassroots and corporate media intersect, where the power of the media producer and the

power of the media consumer interact in unpredictable ways" (Jenkins 2). Positioning these concepts within a broader framework of "participatory culture" (and its attendant role in the production of "collective intelligence" out of a fragmented media landscape), Jenkins explicitly downplays the centrality of technology alone in this global "cultural shift" (2–3). His vision, on the whole, comes across as an optimistic one, given the element of avowed consumer empowerment that it endorses. Critics such as Hay and Couldry, however, question some of the book's assumptions about the genuine "agency of media consumers," especially in light of what they see as its somewhat simplified "universalist understanding of democracy" – one that seems to overlook "the messy contradictions and contingencies of democratic citizenship in the historical and geographic production of convergence/cultures" (481).

5 Moore's feature-length documentary work has, in fact, on occasion made use of animated sequences to satirical effect. A case in point is a three-minute satirical cartoon "A Brief History of the United States of America," included in *Bowling for Columbine* (2002). The sequence presents a vision of gun culture in the United States as a function of historical racism and the legacy of slavery. While beyond the scope of this chapter, this animated sequence (produced by FlickerLab Animation Studio) bears a striking resemblance, in terms of its design, rhythm, character voices, sound effects, and narrative style, to Saló's own online video for *Españistán*. The *Columbine* animated mini-film, for its part, has been seen as following – not without controversy – in the stylistic footsteps of *South Park* by none other than that animated series' co-creators (one of whom, Matt Stone – once a student of Columbine High School – was interviewed for Moore's documentary) (Brett).

6 As cited in press release excerpts included in a 26 May 2011 *RTVE* review of the graphic novel *Españistán*, or on the book's own back cover, Saló's description of Fredo opts for the term "cani" [a boorish suburban youth prone to tawdry style and crass materialism] over "nini" [slacker] (the latter being derived from the phrase, *ni trabaja, ni estudia* [neither working nor studying]): "Fredo representa la síntesis del lugar y el momento en el que vive ... Es a la vez una sátira y un homenaje a un colectivo conocido como los 'canis,' que más o menos podemos identificar con ese sector joven de la clase trabajadora que abandonó tempranamente los estudios para lanzarse al mercado laboral durante el periodo de bonanza" [Fredo represents the synthesis of the place and moment in which he lives ... He is at once a satire and a homage to a collective known as the "canis," whom we can identify more or less with a certain young sector of the working class who abandoned their studies early in order to enter the labour market during the boom period] ("'Españistán ...' el retrato").

7 During the waning days of the Rodríguez Zapatero administration, Saló's internet short reportedly penetrated the confines – and economic conversations – of the Moncloa Palace as well, as noted in the introduction.

8 Among the many amusing techniques employed by Saló in the *Españistán* video short is a string of invented acronyms, such as "SDM" (or "Sueldo de Mierda" [Shit Salary]; see figure 5.6b), which parodies the jargon of trained economists.

9 Gray examines this idea of movie-inspired toys as paratexts by using the original Star Wars action figures as his primary example (21). His work also points to *The Simpsons* (clearly an influence on Saló's own comics sensibility) as a heavily merchandised work complicit in the very consumerism that the series itself critiques (15). This sort of push-pull current is something I have suggested is discernible in Saló's use of media marketing strategies within his broader satirical deconstruction of an economic disaster whose roots he pinpoints as being inseparable from the values of neoliberalism.

10 In various interviews with the press, Saló's "faceta de emprendedor" [entrepreneurial facet] ("Españistán y Aleix Saló") is broached by journalists and the Catalan cartoonist himself (he notes, for example, having spent two years' savings on production costs for the *Españistán* video ["La Ventana"]) in ways that contrast his own "autorrealización" [self-actualization] ("Entrevista Pirata") with the professional stagnation and socioeconomic anxieties of the generational peers whose plights feature so prominently in his work. Moderna de Pueblo, the pen name and comics alter ego of Raquel Córcoles (born in Tarragona in 1986), is noteworthy as another recent graphic satirist whose enterprising development of an intermedial distribution apparatus – arguably building, at least in part, on Saló's example in the Spanish context – has catalysed her prominence in a challenging market. Appearing in digital and paper-form venues, with both short- and long-form manifestations (including, to date, four hardcopy graphic novels), work by Córcoles and her scriptwriter collaborators straddles some classic venue divisions in Spanish comics culture. Many of the motifs and figures introduced not only in her blog and Facebook *viñetas* (a few of which have online animated versions) but also in single-panel and mini-strip contributions to online and paper-form periodicals such as *El Jueves, GQ,* and *Cuore* have served as both teasers and "b-sides" to hardcopy (and subsequent e-book) graphic novels: publications that have averaged around 50,000 copies sold each, with contracts on high-visibility presses including Lúmen, Planeta, Plaza y Janés – not to mention peripheral merchandise deals for coffee mugs, calendars, notebooks, greeting cards, and editions of her books in French, Italian, and Portuguese. More cultural than socioeconomic in their satirical leanings, Moderna de

Pueblo's comics are most often attuned to the "hipsterization" of young adult lifestyles, identities, and practices (sexual, consumptive, environmental, professional, fashion-related, and otherwise) in her adopted city of Madrid – and, specifically, the present-day, cartoonishly commodified neighbourhood of Malasaña. Her work populates this space with a recurring typology of risibly self-conscious, twenty- to thirty-something characters, nearly all of whom swim in – or haplessly struggle to tread – the waters of a global hipster economy where trend-based capital flows frenetically via Twitter, Facebook, Instagram, and WhatsApp (at many turns, platforms that the artist visually incorporates into dialogue in lieu of traditional speech balloons).

WORKS CITED

Acland, Charles. *Screen Traffic: Movies, Multiplexes, and Global Culture*. Duke UP, 2003.

Baetens, Jan. "Other Non-Fiction." *The Cambridge Companion to the Graphic Novel*, edited by Stephen E. Tabachnick, Cambridge UP, 2017, 130–43.

Benson, Thomas W., and Brian J. Snee. "Michael Moore and the Rhetoric of Documentary: Art, Argument, Affect." *Michael Moore and the Rhetoric of Documentary*, edited by Thomas W. Benson and Brian J. Snee, Southern Illinois UP, 2015, 1–24.

Brett, Anwar. "Matt Stone. Team America: World Police." Interview. *BBC*, 13 January 2005, www.bbc.co.uk/films/2005/01/13/matt_stone_team_america_interview.shtml.

Carrier, David. *The Aesthetics of Comics*. Penn State UP, 2000.

Doncel, Luis. "El futuro de 'Españistán.'" *El País*, 8 July 2011, elpais.com/diario/2011/07/08/tentaciones/1310149375_850215.html.

"Entrevista Pirata: Aleix Saló, viñetista y pintamonas." *La Arcadia de Urias*, 28 July 2010, laarcadiadeurias.com/comics/entrevista-pirata-aleix-salo-vinetista-y-pintamonas/.

"'Españistán. Este país se va a la mierda,' el retrato social de Aleix Saló." *RTVE*, 26 May 2011, www.rtve.es/noticias/20110526/espanistan-este-pais-se-va-mierda-retrato-social-aleix-salo/434796.shtml.

"Españistán y Aleix Saló en TVE24h." *YouTube*, 13 June 2011, www.youtube.com/watch?v=uS8Sg0XJy5o.

García, Santiago. *On the Graphic Novel*. Translated by Bruce Campbell, UP of Mississippi, 2010.

García Mongay, Fernando. "Una rosa y un 'ebook.' El libro electrónico comienza a formar parte de la oferta del día de Sant Jordi." *El País*, 23 April 2012, elpais.com/ccaa/2012/04/22/catalunya/1335123181_473202.html.

Giroux, Henry A. *On Critical Pedagogy*. Continuum, 2011. Critical Pedagogy Today Series.

González, Lucía. "Europesadilla (PDF): Aleix Saló, tras Simiocracia y Españistán, explica quién se ha comido a la clase media." *Huffington Post*, 1 April 2013, www.huffingtonpost.es/2013/04/01/europesadilla-nuevo-libro-aleix-salo_n_2990531.html.

Gray, Jonathan. *Show Sold Separately: Promos, Spoilers, and Other Media Paratexts*. NYU Press, 2010.

Grøn, Rasmus. "Literary Experience and the Book Trailer as Intermedial Paratext." *Sound Effects: An Interdisciplinary Journal of Sound and Sound Experience* 4.1 (2014): 90–107. www.soundeffects.dk/article/view/20330/17917.

Hay, James, and Nick Couldry. "Rethinking Convergence/Culture." *Cultural Studies* 25.4–5 (2011): 473–86. doi.org/10.1080/09502386.2011.600527.

Hutcheon, Linda. *A Poetics of Postmodernism: History, Theory, Fiction*. Routledge, 1988.

Jenkins, Henry. *Convergence Culture: Where Old and New Media Collide*. NYU Press, 2006.

Merino, Olga. "Un cómic mordaz sobre la crisis arrasa en internet." *El Periódico*, 12 June 2011, www.elperiodico.com/es/noticias/comi-mordz-sobre-crisis-arrasa-internet-1039884.

Mickwitz, Nina. *Documentary Comics: Graphic Truth-Telling in a Skeptical Age*. Palgrave Macmillan, 2016.

Moreno-Caballud, Luis. "La imaginación sostenible. Culturas y crisis económica en la España actual." *Hispanic Review* 80.4 (2012): 535–55. doi.org/10.1353/hir.2012.0039.

– "Looking Amid the Rubble: New Spanish Documentary Film and the Residues of Urban Transformation (Joaquim Jordà and José Luis Guerín)." *Studies in Spanish & Latin American Cinemas* 11.1 (2014): 61–74. doi.org/10.1386/slac.11.1.61_1.

Nichols, Bill. *Representing Reality: Issues and Concepts in Documentary*. Indiana UP, 1991.

Pons, Álvaro. "El 15-M toma el cómic." *El País*, 10 Sept. 2011, elpais.com/diario/2011/09/10/babelia/1315613564_850215.html.

Ruiz Bartolomé, José Luis. "Desmontando Españistán (1)." *Libre Mercado*, 30 May 2011, adiosladrilloadios.libremercado.com/desmontando-espanistan-1/.

Saló, Aleix. "Aleix Saló: Españistán simplifica por su format, pero no busca culpables." *El Economista*, 3 June 2011, www.eleconomista.es/opinion-blogs/noticias/3126051/06/11/Aleix-Salo-Espanistan-simplifica-por-su-formato-pero-no-busca-culpables.html#.

– *Españistán: De la burbuja inmobiliaria a la crisis*. Film short. *YouTube*, 25 May 2011, www.youtube.com/watch?v=N7P2ExRF3GQ.
– *Españistán: Este país se va a la mierda*. Editores de Tebeos, 2011.
– *Europesadilla: Alguien se ha comido a la clase media*. Debolsillo (Random House Mondadori), 2013.
– *Europesadilla: Alguien se ha comido a la clase media*. Film short. *YouTube*, 3 April 2013, www.youtube.com/watch?v=BF0bGaQCn04.
– *Fills dels 80: La generació bombolla*. Glénat, 2009.
– *Hijos de los 80: La generación burbuja*. Translated by Carlos Mayor, Debolsillo (Penguin Random House), 2014.
– *Simiocracia: Crónica de la gran resaca económica*. Debolsillo (Random House Mondadori), 2013.
– *Simiocracia: Crónica de la gran resaca económica*. Film short. *YouTube*, 12 April 2012, www.youtube.com/watch?v=TfRSfF296js.
Serrano, José A. "Aleix Saló." *Guia del Cómic*, August 2012, www.guiadelcomic.es/s/aleix-salo.htm.
Test, George A. *Satire: Spirit and Art*. UP of Florida, 1991.
"La Ventana: Cansado, pino y los jóvenes." *SER, La Ventana*, 29 June 2011, cadenaser.com/programa/2011/06/29/audios/1309303038_660215.html.
Voigt, Kati. "Becoming Trivial: The Book Trailer." *Culture Unbound: Journal of Current Cultural Research* 5.4 (2013): 671–89. doi.org/10.3384/cu.2000.1525.135671.

6 Urban Ecology and Comics Journalism in Jorge Carrión and Sagar Forniés's *Barcelona: Los vagabundos de la chatarra* (2015)

CHRISTINE M. MARTÍNEZ

[E]l progreso es un mito inmaterial que deja a su paso un grueso y matérico rastro de mierda.

[Progress is an immaterial myth that leaves in its wake a fat and material trail of shit.][1]

Jorge Carrión and Sagar Forniés, Prologue

For Jorge Carrión, writer and professor of journalism at Barcelona's Pompeu Fabra, today's New Journalism is to be found in the non-fiction comic book. He explores this idea in conversation with Joe Sacco, a seminal figure of comics journalism, in the epilogue of *Barcelona: Los vagabundos de la chatarra* [Barcelona: The Scrap Metal Vagabonds], Carrión's comics collaboration with illustrator Sagar Forniés (known as "Sagar") (100). Carrión as writer and Sagar as illustrator shared the investigative work over several months, riding through the streets of Barcelona's ex-industrial Poblenou neighbourhood at a time of economic crisis, resurgence of Catalan nationalism, and grandiose development projects to interview some of the city's most disenfranchised: "los 'vagabundos' de la chatarra," scrap metal collectors working at the margins of legal industry. Javier López Menacho notes that this type of investigative collaboration is not typical in the history of comics journalism, a genre mostly defined by the work of solo investigator/artists like Sacco, Dan Archer, and Josh Neufeld or by solely post-investigative collaborations between illustrators, writers, and journalists such as seen in Emmanuel Guibert, Didier Lefèvre, and Frédéric Lemercier's *The Photographer* and Charles Bowden and Alice Briggs's *Dreamland: The Way Out of Juárez*. Throughout *Barcelona*, the author and illustrator ruminate on the decision to tell the story of Barcelona and the "chatarreros" [scrap metal collectors] in comics form.[2] Reasons why the comics form has been an effective medium for conveying stories conventionally told by journalism abound, including comics' ability to synthesize complex information through the combination of text and image (Archer; Priego 2); the graphic portrayal of space and soundscape (Brister); and the mnemonic power, impact, and "stickiness" of graphic storytelling, capable of exploring in new light complicated and longstanding conflicts, which, because of frequent (but often flat) news coverage, exhaust the attention of news audiences (Schack). While other creative and journalistic forms, such as the documentary film, engage similar verbal and visual possibilities in storytelling – a point also argued in the epilogue of *Barcelona* – the spatiality of the comics page and the illustrator's ability to visually access or imagine moments often closed off to other media are examples of formal possibilities more specific to comics.

This chapter argues that the comics form better enables Carrión and Sagar to engage with the complexities of Barcelona as an urban ecosystem and represent the competing interests of the city's struggles over space. Their engagement is mainly accomplished through the form's construction of an "ecological understanding" of the problems at hand, which works through the relation of heterogeneous voices, sources, and objects and traces the flows of material, inextricable from issues of social import. *Barcelona*'s ecological understanding sketches out the structure to a contemporary problem materialized on the space of the city while remaining open and incomplete, fragmented but juxtaposing sources, images, voices, and texts. While all texts work through composition of diverse voices and elements, the notion of "composing" is an important concept throughout this study, employed along with other terms and concepts – such as Levi Bryant's "black ecology," Nick Sousanis's "ecological" understanding of comics (45), and Manuel Delgado's notion of "lo urbano," the unruly and unfixable "urban" ("La ciudad" 81) – in an attempt to describe an "ecological" mode of meaning-making and representation that emphasizes relation and carries within itself its own incompletion and provisionality. I draw from Bruno Latour's proposal of composition as an alternative to critique, as a form of knowledge-making that does not aim to merely dispel myths – in expectation of some "true beyond" – but seeks to understand relations of heterogeneous elements, always immanent and incomplete. Composition judges not what is constructed, but what is well constructed and what is badly constructed (474–5). *Barcelona* "composes" against the simplified identity of the city as put forth by its politicians, architects, and allied corporate interests in their celebratory and optimistic plans for its economic growth and design by juxtaposing these plans with the expulsion and invisibilization of wasted materials and populations, a task aided by the comics form.

Barcelona opens with a statement that clearly places the work's journalistic incursion into the city and the world of the city's *chatarreros* within a larger context of ecological crisis, meted out by the global economy's voracious appetite for growth and its propensity for generating waste. The prologue begins with statistics from the World Bank's 2012 report on global solid waste management, which stated that 1.3 billion tons of solid waste are produced annually across the globe and projections nearly double that quantity for 2025. After this presentation of monumental numbers, both sobering and difficult to grasp, Carrión concludes, "Por mucho que nos esforcemos en destruir y en reciclar, multiplicamos los desechos, las ruinas de nuestro consumo" [As much as we force ourselves to destroy and to recycle, we multiply waste, the ruins of our consumption] (Carrión and Forniés, Prologue). This statement is consonant with contemporary critiques of "green" politics, which remain optimistic about technological fixes for the social and environmental complications of current consumption patterns, and echoes critiques elaborated by a particularly Southern European environmentalism and the Degrowth movement. Such critiques have highlighted the necessity to challenge the discourses of progress and growth and patterns of consumption and urban planning that, in the span of a few hundred years, have led to an environmental impact of such proportions that some scientists have described it as a new geological epoch: the Anthropocene. Breaching the gap that has often separated questions of material flows and environmental impact from discussions of social politics, Carrión and Sagar argue that it is *our* production of waste that defines *us* as citizens (23).

Barcelona is a text that makes visible the "darker" underside of growth and progress, specifically the Catalan capital's internationally praised urban development projects of recent decades. These projects shaped the gradual transformation from a sprawling industrial centre, marked by authoritarian policies and largely unregulated real estate speculation carried out under the Francoist mayor Josep Maria de Porcioles, towards a post-industrial powerhouse and star child of international tourism and service industries (Illas 6–7, 46). The celebratory narratives of Barcelona's urban renewal and development of past decades – gathered under a term that highlights its desirability and exportability, the "Barcelona model" – have staged popular consensus, telling a story of "innovative" collaboration in urban planning between citizens and public and private investment, and highlighted an emphasis on the improvement of quality of life in certain neighbourhoods at a time when more conservative models of suburbanization and city sprawl were internationally more commonplace (Balibrea, "Urbanism" 187–8; Montaner 48). Since the mid-1980s, with the city's preparations to host the 1992 Olympics, this model of urban development has provided massive funds for the creation of cultural centres and restoration of the city's modernist architecture, capitalizing on the image of a sunny Mediterranean city of culture and modernist beauty, as seen in tourism advertisements and media. Several critics mark the late 1990s and early 2000s as a turning point in Barcelona's urban transformation, characterized by the increased power and sway of multinational capital over the consideration of citizen interests. Since the beginning of the twenty-first century, the city's corporate-aligned plans for urban renewal have received more vocal and visible pushback from neighbourhood associations fearing gentrification and complaining of top-down decision-making and insensitivity to local history and character (Marrero Guillamón 4). Many of the urban development projects referenced in *Barcelona* have their origins in this period.[3]

Barcelona focuses on the people and materials held in the margins of the optimistic narratives of the city's development, while its exploration of the flow of *chatarra* and the precarious *chatarrero* participates in a long tradition of literature and cultural critique that has found in the trash collector, the rag picker, and the gleaner not only a metaphor for artistic and creative practice but also a central figure for understanding the mechanisms and seeming contradictions of modernity, namely, its simultaneous rhetoric of progress and unprecedented production of waste. *Barcelona* also participates in more recent critiques, such as elaborated by Rob Nixon and Zygmunt Bauman, which trace processes between global capitalism's displacement of waste and its displacement of marginalized people through their focus on those spaces where these populations and materials coincide. Carrión and Sagar's text is thus an exploration of the invisibilized "excess" created by neoliberal models of design and development, placed in the context of a Barcelona touched by the market's continued appetite for material and infrastructure growth and a festering social disparity exacerbated by Spain's most recent economic crisis, regional tensions, and the compounding failures of municipal governments to prioritize and provide for the city's most vulnerable populations.[4]

Comics and the City: Towards an Urban Ecology

Jörn Ahrens and Arno Meteling describe comics as a historically urban genre, developing along with the growing urbanization of modern nations and suited to represent particularly urban spaces and subjectivities (6). They observe that by 2010 "every modern metropolis in the world" had been made the subject of a comic book and offer Berlin, Paris, London,

Tokyo, and New York as a handful of well-known examples. *Barcelona* participates in this comics tradition that takes as its subject a major urban centre, while its graphic form offers a particular representation of the experience of city streets and the distinct contradictions and sensibilities of modern urban life. Aptly titled "Barcelona," the author and illustrator propose a counter-narrative to hegemonic, celebratory visions of the city. Carrión and Sagar's collaboration in *Barcelona* was sparked by a mutual contact who suggested Sagar as an illustrator for what Carrión originally intended to be a shorter journalistic project for *La Vanguardia* (Norma Editorial). Outside of Carrión and Sagar's collaboration, the works of both the author and illustrator show longstanding interests in the intricacies of the contemporary city. Carrión is known for his writings on Madrid and Barcelona, having edited a volume of creative and critical texts regarding these two cities, *Madrid/Barcelona: Literatura y ciudad (1995–2010)* [Madrid/Barcelona: Literature and City (1995–2010)] – released in 2009, and subsequently published as a non-fiction book, *Barcelona: Libro de los pasajes* [Barcelona: Book of Passages] (2017), a tribute to Walter Benjamin's *Arcades Project* and Italo Calvino's *Invisible Cities* – which collects conversations between the author and passersby encountered on Barcelona's streets. Sagar is an avid street sketcher who has published his drawings of Barcelona's internationally known and touristic neighbourhoods in collaboration with the Ajuntament of Barcelona. Sagar's *Barcelona Travel Notebook*, titled in English, has also been used to encourage touristic consumption of the city and is promoted on the Ajuntament's website along with other cultural texts about the city.[5] Including comics like *Bajo la piel* [Under the Skin] (2005) and illustrations for the 2017 BCNEGRA festival, Sagar has also worked within the noir genre, notable for its fascination with the "dark side" of the modern city.

The coexistence of text and image ties comics to modern urban subjectivity, particularly the materialization of market capitalism on the cityscape, marked by the prevalence of advertising and the rationalization of space and seen in printed and projected advertising campaigns, for-sale signs, street names, and business fronts. Jens Balzer writes that the mingling of words and images on the same frame reflects "a semiotic shift occurring in the urban living space at the turn of the century." This shift, "forc[ing] the observer to look and read at the same time" is what, for Balzer, distinctly separates comics from earlier pictorial precursors (25). Benjamin has also commented on this coexistence of text and image, which requires the reader to both look and read simultaneously, and the elevation of text onto the cityscape in his writings on 1920s urban life (62). Decades later, David Harvey and Henri Lefebvre have described the city as a spatial materialization of the ever-evolving contradictions and configurations of capital (Harvey 204; Lefebvre 129).

Thanks to Sagar's illustrations in *Barcelona*, which embed the action of the narrative within the built environment of the city, the cohabitation of text and image mirrors the visual semiotic structure of the city and engages throughout with the conflicts struggling to define it. Additionally, because of comics' ability to depict urban waste and access spaces often foreclosed to other more invasive visual media, *Barcelona* is able to bear witness to the dismantling of space for the indigent and disenfranchised, often required by contemporaneous processes of city building.

The working-class and post-industrial neighbourhood of Poblenou serves as ground zero for urban conflict in *Barcelona* (though it is only one of several city neighbourhoods to have experienced such conflict in recent years). Poblenou abuts lucrative coastal real estate and still bears many physical remains of the area's industrial heritage, most notably the shells of empty industrial warehouses and factories (*naves*) that many of the *chatarreros* use for their work and residence. Once nicknamed the "Catalan Manchester," Poblenou is at the heart of Barcelona's twenty-first century post-industrial reconversion outlined by the government-sponsored and corporate-run development plan 22@Barcelona ("Innovación"), launched in 2000 and slated to transform the neighbourhood into a hub for service and technology industries. The plan, explained by Carrión and Sagar in one of three historical annexes included in *Barcelona*, is one of Europe's biggest urban regeneration schemes, covering over 115 city blocks (22). 22@'s vision for the neighbourhood's future, as seen on the Ajuntament's website, employs a vocabulary of "innovation," economic opportunity, job creation, and increased quality of life for the neighbourhood ("Innovación"). The rhetoric of the plan is particularly revealing of the selective values of 22@'s vision: while selling an image of "modern" spaces and "innovation," it describes the warehouses of Poblenou as "obsoletas" [obsolete] and "con usos poco productivos" [with little productive use], claims that seem disconnected from reality when taking into account the value of these spaces for the city's most marginal *chatarrero* communities.

The comics form is adept at communicating atmospheres of tangled conflict as writ upon city space. Following Schack, by "atmosphere" I refer to how the comics form allows artists "to create and maintain an overall feeling for the locative elements via visual cues that remain in panel after panel" (111). Even as *Barcelona*'s narrative may focus on other conversations or as the author and illustrator are shown in transit, visual traces of this conflict accompany the reader's experience of the narrative. Sagar's illustrations of the city streets depict the humanizing and politicizing messages left by the *chatarreros* on these contested warehouses – graffitied messages such as "equality," "no soy un animal somos personas"

[I'm not an animal, we are people] (37) and "Sr. Rajoy, dónde voy??" [Mr Rajoy, where do I go?] (79) – and the corporately printed for-rent and demolition signs erected above the same structures. *Barcelona*'s drawn city orients and accompanies the reader throughout the narrative, illustrating heterotopic cityscapes of soaring towers and shuttered windows, hand-drawn graffiti, political posters, advertising, group occupations of public space, broken glass, and fallen leaves, making ever-present the complex and often nonlinear web of forces, seasons, and interests shaping the city.

In *Barcelona*, as in other well-known comics of place such as Jason Lutes's *Berlin*, Chris Ware's *Building Stories*, and Sacco's *Palestine* and *Safe Area Goražde*, the comics form reinforces the importance of reading the archive of the cityscape and stepping out of the tempos and narratives of linear development and progress in order to develop a useful exploration of the phenomena and politics affecting place. While the processes of development – such as debt and speculation or demolition and construction – seek to temporalize space, the comics page, along with other media such as painting and the printed book, spatializes time (Harvey 205–6). The comics form offers a particular way of spatializing time, primarily through the nonlinear characteristics of the image and the simultaneous placement of frames and images on the page. While the verbal marches in linear time and the viewer of a film in a theatre is subjected to a relentless stream of images, the comics page is capable of presenting sequences of images in the form of a static grid. This technique suggests the possibility that time can be fractured, reconfigured, and read along multiple pathways or considered all at once (Bukatman 89; McCloud 67). The comics page becomes a place where multiple moments and multiple temporalities, including the linearity of the verbal and the nonlinearity of the visual, coexist (Sousanis 58). Given the multiple temporalities that shape the city and are evoked by the cityscape, it makes sense that the vignettes and page spreads that depict Carrión and Sagar's movement through the city are among the most temporally and spatially experimental of the text, whether juxtaposing progressively zoomed-out images of the city streets as seen from above (66) or illustrating various moments of conversation at several points within the same frame (23, 55–6).

In his seminal thesis, *Unflattening*, drawn completely in comics form, Sousanis comments that comics' "expansive way of seeing corresponds to an understanding of ecosystems" (45). His text grapples with the many ways the comics form can turn the flatness of print and the linearity of narrative into arguably new and innovative ways of perceiving time and space. These innovations involve comics' power to mix, combine, and

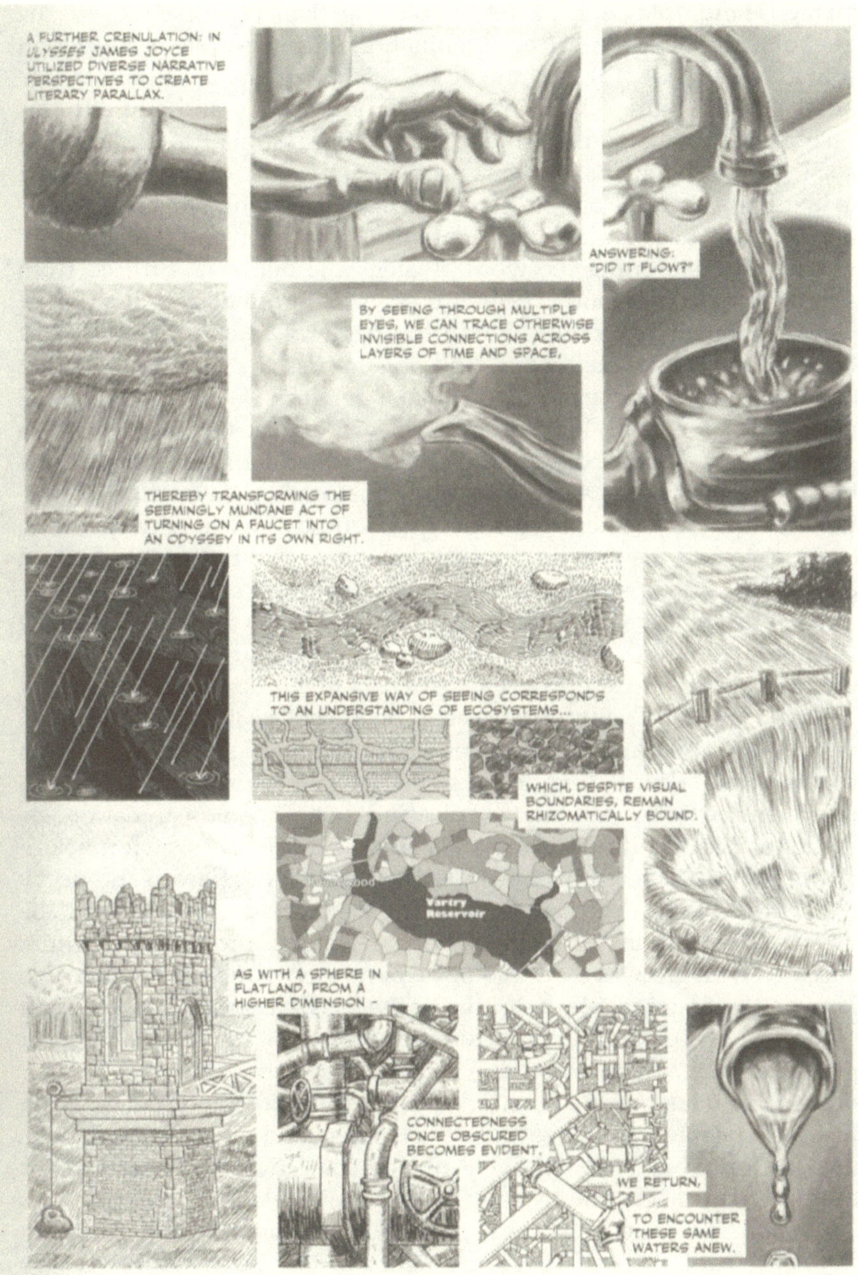

Figure 6.1. *Unflattening* depicts an understanding of ecosystems (Sousanis 45).

juxtapose multiple perspectives, employing "kaleidoscopic views," the phenomenon of parallax (the combination of diverse perspectives that provides visual depth), and the de-privileging of any absolute vantage point (32–9). Figure 6.1 communicates both visually and verbally this "ecological understanding" of the comics form, similar to literary parallax (the employment of diverse narrative perspectives) but also able to juxtapose multiple objects, which, even in fragmentation and opposition, suggest an unlimited combination of connection and relation.

Without mentioning the word "water," the material is traced from several perspectives and explored in an undetermined combination of ways, exponentially suggestive to the reader. Drawing from Thierry Groensteen's work on comics, Sousanis argues that the organization of simultaneous images functions like a network, "a connected space, not reliant on a chain-like sequence linearly proceeding from point to point" (62). In comics, the combination of text and image, dual sequential and simultaneous awareness, and construction via relationality offer effective engagement with the rapid but layered tempos of urban experience and the synchronic and diachronic realities of the modern city, which is no less an ecosystem than a rainforest or a desert.

Bryant coined the term "black ecology" in part to link ecology to the study of the urban and global dynamics of inequality, the inheritances of colonialism, and the externalized costs of neoliberal capital. Black ecology complicates simplistic notions of "green" ecology and idealized nature, thus revealing the impossibility of separating "the social" from the material. "Green" here refers to marketable environmentalism and its preference for the aesthetically pleasing over other more dynamic aesthetics of decay and nourishment, such as manure, the brown muck of rivers, mineral rich reds of the desert, and the greys of death and decay (Buell ix–xii; Cohen xix–xxi). Referencing the hue of a growing plant, the green serves as a convenient metaphor and a pleasing image for a culture obsessed with growth. Black ecology emerges as a sort of antidote to this kind of thinking, capable of disarming the idea that society is something distinct from ecology, and proposes the necessity of thinking in terms of particular human and material ecological formations (Buell x). In their decision to trace *chatarra,* Carrión and Sagar seem to confront head-on Bryant's statement that "we will never understand why social relations take the form they take without also understanding how features of, for example, natural geography contribute to social relations" (294).

Awareness of material flows is present throughout *Barcelona* thanks in large part to the comics form's combination of text and image. *Barcelona*'s prologue, informational text squares, and annexes trace the history of certain objects in time – such as the history of the shopping cart (36) or the quantity of *chatarra* that moves through the city's ports annually

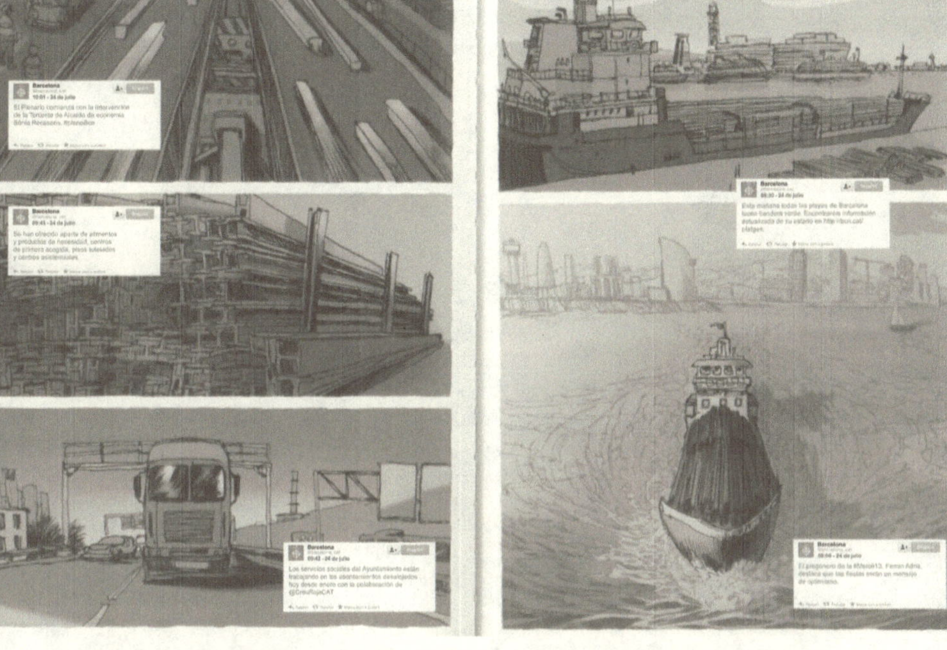

Figure 6.2. Scrap metal in transport in Carrión and Forniés's *Barcelona* (92–3).

(9) – while its images locate these objects spatially at various stages of their relation to subjects and structures, as seen in figure 6.2, which illustrates part of the process of reconversion and export of scrap metal. Metal in various stages appears throughout the book: in the skeleton of naked steel frames of the new Encants, completed in 2013 to house the previously open-air Encants flea market of Poblenou (60–1); in the piles of discarded objects illustrated in the occupied warehouse of Puigcerdà Street (figure 6.3); in the carts of the *chatarreros* (cover page); and in cooling molten beams as it undergoes forging (92). As seen in figure 6.3, the warehouses occupied by the *chatarreros* are repositories of items to be reused, reconverted, and recirculated: circular movements that confound the linear temporalities often associated with development. While the text shows the linear progression of an interview in the succession of text bubbles moving from left to right, the image also suggests spatio-temporal complexity in the multiple layers of discarded and collected items, which, if verbally described, would become a tedious list. As illustrated, each item contributes to a whole while still maintaining the singularity of socks, toy cars, bed frames, and the like, and suggesting a litany of past uses and connections to a multiplicity of unknown lives.

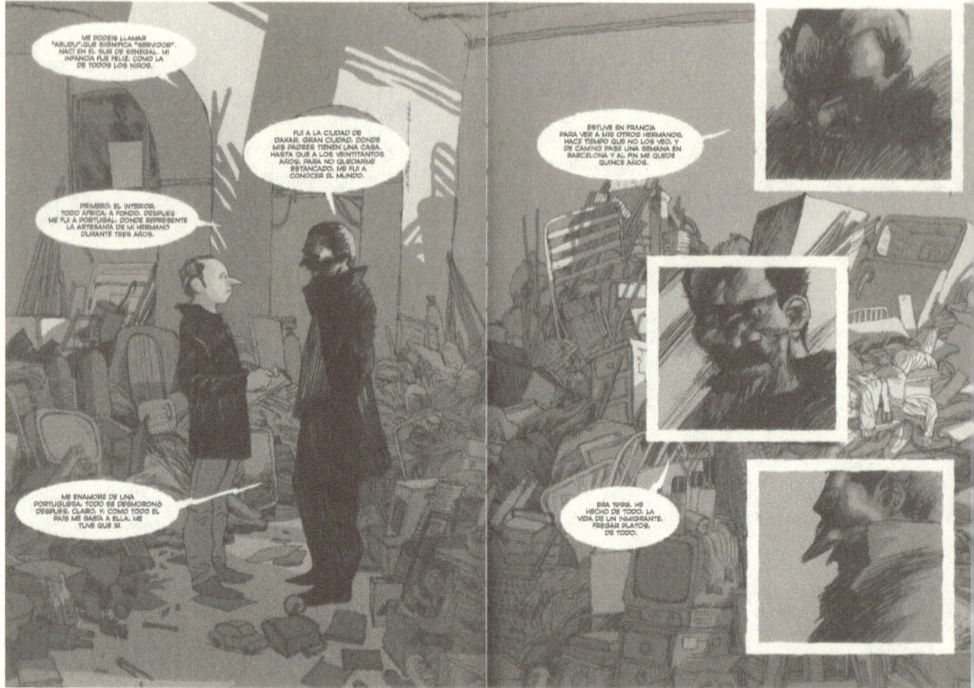

Figure 6.3. Interview at Puigcerdà Street nave in Carrión and Forniés's *Barcelona* (42–3).

Barcelona: Shadows of Design and Urban Wilderness

Barcelona begins as an investigation to trace the movement of material and the circulation of scrap metal in the city, an industry that suffered significant losses with the end of the construction bubble of the 1990s and 2000s and the ensuing economic crisis in which both local demand and availability of scrap metal declined (Blázquez). The narrative thus begins at the city docks in an attempt to trace the flow of material (steel beams, scrap wire, copper, aluminium), the very material required by local and global development, produced by dismantling old industry and consumed in the erection of new structures. Carrión and Sagar find themselves marvelling at the deafening sound of scrap metal and the sheer quantities transported annually while lingering with the morbid fascination of a second-hand observer in the port workers' stories of hard labour and corporate corruption.

The text quickly picks up and follows the trail of the city's "illegal" scrap metal collectors, many of whom are African and Romanian immigrants out of work after the 2008 economic crisis.[6] While *chatarreros* and *chatarrerías* had long existed in the city lucratively, the number of people working as *chatarreros* multiplied in the years of national austerity and unemployment, as revealed in the text (83). Many are long-time immigrant labourers who had found work in construction during the years of the real estate bubble (27–8, 39, 84). Many are also first-time *okupas* [squatters] who had paid years of rent while the work was steady (47, 85; Blanchar). Picking up on a story often covered by local, national, and international press in the one-sided terms of misery and abjection, *Barcelona* focuses on the *chatarreros'* occupation of Poblenou's abandoned warehouses and factories for work and living purposes, and climaxes after a surge in evictions from these warehouses by the Ajuntament in 2012 and 2013 and subsequent protests from the squatters allied with representatives of neighbourhood associations.[7] The forced eviction of the warehouse on Puigcerdà Street in Poblenou, housing over three hundred people, was the most notable eviction, one whose fallout continues to receive media coverage (Altimira; López; Verdú). Carrión describes the collective and community occupation of the Puigcerdà Street warehouse as the "corazón del reportaje" [heart of the journalistic story] in *Barcelona* (Norma Editorial).

Barcelona also juxtaposes this narrative to the timeline of the contemporaneous closure and transference of the city's historic flea market, Encants Vells, where many of these workers sell other collected items, to a new and spectacular neighbouring structure, part of the Ajuntament's renovation of Poblenou's Glòries Catalanes, a large square bordering the Eixample, undergoing massive renovations since the early 2000s. The opening of the new Encants in September 2013 is depicted as the temporal closure of *Barcelona* (94–5). While the text suggests scepticism over several elements and stated motives surrounding the market's construction – such as the imposition of the "marca Barcelona" in the market's new name (Encants Barcelona) and the extent to which the needs of its vendors and patrons were addressed by the new structure – the most troubling aspect is that the new Encants and the redevelopment of the surrounding Glòries received funds for completion at a time of continued economic crisis and record unemployment when little money remained for other civic projects (19). In an interview with *RTVE*, Carrión comments on the faulty logic of this prioritization of development – inflexible, even at a time of economic crisis – and the central irony that drives *Barcelona*'s narrative: "Hay voluntad política para abrir nuevos hoteles pero no para intentar reintegrar a todas esas personas a las que la crisis ha expulsado de la sociedad" [There is political will to open new hotels but not to integrate those persons that the crisis has ejected from society] (RTVE).

Barcelona reflects both visually and textually contemporary critiques of Barcelona as a "bipolar" or "dual" city of ever-increasing disparity, especially as managed under the watch of the Trias government (Mondelo). As Megan Saltzman highlights, *Barcelona* serves to expose the city as an increasingly polarized and "dual" city – one of "order and light" and the other of "disorder and dark." Carrión describes the city council's 22@ plan and the neighbourhood of Poblenou as "dos naturalezas y dos nombres" [two natures and two names], while the physical space of Poblenou, captured in Sagar's illustrations and pieced together by the panels of the book, becomes "un televisor mal sintonizado entre dos canales distintos" [a television set poorly synchronized between two different channels] or a space upon which two conflicting interests overlap in confusion (*Barcelona* 19). Light and shadow are common visual tropes throughout the text as the warm earthy red and golden tones of Sagar's illustrated light rarely reach the spaces inhabited by the *vagabundos*. Visually, the illustrations maintain constant the obscurity that codes these unofficial residents and workers of the city, moving among the long shadows of the city's built environment, for example, as seen in the shadows that cover the *chatarrero*'s face in figure 6.3. Sagar's aesthetic combines the more vibrant colour and descriptive style of his touristic street sketches with the noir genre's fascination with the shadows of the city, suggesting a coexistence and intermingling between these two experiences of the city. While metaphors of the "dual city" in "light and dark" may seem Manichaean, it is precisely this dualism of "black and white" that Carrión and Sagar attempt to escape via the comics form and their engagement with the urban ecology of Poblenou.

It is significant that many of the most important discussions between Carrión and Sagar about the function of the comics form, their hopes for their investigation, and their sentiments on the changing city occur while they are in transit, cycling through the streets of the city (figure 6.4; see also 24, 66, 83). This particular contact with the city street – a space of complexity and contradiction – and the privileged space of knowledge it seems to create for Carrión and Sagar are in line with Michel De Certeau's "rhetoric of walking" and Delgado's description of uncontainable urban life (although the pair are "technically" on bicycles, another form of city traffic that has increased with the growth of international tourism). De Certeau's "walking" describes a practice of immersion in the city that makes impossible any totalizing view and is in stark contrast to the panoptic and ordering view of the city planner, dependent upon maps and designs, which articulates space in the temporal terms of projects and "progress" (framing a future that one can invest in!) (97–8). The danger of this view, similar to that of touristic overlooks

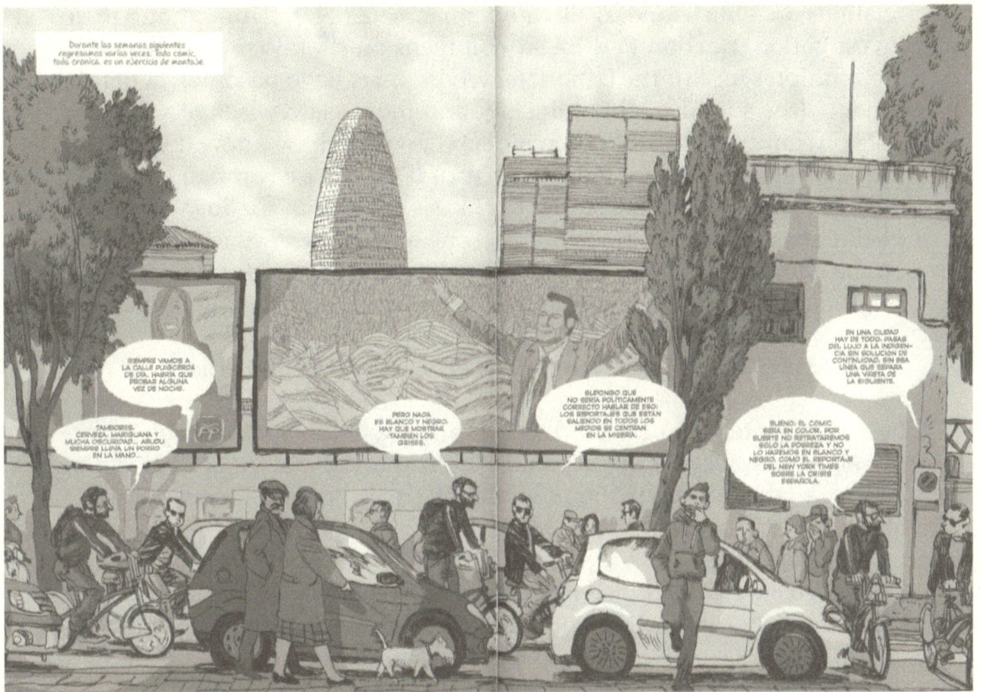

Figure 6.4. "El cómic será en color" in Carrión and Forniés's *Barcelona* (54–5).

and high-rise vistas, is that it clears the city of contradictions and makes static a space that is in constant flux (Stafford 125–8; Frahm 43). Delgado's notion of the urban, drawing from Lefebvre's *Right to the City* (1968), describes the ever-confounding and unfixable element of city life that constantly escapes and undermines the auditing of the organizing powers that shape the city ("El espacio" 4; "La ciudad" 81).

Carrión and Sagar's evolving sentiments and insights revealed in these frames are a direct function of contact with the world around them, making them subjects of Bryant's black ecology, capable of absorbing qualities never fully anticipated or predicted from the relations in which they are immersed. A major task of *Barcelona*, accomplished in the visibilization of waste and its collectors, is the communication of what could be called black ecological subjecthood and urban wilderness: in other words, the urban reader's awareness of her or his own inextricability to ecologies of waste and reported events. For Bryant, "wilderness" is no longer the space outside the city or civilization, but the very unknown and unpredictable element of the networks of social and material relations in which one is already immersed (299). Throughout their investigation, Carrión and Sagar comment on the disconnect between the omnipresence of the *chatarrero*, whose carts have become "la banda sonora" [the sound track] of the city, and their relative lack of visibility. This proximity of the unknown is also echoed in the shadow that covers the face of the foregrounded *chatarrero* of *Barcelona*'s cover page. Even as the figure approaches the reader his face is covered in shadow, while the phallic structure of the Torre Agbar – one of the first icons of new capital on the Glòries Catalanes, designed by the same architectural firm of the new Encants market – looms in the background, drenched in light.[8]

"El cómic será en color": Journalistic Process and Composition

In a video interview for Norma Editorial, Carrión speaks about comics' ability to liberate the journalist from the imperative of objectivity, a move that can even make possible the construction of more complex and contradictory narratives. He states:

> En el comic está claro que no es objetivo ... el dibujo ya distorsiona de modo que parece que eres más libre para trabajar la complejidad de un modo poliédrico y diferentes versiones y voces que se pueden contradecir y que son verbal y visualmente [sic].
>
> [It is clear that the comic book is not objective ... The drawing already distorts in a way that makes you feel freer to work the complexity in a polyhedral manner, and different versions and voices can contradict themselves verbally and visually.]

In its ability to include the author/illustrator within the images of the text – an option not as easily available to other forms of visual journalism such as photography – the comics form permits greater self-reflexivity and awareness of the constructed nature of the storytelling enterprise, drawing parallels with experimental forms of journalism, especially the twentieth century school of New Journalism, which combined investigative reporting with autobiography to counter illusions of the invisible journalist and objective facts (Archer; Faye 211). In addition to comics' ability to include the author and illustrator, the comics form, as Hillary Chute highlights, "always shows its seams." While every representation – text, film, and news article – requires framing, the comics form "crucially makes its framings hand-drawn and *literal*," an aspect that more closely represents the contingencies and constructed nature of the journalistic process (408).

As Sagar's illustrations of himself and Carrión reveal, the process of finding out information is as much a part of comics journalism as the story itself. The comics form, in this sense, is adept at illustrating journalism's construction of knowledge through the composition of diverse and often contingent or contradicting elements. Pieced together through fragments and assemblage, journalistic comics thus serve to communicate both the product of that process (a narrative) and many parts of the process itself, though the painstaking time it takes to edit and draw each frame of a comic book is not as frequently depicted. The narrative, presented in this fragmented form, has a different, more ecological truth effect than that of the linear narrative, arguably allowing readers to be more critical in their engagement with multiple possibilities of information.

In one of the street-riding vignettes (figure 6.4), after Carrión and Sagar's first visit to the occupied warehouse on Puigcerdà Street, Sagar mentions that nothing is "black and white" and that he intends to show "the greys" of the *vagabundos'* situation. At this moment, the pair are cycling among a crowd of pedestrians on a city street. The visual cues offer layers of entanglement: political ads hinting to the figure of Artur Mas, then president of Catalonia, and the contemporary resurgence of Catalan nationalism; shuttered buildings; the tip of the Torre Agbar; and a sea of pedestrians, each with a different face. Carrión picks up on the metaphor and complains to Sagar about the simplicity of the reports on the Spanish economic crisis and the typically one-sided misery of its affected. Sagar replies, continuing to employ metaphors from his craft, "Bueno, el cómic será en color" [Well, the comic book will be in colour].[9] Carrión's response directly ties this envisioned nuance of Sagar's colour palette to the lived and irreducible complexity of the city. He states, "En una ciudad hay de todo, pasas del lujo a la indigencia sin solución de continuidad, sin esa línea que separa una viñeta de la siguiente" [In a city, there is everything, you pass from luxury to destitution without interruption, without that line that separates one vignette from the next].

Carrión here recognizes the limits of the comic book in reflecting the continuity and seamlessness of the city: it must parcel off images and separate moments to construct its narrative, a technique that, as previously mentioned, offers many strengths to comics journalism in maintaining the contingent, constructed, collaborative, incomplete, and fragmented reality of its truth-telling enterprise, but one that too cleanly fits irreducibly messy subjects into boxes and two-page spreads.[10] Echoing Carrión's statement, Sagar imposes no line upon the separate moments of the conversation in figure 6.4. In a vignette that critiques the simplicity of journalistic narratives – often the product of gruelling temporal and spatial constraints like deadlines, sound bites, and word counts – the pair appears spatially, at three points in the same crowd. As the author and illustrator make explicit that it is complication and multiple resonance the book is aiming for, open and public space is given priority, an emphasis that recalls Sousanis's description of the relationality of the image, inscribed in space rather than time. This relationality within images and between images provides the knottiness that clean framing and linear narrative would otherwise foreclose, techniques extended especially to the visual and verbal depiction of the *chatarreros*.

Figure 6.3 illustrates part of an interview with the Senegalese *chatarrero* Mamadou Kheraba Drame, who gives the author and illustrator a tour of the occupied warehouse at Puigcerdà Street. His identity and role in the community is never quite fixed in the text: he initially goes by a pseudonym "Abudu" (meaning "he that serves"), and, while he presents himself as leader of the community of *okupas* at the warehouse, interviews with other members of the community that question his role as servant and leader also appear in the text. A newspaper article is reprinted to corroborate Kheraba's story about Desiré, a Senegalese youth killed by the local police in 1999, though it also reveals the contested nature of the facts in the particular legal case (48). Throughout *Barcelona*, even as the text aims to shed metaphorical "light" on their situation, Sagar's illustrations repeatedly visually code the *chatarreros* with suspicion inherited from noir: furtive gazes, faces draped in shadow, and quick successions of multiple frames, building tension. He initially drenches their faces in shadow, employing perspectives that set their eyes at furtive and gleaming angles (figure 6.3), only to later empathize with the subjects, drawing their features in greater detail, after the climax of their stories of struggle, as they mention their children and families, fears, hopes, and regrets (27–30, 49–51). This aesthetic also adds a dynamic complexity to the representation of these subjects, who emerge ultimately irreducible to any sole affect of pity, suspicion, admiration, or identification. This complexity is perhaps, in part, what Sagar means by a comic book "en color": capable of not only showing the misery but also the creativity and resilience, and even the complicity that these subjects might have with the very systems that prescribe their precarious status. Sagar and Carrión considered illustrating *Barcelona* in black and white but opted for colour for various reasons: for Sagar, "endulza la lectura" [it makes for a more enjoyable read], while for Carrión, "la realidad es en color" [reality is in colour] and creates an interesting and dynamic contrast between the pleasing and ludic aesthetic of the illustrations and the bleak reality of the text's subject matter (Norma Editorial).

The *chatarreros* are complex subjects in multiple kinds of relation to the system that marginalizes them, and they are are coded in *Barcelona* accordingly.[11] Though there may be a certain level of freedom and autonomy in their labour, the *chatarreros'* transit through the streets of the city is not the liberating walking of De Certeau, but is defined by their precarious existence apart from the system of legalized labour, one that is physically exhausting and not without its risks: the average *chatarrero* walks for upwards of ten hours a day among the city streets to earn between five and fifty euros, while the unlicensed recollection from the streets has been made illegal by a number of ordinances throughout the previous decade.[12] Additionally, many *chatarreros* work for abusive mafias, an element mentioned but mostly sidestepped in *Barcelona* (29; Blázquez). The scrapped material upon which the *chatarreros* depend and their main tool of labour – the shopping cart – are symbols of the very system of consumption that produces them as marginalized subjects, symbols that they creatively alter and repurpose for functions never previously intended by these objects' designers. Another ostensible irony is that many of the city's contemporaneous *chatarreros* once found work in construction during the very housing boom that led to Spain's financial ruin: as Daniel Verdú writes, "buscan fortuna desguazando los restos de la bonanza española que ellos mismos ayudaron a construir" [they survive by breaking up the remains of the very Spanish prosperity that they themselves helped construct].

Kheraba's story and the multiple connections drawn from it give depth to the present struggle of the Poblenou *okupa* and *chatarrero* communities by referring to other events and other interests connected to their situation. Kheraba mentions events from previous decades that point to racial discrimination and reminds the author and illustrator that the occupation of Poblenou's industrial buildings had been going on for well over a decade. Kheraba, surrounded by the junked items of the warehouse (figure 6.3), tells narratives of activism, collaboration, and resilience – speaking of community efforts to self-organize and the foundation of an organization for immigrant rights in Catalonia (La Federación Panafricanista). He also mentions that the owners of the warehouse are connected to a non-governmental organization (NGO) that assists women of limited resources in African nations. Regarding a previous attempt at eviction by representatives of the owners, Kheraba expresses incomprehension and hints towards the state of disconnection between the owners and the *nave*'s residents.

Despite their relative silence and facelessness in *Barcelona*, these corporate interests are depicted with a degree of complexity. Later on in the text, Carrión and Sagar include another annex that researches the owners of the Puigcerdà Street *nave* and their NGO – La Fundación Maite Iglesias Baciana – founded after the untimely death of the family's daughter. Carrión also describes this story as one of "pérdida" and "duelo" [loss and mourning] as he introduces the annex (73). Contrasting emotions are elicited as the section includes a screenshot of the foundation's webpage with what is presumably a photograph of the deceased daughter, embedded into notes that detail the multiple business ventures and management positions of the family. This section paints the picture of a mourning family and financial powerhouse attached to some of the economic crisis's most controversial industries: venture capital and real estate. Another reference to the father's involvement with the "La Caixa" Group, which provides social assistance to immigrants without housing, offers yet another incongruity that highlights the disconnect between the family's corporate rhetoric and actual attempts to evict the three hundred mostly immigrant *okupas* from their own unused property. There is an obvious tension when Carrión later mentions the 196,000 euros in social assistance given by the Iglesias Baciana Foundation the previous year (73), considering the prologue's mention of Nuria Güell's project that, with 3,000 euros, was able to create a legal framework within which the *chatarreros* could work and self-employ.

The inclusion of such sources and elements in *Barcelona* ultimately suggests the indictment of corporate (and municipal) interests and their indirect manners of action, primarily by showing them in verbal and visual relation or dis-relation – a type of relation either ignored or rendered invisible – to the situations that Carrión and Sagar encounter on the streets of Poblenou. It is significant that the interests of capital and political power, rather than the *chatarreros*, remain invisible or refuse to speak directly in conversation throughout *Barcelona*. Politically aligned corporate influences over the cityscape emerge in printed posters announcing business transactions, for-rent signs, and demolition announcements, while their goals and intentions appear indirectly in curated websites or Twitter feeds. The manager of an established *chatarra* factory refuses to speak with Carrión and Sagar (as illustrated on pages 20–1) and redirects the pair to the company website, not updated in thirteen years. In Poblenou, Carrión and Sagar only manage to encounter the hired staff of the companies guarding the remains of evicted sites, while it is only through Twitter that the Ajuntament communicates its public plans to "manage" the social costs of the eviction of the *nave* at Puigcerdà Street.

Just as the comic strip was suited to represent new print and visual technologies of the nineteenth and twentieth century, *Barcelona* takes up and includes in its narrative recent textual phenomena related to the rise of internet technology and social media, the very industry threatening to overtake Poblenou. These technologies reveal a particular mode of neoliberal power and impersonal communication – mediated through invisible data waves and undisclosed servers – that executes simplified image control and hides behind supposed "transparency." In *Barcelona,* these phenomena are most clearly seen in the Ajuntament's Twitter feed and the corporate websites of Chatarras Sánchez and La Fundación Maite Iglesias Baciana. The corporate and municipal interests appear faceless, as if hiding behind their technologies of communication that carefully curate and emit rhetoric in one-sided, enunciative rather than communicative, contexts lifted from the conversation desired by the community of *chatarreros* and the neighbours of Poblenou.

For Thomas Faye, the juxtaposition of the Ajuntament's tweets with the illustrated process of collection, reconversion, and export of *chatarra* offers a representation of the city's flawed rhetoric and lucrative expulsion of excess materials *and* persons: the barge in figure 6.2, depicting the final stages in the conversion cycle of *chatarra,* sails away from the city. The tweets from the Ajuntament are presented in temporal reverse, promising social assistance to the evicted residents of Puigcerdà Street and, in anticipation of upcoming *fiestas,* commenting on the beauty of the city's public beaches – a public resource, expanded by various development plans associated with the Barcelona model, which is of little interest to the homeless and jobless (Carrión and Forniés 89–93). Social and ecological concerns emerge as one and the same as this clash makes "cynically manifest" the incomprehension "entre los que preconizan el reciclaje como fuerza de vitalidad e integración y los que resultan excluidos de este círculo" [between those who profess recycling as a force of vitality and integration and those that remain excluded from this circle] (Faye 215). The Ajuntament's "green" rhetoric of recycling and progress is thus revealed as superficial and flawed, while *Barcelona* seems to suggest a rhetorical question: what environmental responsibility is there without social justice, and what social justice exists without an awareness of material flows?

Conclusion: Comics and Ecology in Colour

Sacco comments in the illustrated epilogue of *Barcelona* that though he considers himself to be of the Left (which is to say, "progressive"), "las soluciones apestan" [solutions reek] (101). While this comment could be articulated as a cynical, postmodern, exhausted, and counter-productive take on the question of social commitment, there is something salvageable and necessary in his statement. If taken beneath the signs of the wilderness and melancholy of black ecology, which is the rejection of closure and optimism obtained by simplification and invisibilization, or beneath the ever-unfixable and ever-incomplete ecology of urban life, the search for "solutions" emerges as a mistaken or at least poorly articulated enterprise. *Barcelona* as a comics work conveys the "solution" as designer thinking. The "solution" is the pretention of the "model" and the imposition of the imagined city over its ever-unfixable urban life. It is the "success story" of the NGO, measured in euros and recounted on the Iglesias Baciana website. It is also "green" thinking and the illusion of stasis, the coveted and impossible horizon of natural homeostasis that drives neoliberal economics and green ecology alike (Bryant 291).

In a text that ultimately counters the type of thinking that imposes static "solutions" on urban space and communities, the ecological understanding of the comics form – which composes meaning through relations of text and image, and recognizes the ever unfixed nature of the urban – lends coherence to *Barcelona*'s form and content. The choice of the comics form could be described as a performance of antidotal thinking, a refusal to participate in the mode of hierarchical, managerial thought that the text ultimately complicates. In an interview about *Barcelona*, Carrión describes the real city as "una negociación constante" [a constant negotiation] and signals the extreme contrasts that define his contemporary Barcelona, separating the official discourse from the life in the streets (Carrión qtd. in RTVE). Carrión is signalling a disconnect and lack of relation between the city (as planned) and the urban (as lived). Similarly, Bryant writes that "many of our central political problems arise from the fact that people and other living beings are *not* related." Activist work thus requires getting people, governments, and businesses not only to recognize relations but also to forge, judge, and preserve relations (304). Through comics journalism and the ecological understanding of the comics form, *Barcelona* confronts the necessity of composition: linking causes and effects, linking the rhetoric of corporations with their multiple consequences, and showing the lack of relation where it should exist or already exists (such as between government projects and the lack of legal work and affordable housing). This composition is a task of ecology and journalism alike, complemented by the comics form.

The condition of the hundreds evicted from the *nave* at Puigcerdà Street has received continued press coverage over the years, in part thanks to works by writers and artists like Carrión and Sagar, and in larger part thanks to the continued resistance of community alliances and neighbourhood associations (Altimira; López; Verdú). Of the several hundred *chatarreros* who were evicted, a few dozen were able to receive papers to legally work with the assistance of the municipality, a couple dozen received work in a *chatarra* cooperative eventually founded by the Ajuntament, as promised in 2013, and a handful have been featured in artistic endeavours meant to raise awareness or make performative interventions (Altimira; García; López).[13] Trias announced ambitious plans to expand the city's offering of affordable housing that same year, which were not carried out during his tenure as mayor. Some place more hope for the prioritization of such projects with the current municipal government of Ada Colau and her party Barcelona en Comú, elected in 2015. But, for the majority of the *chatarreros* evicted from Puigcerdà Street, the fundamental problems of how to meet basic needs still remain. In a 2015 interview with VICE News, a young Senegalese man confirms that "cuando nos echaron de la nave, nos prometieron muchas cosas pero, al final, nada, yo sigo sin papeles, ni trabajo" [when they threw us out of the warehouse, they promised us many things but, in the end, nothing. I remain without papers or work] (Altimira). *Barcelona* begins at its improvised end, provisionally circular, in a prologue written three years after the events of the text itself, describing not solutions but a handful of specific and limited relations given at the time of publication – between resources and a few jobs, between a problem and public awareness – that were eventually able to be made. Above all else, the most powerful relations made in *Barcelona* are those that trace the structure of a contemporary problem. Sagar's words echo: "Supongo que esa será la function del cómic: señalar un problema" [I suppose this must be the function of the comic book: to point out a problem] (83).

NOTES

1 All translations are by the author unless otherwise noted.

2 Throughout this chapter I will use both the terms "vagabundos" and "chatarreros" to refer to the subjects of *Barcelona*, though "vagabundos" nods to the homelessness and precarity of the residents of the occupied warehouses and unofficial "chatarra" [scrap metal] workers while "chatarrero" refers simply to the collector of "chatarra" and describes a wider set of labour situations, which are not precarious per se. The subtitle "vagabundos de la chatarra" also makes reference to Steinbeck's 1936 journalistic work on

migrant workers of the American Great Depression, recently re-edited and published in Spain as *Los vagabundos de la cosecha* (2007).

3 Josep Maria Montaner argues that, even if beginning with socially responsible and committed models for urban renovation under the governments of the 1980s and 1990s, the Fòrum 2004, the strategic plans put into practice from 1988, and the introduction of the city into branding strategies with the Barcelona trademark (marca BCN) show "a tendency to favour the power and benefits of private interests, as opposed to public and administrative ones" (53). Mari Paz Balibrea describes the "marca BCN" as a simplified and spectacularized image of what had previously been the "modelo Barcelona" and traces its rise to the 1992 Olympic games and their effect on mass tourism in the city and the presence of the city in global markets ("¿Somos iguales?" 265). Both Balibrea and Edgar Illas, in light of the Barcelona model's limitations and achievements, explore possible elements to "recuperate" and retain from the city's experience of urban transformation (Balibrea, "¿Somos iguales?" 266; Illas 181–217).

4 While the contemporaneous municipal government of Xavier Trias (CiU [Convergència i Unió / Convergence and Union], 2011–15) is criticized for prioritizing large-scale development projects at a time of economic austerity and public need for affordable housing, the proposal and planning of such projects addressed in *Barcelona* happened under previous municipal governments, most notably, that of Joan Clos (PSC [Partit Socialista de Catalunya / Socialist Party of Catalonia], 1997–2006). *Barcelona* also points to a mix of national and regional events and figures that are necessary to understand the political management of the economic crisis, which forced the regional government to pass significant and unpopular cuts in social spending. The crisis exacerbated already extant political and financial tensions between the regional and national government, contributing heavily to the resurgence of Catalan nationalism and calls for independence. The political support of an independence referendum has been variously interpreted as a political reflection of the will of the people and as a move to distract the public's attention from the unpopular austerity measures. The 2012 *Diada* celebration (the national day of Catalonia) and the regional elections of that same year, in which the independence referendum was a major campaign issue, mark important moments in the renewal of calls for independence and are illustrated in *Barcelona* (Rico and Liñeira). *Barcelona*'s inclusion of these references in images that foreground the *chatarreros* (6–7, 55, 78) points to a popular context in which the plight of the *chatarreros* is further overlooked and seems to refocus attention on the lived experience of economic crisis and austerity politics.

5 See a description of the book at ajuntament.barcelona.cat/barcelonallibres/es/publicacions/barcelona-travel-notebook.

6 As Megan Saltzman has mentioned in a conference presentation, ordinances issued around the mid-2000s made it illegal to retrieve discarded waste in public, including from garbage bins (see article 63.2d of the *Ordenanza sobre el Uso de las Vías y los Espacios Públicos de Barcelona*), a fairly unpopular statute that subjects violators to steep fines. Saltzman describes an increase in the frequency of these fines since 2011, during the deepening of the economic crisis.

7 Carrión notably describes the occupied warehouses as "okupadas" [okupied], a term with particular significance in connecting these communities' occupation of industrial spaces with international communities of squatters in the privatized, neoliberal city. *Okupas* and *okupation* with a "k" first appeared around the mid-1980s in Spain to give a coherence and identity of resistance to the act of such occupation (Adell Argilés 25–6), at times linked to anti-war protests, the anti-capitalist and anti-globalization movement, or protests against real estate speculation (Adell Argilés 27; Illas 187). Many of the *okupas* in *Barcelona* share only partial identities with these movements, epitomized in the words of the Gambian/Senegalese *chatarrero* Katim who found himself living as an *okupa* after ten years working in agriculture and construction. In a 2012 interview with *El País*, he notes the irony of his situation as *okupa*, "yo, que pensaba que esto era de *hippies* blancos anticapitalistas" [me, who thought this was for white anti-capitalist hippies] (Blanchar).

8 My use of "unknown" and "urban wild" not only refers to those elements of an urban ecology that are invisibilized, marginalized, or beyond human vision, but also to the multiplicity of ways in which these elements are attached and inextricable to more visible elements. The marginalization and shadow I speak of in this section are products of structures and discourses that conceal relations where they exist, while black ecology and the embracing of the urban wild and the unknown recognize the contingency and incompletion of current visibilities.

9 Sagar's rich colour palette is also an element that separates the aesthetic of *Barcelona* from that of Sacco, in all other matters an obvious influence for Carrión and Sagar. Sacco's work, mostly published in black and white, is arguably bleaker and shares many similar visual elements with the American underground comix tradition of the 1960s and 1970s, such as distorted human features, warped bodies, grotesque faces, and roughly drawn gutters and margins. The images of *Barcelona*, while greatly exaggerating certain features of their subjects, most notably the elongated noses of all of Sagar's subjects, appear less distorted and tend towards realism, employing a colour palette of rich earthen hues, which – even in the text's critique of the touristic co-option of the city's identity – echoes that of its most renowned modernist architect, Gaudí.

10 As formerly discussed, Sousanis's *Unflattening* takes on the multiple ways in which comics escape this two dimensionality and the restrictions of the frame.

11 Megan Saltzman explores these dualities and the particular precarious freedoms of *chatarreros* and other populations in the context of neoliberal Barcelona in her forthcoming book, *Everyday Agency in the Discarded: Cultural Politics in the Public Spaces of Neoliberal Barcelona.*

12 Illas writes about the insufficiency of the much popularized walking-in-the-city strategy of urban critique (easily co-opted for touristic uses) and stresses the utility of also comprehending the city as totality, considering wider networks of political economy and structural forces (13–14).

13 Kheraba also appears in Francesc Torres and Mercedes Álvarez's multimedia project *25%*, shown at the Venice Biennial (2013) and making reference to the contemporaneous 25 per cent of unemployed able-bodied residents of Catalonia, while Núria Güell created a legal framework for *chatarreros* to legally employ themselves on display at the Museo de Arte Contemporáneo de Barcelona (MACBA).

WORKS CITED

Adell Argilés, Ramón. "La vivienda sí preocupa: Ocupantes y okupas." *Libre pensamiento* 54 (Spring 2007): 24–31.

Ahrens, Jörn, and Arno Meteling. *Comics and the City: Urban Space in Print, Picture and Sequence.* Continuum, 2010.

Altimira, Maria. "La Barcelona marginal que persiste: Los chatarreros africanos que malviven ocupando." *VICE*, 28 Sept. 2015, www.vice.com/es_latam/article/qv9dzd/la-barcelona-marginal-que-persiste-los-chatarreros-africanos-que-malviven-ocupando.

Archer, Dan. "Knight Fellowships Talk – Dan Archer." *YouTube*, uploaded by John S. Knight Journalism Fellowships at Stanford, 31 May 2011, www.youtube.com/watch?v=Adjwk91hGWc.

Balibrea, Mari Paz. "¿Somos iguales o somos diferentes? Barcelona entre las ciudades (extracto)" *Desacuerdos 3. Sobre arte, políticas y esfera pública en el Estado español*, edited by Jesús Carillo et al., San Print SL, 2005, 263–6.

– "Urbanism, Culture and the Post-Industrial City: Challenging the 'Barcelona Model.'" *Journal of Spanish Cultural Studies* 2.2 (2001): 187–210. doi.org/10.1080/14636200120085174.

Balzer, Jens. "'Hully Gee, I'm a Hieroglyphe': Mobilizing the Gaze and the Invention of Comics in New York City, 1895." *Comics and the City*, edited by Jörn Ahrens and Arno Meteling, Continuum, 2010, 19–31.

Bauman, Zygmunt. *Wasted Lives: Modernity and its Outcasts*. Polity, 2004.

Benjamin, Walter. *One Way Street*. Harvard UP, 2016.

Blanchar, Clara. "La crisis lleva a centenares de africanos a recoger hierros por las calles de Barcelona." *El País*, 27 Feb. 2012, elpais.com/ccaa/2012/02/25/catalunya/1330198632_698695.html.

Blázquez, Susana. "Los chatarreros más tecnológicos." *El País*, 15 May 2016, elpais.com/economia/2016/05/12/actualidad/1463051214_327090.html.

Brister, Rose. "Sounding the Occupation: Joe Sacco's *Palestine* and the Uses of Graphic Narrative for (Post)Colonial Critique." *ariel: A Review of International English Literature* 45.1–2 (2014):103–29. doi.org/10.1353/ari.2014.0009.

Bryant, Levi R. "Black." *Prismatic Ecology: Ecotheory beyond Green*, edited by Jeffrey Jerome Cohen, U of Minnesota P, 2013, 290–310.

Buell, Lawrence. Foreward. *Prismatic Ecology: Ecotheory beyond Green*, edited by Jeffrey Jerome Cohen, U of Minnesota Press, 2013, ix–xii.

Bukatman, Scott. "Comics and the Critique of Chronophotography, or 'He Never Knew When It Was Coming!'" *Animation* 1.1 (2006): 83–103. doi.org/10.1177/1746847706065843.

Carrión, Jorge, and Sagar Forniés. *Barcelona: Los vagabundos de la chatarra*. 2nd ed., Norma Editorial, 2015.

Chute, Hillary. "Graphic Narrative." *The Routledge Companion to Experimental Literature*, edited by Joe Bray et al., Routledge, 2012, 407–19.

Cohen, Jeffrey Jerome. "Introduction: Ecology's Rainbow." *Prismatic Ecology: Ecotheory beyond Green*, edited by Jeffrey Jerome Cohen, U of Minnesota P, 2013, xv–xxxv.

De Certeau, Michel. "Walking in the City." *The Practice of Everyday Life*, by Michel De Certeau, translated by Steven F. Rendall, 3rd ed., U of California P, 2011, 91–110.

Delgado, Manuel. "La ciudad mentirosa." *Madrid/Barcelona: Literatura y ciudad (1995–2010)*, edited by Jorge Carrión, Iberoamericana Vervuert, 2009, 73–81.

– "El espacio público como representación." Lectures on Urban Regeneration. *Ordem Dos Arquitectos Secção Regional Norte. Porto*, 15 May 2013, www.oasrn.org/pdf_upload/el_espacio_publico.pdf.

Faye, Thomas. "El reportaje gráfico: Una alternativa del compromiso periodístico." *Diablo Texto Digital* 1 (2016): 206–21. doi.org/10.7203/diablotexto.1.8860.

Frahm, Ole. "Every Window Tells a Story: Remarks on the Urbanity of Early Comic Strips." *Comics and the City*, edited by Jörn Ahrens and Arno Meteling, Continuum, 2010, 32–44.

García, Ángeles. "Los desastres de la crisis, escaparate del arte español en Venecia." *El País*, 29 May 2013, elpais.com/cultura/2013/05/24/actualidad/1369404882_019292.html.

Groensteen, Thierry. *The System of Comics*. Translated by Bart Beaty and Nick Nguyen, UP of Mississippi, 2007.
Harvey, David. *The Condition of Postmodernity*. Blackwell, 1989.
Illas, Edgar. *Thinking Barcelona: Ideologies of a Global City*. Liverpool UP, 2012.
"Innovación urbana." *22@ Barcelona*. Ajuntament de Barcelona, 2006. www.22barcelona.com/content/blogcategory/50/281/lang,es/.
Latour, Bruno. "An Attempt at a 'Compositionist Manifesto.'" *New Literary History* 41.3 (2010): 471–90.
Lefebvre, Henri. *The Production of Space*. Translated by Donald Nicholson-Smith, Blackwell, 1991.
López, Helena. "La cooperativa de la chatarra cumple un año." *El Periódico*, 8 July 2016, www.elperiodico.com/es/barcelona/20160708/la-cooperativa-de-chatarreros-del-poblenou-cumple-un-ano-5254979.
López Menacho, Javier. "Los vagabundos de la chatarra, de Jorge Carrión y Sagar." *La Réplica*, 15 May 2015, lareplica.es/los-vagabundos-de-la-chatarra-de-jorge-carrion-y-sagar/.
Marrero Guillamón, Isaac. "¿Del Manchester catalán al Soho Barcelonés? La renovación del barrio del Poble Nou en Barcelona." *Scripta Nova: Revista Electrónica de Geografía y Ciencias Sociales* 7.146(137) (Aug. 2003): 1–20. www.ub.edu/geocrit/sn/sn-146(137).htm.
McCloud, Scott. *Understanding Comics: The Invisible Art*. Tundra, 1993.
Mondelo, Víctor. "Y Barcelona se partió en dos." *El Mundo*, 11 May 2015, www.elmundo.es/cataluna/2015/05/10/554fa9c7ca4741b9648b456c.html.
Montaner, Josep Maria. "The Barcelona Model Reviewed: From the beginning of democracy to now." *Transfer: Journal of Contemporary Culture* 7 (2012): 48–53. llull.cat/IMAGES_175/transfer07-foc03.pdf.
Nixon, Rob. *Slow Violence and the Environmentalism of the Poor*. Harvard UP, 2011.
Norma Editorial. "Barcelona: Los vagabundos de la chatarra de Jorge Carrión y Sagar." *Vimeo*, uploaded by Norma Editorial, 08 May 2015, vimeo.com/127245347.
Priego, Ernesto. "Comics as Research, Comics for Impact: The Case of *Higher Fees, Higher Debts*." *The Comics Grid* 6.1 (2016): 2–15. doi.org/10.16995/cg.101.
Rico, Guillem, and Roberto Liñeira. "Bringing Secessionism into the Mainstream: The 2012 Regional Election in Catalonia." *South European Society and Politics* 19.2 (2014): 257–80. doi.org/10.1080/13608746.2014.910324.
RTVE. "La vida de los buscadores de chatarra de Barcelona en un cómic." *RTVE*, 18 May 2015, www.rtve.es/rtve/20150518/vida-buscadores-chatarra-barcelona-comic/1146980.shtml.

Saltzman, Megan. "Reading the Waste of the Global City: Jorge Carrión and Sagar's *Los vagabundos de la chatarra*." From the seminar "Nomadic Waste & Ecological Materiality in Neoliberal Space (Hispanic Studies)," organized by Megan Saltzman, American Comparative Literature Association Conference, Harvard University, 20 March 2016.

Schack, Todd. "'A Failure of Language': Achieving Layers of Meaning in Graphic Journalism." *Journalism* 15.1 (2014): 109–27. doi.org/10.1177/1464884913486022.

Sousanis, Nick. *Unflattening*. Harvard UP, 2015.

Stafford, Richard Todd. "The Politics of Space in Joe Sacco's Representations of the Appalachian Coalfields." *The Comics of Joe Sacco*, edited by Daniel Worden, UP of Mississippi, 2015, 123–38.

Verdú, Daniel. "Refugiados de la chatarra." *El País*, 24 May 2016, elpais.com/ccaa/2016/05/23/catalunya/1464020438_133524.html.

PART THREE

Comics and Personhood

7 Post-op in the Real World: Cancer and Queer Resistance in Isabel Franc and Susanna Martín's *Alicia en un mundo real* (2011)

EMILY DIFILIPPO

According to its most rational definition, cancer can be understood as a mass of abnormal cells: a thing that can be located, excised, and studied. The human experience of the disease, however, is more phenomenological. It is an assault upon the body that cultivates anxiety and pain, orienting patients in new and unexpected ways towards both their fellow human beings and the environment they inhabit. The focus of this chapter is the 2011 graphic novel *Alicia en un mundo real* [Alice in a Real World],[1] created by well-known lesbian author Isabel Franc and artist Susanna Martín. This novel tells the story of Alicia, the queer protagonist who is diagnosed with breast cancer and undertakes a taxing treatment journey that includes chemotherapy, radiation, and a unilateral mastectomy. The graphic form of this work obliges the reader to behold and consider post-mastectomy embodiment, presenting breast cancer as a force that at once creates disability and erodes and destabilizes gender performance. Through its portrayal of an array of queer characters, *Alicia en un mundo real* presents a flexible concept of gender that transcends the binary model. The protagonist's resistance against norms of gender and female sexuality contrasts with mainstream cancer narratives in which the disease and its treatment often decimate women's sexual desire and sense of attractiveness. This graphic novel, by exposing and eschewing cultural imperatives of compulsory able-bodiedness and compulsory heterosexuality, serves to validate a variety of diverse breast cancer experiences, particularly those that lie outside the realm of the commonplace and the normative.

In order to coherently perform heterosexuality, the subject requires a perfectly able and medically "normal" body. Robert McRuer draws on Adrienne Rich's 1980 essay "Compulsory Heterosexuality and Lesbian Existence" to develop the concept of "compulsory able-bodiedness." Just as Rich proposes compulsory heterosexuality as an ideology that requires women to desire men in return for social acceptance, inclusion, and recognition, compulsory able-bodiedness denotes the culturally imposed necessity for the body and mind to be capable of a certain level of productive activity. McRuer emphasizes that these systems work in the same manner and are actually intertwined, since "the system of compulsory able-bodiedness, which in a sense produces disability, is thoroughly interwoven with the system of compulsory heterosexuality that produces queerness" (2). Compulsory heterosexuality and compulsory able-bodiedness work together to construct an ideal subject who is defined by what he or she is not: queer and/or disabled. In fact, it is this process of negative definition that generates the concepts of queerness and disability. McRuer establishes that a "perfect" performance of heterosexuality relies on able-bodiedness as part of its execution, felt as a sense of culturally approved "wholeness" (12). Furthermore, following Butler's theory of gender performativity, McRuer holds that the heterosexual, able-bodied norm does not represent an achievable goal, but rather an unattainable fiction ever in the process of construction: "able-bodied norms are 'intrinsically impossible to embody' fully," given that "able-bodied status is always temporary, disability being the one identity category that all people will embody if they live long enough" (30). Just as it is impossible to flawlessly perform gender and sexuality, it is also impossible to inhabit a body that conforms completely to models of medical normalcy.

Franc and Martín's graphic novel celebrates bodies that are non-normative in terms of gender presentation, sexual desire, and conformity to standards of medical "normalcy." In this sense, the graphic novel provides a counterexample to McRuer's assertion that, in contemporary cultural production, while "disabled, queer figures no longer embody absolute deviance," they "are still visually and narratively subordinated, and sometimes they are eliminated outright" (18). In fact, in a reversal of the typical situation, it is the heterosexual figure that is narratively subordinated in Franc and Martín's novel, which does not include any openly straight characters and only a very few men. This reversal is an unusually transgressive use of a genre, the comic book, whose production has long been dominated mostly by heterosexual males and whose roster of characters has been dominated by hyper-masculine and uber-athletic superheroes. The powers and achievements of twentieth century female superheroes like Wonder Woman and Mary Marvel pale in comparison to those of their male counterparts; furthermore, these female characters were often defined by their relationships with men (Moix 331). A noted inspiration for feminist and queer women comics artists worldwide is the American author Alison Bechdel, most famous for *Dykes to Watch Out For*, a comic strip launched in 1983 and first published in book form in 1986. The "Bechdel test," named for the author, assesses comics for their degree of female involvement, asking whether texts feature more than one named female character and whether those characters interact with one another discussing topics unrelated to men. To approach comics from this angle challenges the sexist and heterosexist norms of the genre while also drawing attention to counterexamples, which have existed throughout comics history but are often less prevalent.

While comics have been largely male-dominated in Spain as well, they have also served as a vehicle for subversive content, particularly during the years of the Transition, which saw a flourishing of the comics form. Two notable queer comics from this time period are the publications *El Víbora* and *Madriz*. *El Víbora*, published from 1979 to 2005 in Barcelona, was an "underground" comics magazine associated with queer counterculture. Gema Pérez-Sánchez notes that the emergence and popularity of comics featuring LGBT characters and lives, while not necessarily signalling their unequivocal acceptance, was emblematic of the wider cultural shift in Spain: "the representation of these radical themes without censorship serves to confirm that Spain had reached a high level of democracy and freedom, finally breaking away from Francoism" (179). *Madriz*, in fact, was funded by the socialist government, precisely in an effort to cultivate the image of a pluralist, progressive nation that could include diverse expressions of sexuality and non-traditional gender roles. To this end, numerous female artists were employed, thus creating a space for women comics artists that had not previously existed, but that quickly disappeared when government funding for the project was cut (Pérez-Sánchez 171).

In 2013, in response to the lack of recognition for women comics artists in the Spanish state, the Colectivo Autoras de Cómic [Women Comic Artists' Collective] was formed. The Colectivo's dual purpose is to seek greater visibility for contemporary female comics artists, while celebrating women of the past whose work went without due appreciation ("Sobre El Colectivo"). In a documentary produced by the Colectivo Autoras, Susanna Martín describes the comics form as a potential vehicle for activism and protest (*Presentes*). Four years after the publication of *Alicia*, Martín was involved in the coordination of the "Wombastic" project, a graphic response to proposals by the Spanish Partido Popular [People's Party] in 2014 to restrict access to abortions. The artist, who self-identifies as an activist for feminist and lesbian causes, says her comics creations cannot be separated from her political consciousness (*Presentes*). Isabel Franc, who has also published under the pseudonym

Lola Van Guardia, has been qualified as "la autora lésbica de mayor renombre en España" [the most renowned lesbian author in Spain] (Arroyo Pizarro). Her body of work includes a trilogy that follows the lives of a group of urban lesbian friends (*Trilogía de Lola Van Guardia* [Trilogy of Lola Van Guardia]), a collection of queer fables (*Cuentos y fábulas de Lola Van Guardia* [Stories and Fables of Lola Van Guardia]), and a lesbian novela negra (*No me llames cariño* [Don't Call Me Darling]). Her 1992 novel *Entre todas las mujeres* [Among Women], which tells the story of a mystical lesbian relationship between St Bernadette and the Virgin Mary, was a finalist for the Sonrisa Vertical prize for erotic fiction in Spain. *Alicia en un mundo real* is yet another example of Franc's project of producing queer variants of conventional genres: the fable, the detective novel, the hagiography, and, in this case, the graphic novel.

My analysis of *Alicia* begins by considering cancer as an experience of disability in addition to one of life-threatening illness. I am not the first scholar to approach the disease from this perspective: McRuer recalls in his discussion of disability the "army of one-breasted women" from Audre Lorde's *The Cancer Journals*, aligning cancer with conditions more commonly considered disabilities such as blindness, deafness, and compromised mobility (31). Also, Rosemarie Garland-Thomson refers to the post-mastectomy body as having a "disabled breast" (24). After a mastectomy, the absent mammary glands can no longer serve their natural purpose of milk production, thus leaving the body technically disabled in that capacity. In general terms, the post-operative body fails to conform to gendered norms, which prescribe that two healthy symmetrical breasts should be present on the female torso. The post-mastectomy body might thus also be considered disabled in its capacity to attract sexual partners, since breasts are culturally intrinsic to female sexual attractiveness. In a sense, mastectomy can be understood in similar terms to other types of amputation – Lorde also employs this term to describe the surgery (14). Anthropologist S. Lochlann Jain observes that "women's mastectomy scars cite the amputation of gender" (82). Regardless of mastectomy, other markers of gender remain beyond the breast; the reading of gender becomes scrambled in the text of the post-operative body, resulting in a kind of unthinkable, unsettling embodiment.

Generally speaking, amputation of any sort tends to elicit horror in those who perceive or imagine it, as it draws attention to the frailty of the human body. Nancy J. Hirschmann explains that, "as opposed to racism and sexism, which is fear of the not-self, of the different-from-self, fear of the disabled is fear of oneself, a fear of what might happen to one's own body" (141). The spectacle of differently abled embodiment can at once inspire fear of the other and apprehension of disability that may

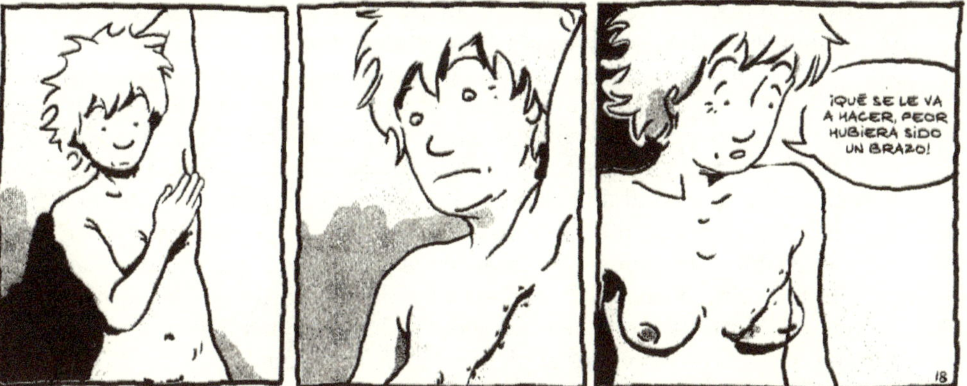

Figure 7.1. "An arm would be worse!" in Franc and Martín's *Alicia en un mundo real* (34).

one day come to reside in the self. Franc and Martín's graphic novel, in its unabashed visual representation of the results of mastectomy, forces the reader to face these fears. Rocco Versaci notes the unique capacity of comics, as a genre, to "challenge" the reader to view the non-normative body "without turning away" (55). A page divided into six panels shows Alicia's reaction to the first view of her post-operative body, as reflected in a mirror. The antique mirror that precedes the sequence recalls the Lewis Carroll trope, evoking his sequel to *Alice in Wonderland*, entitled *Alice through the Looking-Glass*, in which the mirror serves as a portal to a magical world. The antique mirror appears to be symbolic, since Alicia is shown in another panel to be standing nude in a modern bathroom. What she sees is not a fantasy, but is part of the "mundo real" [real world] referenced by the work's title. In the first panel, the protagonist covers her eyes. In the second, when her hands are removed, her eyes appear wide with shock. A close-up image of Alicia's wide eyes offers the reader intimacy with her emotional response, suggesting anxiety, horror, denial, and very possibly sadness at the sight of her one-breasted body. Below this detail is a point of view image of the intact right breast and a surgical incision where the left breast had been. Subsequent panels show Alicia touching the surgical site and considering her new appearance. The ghostly outline of the absent breast is drawn into the page's final panel, and Alicia says: "¡Qué se le va a hacer, peor hubiera sido un brazo!" [What can be done, an arm would be worse!] (Franc and Martín 34). The heroine consoles herself with the fact that it would have been worse to lose a body part with more crucial functionality (figure 7.1).

Undoubtedly, the role of breasts in personal aesthetic and gender performance varies for different individuals. For example, Lochlann Jain, who describes herself as a butch (or "masculine"-identified) lesbian, claims that, throughout her life, "breasts had forced me to live in a sort of social drag" (75). While she admits that she had never wanted "to actually *be* a guy," breasts were also culturally read as feminine in a way that conflicted with her cultivated self-image. In fact, she describes the advantages brought by her post-mastectomy physique, such as an increased ability for yoga, now that breasts were no longer in the way (75). In featuring a cast of characters who are primarily queer women, Franc and Martín's work also presents a flexible portrayal of gender. While the protagonist never explicitly labels herself as a certain "type" of lesbian (that is, "butch" or "marimacha"), she consistently maintains short hair, wears androgynous clothing, and confesses that she has never worn a bra (91). Her friends and female lovers also present an assorted range of gender performances. Some are marked as typically feminine (having long hair, wearing dresses and skirts), while others adopt a decidedly butch style; one woman in particular even describes herself as "masculina performativa, y a mucha honra" [masculine performative, and proud of it] (123). Lochlann Jain emphasizes that breast cancer is an undeniably gendered disease (despite the fact that it also occurs in men, though with far less frequency). She cites Eve Kosofsky Sedgwick, another queer scholar who, upon receiving her breast cancer diagnosis, declared: "*Shit, I am a woman*: I am the person whose wheel of fortune pointed to the illness not only of cancer but of femininity" (Lochlann Jain 85). Despite Sedgwick's (or Lochlann Jain's, or Alicia's) attempts to foster a subversive gender performance, a breast cancer diagnosis signifies the interpellation of the patient as "woman" – a category that is problematically reliant upon the presence of breasts.

While much of the cultural discourse that surrounds breast cancer interpellates the patient as a woman, the effects of the disease and its treatment, including hair loss and mastectomy, bring female embodiment under attack. Gender and sexuality are thus easily destabilized by the body that has been distanced from medical normalcy as the result of disease. Jennifer K. Stuller points out that, in comics, the role of the body's ability in scaffolding coherent, binary gender and heterosexuality (more specifically, male heterosexuality) is particularly evident: "the focus on male bodies in comics emphasizes the power of their physique, whereas the focus on female bodies in comics is meant to titillate the presumed male reader, as well as privilege his interests as consumer and audience" (237). The male body is almost entirely absent from *Alicia*, and the primary stated audience is composed of women who have had breast cancer, rather than heterosexual male consumers. Franc and Martín's graphic novel, in highlighting the body's resilience rather than its physical prowess or aesthetic appeal, questions the validity of able-bodied and gendered norms.

The title page of *Alicia*'s Chapter 9 questions notions of the medically normal human body with a queer interpretation of an easily recognized classical art piece: Leonardo DaVinci's *Vitruvian Man* (Franc and Martín 99). DaVinci's famous original depicts a man circumscribed by a circle and square, with two sets of arms and legs outstretched. As it demonstrates the ideal geometrical proportions of the human body, this image has often been employed by popular culture to denote health. In Martín's version, Alicia's female figure replaces DaVinci's male; she wears a crooked scowl and her mastectomy scar disrupts the Vitruvian symmetry (Franc and Martín 99). Alicia's body can be read here as both queer (female in the expected place of a male) and disabled (female but with only one breast) in its transgressive deviance from the classical archetype. Norms of gendered embodiment are undeniably intertwined with standards of beauty, which are employed to measure the individual's level of sexual attractiveness. Garland-Thomson observes that women with disabilities are stereotyped as asexual, "as generally removed from the sphere of true womanhood and feminine beauty" (30). The breast cancer patient is isolated from what is understood to be the desired female embodiment in a very specific way, given the possibility for losing hair and one or both breasts. One advantage of Alicia's queerness is that she remains mostly unaffected by oppressive female beauty practices, ostensibly because they are intertwined with a feminine performance to which she does not subscribe. While Franc and Martín's protagonist appears comfortable remaining outside the realm of traditional femininity, it is important to recognize that many disabled women, regardless of sexual orientation, are dismissed by mainstream culture as unfeminine, no matter their desire to be or not be so. In her capacity as journalist, Alicia writes an article about shifting beauty standards, presumably in reflection upon societal pressures that commonly affect breast cancer patients. The first two pages of the chapter introduced by the Vitruvian Alicia present the protagonist's article, entitled "¿Quién es la guapa?" [Who Is the Pretty One?], and are accompanied by illustrations of changing beauty standards from prehistoric times to the present day (Franc and Martín 100). In her journalistic voice, Alicia establishes that beauty is a cultural construction: "el conjunto de atributos que determina que una mujer sea guapa está a merced, única y exclusivamente, de los caprichos de la sociedad; según su cultura las tendencias políticas, la clase social o la ideología imperantes, resultará más o menos atractiva" [the set of attributes that determines whether a woman is beautiful is at the unique and exclusive mercy of society's whims; according to her culture's political tendencies, her social class, or dominant ideologies, she will end up being more or less attractive] (100). Panels on subsequent pages reflect upon other beauty standards, although they incur the use of gendered cultural stereotypes, such as the association of bound feet with China: "menos mal que no hemos nacido en China donde a las mujeres se les vendaban los pies" [good thing we weren't born in China where they used to bind women's feet] (101). A reductive parallel is then made between foot binding and the use of high heels, as Alicia's boss is shown wearing stilettos that shoot stars, denoting pain in the visual language of comics. Alicia's feet, however, wearing sneakers, appear comfortably beside those of her boss – Alicia is not the type of woman to be bothered with stilettos. The protagonist's queer nonconformity suggests that she is a person whose sexuality and sense of attractiveness have never relied upon traditional norms of female beauty. On the one hand, Alicia's seemingly self-imposed "banishment from femininity" is beneficial to her, excusing her from the societal pressures of painful or inconvenient beauty practices (Garland-Thomson 24). On the other, the narrative fails to recognize people who, regardless of sexuality, *do* identify with traditional notions of femininity, and who may experience distress upon being banished from the realm of female beauty due to illness or disability.

Despite the novel's attempts to defy traditional norms of female beauty, its portrayal of cancer-related baldness ultimately reinforces negative perceptions of the disease's effects on the body. Many cancer patients – especially women – fear hair loss as a side effect of chemotherapy, both because hair is culturally associated with female beauty and because baldness becomes a marker of cancer itself. Lochlann Jain observes that, "for women, baldness has become a signifier of either illness or aggression" (210). Bald women run the risk of being marginalized as diseased, dismissed as unattractive, or resented for appearing threatening and "unfeminine." The stigma of female hair loss is evident in consumer culture; one such example is found in an advertisement for Danien wigs, aimed at women who have had cancer. The wigs are promoted on the first page of a 2010 issue of *Àgata*, a publication of the Catalan Grup Àgata, an organization based in Barcelona (Alicia's home town) that supports women who have breast cancer. Danien claims to be working to "minimize the aesthetic change" in cancer patients, thus improving their self-esteem: "se et veus bé, et sentiràs millor" [if you look good, you will feel better] (Danien 2). With their wigs, Danien offers to help customers appear more "radiant," and to "hide" their hair loss (2). The idea is that, with the wigs, the customer will be able to disguise the evidence of disease and its toxic treatment, and will thus, in performing wellness, feel "better." The implied message is also that one can spare others the uncomfortable experience of observing cancer, which, following Hirschmann, inspires fear of the potential for cancer in the observer's own body.

Alicia wears her wig in social situations and when she is drawn as a superhero; baldness is used visually to accentuate moments of suffering and vulnerability. At first, the text does approach Alicia's chemotherapy-induced hair loss with black humour. A panel of the protagonist holding a handful of blonde hair, her black T-shirt covered in fallen strands, is juxtaposed with an image of her shedding cat, scratching himself and surrounded by flying hair. In the shower, now completely bald, Alicia smiles and gives a "thumbs up," pointing out her savings on shampoo and haircuts (Franc and Martín 55). When she obtains a ridiculously enormous shaggy wig, a hairdresser friend promises to fix it with a "corte más moderno" [more modern cut], and the wig shop owner assures the client that "le quedará monísima" [it will look beautiful on you] (53). Once it is styled, the wig comes to replicate Alicia's natural hair before chemotherapy, and she is drawn both with and without it throughout the duration of her treatment. It is notable that she often appears without the wig at times of greatest despair, such as when she cries in the office of a homoeopathic doctor, or when she is at home feeling weak and nauseated, or when she faces herself naked in the mirror, emaciated and missing a breast (54, 62, 72). Ultimately, the wig operates in a culturally normative way within the text, as Alicia uses it to disguise her disease in public and in social situations. Other than signalling illness, Lochlann Jain points out that baldness can also be read as queer, since some butch women choose to shave their heads or wear their hair extremely short (46). *Alicia en un mundo real* neither engages with the subversive possibilities for baldness nor does it explore the queer possibilities for wigs, which can be employed (for example, by drag queens) to pursue a camp effect. In the context of Franc and Martín's graphic novel, baldness primarily signifies malady and fragility, rather than boldness, defiance, or queerness.

Notwithstanding its conventional treatment of cancer-related baldness, the work does in fact embrace the aesthetic of the post-mastectomy body. Alicia personally prefers neither to have reconstructive surgery nor to wear breast forms in her clothing, thereby resisting what Garland-Thomson describes as "the sexist assumption that the amputated breast must always pass for the normative, sexualized one either through concealment or prosthetics" (24). Alicia confronts her friends with a particular cultural challenge when she asks them: "¿Tengo que implantarme una prótesis para seguir haciendo topless?" [Do I have to get implants to continue going topless?] (Franc and Martín 92). While the practice of topless sunbathing is common in contemporary Spain, it would be a less common concern for mastectomy patients in other countries such as the United States, where most women cover their breasts in all public spaces. Despite the arguably relaxed environment of the beaches in Cataluña, Alicia wonders whether it is acceptable to be topless in a body that does not conform to cultural expectations of female breasts.

Ultimately, the protagonist chooses precisely to draw attention to her surgical scar by adorning it with a tattoo. Alicia reports feeling empowered when her tattoo artist suggests that she think of body art not as hiding her mastectomy scar, but instead as an adornment that will actually draw people's attention to it: "No tienes que tapar la cicatriz, tienes que decorar la zona. En tu caso, el tatuaje representa un discurso, estás invitando a la gente a que mire tu cuerpo sin apuro" [You don't have to cover the scar, you have to decorate the area. In your case, the tattoo represents a discourse, you are inviting people to look at your body without embarrassment] (Franc and Martín 96). Alicia believes that her tattoo will offer "presence" where previously there was "absence," musing: "El efecto psicológico que produce en la persona que te mira es el de decir: ¿qué tiene esa chica? En lugar de ¿qué le falta?" [The psychological effect that it produces in the person who looks at you is that of saying: what does that girl have? Instead of what is she missing?] (96). Considering the decorated scar in this manner upturns the notion that mastectomy patients are "insufficients dependent on pretense," as suggested by the adoption of prostheses (Lorde 62). By the end of the novel, Alicia does indeed go topless at the beach with her queer friends. Furthermore, a photo of her posing nude, with her mastectomy scar tattoo, is hung in a cancer treatment centre as a courageous inspiration to other patients (Franc and Martín 96). These initiatives exemplify the ways in which the mobilization of "the inevitable failure to approximate the norm" (both heterosexual and able-bodied) can give way to "a newly imagined and newly configured public sphere where full participation is not contingent on an able body" (McRuer 30). The graphic novel, by including these images, can assist the reader in envisioning a greater diversity of desirable post-cancer embodiment, rather than limiting the imagination to images provided by dominant culture, which tend to shy away from the post-operative body.

Of course, not every woman who undergoes a mastectomy will find herself disposed to embrace post-operative embodiment in the same way as Alicia. The page of the Grup Àgata website dedicated to "cirurgia plàstica i reparadora" [plastic and reparative surgery] recognizes the very real detrimental effect that mastectomy can have on one's body image. Two primary responses to the surgery are described: acceptance and the ability to live in peace with the surgery's results; and, alternatively, failure to accept, leading to the choice of mammary reconstruction. According to this perspective, the reason for reconstruction is to preserve quality of life, which is compromised by one's body image after mastectomy. Grup Àgata describes the goal of prosthetics as recreating the appearance of the pre-treatment body, thus improving one's emotional, social, and even professional well-being. While Lorde recognizes that prosthetics offer the mastectomy patient the prospect of escaping "the loneliness of difference," she strongly opposes them because she believes they foster denial and encourage women to hide the experience of illness (3). Unlike other prosthetics, which exist to help the wearer functionally perform certain activities (that is, prosthetic limbs for walking, eyeglasses for seeing, or dentures for chewing), the only function of the prosthetic breast is to make the woman look "normal" in the eyes of others (65). Lorde points out that the implicit message behind the promotion of these products is that the pre-cancer female body is more valuable, and thus must be approximated (42). While the Grup Àgata website recognizes that some women will be able to resist this ideology and accept the appearance of mastectomy, it also acknowledges that reconstructive surgery exists as a support for those who, for whatever reason, wish to continue their lives with two breasts. It is important to recognize that the freedom to openly display one's mastectomy is not available to all; some women may feel compelled to conceal the effects of cancer in order to function in environments that actively discriminate against disability. For example, some may be forced to "masquerade" through the use of prostheses in order to retain opportunities in the workforce. Others may simply prefer to maintain the appearance of symmetrical breasts, for reasons of their own gender performance and personal aesthetic.

While Alicia herself chooses to forego both reconstructive surgery and wearing a prosthesis, the novel avoids being prescriptive in regard to the options facing mastectomy patients. When Alicia visits the "Asociación de Mastectomizadas Insurrectas" [Association of Insurgent Mastectomy Patients], she meets two other women who have undergone mastectomies and taken subsequent action different from her own. In a panel with the caption "Somos muchas y existen soluciones

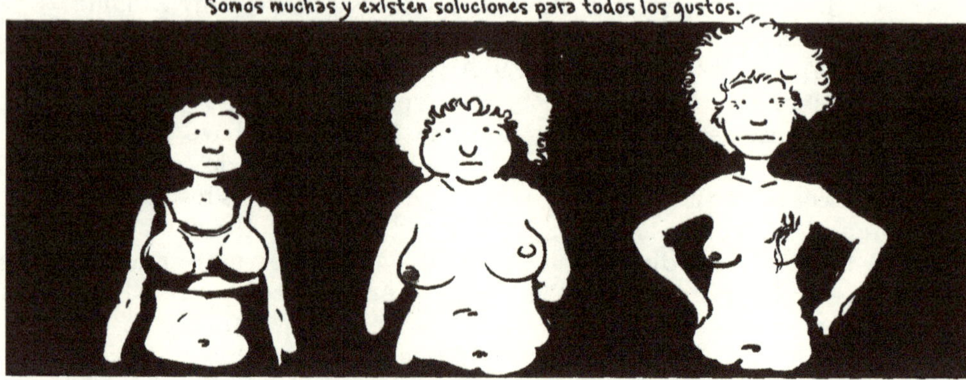

Figure 7.2. Diverse solutions for post-mastectomy in Franc and Martín's *Alicia en un mundo real* (113).

para todos los gustos" [We are many and there are solutions for all tastes], three women display distinct options for the mastectomy patient (figure 7.2): one wears a bra with breast forms; another has had reconstructive surgery and appears to have two breasts (even though they are not identical); and, finally, Alicia displays her mastectomy scar tattoo (Franc and Martín 113).

Personally, Lorde chose to embrace her post-mastectomy body as the physical manifestation of her cancer experience, which she wanted in order to orient herself towards community. "It is that very difference which I wish to affirm," she wrote, "because I have lived it, and survived it, and wish to share that strength with other women" (62). The fellowship among *Alicia*'s Mastectomizadas Insurrectas proves that prosthetics and reconstructive surgery do not have to stand in the way of feminist community. Granted, three decades had passed between the publication of *The Cancer Journals* and of *Alicia*, during which time cultural attitudes towards breast cancer have shifted, helping to dissipate the silence and shame that separated women from one another's experience.

In and of itself, Franc and Martín's graphic novel forms part of an effort to foster connection with those who have shared the experience of breast cancer. In the introduction, Franc recognizes the continued stigma associated with cancer, and offers her and Martín's work as a source of humour to those whose lives it has touched (5). She explains that Alicia's story is based on her own, and hopes that her readers will identify in some way with the character. In this sense, the novel functions as a kind of survivor testimony, since the reader knows that the author went on to live beyond her diagnosis and treatment. Within the narrative itself, it is also clear from the beginning that the protagonist will survive; the primary narrative is framed by the story of Alicia, who is a journalist writing a "novel" about the disease, as requested by her boss. She establishes in the prologue that she is writing from the tropical tranquillity of Mexico, and appears in various panels throughout the book working at her laptop with the beach in the background. In these drawings, Alicia appears healthy, thus suggesting that she is recalling her story from the safe space of a cancer-free present. In reality, when the word "cancer" is spoken, it often conjures the spectre of death, considering that the disease's various forms claim so many lives. In 2012, the year after Franc and Martín's book was published, 102,762 Spaniards died of cancer, and breast cancer accounted for 15.5 per cent of those deaths (Sociedad 14, 15). Within the narrative, however, cancer is aligned more with disability than with life-threatening illness. When Alicia meets with her breast surgeon, he prepares her for the prospect of losing time and hair, but not life itself. In matching panels numbered one through three, the male surgeon dictates to his patient what the experience of cancer will entail. First, he informs her: "Tienes una enfermedad que antes era mortal" [You have a disease that, before, was fatal], while making a gesture of cutting the throat (Franc and Martín 22). The word "antes" [before] implies that, while in the past Alicia's diagnosis would have signified a likely death, in the present day it does not typically carry this threat. Granted, details of her cancer (what stage, the presence of aggressive cancer cells, and so on) are not disclosed. On the one hand, this lack of specificity allows for a wider range of readers to identify with the narrative. On the other, the narrative does not account for worse prognoses.

In the second panel, the surgeon points his finger and warns: "Perderás un año de tu vida" [You will lose a year of your life] (Franc and Martín 22). Rather than losing her life, the patient should expect to lose only a year. Colloquially, the idea of "losing a year of one's life" implies wasting time, in the sense of being unproductive. The surgeon is thus preparing Alicia for a period of disability, in which her career will be put on hold. The work meditates visually on what this time loss means, in the context of the capitalist economy. Chapter 1 is announced with a panel whose caption reads, in bold black letters, "¿Quién dijo planes?" [Who said plans?] (17). Alicia's calendar (a plain book labelled "Agenda") is shown on her desk, amidst other office supplies. As an object, the calendar acts as the guiding organization of her busy professional life as a journalist. The title page for Chapter 12 then visually

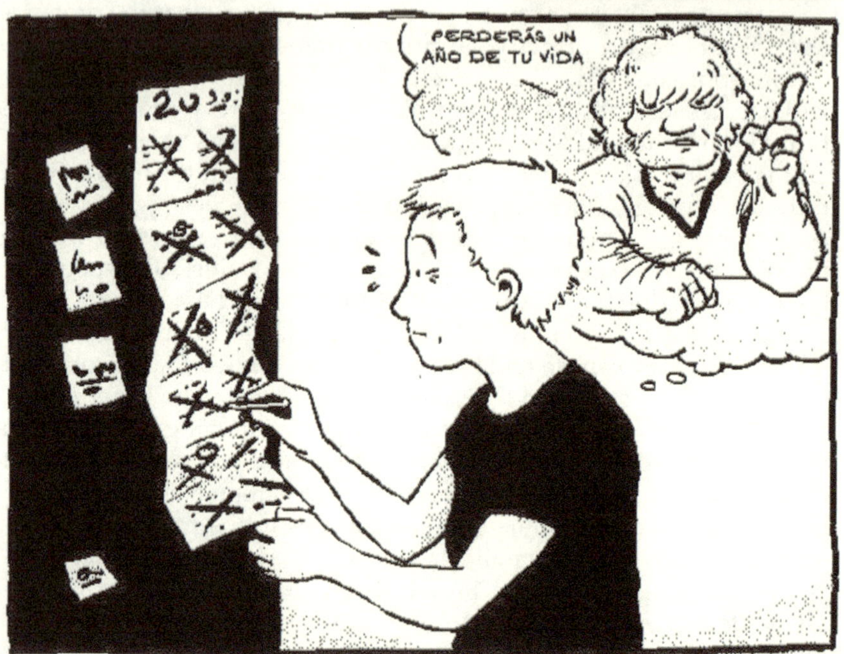

Figure 7.3. A lost year in Franc and Martín's *Alicia en un mundo real* (127).

reflects Chapter 1: a panel shows Alicia crossing off twelve months of a hanging calendar, while a caption reads, "¿Quién dijo agenda?" [Who said agenda?] (127). In a thought bubble, she sees the surgeon, prophetically proclaiming "Perderás un año de tu vida." This image proves the surgeon was right, at least in terms of capitalist notions of gain and loss: Alicia's agenda has been erased, replaced by visual evidence that she has "lost" twelve months to cancer treatment (figure 7.3).

The power dynamics of medicine are evident in the exchange between the protagonist and her surgeon. In the final panel of their conversation, the surgeon prepares Alicia for a change in appearance as he commands her to "ponte peluca" [put on a wig], while indicating his own full head of curly hair (Franc and Martín 22). The surgeon's own abundance of hair separates him from the fate of the patient, as he strongly suggests the normalizing practice of wearing a wig to disguise chemotherapy-related hair loss. The medical establishment has the capacity to unmoor the patient's very identity, as "white coat and hospital gown divide those who define the bureaucratic and medical realm of illness from the one who necessarily, if perhaps not wholly, comes to be defined by it ... [A]s doctors and/or patients, we all play roles in this script" (Lochlann Jain 15). In these images, the surgeon is drawn by himself in the centre of the page, looking directly at the reader as he would at Alicia, rather than having the two figures both drawn in the same panel and appearing to converse with one another. Her reaction appears below his directives in three corresponding panels. At first, Alicia's figure is small, about two-thirds the size of the surgeon, against a black background, mouth agape in fear. The second and third panels show her face morphing into Edvard Munch's easily recognizable painting *The Scream*. No words accompany these panels; Alicia's anxiety is represented only visually. The progression of the protagonist's transformation from a scared patient into the distorted anguish of *The Scream* evidences the power wielded by the surgeon and his unemotional predictions of her immediate future.

This series of panels manages to capture the emotional transformation of cancer, which is also described on Grup Àgata's website: "L'impacte de la malaltia fa que la persona 'es desdibuixi' i deixi de sentir-se 'normal,' tot i mantenir la seva essència intacta" [The impact of the illness causes a person to "blur" and to stop feeling "normal," even while maintaining their essence intact] (Grup Àgata). In these panels, Alicia is literally "undrawn," becoming blurred and diminished, her image twisted from that of a "normal" woman to a screaming expressionist figure. Versaci emphasizes that serial images incorporated by the graphic form, particularly in the case of memoir, lend themselves well to the representation of "the complicated and shifting nature of the self" (49). Distinct images contained within frames allow for different facets of the character to be read coherently in the same text. In addition (and in contrast) to her appearance as *The Scream*, Alicia is also portrayed at certain points in the work as a superhero. In the cover art, she appears wearing a black cape, gloves, and a yellow suit emblazoned with a radiation symbol. While patients are often said to "battle" cancer, in Franc and Martín's graphic novel Alicia is shown to battle the challenges of everyday life, rather than the disease itself. On the title page of Chapter 6, which is entitled "Lo cotidiano después de la catástrofe," [The Everyday After the Catastrophe], Alicia appears in a wrestling ring, wearing a costume that can be associated at once with wrestling (it includes gloves and laced-up boots) and with a superhero aesthetic (it includes a cape) (71). She is facing off with a personified planet Earth, suggesting battle between the cancer patient and the world in which they live.

The graphic novel presents the built environment and the requirements of remunerated labour as forces with which Alicia must do "battle." Peter Coogan discusses the role of genre fiction in representing and normalizing cultural values, often through the dramatized conflict between hero and villain (207). In these images, it is not exactly cancer but the challenges of day-to-day survival in the modern world, along with the neoliberal demands of independent wage-earning, that are personified as the enemy to the recovering cancer patient. The chapter's first panel shows the heroine looking dejected, facing her reflection with its mastectomy scar and bald head. The caption reads: "Superado el tifón, había que recolocarse en el mundo y, entonces, me di cuenta de que mi cuerpo se había convertido en un gran desconocido" [Having overcome the typhoon, it was necessary to be repositioned in the world and, then, I realized that my body had become a complete stranger] (Franc and Martín 72). The body is here understood as another entity that can be known or unknown to the subject who inhabits it. This phenomenon signals the great shift in embodiment brought on not only by the visual difference of the mastectomy and hair loss but also by diminishing ability, as Alicia's body can no longer do the things it once did. In the introduction, Franc explains the connection between her use of the graphic form and the acknowledged change in ability brought on by cancer treatment. She expresses the hope that using images will make the narrative more easily consumable for potential readers who are, themselves, undergoing treatment for cancer: "Cuando se está en tratamiento de quimioterapia se tiene mucho más tiempo para leer, pero pocas energías para hacerlo, y entrar en la historia a través de la imagen siempre ayuda" [When one is under chemotherapy one has much more time to read, but less energy to do it, and getting into a story through images always helps] (Franc and Martín 5). In this case, the choice of the graphic form takes accessibility into consideration, recognizing that the cancer patient will experience reduced energy levels.

The protagonist's body, which has been altered by surgery and a debilitating regime of chemotherapy and radiation, is now situated in a new relationship to the physical environment. In addition to keeping track of a complex assortment of medications, Alicia also has to protect the site of her surgery while performing everyday activities such as getting dressed or carrying groceries. Her low energy levels affect both her social and professional life. When she returns to her job as a journalist, she faces the challenge of a travel assignment. A series of panels shows her unexpectedly struggling to navigate a train station: "No contaba con la serie de obstáculos que me salieron al paso. En mi nueva situación los desplazamientos con equipaje requerían unas estrategias que antes ni se consideraban" [I didn't count on the series of obstacles that came my way. In my new situation, moving around with luggage required strategies that before had never been considered] (Franc and Martín 76). She encounters non-working elevators and searches for an accessible train door, all the while grappling with two large suitcases. These images correlate with the social model of disability, which holds that the source of impairment is found in society and its spaces, which are designed for the able-bodied majority. Nonetheless, Alicia devises "strategies" for compensating, demonstrating resilience and ingenuity. The protagonist alone carries graphic weight in these panels; even the herringbone print of her coat is distinguishable. In contrast, other travellers are mere outlines, partial sketches that disappear into the background. This technique is a strategy often employed in the graphic novel, as Versaci points out that differences in the style in which figures are drawn can serve to emphasize difference between the characters (52). Alicia's apparent isolation from the able-bodied majority emphasizes her distinct relationship to travel. After two facing pages of panels portraying her difficulties catching a train to Donostia, Alicia thinks: "Creo que mi próximo reportaje será sobre la supresión de barreras aquitectónicas" [I think my next report will be about the removal of architectural barriers] (Franc and Martín 77). Since the graphic novel represents Alicia's telling of her story, making architectural barriers visible precisely forms part of the book's project. Because inaccessible public spaces are not a unique challenge to breast cancer, but rather affect people with many kinds of disabilities, this sequence aligns Alicia's story with a wider range of impairment.

Another challenge Alicia faces is the reorientation to sex and romantic relationships after cancer. Lochlann Jain acknowledges that one outcome of the mastectomy is the "undermining" of sexuality – not only in terms of the patient's level of physical attractiveness, but also in their ability to experience pleasure (82). The breast is not merely functional as a mammalian source of nutrition for offspring; neither is it purely aesthetic and exciting to the woman's sex partner. Lorde reminds her readers of the breast's importance also as a pleasure point for the woman herself (43, 79). Franc and Martín's portrayal of sex after cancer is optimistic but realistic: while Alicia resists the truncation of her sexuality due to mastectomy, her experiences are not exclusively positive. In Alicia's words, with her various pains, medications, and complications from her recent treatment, "follar es complicado" [fucking is complicated] (84). Her first attempt at sex after cancer, with a critical and impatient partner, ends in frustration. The partner, who is drawn in three out of four panels seated on the edge of the bed with her back towards Alicia, throws up a hand and declares: "Así no hay forma de correrse" [It's impossible to come like this] (84). Alicia, in the background, covers herself with sheets, a tear falling from one eye. The repeated image of the partner, with her dishevelled hair and angry facial expression, physically refusing connection with Alicia, highlights the lack of empathy met by some cancer patients. In this scenario, the graphic novel at once acknowledges the protagonist's post-cancer embarrassment and lack of sexual pleasure, while also emphasizing the problematic behaviour of the non-accommodating partner.

While the text shares other negative sexual experiences of women who have had breast cancer, they all happen to occur with men. One woman crosses her arms over her chest, forbidding her male partner to touch her. Another cries into her hands while her husband, who himself is drawn as an overweight man with thinning hair, accuses her of being an "incomplete woman" (Franc and Martín 97). Because these are the only examples of heterosexual relationships that appear in the novel, the text seems to imply that the outlook is bleak for the sexuality of women who have had cancer and are sexually attracted to men. Alicia, however, does eventually find a loving partner and explains that an unconventional approach is key to recuperating an enjoyable sex life: "A veces, ni siquiera es necesario follar en sentido estricto. Con un poco de complicidad y comprensión por ambas partes, hasta resulta sencillo" [Sometimes, it's not even necessary to fuck in the strict sense. With a little mutual understanding, it's very simple.] (119). The idea of questioning the necessity to "fuck in a strict sense" is essentially queer, considering that dominant notions of sexual intercourse are undeniably heteronormative. This idea, along with the narrative's failure to present a positive experience of post-cancer sexuality in a traditional heterosexual context, suggests that queerness – in this sense, non-normative sexual activity – is key to a satisfying sex life after illness alters the body.

Franc and Martín's graphic novel also uses superhero imagery to represent cancer's transformation of Alicia's body and persona. The protagonist is drawn as a cape-wearing superhero on the book's cover, with her eyes wide, eyebrows raised in an expression of ambivalent fear, surprise, or both. She is holding her remaining breast, the other's absence evident. Her cat sidekick, who also appears throughout the novel, leans against her. The first superhero image within the text itself appears again at the end of Chapter 4, which is actually entitled "No soy una heroína" [I Am Not a Heroine]. On the title page of the

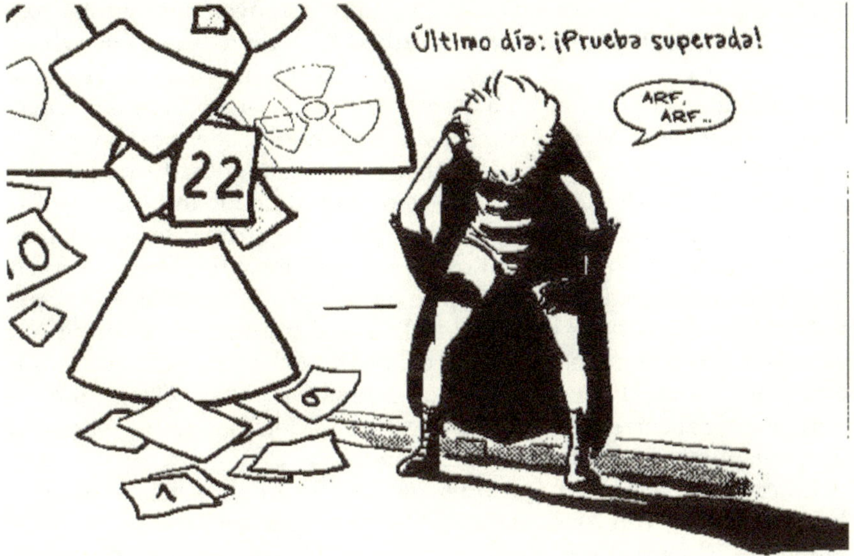

Figure 7.4. "Challenge complete!" in Franc and Martín's *Alicia en un mundo real* (57).

chapter, Alicia does not appear heroic; instead, her face is placed at the extreme left edge of the panel, she wears a cap pulled low, covering her hairless head, and looks out a window at what might be the ocean. The first page of the chapter is without words; it shows six panels of Alicia receiving chemotherapy treatment. On the facing page, one large panel appears to show another angle of the image that opened the chapter: Alicia gazes out the window of the treatment centre, her hand touching the glass. The windowpane can perhaps be understood as a barrier between the protagonist and the cancer-free world.

Once she finishes with chemotherapy, Alicia passes through the "recta final" or "last stage" of her journey, which is that of radiation (Franc and Martín 57). Loose calendar pages float among radiation symbols to demonstrate the passage of radiation time: "No es tan duro, pero se te hace interminable" [It's not that tough, but it seems endless] (57). Finally, Alicia appears in full body, not contained within a frame but as a lone figure in the bottom right corner of the page, dressed in her superhero costume, hunched over (figure 7.4). A speech bubble contains the sounds "Arf, arf," indicating gagging, coughing, or exhaustion, and a caption announces: "Último día: ¡prueba superada!" [The last day: challenge complete!]. (57).

Cancer is here presented as a kind of endurance test or challenge through which the superhero figure must pass in order to prove herself worthy of her powers of survival. In addition to overcoming this challenge, radiation therapy has transformed Alicia into a heroine whose superpower is the ability to survive life-threatening disease. The idea that radiation should morph a mere mortal into a superhero is a reflection of early 1960s Marvel comics: a high school student becomes Spiderman when bitten by a radioactive spider; a scientist turns into the Incredible Hulk after contact with gamma radiation; and participants in an experimental space flight are exposed to cosmic rays and turn into the Fantastic Four. Robin Rosenberg explains it this way: "At their best, superhero origin stories inspire us and provide models of coping with adversity, finding meaning in loss and trauma, discovering our strengths and using them for good purpose. (Wearing a cape or tights is optional)." Beyond generating a non-normative physical body, the experience of cancer and its treatment can be understood to have imbued the protagonist with superhuman qualities.

Chapter 4's title ("No soy una heroína") signals Alicia's ambivalence about her role as superhero. She at once demonstrates physical vulnerability and the capacity to overcome extraordinary obstacles. Fear and anxiety, nonetheless, are certainly present in her narrative. These emotions are evident in the protagonist's facial expression on the book's very cover, and continue to manifest themselves in the verbal and graphic aspects of the text throughout. That a cancer patient should experience fear is not surprising, even though it is an emotion not traditionally associated with superheroism. This chapter can also be read as a questioning of the "sadcrip/supercrip" dichotomy that Charles A. Riley discusses in the context of film and media. Riley explains that "the 'sadcrip-supercrip'" are "two sides of the same coin – one is dependent on caregivers while the other is a miraculous triumph of medical progress teamed with willpower" (4). Both dimensions of Alicia's character are portrayed visually: the "sad," sick person who is weak and frightened, and the literal superhero in full costume. The simultaneous presence of these images in the graphic novel establishes them both as valid aspects of the experience of illness and disability, rather than privileging one over the other. In this way, Franc and Martín's text acknowledges the stark medical and physiological reality of cancer, while at the same time offering the optimistic fantasy of the superhero.

The role of superhero in this work is furthermore intertwined with the interpellation of the cancer survivor. When Alicia is pronounced cancer-free, she appears once again as a superhero, once again in the bottom right corner of the page, not enclosed by a frame. Here, she holds her arms up in victory like the winner of a wrestling match, accompanied by a bow tie–wearing referee. This "victory" over cancer interpellates Alicia into the role of "survivor," even though this word is absent from the text and is more prevalent in the English-language discourse surrounding cancer. Lochlann Jain notes that the "survivor" identity is built upon statistics that stand in for the invisible presence of those who did not survive (31). This interpellation invites survivors to feel triumphant for finding themselves on the desirable side of the statistics, rather than identifying with those fellow cancer patients who lost their lives to the disease (31). McRuer uses the term "compulsory individualism" to describe the stark division between persons with disability and their caretakers, between the sick and the well (49). This individualism is a product of neoliberal policy, which, through the deregulated flow of capital and the elimination or privatization of social services (including healthcare), promotes "independence" as the ideal state of achieved human progress. The survivor, then, can be understood as a victorious individual, burdened neither by the shadows of exhausted caretakers nor by the cancer battle's "losers." This interpellation thus promotes individualism, insulating the survivor by erasing the dead.

Idealized neoliberal "independence" is realized by the labourer who is also a consumer, and who lives independently by the fruits of their own labour and the subsequent accumulation of capital. For some individuals, however, independence and survival (or even comfort and happiness) are incompatible. Neoliberal narratives also frame disability and illness as the private responsibility of the family, assuming traditional, heteronormative kinship structures. In *Alicia en un mundo real*, queer notions of community provide an alternative support system to the individual facing health-related challenges. Alicia is cared for by a support network of queer women, who include past and present lovers as well as friends, co-workers, and neighbours; none of her biological family members ever appear, however. The work can thus be said to gesture towards a model of alternative, non-heteronormative family that is able to provide support for this doubly marginalized queer-disabled subject.

Absent from the narrative, however, are financial concerns; the reader knows from the beginning that Alicia will survive her disease to enjoy a trip to the beaches of Mexico. Of course, as a Spanish citizen, she would have access to public healthcare; in contrast, in the United States, an estimated 60 per cent of personal bankruptcies are attributed to "the catastrophic financial burden of illness" (Lochlann Jain 11). Ironically, cancer actually brings Alicia profit in the form of the memoir she writes: presumably, the graphic novel in the reader's hands. Her

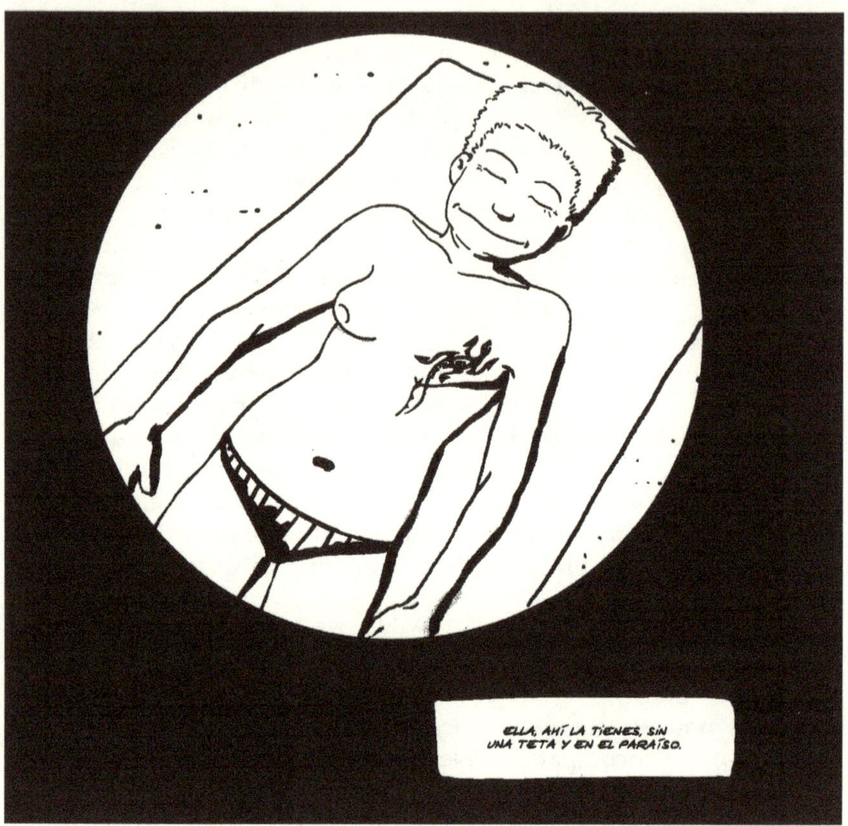

Figure 7.5. "Without a tit and in paradise" in Franc and Martín's *Alicia en un mundo real* (137).

boss repeatedly pressures her into the project, and is even drawn at one point with Euro signs for eyes, drooling as she entreats Alicia to write a dramatic memoir that will sell copies: "Que sea muy desgarrada, muy dramática, que vende más" [Make it terribly dramatic, which sells more] (Franc and Martín 94). This image suggests a critique of those who seek to profit from sensational narratives, rather than delving into the nuance and complexity of illness and disability. Alicia's book project is the reason she decides to go to Mexico – in order to write in luxurious solitude. Not only does she survive cancer, but she finds herself, as described in the epilogue, "sin una teta y en el paraíso" [without a tit and in paradise] (137; figure 7.5).

Alicia retains her position as a journalist throughout her treatment and never seems concerned about the destruction of her career. A series of panels in which she argues with her boss about her decreased productivity is introduced by the observation: "Tampoco es fácil volver a la vorágine laboral" [It's not easy to get back to the daily grind either] (Franc and Martín 111). In the first panel, Alicia leans back in an armchair, insisting that her boss understand she is unable to work as much as before: "Es que no puedo asumir tanto trabajo, Maru, entiéndelo. No tengo la misma energía que antes" [I can't take on so much work, Maru, please understand. I don't have as much energy as before] (111). Granted, in an ideal world, those who have disabilities should have access to accommodations in the workplace. In practice, however, in a profit-driven economy, many workers are not in a position to insist that their boss recognize their limitations. Lochlann Jain speaks of the hardship that young adults experience when they have to unexpectedly "drop out" of the workforce due to cancer at a moment that is culturally assumed to be their most productive in terms of generating income and saving for retirement (52). Given this context, the flexibility shown in Franc and Martín's portrayal of the labour force is especially idealistic. Ultimately, this text's representation of the cancer patient's financial and professional prognosis offers a kind of fantastic, best-case scenario, rather than engaging with less fortunate outcomes.

Despite the pressing issues that remain outside the scope of *Alicia in un mundo real*, its unconventional cancer narrative suggests empowerment through alternative ways of being to those affected by the disease. Like the original Alice in Lewis Carroll's 1865 novel *Alice in Wonderland*, Franc and Martín's Alicia finds herself on an absurd journey that shatters her accustomed reality. Both protagonists must travel through a space of darkness and danger in which they are both altered physically by "magical" substances and threatened with the loss of body parts and of their very lives. In *Alicia*'s prologue, a panel shows the wing of a plane advancing down a runway, with a caption that explains: "Cada vida es un viaje y su itinerario no es siempre el deseado" [Every life is a voyage and its itinerary is not always the one that is desired] (Franc and Martín 9). Alicia's story is perhaps idealistic, but it is also optimistic. Versaci speaks of the "escapism" of the comic book, designed to transport the reader into an alternative realm (4–5). In Alicia's world, the woman who is diagnosed with breast cancer is condemned neither to death nor to a sexless existence. To share her journey is to accept an invitation to participate in the "madness" of questioning heteronormative promises of happiness and fictions of able-bodied wholeness.

NOTE

1 All translations from Spanish to English and Catalan to English are by E. DiFilippo.

WORKS CITED

Arroyo Pizarro, Yolanda. "Yolanda Arroyo Pizarro entrevista a Isabel Franc." *Aurora Boreal*, www.auroraboreal.net/actualidad/entrevistas/1493-yolanda-arroyo-pizarro-entrevista-a-isabel-franc. Accessed 29 Apr. 2017.

Coogan, Peter. "Reconstructing the Superhero in *All-Star Superman*." *Critical Approaches to Comics: Theories and Methods*, edited by Matthew J. Smith and Randy Duncan, Routledge, 2012, 203–20.

Danien. Advertisement. *Revista Grup Àgata* 28 (2010): 2. www.grupagata.org/images/revistes/28_AGATA_web.pdf.

Franc, Isabel, and Susanna Martín. *Alicia en un mundo real*. Norma Editorial, 2011.

Garland-Thomson, Rosemarie. "Integrating Disability, Transforming Feminist Theory." *Feminist Disability Studies*, edited by Kim Q. Hall, Indiana UP, 2011, 13–47.

Grup Àgata. Grup Àgata: Associació Catalana de Dones Afectades de Càncer de Mama, www.grupagata.org. Accessed 7 Apr. 2017.

Hirschmann, Nancy J. "Queer/Fear: Disability, Sexuality, and The Other." *Journal of Medical Humanities* 34.2 (2013): 139–47. doi.org/10.1007/s10912-013-9208-x.

Lochlann Jain, S. *Malignant: How Cancer Becomes Us*. U of California P, 2013.

Lorde, Audre. *The Cancer Journals*. 1980. Special ed., Aunt Lute, 1997.

McRuer, Robert. *Crip Theory: Cultural Signs of Queerness and Disability*. New York UP, 2006.

Moix, Terenci. *Historia social del cómic*. Brugera, 2007.

Pérez-Sánchez, Gema. *Queer Transitions in Contemporary Spanish Culture*. SUNY Press, 2007.

Presentes: Autoras de tebeo de ayer y hoy. Autoras de Cómic, AECID, 2016, vimeo.com/206609128.

Riley, Charles A. *Disability and the Media: Prescriptions for Change*. UP of New England, 2005.

Rosenberg, Robin. "The Psychology behind Superhero Origin Stories." *Smithsonian Magazine*, Feb. 2013, www.smithsonianmag.com/arts-culture/the-psychology-behind-superhero-origin-stories-4015776/.

"Sobre el Colectivo Autoras de Cómic." *Autoras de Cómic*, asociacionautoras.blogspot.com/p/sobre-la-asociacion.html. Accessed 29 Apr. 2017.

Sociedad Española de Oncología Médica (SEOM). *Las cifras del cáncer en España 2018*. SEOM, 2018, seom.org/seomcms/images/stories/recursos/Las_Cifras_del_cancer_en_Espana2018.pdf.

Stuller, Jennifer K. "Second-wave Feminism in the Pages of *Lois Lane*." *Critical Approaches to Comics: Theories and Methods*, edited by Matthew J. Smith and Randy Duncan, Routledge, 2012, 235–51.

Versaci, Rocco. *This Book Contains Graphic Language: Comics as Literature*. Continuum, 2012.

8 How to Explain Comics to a Dead Hare: Intertextuality and Crisis in Rosana Antolí's Neo-surrealist Graphic Novel *Pareidolia* (2014)

EDUARDO LEDESMA

Introduction: *Pareidolia's* Radical Intertextuality as Critique

The 2014 self-referential graphic novel *Pareidolia*, by Rosana Antolí (born in Alcoy, Spain, in 1981), places readers within the subject position of an unravelling consciousness as witnesses to the protagonist's descent into the irrational.[1] The character's delusions are triggered by pareidolia, the tendency – acute in those who suffer from cognitive disorders (dementia, stroke, schizophrenia) – to recognize human shapes within random patterns. The unnamed protagonist (who stands in for the author) experiences visual and auditory pareidolia as wall stains, cracks, and rumpled clothing transform into characters with whom she interacts.[2] These imaginary interlocutors include a former lover, herself as a child, and assorted pop icons, including late glam rocker and master of transformation David Bowie (1947–2016), musician and cultural critic Jarvis Cocker (1963–), enigmatic performance artist Bas Jan Ader (1942–75), self-proclaimed mystic and Zen popularizer Alan Watts (1915–73), conceptual artist Joseph Beuys (1921–86), and even Beuys's dead hare, a reference to his neo-surrealist performance *How to Explain Pictures to a Dead Hare* (1965).

Patently, this graphic novel's most salient device is its radical intertextuality, as it draws on an eclectic mix of cultural referents to investigate aesthetic and existential questions, and also to reflect on contemporary issues.[3] This essay will focus on tracing and analysing intertextuality's role(s) in *Pareidolia*, including how the device functions to indirectly reference Spain's current socioeconomic crisis. Identifying intertexts will serve both to unravel Antolí's web of American and European cultural referents and, more importantly, to explicate the motives that move her to redeploy them. More critically, by tracing the novel's intertexts of

American and European cultural icons of rebelliousness from the sixties and seventies, this essay seeks to understand whether Antolí redirects that spirit of revolt against today's crisis or if this network of referents functions as a mere pastiche of high and pop culture.[4] I will argue the former, suggesting that, although Antolí displays a sceptical attitude towards dogmatism and overt political stances, refusing to convert her graphic novel into an outright political tract, her politics come by way of a philosophical reflection on a state of crisis that is rooted in broader socioeconomic and existential problems. Thus, her novel tackles multiple philosophical questions, such as the mythification of suicide in Western culture, art's potential to heal humanity's alienation, the search for (artistic) authenticity, and the possibility for transcendence through art. Definitive solutions are not provided, but these (timeless) questions are implicitly linked to more prosaic contemporary issues, such as the crisis in Spain, through the choice of intertexts. Moreover, following the Surrealists, Dadaists, and Neo-Dadaists' embrace of contingency and irrationality, *Pareidolia* presents the anarchic potential of madness, drug use, musical trance, and mystical experience, not as a misperception of reality but as an expansion of consciousness that can lead to a more present reality and, potentially, may show a way out of the current state of crisis.

In that sense, *Pareidolia* is not only about one individual's confrontation with larger philosophical questions, but also about how these philosophical issues are produced by an ever-mounting consumerism and alienating market logic. Antolí declares her commitment to broaching the political via the aesthetic in a press release for a June 2016 exhibition at Barcelona's *Fundació Joan Miró*: "My focus of attention lies in the intersection between art, politics and everyday life" (Espai 13). Underlying the novel's existential and aesthetic preoccupations are implicit political concerns. Published in 2014, *Pareidolia* is born out of a Spanish socioeconomic crisis characterized by youth unemployment, austerity, social inequality, and a defunding of the arts, leading to widespread generational anxiety. Although the graphic novel's protagonist at first turns away from dealing with Spain's crisis by escaping into a kind of "madness" or fantasy world, there are frequent reminders of the economic situation throughout, and, finally, in the last panel she returns to squarely face that reality. The key to understanding both the character's progression and the novel itself is through its intertextuality.

Despite the episodic nature of its eight chapters (with independently themed, bilingual titles: "La presentación" [The Presentation], "The Crazynest," "The Simplification," "La regresión" [The Regression], "Las caídas" [The Falls], "The Absence," "La impersonation," "The

Final Dance"), *Pareidolia* has a continuous narrative as a psychological bildungsroman charting the protagonist's metamorphosis towards greater self-awareness. Intertexts, in addition to motivating existential questions, are used to establish autobiographical references and suggest alternatives out of the crisis (some, like the notion of suicide, will be discarded; others, such as embracing a collective spirit, will be endorsed).

The novel opens with the lyrics of Bowie's 1971 "Changes," a song that signifies life's impermanence and gestures to the incessant mutability of subjectivity (the protagonist's, Antolí's, Bowie's). The first text box displays the verse "I still don't know what I was waiting for and my time was running wild," signalling the protagonist's disorientation and the "changes" she will undergo as the novel progresses. This disorientation is further emphasized by the way in which *Pareidolia* departs, in its opening panels, from the standard features of the graphic novel as a medium. Here, the grid layout with multiple panels and the usual white gutters are replaced by two large, full-page panels depicting a bedroom, set against a black, rather than white, gutter; even the text boxes are inverted, utilizing a black background with white lettering. These dark colours and the departure from the tabular layout are motivated by the need to echo the sense of psychological angst and crisis present in the narrative and by the desire to emphasize the importance of flux, of change, of irregularity so that "the size of the images, their distribution, the general pace of the page, all must come to support the narration" (Peeters, par. 19).

The protagonist's changes are triggered by an existential crisis, by artistic self-doubt, and by her unstable psyche, set against a backdrop of national instability. When the character's subjectivity dissolves into an insubstantial world of abstract self-reflection, she enters a porous state of awareness in which imagination and reality become indistinguishable. The word "wild" seen in the text box refers to a process of animalization, a return to a primitive condition experienced by the protagonist as she tries on various human and animal masks (identities).[5] The recurring themes of transformation and impersonation revolve around the protagonist's attempts to adapt to her personal and social situation, including the end of a romantic relationship, and the hardships of being an artist during Spain's economic collapse. In that sense, Antolí's protagonist makes no distinction between her personal crisis and the social upheaval around her, seeking a solution for the latter by addressing the former. This overlap between personal and public crises echoes both Dean Allbritton's reference to the "publicly personal experience with vulnerability" (104) and Germán Labrador Méndez's notion of the existence of a shared cultural experience of the Spanish crisis, which results in a "colectiva inundación de microliteraturas del yo" [collective flooding of microliteratures of the self] ("Las vidas" 571). The novel will capture Spain's profound social transformation through the recurring theme of impermanence. Other characters will also embody transformation (individual and societal), most notably Bowie, who reinvented himself into multiple personae during his career.

The protagonist tries on a variety of personae, precisely to understand her own contemporary moment from multiple perspectives; of course, Antolí also explores these subject positions through her narrative and stylistic choices. As an authorial self-exploration, *Pareidolia* continues an auto-fictional vein originating in American underground comics from the sixties and seventies by cartoonists such as Robert Crumb (1943–), Aline Kominsky (1948–), Justin Green (1945–), and Harvey Pekar (1939–2010) (García 193). This genre, called "autobio," typically displays a "minimalismo confesional ... historietas que tratan la propia vida aparentemente sin distanciamiento en el contenido ... y con una gran inmediatez en el aspecto gráfico" [confessional minimalism ... comics that address the content (of the author's) own life without any apparent distance ... and with a sense of immediacy in the graphic elements] (García 237–8).

The graphic novel's minimalist style becomes apparent from the first panels, which depict its bare mise-en-page: a dark and sparsely furnished room, an unmade bed, a dresser, a desk, and a few scattered posters. This setting, coupled with the black background of the first five pages, strikes a starkly sombre mood that captures the moment of personal and collective crisis and suggests "a visual equivalent of what happens at story-level" (Baetens and Frey 116). At first, Antolí's unnamed protagonist appears as a shadow blocking a crack of light discernible under the doorway. Such lack of definition anticipates the novel's fascination with the blurred contours of existence and the protagonist's shifting identities. Uncertainty and fluidity are thematized in content and style, as shadows, stains, and diffuse shapes trigger the protagonist's visual hallucinations and reveries, providing a "mirror" for her existential journey. Once inside, the protagonist utters a strange "Hola a todos" [Hello everyone] (*Pareidolia* 12), a greeting seemingly directed at the readers but also meant for other characters who materialize in subsequent panels, conjured by the protagonist's pareidolia. An ex-boyfriend emerges from a wall stain, a pile of rumpled clothes transforms into the protagonist's childhood self, and soon an entire repertoire of figures materialize and engage with the protagonist in philosophical debates. The opening chapter thus sets a tone of impermanence for the entire novel as the protagonist "works through" a recent break-up, bemoaning that everything in life is flux – her lover has changed, and her desires have also changed – and concluding that "nada es eterno, ni para siempre" [nothing is eternal or forever] (19).

Antolí's sense of unstable impermanence is seemingly endemic for Spain's millennial generation, which suffers from unemployment rates of more than 50 per cent and a vanishing social safety net. Spain's crisis, by now amply theorized, has had a profound effect on the cultural field because, "for the vast majority of Spaniards, neoliberal policies have produced a strain of cultural pathology (due to the consequences of staggering unemployment, foreclosures and evictions, poverty and hunger, depression, an increased suicide rate, etc.) that can no longer be ignored" (Cameron 4). Although this first chapter initiates the theme of inward self-discovery, as captured by Bowie's lyric "So I turned myself to face me" (Antolí, *Pareidolia* 9), Antolí will link these self-reflexive issues to the present moment's crisis, a crisis whose sombre mood permeates and inflects the protagonist's existential quest and the novel's visual style.

As mentioned, the conceptual art of the sixties and seventies provides Antolí with potential responses for present-day issues. A paradigmatic concern of that earlier period was how to negotiate the dissolving boundary between the artistic and the mundane, reconciling aesthetics and commitment; for instance, Fluxus, represented in the novel by Beuys, was a movement that sought to transform reality through happenings and art actions.[6] Antolí recovers the ways American and European post-war avant-gardes (that is, Neo-Dada and Fluxus) questioned Western rationalism, rebelling against rapid industrialization, man's alienation from nature, reified social orders, and global militarization. Antolí, then, redirects these discourses of resistance from avant-garde art and popular music against the contemporary crisis of late capitalism.

Joseph Beuys and Anti-rationalism: The Artist as Shaman-Healer

The second chapter, "The Crazynest," portrays a dream sequence that exemplifies the graphic novel's anti-rationalism embodied in the intertextual presence of the German conceptual artist Joseph Beuys. The chapter's anti-rationalist stance also functions as a reaction against a global crisis that, Antolí seems to suggest, is caused by a rigidly rationalistic world and the egoism promoted by its capitalist logic. Accordingly, her intimate drawing style – quasi-abstract, loose, pen and ink drawings that emphasize line over volume – represents a complete rejection of what, in traditional American comics, is an unyielding rule: the interchangeability of artists. Marvel or DC comics' superheroes should always look more or less the same regardless of who draws them. Repetitive and standardized, these comics are the very embodiment of a rational system, a "studio system" in which "style tends to be controlled as much as possible in order to enable the smooth functioning of the production line" (Baetens and Frey 135).

This stylistic revolt against rationalism and standardization is accompanied by the surrealist tone of the narrative. Set in a dense jungle, the surreal scene depicts the naked protagonist swinging from trees and crawling on all fours, then capturing and devouring a live bird: pursuing her animal instincts, the protagonist reconnects with her animal nature. The oneiric scene, which resembles a strange initiation rite, hearkens to a primeval time, a savage lost paradise. In the next panels, the arrival of an enigmatic monkish figure wrapped in a felt cloak and holding a shepherd's staff interrupts the ritual feast. Only the staff is visible protruding from the cloak, conferring on the faceless shape (later identified as Beuys) a prophetic or mystical look and a hint of surrealist absurdity (figure 8.1).

Antolí's panel cites Beuys's 1974 performance, *Coyote: I Like America, and America Likes Me* (figure 8.2), not as a slavish homage but as an intricate part in her sophisticated redeployment of anti-rationalist discourses. The panel is an explicit reconstruction of the photograph that documented Beuys's performance into which Antolí has inserted herself. This gesture of including photographic references is characteristic of "radically experimental hybrid forms that exceed the traditional boundaries of genre and media" (Baetens and Frey 141) and also serves to connect these artists from two different temporalities. As artists, Antolí and Beuys share many affinities: Both combine drawing, painting, photography, sculpture, dance, and performance art. They favour process-oriented art that de-emphasizes the object, focusing on the underlying concept. They both create work that blurs fact and fiction, mixing art and life, autobiography and myth. They believe in art's potential for healing our alienation from nature, bringing us closer to the animal world, and even restoring spirituality to lived experience. Finally, insisting that art, like mystical experience, is ineffable, both artists sustain that the irrational and the absurd provide an escape from a (failed) rigid and materialistic Western rationalism, serving as gateway to a "miraculous" reality. Most importantly, they share a belief in the critical potential found in collective action through art.

Some background on Beuys is needed to fully grasp this intertext's function. While in the Luftwaffe during World War II, Beuys's plane was shot down over Crimea. He claimed he was found and kept alive by Tartar tribesmen who wrapped him in felt blankets and animal fat. Although the story was apocryphal (he was rescued by a German unit), Beuys built a mythology around it. Felt, fat, honey, and other organic

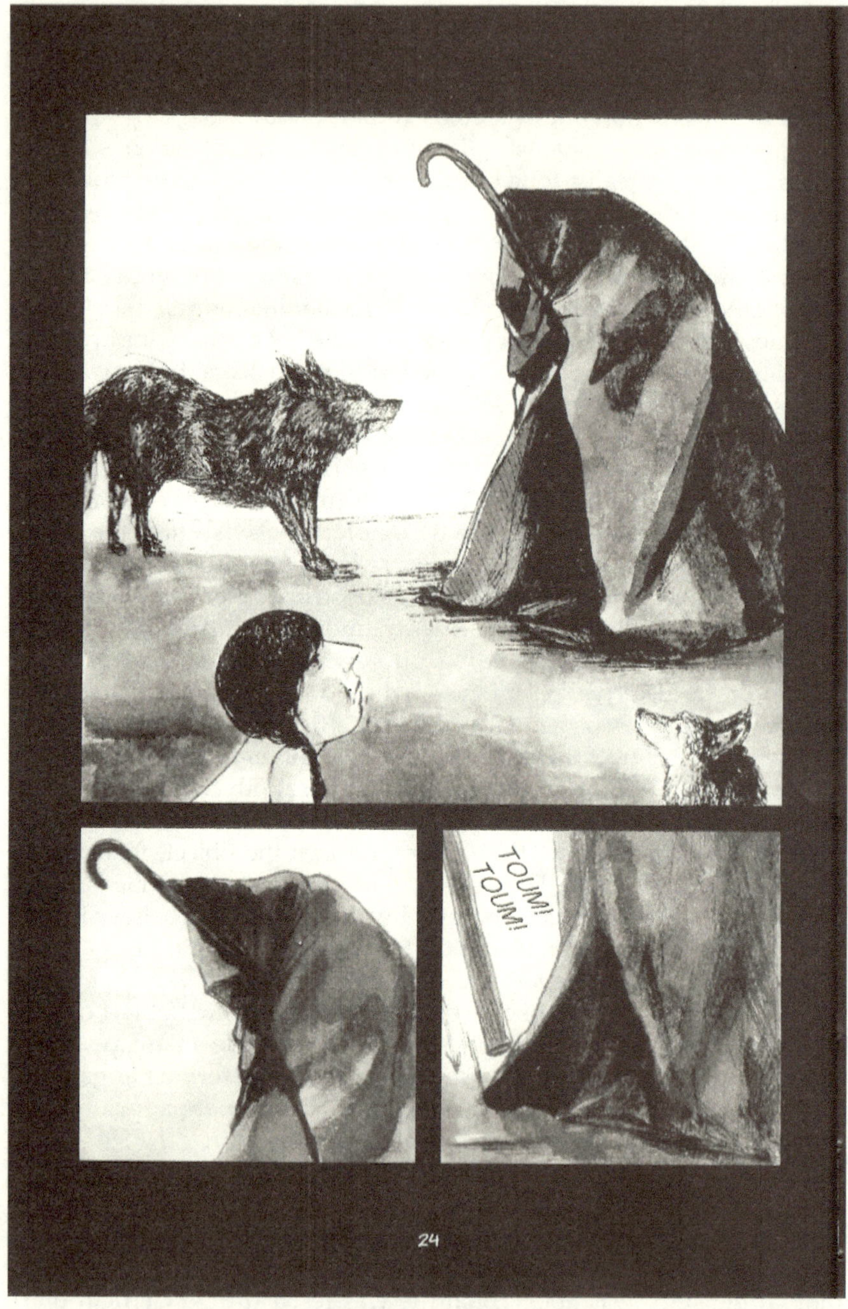

Figure 8.1. The protagonist's surreal encounter with Beuys in Antolí's *Pareidolia* (24).

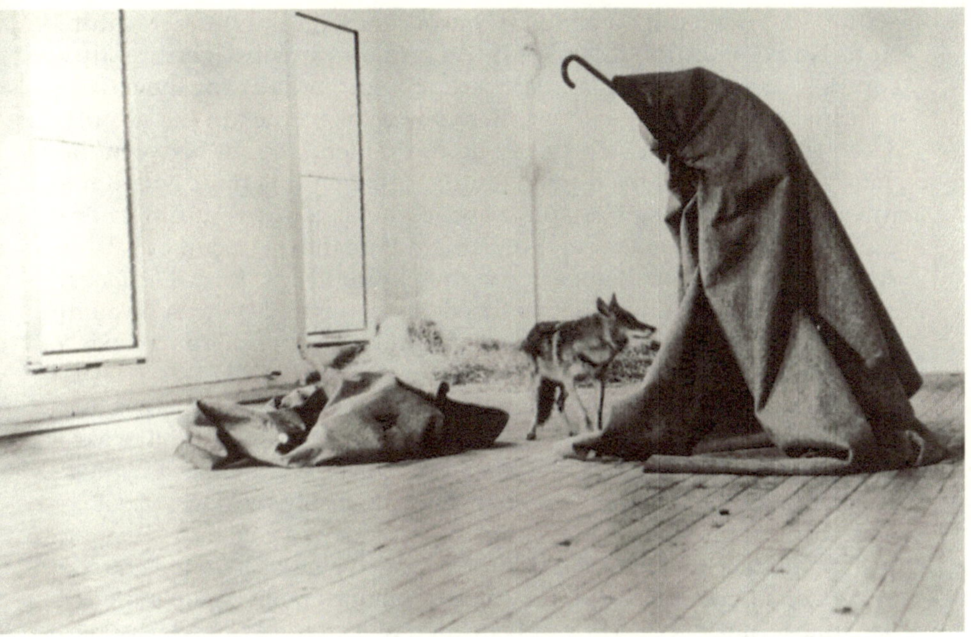

Figure 8.2. Joseph Beuys performs *Coyote: I Like America and America Likes Me* (1974). Photographer: Larry Qualls. Image: ARTStor. Collection: Contemporary Art (Larry Qualls Archive). Source image and original data provided by Larry Qualls.

materials acquired symbolic value in his art. By virtue of his (false) miraculous resurrection, Beuys adopted the role of shaman, insisting that he could deploy art's healing power by bringing his audience closer to nature (Buchloh 45–7). Referring to his art actions as "social sculpture," he sought, through them, to induce a transformative mystical experience that would restore a sense of ethics, respect for the environment, and regard for animal and human life, as well as a spirit of collectivity. Martin Crowley theorizes that Beuys's "path" to renewing a sense of the collective and creating social cohesion entailed minimalist materials and a return to the primitive and animalistic, to the irrational (46), exactly the elements that Antolí's graphic novel emphasizes in this intertext.

In *Coyote*, Beuys arrived at New York's Kennedy airport and was taken by ambulance to René Block's Manhattan gallery. The ambulance signalled humanity's illness and Beuys's role as healer. For three days, while spectators watched from behind glass, Beuys shared a small space with a wild coyote and sought to communicate with it (Tate Modern). Enveloped in a felt blanket and grasping a shepherd's staff, Beuys prayed for a genuine "encounter with a mythical creature from Native culture" (Mesch 51). As an anti-capitalist gesture, fifty copies of the *Wall Street Journal* were brought in daily for the coyote to urinate on. After three days, Beuys was taken back to the airport. As artist-shaman, Beuys believed he could mend the rift between the natural (coyote) and the human (audience), reuniting our divided natures. Besides healing our split psyche, the action was meant to critique the US involvement in the Vietnam War, the treatment of Native Americans, and our disregard for the environment. With *Pareidolia,* Antolí emulates the way Beuys fused aesthetics and politics through an art action that explored the fundamental questions of human existence and sought to heal our alienation in a time of crisis.

In *Coyote,* Beuys synthesizes the natural with the mystical; appropriating the shaman's role, he arguably "communes" with a coyote. Antolí retakes the figure of the coyote, as its shape-shifting skills speak to *Pareidolia*'s own metamorphosis and impersonation themes; invariably, the novel's protagonist also impersonates the role and appearance of a coyote, associating such mimicry with a return to primitive group values: "el sentimiento de permanecer o de ser parte de un grupo es un buen motivo para impersonar" [the feeling of belonging or being part of a group is a good reason to impersonate] (152). Such a return to collectivity, to "our animal nature," is undoubtedly seen as a corrective to the depersonalizing effect of the Spanish crisis, where isolated individuals are valued by their economic worth, or lack thereof, rather than by how they contribute to the collective good. In Antolí's graphic novel, self-worth is brought to a spiritual plane, and a tribe-like communalism provides the key for a new social organization.

In Claudia Mesch's assessment, Beuys's *Coyote* performance and his earlier *How to Explain Pictures to a Dead Hare* (1965) "reveal Beuys's familiarity ... with the shaman's range of action" (50). Through dreams and visions, the shaman is initiated into the world of the spirits, enlists the help of animal spirits, and "mimics their cries and movements in a dance" (50). In Antolí's novel, Beuys becomes the protagonist's artistic and spiritual guru, guiding her and providing insights into art's curative power. Echoing *Coyote, Pareidolia* depicts dance, animal mimicry, and music as components in the performance of healing rituals, summoning various human and animal "spirits," including Beuys, Ader, Bowie, Cobain, and also wolves, birds, and a dead hare. Likewise, Antolí draws on irrational shamanistic beliefs to restore a lost link to communitarian ideals (which emphasize the unity between individuals and their community) and an organic relation to the world not based on capital. This, I suggest, echoes not only a 1960s understanding of collective action (for instance, in the wake of anti–Vietnam War movements, May '68, and so on) but also the emergence of a contemporary vision of participatory democracy that has its origins in the *indignados* [outraged] movement, followed by the 15-M movement, which initiated the 15 May 2011 occupation of public squares, first in Madrid's Puerta del Sol and later throughout Spain, and whose latest consequence is, arguably, the rise of the Podemos party.

Antolí, therefore, includes this intertext for several important reasons: to establish a network of avant-garde referents that contextualize and legitimate her graphic novel and artistic practice; to reaffirm Beuys's neo-surrealist discourse on anti-rationality; to evoke his animistic and mythologizing approach to art; and to tap into its curative potential to mend our sense of lack through a renewal of the collective. Antolí's statement for another project provides an additional interpretative key for *Pareidolia*. Regarding *I must obey the inscrutable exhortations of my soul: MY ANIMAL DANCE* (2012), she states:

> [Este proyecto] es un encuentro con las formas de ser más instintivas, un "back to the wild," un regreso a nuestros orígenes. Las exhortaciones entendidas como tendencias irracionales que nos conectan con nuestro "yo" más primitivo y esencial ... busca recrear un paraíso perdido. Se cuestiona nuestro rol y nuestros propios límites a través de máscaras o suplantaciones de identidad. La tentación de dar unos pasos hacía atrás, lejos de los modales y hábitos civilizados, parece ser la única forma de encontrarnos a nosotros mismos. (Mariani, "My Animal")
>
> [This project is a reunion with the most instinctual ways of being, a "back to the wild," a return to our origins. The exhortations are understood as irrational tendencies that connect us to our most primitive and essential "I" ... It seeks to recreate a lost paradise. It questions our role and our limits through masks or substitute identities. The temptation of taking a few steps back, away from good manners and civilized habits, seems to be the only way to find ourselves.]

Antolí believes that the artist-shaman, embodied by Beuys and herself, can mediate the return to a primitive state and, through it, to a "truer" original self, leading ultimately to a better society. For Antolí, art cannot be understood rationally, only experienced phenomenologically and internalized, as with dance, through embodied interactions; art must be apprehended as a quasi-primitive and instinctive knowledge that combines aspects of mystical illumination (such as Zen enlightenment) with primordial animal intuition. This reconnection with animal nature, with our "animal dance," entails a return to a mythical prelapsarian unity in which the individual is not only reconciled with his or her underlying primal instincts but also restored as a member of a tribe.[7] In the graphic novel *Pareidolia*, Antolí's protagonist rearticulates a need for collective resistance, but admits it will require the sacrifice of part of her individuality: "Somos más fuertes en grupo, pero también más anónimos. Sacrificamos nuestra individualidad a favor de una identidad colectiva más fuerte" [We are stronger as a group, but also more anonymous. We sacrifice our individuality in favour of a stronger collective identity] (157).

Deadly Intertextualities: Suicide, Comics, and Rock 'n' Roll

As we are beginning to see, Antolí wishes to repair an ailing society, exemplified by Spain's crisis, by bringing us closer to our animal nature and rekindling a tribe-like sense of cooperation. But *Pareidolia* investigates other potential forms of escape out of the crisis, even the irrational act of suicide. During the protagonist's dream in the novel's first chapter, Beuys sings "Ghost Rider" by the all-but-forgotten seventies electronic synth-punk band Suicide. Antolí reproduces this song's lyrics from the band's first album, also titled *Suicide* (1977). In fact, Antolí places the lyrics in a prominent dialogue balloon that is in turn superimposed on a reproduction of the vinyl record's jacket, taking up a full-page panel. By evoking vinyl, the (obscure) reference to "Ghost Rider" also establishes a nostalgic association and longing "for the old comics and other vintage popular culture" (Baetens and Frey 224). The representation of music and song through the word balloon suggests that the character is singing, but also seeks to trigger the reader's own nostalgic evocation of 1960s rock. The song "Ghost Rider" emotes sixties freedom imagery associated with motorcycles and their link to violent death, as seen in films such as Dennis Hopper's *Easy Rider* (1969) or Kenneth Anger's *Scorpio Rising* (1964).

The song's repetitive lyrics ("America, America is killing its youth") also express a post–Vietnam era rebelliousness regarding the (self-) destruction of young Americans, which Antolí implicitly reassigns to the Spanish context. Like a ritual incantation, the melody's repetitious tone channels hopeless generational despair. Here, present reality filters through the fiction. Relating past despair with the dark mood stemming from the present-day economic crisis, Antolí foregrounds a parallel instance of generational angst and alienation for Spanish youth; just like America, she seems to say, Spain is killing its youth, or at least rendering them economically, politically, and socially dead. Through this intertext, she also re-engages with the rebellious spirit of the sixties and seventies. *Pareidolia* makes this association evident, as the "Ghost Rider" lyrics immediately follow a 2014 news report about Spain's worsening crisis (figure 8.3): "si las cosas siguen como hasta ahora y persisten las dudas de los inversores hacia España, provocando que la prima de riesgo se desboque, el rescate será inevitable" [if things continue as they

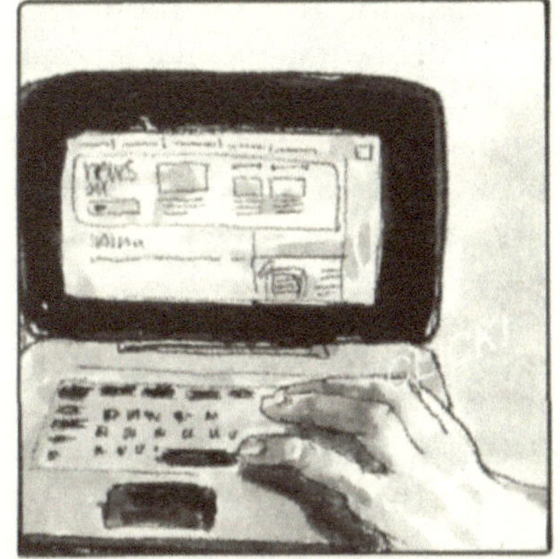

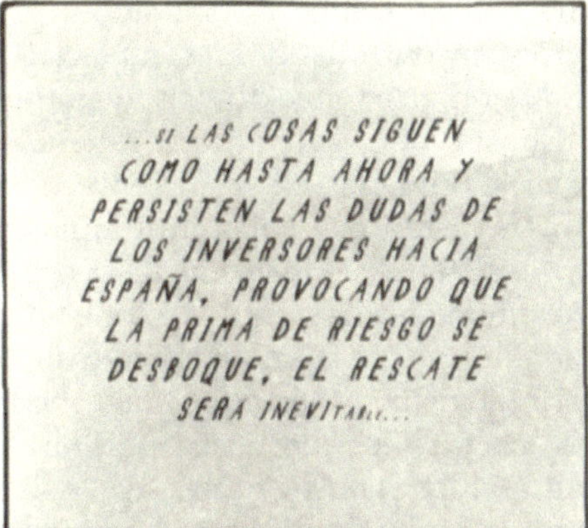

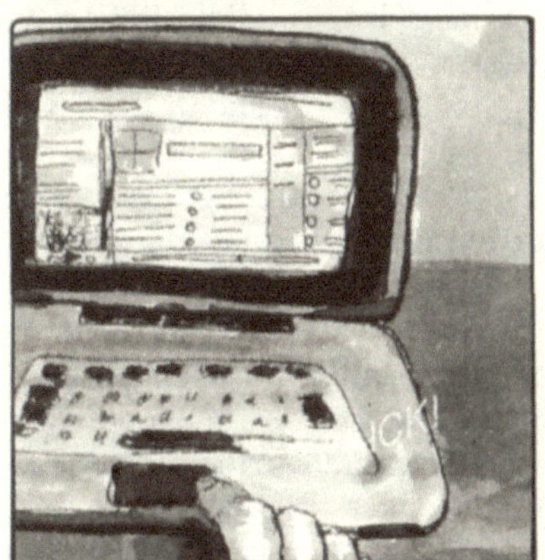

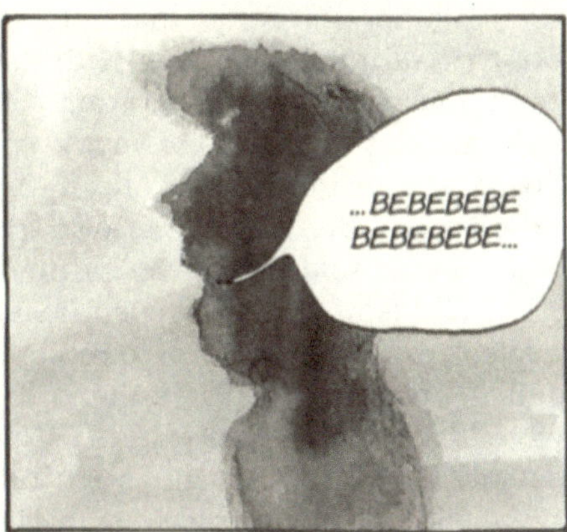

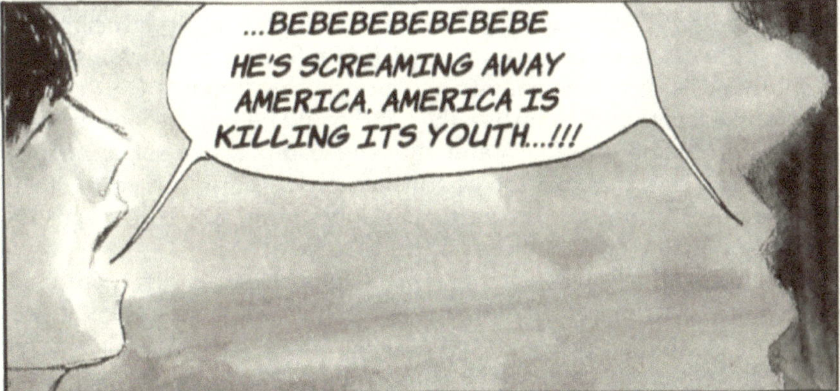

Figure 8.3. The protagonist sings "Ghost Rider" as an escape from the news in Antolí's *Pareidolia* (32).

are and investors' doubts about Spain persist, the risk premium will grow uncontrollably, and (financial) rescue will become inevitable] (32). Rather than engage directly, the protagonist turns the news off and sings "Ghost Rider," substituting rational discourse with an affective reaction that should not be mistakenly read as escapist. Neil Eriksen argues that anti-rational subculture music (punk, grunge) carries a potential for resistance: "Music has tended to become a powerful vehicle for this rebellion because it can provide an expression for the focal concerns of youth." Music is an affective response in tune with Antolí's return to primal instincts and fully enmeshed in the tribal collectivity she wishes to enact. Thus, Antolí's graphic novel displays a desire to build community, which is nevertheless, as we shall see, still dogged by a paradoxical sense of individualism and bound up in a preoccupation with the self.

In another self-referential turn, *Pareidolia*'s intermedial citation of early punk music overlaps with its intertextuality about comics. The band Suicide took its name from "Satan Suicide," an issue in the *Ghost Rider* series published by Marvel in the seventies. "Ghost Rider," the title character in the song and the comic book, was the fictional stunt rider Johnny Blaze, a leather-clad, chain-twirling, skull-faced anti-hero who, having sold his soul to the devil, rode his fiery motorcycle to fight crime and (sometimes) perpetrate it (Schoell 188–90). The band Suicide played up this connection to motorcycle death culture associated with both a punk and biker aesthetic. The lead singer, Alan Vega (1938–), wore black leather and wielded a motorcycle chain during concerts to defend himself from aggressive punk audiences, as self-destructive, ritualistic violence mingled with performative self-mythologizing. Becoming a satanic shaman or mediator between the audience and its dark impulses, Vega would cut himself on stage – although carefully, so as not to cause real damage. *Pareidolia*'s reference to Suicide's antics is another attempt to regenerate rebelliousness in today's youth, since, despite their violent tendencies, the band could be said to have brought societal problems into focus and challenged repressive social norms.[8] Through its clash against the established order, punk served to create a sense of community in its particular subculture, sparking a sense of unity that Antolí's protagonist wishes to recover.

But, although *Pareidolia* interweaves performance art, youth suicide, and rock 'n' roll, Antolí's graphic novel is also critically self-aware of the danger posed by romanticizing suicide and aestheticizing self-destructive violence. While *Pareidolia*'s protagonist, in her search for meaning, never (seriously) considers suicide, there are "mock" (and rock) suicides in the narrative. Non-existence remains a key theme throughout, as the main character, in her words, engages with "la persistente búsqueda de nuestra trascendencia" [the persistent search for our transcendence] (104), acquiring "la conciencia de nuestra fragilidad" [the awareness of our fragility] (103). Fragility, error, and the fall contained within efforts to transcend are recurring existential themes, as is the absurdity of existence itself, symbolized by the myth of Sisyphus. Suicide is briefly considered as a possible escape from life's absurdity, but ultimately the graphic novel's protagonist rejects this nihilist option as flawed, selfish, and immature. In a panel that casts a critical glance at the mythology of suicide, we see the protagonist's hand holding a photo of herself as a teenager. The collapse of temporalities allows Antolí to critique her younger self by introducing annotations with arrows that point to the clothes and gestures in the photograph in a kind of meta-commentary. For instance, an arrow points to the heavy metal hand gesture, and the annotation reads: "No sabía qué significaba esto, pero me daba carácter" [I did not know what this meant, but it gave me character] (61). In the photo shown in the top panel, she also wears a Nirvana T-shirt that displays Kurt Cobain's suicide note, which closed with Neil Young's lyric "It's better to burn out than to fade away" (figure 8.4).[9] Aware of how the shirt idealizes suicide, turning Cobain's death into a commodity (it "sells" a romantic view of suicide), the protagonist disavows her adolescent naiveté, tenderly observing, "y los 15 nunca vuelven" [and 15 never returns] (61). The full-page layout thematizes this process of change, the evolution of the character towards greater self-knowledge. This transformation is reinforced by the way the gutters synthesize the different time periods through their T-shaped layout. As Scott McCloud observes, "in the limbo of the gutter [in comics] human imagination takes two separate images and transforms them into a single idea" (*Understanding* 66). Thus, the upper panel echoes the past, while the bottom two panels are set in the present, as the character recognizes her error and, in the final blank panel, disavows and erases her past self, allows the past to "fade away."

In the narrative, Cobain embodies a ghostly sign of impermanence and change as someone who (some speculate) may have intended for suicide to be his last performance, a radically irreversible and self-delusional escape from rationality.[10] Cobain "performed" the unspeakable act that the protagonist rejects, choosing instead to take a "leap of faith" into the miraculous, as we shall see.[11] Antolí does not advocate but recognizes the danger of self-destructive "solutions" to either personal crisis or to the collective angst spurred by the global economic crisis. A rise in youth pathologies – including depression and suicide – stemming from the vulnerable state of Spain's population during the crisis has been analysed in regard to Spanish cultural production by critics such as

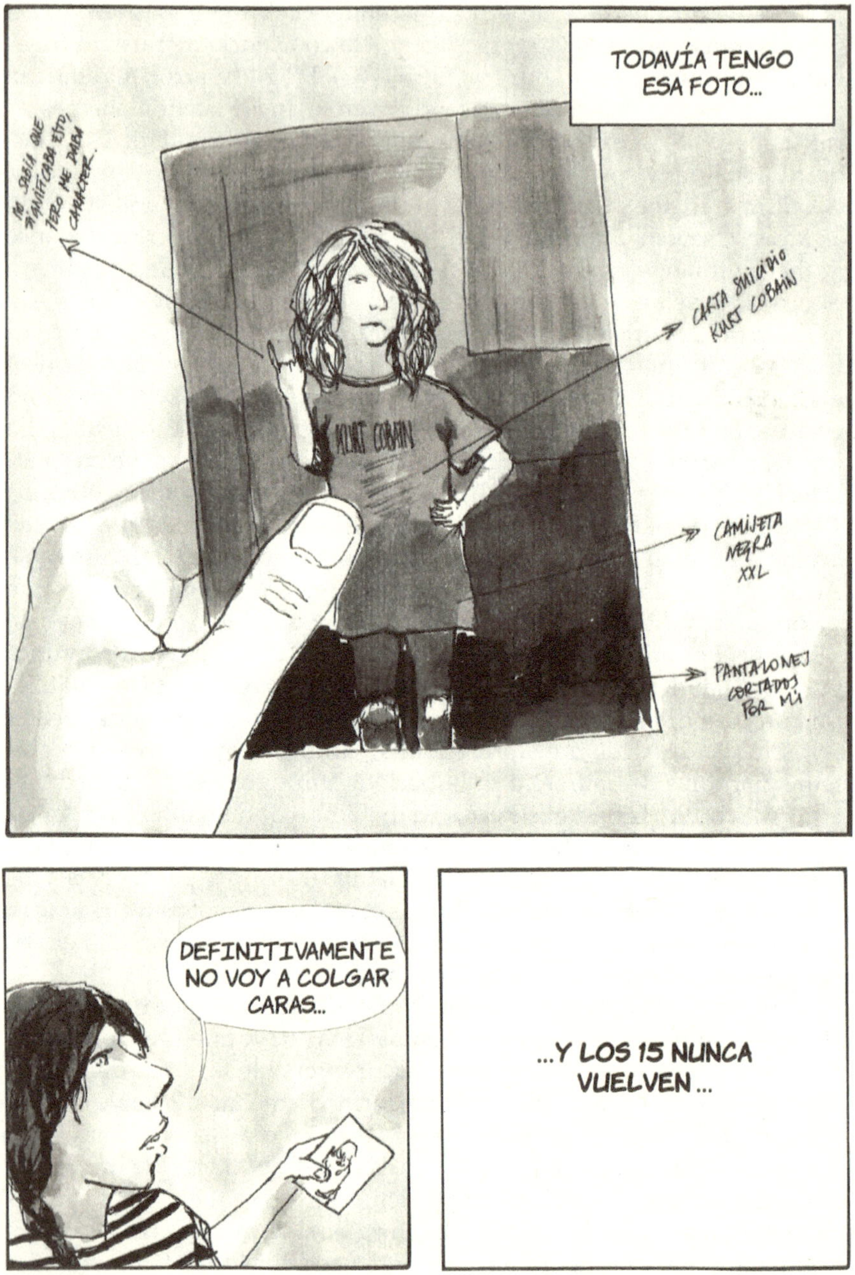

TODAVÍA TENGO ESA FOTO...

KURT COBAIN

CARTA SUICIDIO KURT COBAIN

CAMISETA NEGRA XXL

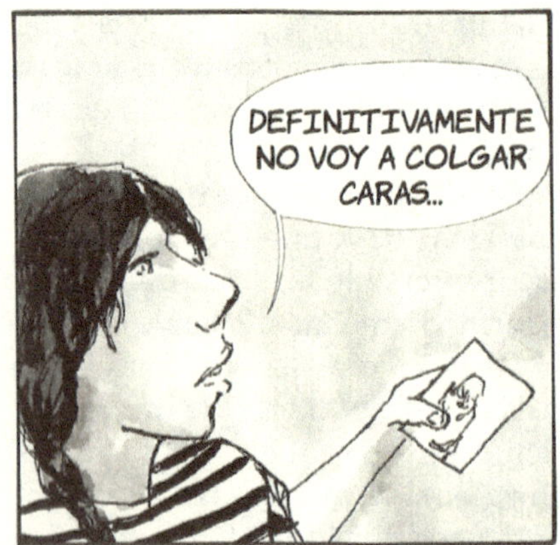

...Y LOS 15 NUNCA VUELVEN...

Figure 8.4. The protagonist being self-critical in Antolí's *Pareidolia* (61).

Germán Labrador Méndez, Luis Martín-Cabrera, Elena Delgado, Bryan Cameron, and Dean Allbritton, among others.[12] These critics propose solutions related to community building or to creating alternate social cohesion models that could offset the state's neglect. Allbritton believes that "the emphasis on interaction – social, physical, activist – that the *indignados* movement calls for thus serves to foreground how important the concept of collective vulnerability has become in contemporary Spain. Beyond this emerging movement, certain mediated representations of the Spanish Crisis seek to further localize the physicality of living in precarity" (102). *Pareidolia* translates this precarious state into its protagonist's self-doubt. Irrationality, for Antolí, suggests a way to escape desperation and reconnect with collective hopes.

Philosophically speaking, the protagonist's existential position is influenced by Albert Camus's *The Myth of Sisyphus* (1942), which associates suicide with the absurd, but also with art: "An act like this [suicide] is prepared within the silence of the heart, as is a great work of art" (4). Suicide becomes possible once the subject is awakened to life's absurdity, to the meaninglessness of daily habit, and to the repetition of routine. As Camus states, "At the end of the awakening comes, in time, the consequence: suicide or recovery" (13). Despite the risk of suicide, the awakening of consciousness is imperative, since "everything begins with consciousness and nothing is worth anything but through it" (13). Like the protagonist, Camus wrests the will to live from the concept of absurdity (from the irrational), rejecting suicide as a viable solution. In the will to live, even when faced by the irrational meaninglessness of existence, he sees a defiant revolt that carries its own redemption. Camus links this act of rebellion to art's transformative force, which renders life worth living and contains something mad and quasi-divine (64). In the novel's final panels, Antolí proposes a group dance as a life-affirming way to embrace the irrational, the mystical, even the miraculous; dance is embodied, irrational, and absurd, but through it, Antolí proposes, one can heal and reconnect with the social body. What is relevant in light of Camus is that suicide may spring from crisis, like art, but it isn't art. Cobain's action cannot be read as performance, only as self-destruction.

Bas Jan Ader and Ziggy Stardust: On Falling, Impersonation, and the Fragility of It All

For Antolí's protagonist, who is beset by self-doubt, mired in feelings of despair, and questioning her own existence, recapturing hope seems like an unreachable miracle. This "miracle" is summoned through yet another intertext found in the chapter "Las caídas" [The Falls], based on the work of Dutch conceptual artist Bas Jan Ader. I argued that Antolí's novel seeks to re-establish a connection between the individual and the collective. As Allbritton sees it, through sharing narratives of crisis, "the pain of being a vulnerable citizen can ... be transformed into a practice that releases hope and a way to mitigate one's individual devastation onto the shoulders of a collective" (104). In the graphic novel, the protagonist discusses the work of Ader as a type of crisis narrative (an existential crisis) that she draws on for inspiration. Ader, for Antolí, represents that "miraculous" potential – an artist who embraced the concept of fragility and the practice of "letting go." Ader found artistic authenticity in fragility and failure, as failure itself was a common, even collective experience, much as today's crisis and its narratives of failure can be said to be "experienced as a collective trauma" (Labrador Méndez, "The Cannibal Wave" 267).

As a way to introduce Ader, Antolí contrasts him with the Neo-Dadaist Yves Klein (1928–62), best known for his monochromatic blue paintings. Both artists were interested in "falling" or "gravity art." The chapter's title panel duplicates Klein's photograph *Leap into the Void* (1960), which shows the artist diving from a wall, arms outstretched. Klein's leap, however, is "fake," a photomontage concealing several assistants waiting to catch him; the photograph is a mere "representation of the dream of overcoming gravity" (Brezavšček 58). In contrast to Klein, who never "falls" and remains forever suspended in a triumphant instant of flight, Ader's performances approximate reality by focusing on the "fall," rather than the "leap."[13] Antolí draws a three-panel sequence from one of Ader's filmed gravity experiments, which comprised "accidental" falls from roofs, bridges, and trees.

The three-panel sequence in *Pareidolia* shows Ader riding a bicycle and falling into a canal. The drawings are Antolí's faithful rendition of *Fall 2* (1970), a nineteen-second film made by Ader of this art action unfolding (figure 8.5). What the graphic novel fails to depict, however, is the key moment. The filmed performance reveals a precise instant when Ader allows himself to lose balance ("letting go") as free will yields to the unavoidable. Here, the reader must imagine that moment through the process that McCloud calls "closure." McCloud states that comics panels "fracture both time and space, offering a jagged, staccato rhythm of unconnected moments. But closure allows us to connect these moments and mentally construct a continuous, unified reality" (*Reinventing* 67). Antolí attempts to capture this moment of authenticity that "falls" somewhere between the second and third panels, but her success or failure rests with the reader's capacity to envision it, to provide closure.

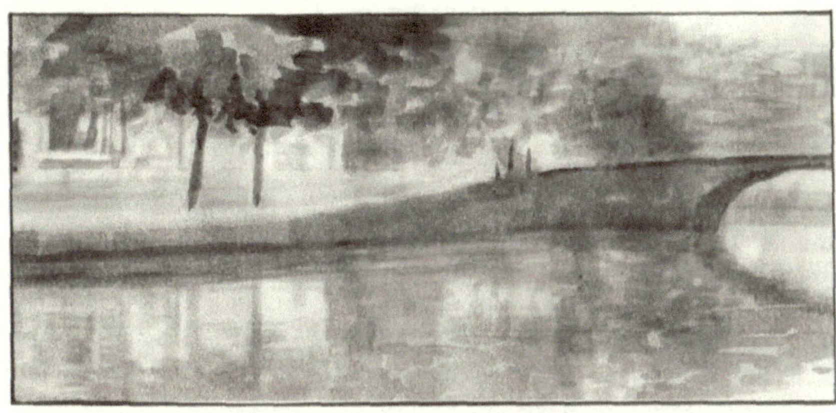

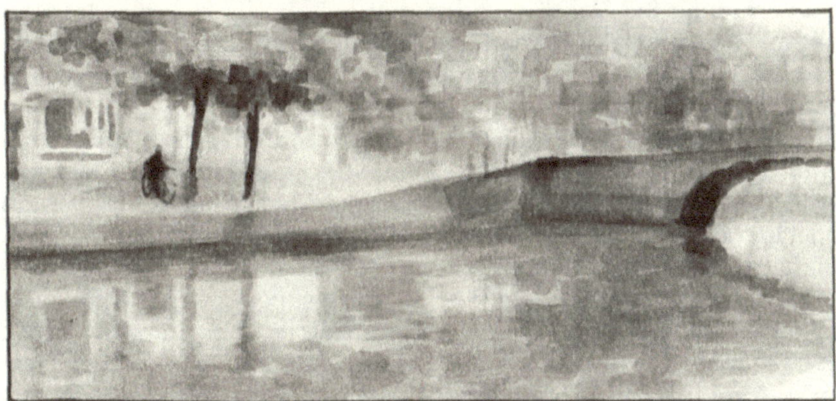

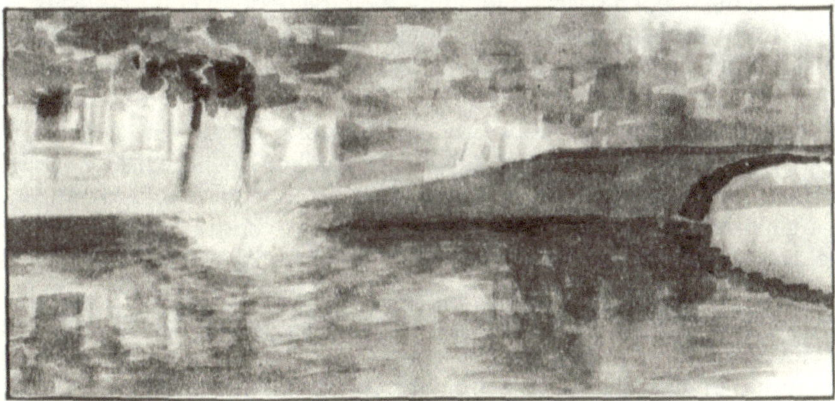

Figure 8.5. Antolí's rendition of Bas Jan Ader's 1970 falling performance, *Fall 2*, in *Pareidolia* (84).

In another performance, *Fall 1* (1970), Ader sits on a chair atop his roof, which becomes unstable and hurls him to the ground. As Alexander Dumbadze contends, "Ader's interest in falling was tied to the philosophical problem of free will and determinism" (6). Integrating art into life, Ader sought to "rid his practice of artifice" and achieve artistic authenticity (7). When asked what she likes about Ader's "falls," *Pareidolia*'s protagonist replies, "lo absurdo de la caída, del fracaso, el drama" [the absurdity of falling, of failure, its drama] (86). The drama of failure, or the failure of drama (performance): Ader realized that the "fall" as a performance trying to be authentic was predestined to fail, to be mere representation.[14] For Jan Tumlir, this failure enhances the falls, since "failure is so much more poignant, so much more successful, than success ever could be" (26).

Interpreting the "falls" as failure not only posits failure as tragedy, but as fundamentally human and essential to understand Ader's art and life. His falls expose the fragility of our human condition, revealing Ader's "existential task" as the quest for transcendence through "letting go" (Brezavšček 59). Letting go meant accepting risk, but did not entail suicide or self-destruction. Charlie Fox considers Ader's falls as a vulnerable anti-heroism: "In the gap exposed by the fall, a brief caesura opens, and human perception and certainty collapses into a glimmer of flight. We can read this as failure or as ... a moment of affirmation. In acts of human defiance, they demonstrate with a superhuman anti-heroism, the brief duration of another truth, miraculous, even immortal" (68). Such anti-heroism evokes Camus's revolt and represents the rebellious spirit Antolí wishes to revive today, at a time when hope and affirmation are the needed basis for creating the type of democratic collectivity seen in the initial phases of Occupy or 15-M.[15] Indeed, Antolí's protagonist adopts Ader as a model for "letting go" of reason and accepting the miraculous, the moment of authenticity in art, precisely because that letting go also represents a renewal of the miraculous, of hope.

After considering Ader's falls, the protagonist's discussion shifts from artistic authenticity to impersonation. For the protagonist, impersonating others (humans or animals) is a matter of survival, a way to acquire additional skills and, perhaps more importantly, a way to belong to a community. It is "el sentimiento de permanecer o de ser parte de un grupo" [the feeling of belonging or being part of a group] (Anatolí, *Pareidolia* 152), fulfilling our "necesidad de pertenecer a una comunidad" [need to belong to a community] (156). The risk associated with belonging to a collective, as presented by the novel, is the dissolution of the self, the loss of part or all of one's individuality. Antolí's character, however, will uphold the Marxian belief that the individual and the collective are mutually constitutive and dependent, and forge ahead exploring a series of impersonations. For instance, *Pareidolia* borrows scenes from *David Bowie and the Story of Ziggy Stardust* (2012), a documentary narrated by musician-critic Jarvis Cocker that focuses on Bowie's multiple personae. Introducing Cocker as a character, *Pareidolia* recreates his explanation about how Bowie's fictional alter ego, Ziggy Stardust, was "killed" during a 1973 concert at London's Hammersmith Odeon when Bowie announced that it was his last show as Ziggy. As Cocker states in Antolí's graphic novel, "So ... la figura a la que se adoraba, ese tótem erguido, desapareció, cayó" [So ... the figure of worship, that erect totem, disappeared, fell] (*Pareidolia* 43). Cocker's narration of Stardust's murder-suicide, his "rise and fall," casts a retrospective light on the novel's previous discussions: the failure and destruction of myths, the notion of tragic endings, the wearing of masks, existentialism, and suicide.[16] Antolí and her protagonist alter ego also mimic (impersonate) Bowie's skill to reinvent himself into multiple personae. As with Bowie, the characters created by Antolí and her protagonist are also reflections of their own identity, appearing in an endless specular game. Joseph Witek has theorized that the form of the graphic novel "provides a stage to act out the multiple roles that people play to each other and to themselves in daily life ... [but these] shifting visual manifestations are not masks concealing an underlying unified truth but a series of candid but inevitably partial revelations" (41).

In the chapter "The Absence," *Pareidolia*'s protagonist quotes from "Rock 'n' Roll Suicide," the final song in the last Stardust concert, whose lyrics imply Ziggy's suicide. Bowie, like Antolí, was a self-referential artist whose work can be read as autobiographical. The verse "You're not alone," from "Rock 'n' Roll Suicide," is multivalent, signifying the multiplicity of identities (Bowie, Ziggy, Major Tom) *and* our interconnectedness with others, our dual status as individual and collective subjects. Here, however, Antolí seems to caution against the erasure of the individual by the collective. Regarding Bowie's "multiplicity," Shelton Waldrep argues that, in "Space Oddity," "multiple voices are echoed in the choric aspects of the song and in Bowie's schizophrenic doubling of his own voice – he sings the lyrics and then repeats them, one step behind, in a resigned spoken voice as though he is a shadow of his own self" (91). Bowie, indeed, feared developing a multiple personality complex, not wishing for his "self" to vanish into some collective "all." Antolí includes Ziggy's murder-suicide because it demonstrates that Bowie dreaded his inability to distinguish his real self from his stage persona, of being unable to remove the mask. Slipping into schizophrenia, affected by stress and drugs, Bowie's identity was dissolving into

Ziggy's. Retiring Ziggy's persona might be read as a temporary return to the rational, re-establishing a demarcation between fictional and factual. This *rappel à l'ordre* seems contradictory to Antolí's investment in the irrational. Its purpose, however, is twofold. First, it anticipates the return to the real world that will transpire in the novel's last panel, as daydreams and fantasy yield to a sober acceptance of crisis. The irrational functions as a temporary space that expands one's consciousness but must eventually be left behind to avoid (self-)destruction. Second, it is a cautionary tale of what might happen if the protagonist loses her own subjectivity to pareidolia. Such ego-death, whether instigated by mystical experience, psychedelics, or psychopathology, is equated in Zen with enlightenment (nirvana), with what philosopher David Loy describes as "a letting-go and falling into the void," becoming nothing and everything (164).

Pareidolia, however, does not advocate for an immediate or complete restoration of rationality. In the chapter "The Absence," the protagonist realizes that her imaginary companions, the collective she created, have disappeared, and she begins to experience loss: Where is her younger self? Where is her ex-lover? Where did Bowie and the other visions go? In a three-panel page, Antolí graphically represents absence and loss. The page's top two panels display only the text "No está" [He is not here] and "Ellos no están" [They are not here] (116), respectively. Both panels are otherwise blank, one solid white, the other grey. The last panel contains no text, only three faces rendered as photographs, Cobain, Bowie, and Ader, all departed cult figures. The use of photographs – typical in Italian *fumetti* comics, as well as Spanish and Latin American *fotonovelas* – has long been deployed to adapt film and video material to graphic novels, and here serves to depict these figures realistically and to confer a sense of their status as (departed) pop culture icons. Also, despite being decoupled into three panels, the words and images still work in unison. The top two panels present absence through their lack of images, and the last panel reinforces absence through its lack of text and by depicting dead icons. Seeing these signifiers of emptiness, the protagonist mourns, "¿Por qué guardo las cosas y los recuerdos si ya no están? ... ¿Por qué ese empeño en hacerlos presentes?" [Why do I keep objects and memories if they are no longer here? ... Why the insistence on making them present?] (117–18). Bemoaning her inability to "let go," the protagonist questions the feeling of emptiness, of the void: "Dicen que el vacío puede también ser el todo, porque todo tiene cabida en el vacío" [They say the void can also be everything, because everything can fit into the void] (122). Her words, not coincidentally, echo Buddhist thought. "According to Buddhism," Loy observes, "letting go of myself and merging with that no-thing-ness leads to something else: when consciousness stops trying to catch its own tail, I become no-thing, and discover that I am everything" (164).

As if to answer her doubt about the "void," a levitating "vision" dressed as a monk appears. The figure is Alan Watts, who popularized Zen in the West with *The Way of Zen* (1957).[17] Another intertext in the graphic novel, Watts's book outlined Zen's principles for a Western audience. Two chapters in his book, "Empty and Marvelous" and "Sitting Quietly, Doing Nothing," explore nothingness and impermanence, salient concerns for Antolí. Watts believed Zen could heal humanity back to originary wholeness:

> In both life and art the cultures of the Far East appreciate nothing more highly than spontaneity or naturalness (*tzu-jan*) ... For a man rings like a cracked bell when he thinks and acts with a split mind – one part standing aside to interfere with the other, to control, to condemn, or to admire. But the mind, or the true nature of man cannot actually be split. (*The Way* 149)

Watts's point about the unified mind suggests a cure for the protagonist's split psyche, one in which she may reunite with her "visions" or alter-egos. This Zen-based restored wholeness resembles Beuys's shamanistic reconciliation of humans with nature, returning to a lost Eden.[18]

Antolí summons Watts to provide another take for the existential enquiry that has occupied the protagonist throughout *Pareidolia*. But this return to a prelapsarian "unity" or coherence brings us full circle, not only to Beuys's desire to reunite mankind and nature but also to Ader's insistence on achieving a miraculous experience of the real through art. These artists believed in an original authenticity that can only be recuperated through "letting go" of material attachments. *Pareidolia*'s protagonist resists this proposition, proclaiming that she wishes to hold onto both her illusions and the material, resisting Watts's concept of the "void" and Camus's existential "nothingness." Given the protagonist's insistence on the tactile materiality of "las cosas" [things], on permanence, Watts warns her (echoing Bowie's "Changes") that "la vida es cambio, la vida es movimiento. Resistirse al cambio es como retener el aliento. Si persistes mueres" [life is change, life is movement. To resist change is like holding your breath. If you persist, you die] (*Pareidolia* 126). She disagrees: "quiero vivir con cada cosa que me ha llevado aquí y ahora" [I want to live with everything that has brought me here and now] (134), suggesting that identity depends on the experiences and material objects that confer a memory and history of the past. From a postmodern materialist angle, objects constitute her identity.[19] Reasserting the protagonist's attachment to past memories, the chapter closes with a full-page panel depicting her embracing the returned images of Bowie, her ex-lover, and her younger self, surrounded by the text "you're not alone" from Bowie's "Rock 'n' Roll Suicide" (139). Lyrics in *Pareidolia* approximate readers to the "magic" of the scene by evoking "sound" in a mental synaesthesia. The sketch engulfs the page and the gutter, immersing readers in this communal image so that once again we return to the collective: "you [we] are not alone." The elimination of the gutter here is telling, since it breaks down the traditional arrangement of space in a graphic novel. If, as Lefèvre has observed, the inside of a panel represents the diegetic space "in which the characters live and act" and the gutter is the extra-diegetic space (157), then by breaking down this separating function, Antolí seeks to include us in the diegesis, at least symbolically.

Conclusion: The Final (Magic) Dance

As we recall from the scene when, faced by Spain's social, political, and economic crisis, she turns off the news, *Pareidolia*'s protagonist initially chooses to escape into the irrational, the surreal, and the absurd. The economic crisis itself, however, is implicitly part of the absurd and the irrational landscape of the graphic novel, an underlying joke of tragic proportions. The last chapter, "The Final Dance," explicitly mentions the crisis: "recortes en sanidad, reducción de las ayudas a enfermos crónicos, no fomentar las investigaciones científicas ... privatización de la educación, subir el IVA cultural" [cuts in public health, reductions to help for the chronically ill, privatization of public education, an increase in the culture tax] (169). As the protagonist demands a solution to the irrational state of crisis, Beuys hands her a dead hare, with which she begins to dance (see figure 8.6), an intertextual re-enactment of Beuys's most recognized performance.

In *How to Explain Pictures to a Dead Hare* (1965), performed at the Schmela Gallery, Düsseldorf, Beuys again sought to remedy our alienation from nature. This neo-surrealist action was an outright rejection of rationality. Beuys, his head covered in honey and gold leaf, performed as shaman, mediating between the dead hare and the audience, between the space beyond death and the space of the living. He walked around cradling the dead animal in a room whose walls were lined the space of the living. He walked around cradling the dead animal in a room whose walls were lined with his drawings. Whispering into the animal's ear, Beuys "explained" the meaning of (his) art. Beuys maintained that the hare "preserves more powers of intuition than some human beings with their stubborn rationality" (Feldman 110). His actions

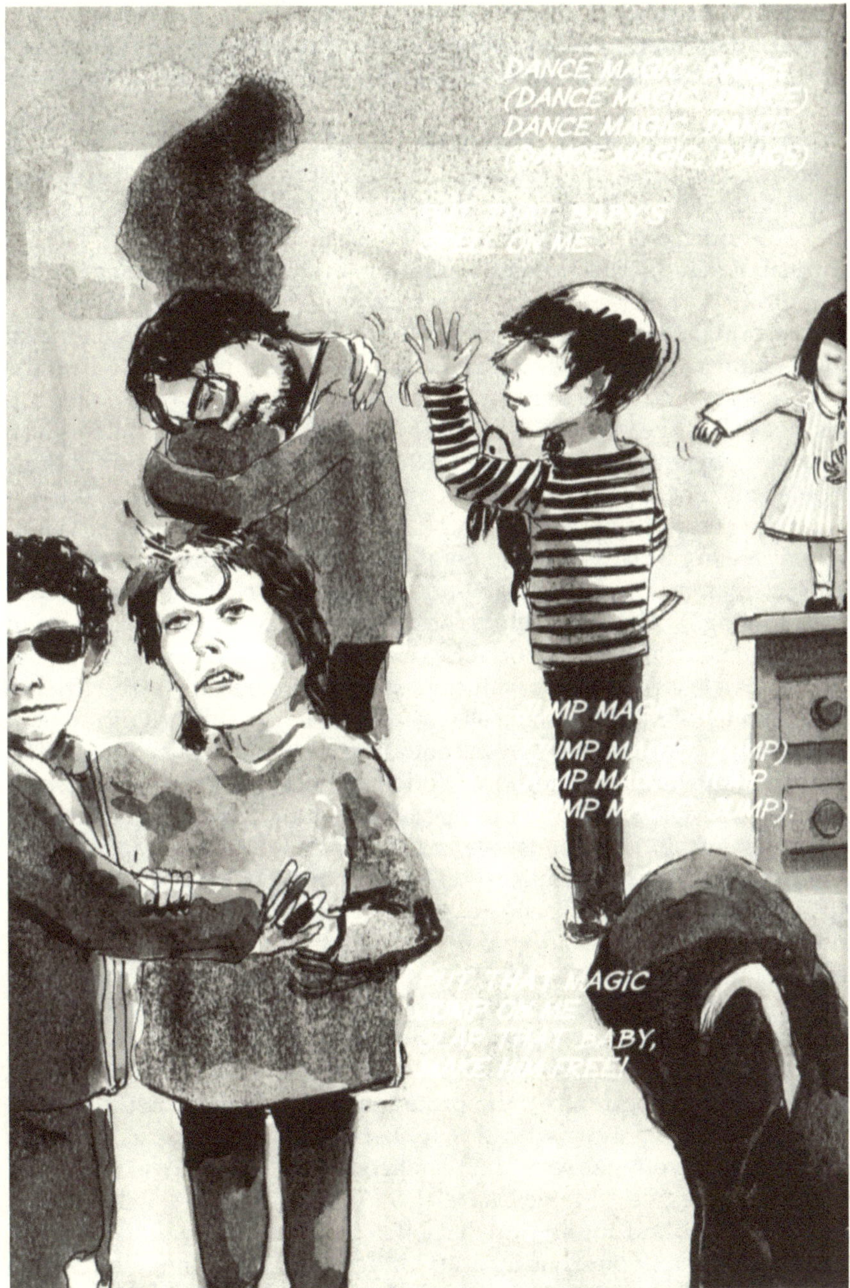

Figure 8.6. "Magic dance" in Antolí's *Pareidolia* (139).

seemed absurd when decontextualized, exposing a gap between the miraculous experience he sought and the apparently meaningless pantomime seen by the audience. His performance was no more "explainable" than his art – it just needed to be phenomenologically experienced. What *Dead Hare* demonstrated, its relevance for *Pareidolia*, is that if there is meaning in the performance, it is not to be found in its rational explanation but in the irrational experience: the "real" message cannot be communicated – it is ineffable. Like Ader, Beuys wished to find the miraculous in the absence of the intellect, outside of the rational.

Antolí approaches Beuys's shamanism with (some) irony, reading it as performance rather than "magic," yet *Pareidolia* also seeks a kind of "miraculous" effect. The miracle for Antolí entails using art to heal the personal and the collective wounds: to lessen the trauma of Spain's crisis, as well as the existential crisis of the modern subject (which is also her own), by engaging with the irrational, the instinctual, and the corporeal. Such healing through art is a fragile, vulnerable process, fraught with the certainty of failure. Antolí states: "My work is about the inherent feeling of lack in my generation ... Because of the nature of this subject matter, I work with mainly ephemeral and fragile materials" ("Following"). Appropriately, ephemerality, fragility, lack, a fraying of consciousness, and plural identities define her graphic novel. In one of *Pareidolia*'s last panels, the wall stain that "channels" the ex-boyfriend, in a display of metafictional self-awareness, laments his (doubly) fictitious status (wall stain, ex-lover), equating it with the collective ephemerality of the human condition: "Todos aparecemos para desaparecer" [We all appear to then disappear] (185). Our material consistency, suggests Antolí, is tenuous; we are only here to soon disappear, like the protagonist's hallucinations. The fictitious Cocker asks, "¿Cuál es tu solución ante éste sinsentido, pues?" [What is your solution to this nonsense?]. And the shadow replies, "Bailar" [To dance] (185). The answer to the meaningless absurdity of existence, proposes Antolí, is to dance, to melt into the embodied phenomena of the everyday and the immediacy of the now, to move together in synchronized rhythm. In what initially seems to be the graphic novel's concluding panel, everyone is dancing (figure 8.6): the protagonist dances with Beuys's dead hare, Lou Reed dances with Bowie, Beuys dances alone, as does the protagonist's younger self. The panel contains, as the novel's final intertext, the lyrics to "Magic Dance" (1986), sung by Bowie in his role as Jareth the Goblin King in Jim Henson's *Labyrinth* (1986). In *Labyrinth*'s hero-quest, the adolescent Sarah (Jennifer Connelly) finds her way to the labyrinth's centre to rescue her baby brother, who was kidnapped by the Goblin King. *Labyrinth* amalgamates elements from oneiric and psychedelic fairy tales that allegorize the passage from childhood into adolescence, such as *Alice in Wonderland* (1865) and *The Wizard of Oz* (1900), and, more to the point, *Pareidolia*. This intertext parallels *Pareidolia*'s plot (also a hero-quest), once again destabilizing rationality. With its uncanny puppets (Who pulls their strings? Do they have free will?), its Escheresque sets, and an androgynous but sexualized Bowie, *Labyrinth* is a surrealist juxtaposition of high and low culture, like *Pareidolia* itself. Irrationality incorporates social critique, not just because it casts aside the "logical" but also because it opens up to the radically unconventional in form and content. Nonsense, irrationality, and absurdity entail critique in *Pareidolia* as in *Labyrinth*.

The reference to *Labyrinth*'s "Magic Dance" in *Pareidolia*'s ending establishes a correspondence between the graphic novel and the film's final scenes: Sarah, alone in her room, discovers that her fantasy world vanished as she crossed into adulthood. Like Sarah, *Pareidolia*'s protagonist and Antolí mourn throughout the novel the passing of childhood, a life stage with access to the miraculous. Looking into the mirror – perceiving her troubled "self" in the "looking glass" – Sarah regrets the end of this magical period, but then the puppets reappear, and the scene closes with a celebratory dance party set to "Magic Dance," again, as in *Pareidolia*.

In *Pareidolia*, however, the magic dance is not really the final panel. A black page serves as an interlude, and then, in a demonstration of stylistic flair, Antolí once again eliminates the gutters and forces her drawing to the very edge of the page, as if to break out of the frame. Mirroring the novel's opening, a two-page single-panel spread shows the room's return to "normalcy": a shapeless wall stain, a pile of rumpled clothing, and a crack in the wall (formerly Bowie). We must accept life's changes, the eternal flux, as Bowie, Watts, and Beuys said. Now alone, the protagonist's visions have vanished, this time not to return. But not all is lost, as the experience remains. The irrational has shown the way to the labyrinth's centre, and the protagonist has learned from the miraculous and the absurd. The shamanistic power of Beuys's hare dispelled her pareidolia; now she must complete her metamorphosis into a "unified" self and face a world where the crisis rages on. That unified self will also be linked to a group of like-minded individuals, others willing to resist the impetus of the neoliberal logic. Thus, while the novel betrays some optimistic elements also present in other cultural representations of the crisis, such as "the hope placed in love, in human communications and connections to each other, and hope that the next generation will get it right" (Allbritton 112), it also bravely turns to face a bleak present. In that present world, Antolí suggests, nothing short of the "miraculous" will bring the magic back. That may just be the role of art – to bring it back.

NOTES

1 All Spanish to English translations are my own.
2 Antolí has stated in several interviews that the novel and her artwork in general contain a significant autobiographical component.
3 Other references include Nirvana's Kurt Cobain (1967–94), the proto-punk band Suicide, Lou Reed (1942–2013), the Velvet Underground, Norwegian electronic music guru Todd Terje (1981–), New York photographer Nan Goldin (1953–), and films such as *8½* (1963) by Fellini (1920–93), *Zelig* (1983) by Woody Allen (1935–), and *Labyrinth* (1986) by Jim Henson (1936–90).
4 Antolí does not foreground her Spanish origin in her work, although she makes frequent references to Spain's crisis. Instead, she juggles a network of global referents that draw on American and British pop music and conceptual art, existential philosophy and theories of the absurd, and philosophical approaches rooted in an Anglo-American understanding of Eastern philosophy. Santiago García observes that a global outlook is typical in today's graphic novels: "Hoy en día es más apropiado relacionar a los historietistas por afinidades estéticas o temáticas que por su localización nacional" [Today it is more appropriate to associate comic book artists with their aesthetic or thematic affinities than with their national origin] (176). Antolí's graphic novel reflects her international training and her transnational trajectory.
5 The protagonist becomes as chameleon-like as Zelig in Woody Allen's film by the same name, another of *Pareidolia*'s intertexts. She even changes herself into a chameleon in one panel. The novel's chapter "La impersonation" cites the film's song "You May Be Six People, But I Love You."
6 Fluxus was predicated on constant artistic flux, with artists such as John Cage (1912–91), Nam June Paik (1932–2006), Yoko Ono (1933–), and, more relevant for this graphic novel, Joseph Beuys.
7 Antolí's wish to recapture primitive impulses is reflected by her drive to simplify form and materials, relying on ink drawings that appear to spring from the instinctual: "Formalmente los dibujos en blanco y negro han surgido de un largo proceso en el que he pasado de la pintura más colorista y expresionista a la simplificación de la forma y material, a algo que me permitiera conectar mejor y de forma más inmediata con mis propias pulsiones o impulsos" [Formally, the black and white sketches emerge from a long process in which I went from the most colourful expressionist painting to a simplification in form and material, which allowed me to connect more immediately with my own impulses] (Mariani, "My Animal").
8 Moreover, life imitated art as the death-driven fictional motorcyclist antihero became embodied in Vega's self-destructive personality, who in turn impersonated his comic-book idol. The band's concerts abolished barriers between audience and performers, often through violence, and Suicide

"worked as supercolliders in which ideas from minimalism, auto-destructive art, living theater and pop art clashed" (Reynolds 143).

9 The protagonist also has a Nirvana poster with Cobain's face on the wall. In one panel she listens to the Bowie song "The Man Who Sold the World" (1970), which Nirvana famously covered in MTV Unplugged in 1993. The song, linked to identity crisis and multiple personality disorder, obviously underscores the narrator-protagonist's own identity confusion.

10 This conflation of suicide and art is not outrageous, considering that one of the band's last televised performances (MTV Unplugged, New York, 1993) has been read as being staged like a funeral: candles, lilies, and Cobain's unusually "raw" and fragile performance (Cottingham).

11 Cobain's escapism was, of course, consequent with Nirvana's anti-materialist punk (grunge) ethos, as signified by their name, which in Sanskrit means to "blow out" (a candle), to escape suffering and the eternal cycle of wandering known in Buddhism as samsara.

12 See, for instance, the special issue, "Spain in Crisis," of the *Journal of Spanish Cultural Studies*, vol. 15, nos. 1–2, 2014.

13 Klein, among the most influential painters and performance artists in post-war Europe, was a precursor for minimalism and pop art.

14 Mimicking Ader's search for authenticity, *Pareidolia*'s protagonist (as child) stages a similar "fall" from a dresser. This derivative performance parodies Ader's own falling failures.

15 Ader, committed to existential art and to achieving an unmediated experience of the "real," punctured through the delicate boundary separating art and life to its final consequences. Antolí's novel refers only to his "falls," but Ader's disappearance during the performance *In Search of the Miraculous* (1975) is an implicit intertext for *Pareidolia*'s query into the irrational. *In Search of the Miraculous* was a three-part performance investigating the romantic sublime (Antolí created a mixed-media award-winning work composed of painting and sculpture entitled *In Search of the Miraculous: Tribute* as a tribute to Ader in 2015). In the second part, Ader left on a solo crossing of the Atlantic, from Massachusetts to Holland. His small vessel was found adrift months later, but Ader had vanished. We can't know whether Ader intended this crossing as a last performance culminating in his suicide, but this reading of the event is unlikely according to those who knew him (Dumbadze 130–5). But Ader knew that the performance entailed a possibility of death; indeed, the chance of vanishing was a key aspect of the project's revolt against rationality, an "inextricable" part of the performance, "not by choice but by fate" (Dumbadze 133). The work hinged on life's fragility, on its impermanence before nature. Thus, although Ader's *In Search* returns to the question of suicide, it is more productive to see his tragic end as a contingency that, in Dumbadze's view,

renders the performance unrepresentable, incomplete, difficult to comprehend: "Ader attempted to distill art to its most basic state. It was him, his actions, his will in the face of nature that made *In Search of the Miraculous* as it is now conceived. But to think of it as complete – made such by events known only to Ader – allows one to understand it as offering a reorientation of the conception of an artwork, how it is constituted, and how it communicates" (142). Ader captures the fragile contingency of meaning itself, and the futility of interpretation.

16 Cocker sustains that Bowie's creation of Ziggy (an "alien" persona) and the transformation of his band into the "Spiders from Mars" was essentially performance art. It was a performance piece steeped in a pop art aesthetic and inspired by an eclectic mix of referents, including Romanticism, Surrealism, Andy Warhol's art, Kubrick's *A Clockwork Orange* (1971), science fiction, Japanese Kabuki Theatre, and rock music "theatricality" modelled on Iggy Pop.

17 Watts was associated with the Beats, especially Gary Snyder, and, like other sixties intellectuals, had been a frequent user of psychedelics. He was close to US avant-garde circles at a time when Zen was seen as a refreshing new influence for philosophy, mysticism, and the arts in a bleak post-war period. Zen left an aesthetic imprint on the Beats, on John Cage, and on the Fluxus movement, including Beuys.

18 For Watts, this "cure" makes Zen appealing: "To the Westerner in search of the reintegration of man and nature there is an appeal far beyond the merely sentimental in the naturalism of Zen ... in an art which is simultaneously spiritual and secular, which conveys the mystical in terms of the natural, and which, indeed, never even imagined a break between them" (*This Is It* 85–6). Locating the mystical within the natural familiarly returns us to Beuys, Ader, and Antolí.

19 Such insistence on materiality seems to counter the aims of conceptual art, which in the sixties privileged "a logic of subtraction as the materiality of the art object is systematically reduced or redefined, and the concept 'art' and the context increasingly carry the burden of meaning" (Bird and Newman 4). Instead, *Pareidolia* foregrounds its materiality as graphic novel, as art object, although it also functions as a conceptual piece about existential issues.

WORKS CITED

Allbritton, Dean. "Prime Risks: The Politics of Pain and Suffering in Spanish Crisis Cinema." *Journal of Spanish Cultural Studies* 15.1–2 (2014): 101–15. doi.org/10.1080/14636204.2014.931663.

Antolí, Rosana. "Following the Fox." *Afasia Archzine*. 9 June 2012. afasiaarchzine.com/2012/06/rosana-antoli/. Accessed 8 Dec. 2018.

– *Pareidolia*. Edicions de Ponent, 2014.

Baetens, Jan, and Hugo Frey. *The Graphic Novel: An Introduction*. Cambridge UP, 2015.

Beuys, Joseph. *Coyote: I Like America and America Likes Me*. 1974. library.artstor.org.proxy2.library.illinois.edu/asset/LARRY_QUALLS_10310850541. Accessed 19 Jun 2018.

Bird, Jon, and Michael Newman. *Rewriting Conceptual Art*. Reaktion Books, 1999.

Bowie, David. "Changes." *Honky Dory*, Virgin/EMI, 1999.

– "Magic Dance." *Labyrinth*, Virgin/EMI, 1986.

– "Rock 'n' Roll Suicide." *Ziggy Stardust and the Spiders from Mars*, Virgin/EMI, 1999.

Brezavšček, Pia. "Three Falls and the Event: Yves Klein, Bas Jan Ader and Tehching Hsieh." *Performance Research* 18.4 (2013): 56–62. doi.org/10.1080/13528165.2013.814330.

Buchloh, Benjamin. *Neo-Avant-Garde and Culture Industry*. MIT P, 2003.

Cameron, Bryan. "Spain in Crisis: 15-M and the Culture of Indignation." *Journal of Spanish Cultural Studies* 15.1–2 (2014): 1–11. doi.org/10.1080/14636204.2014.1002601.

Camus, Albert. *The Myth of Sisyphus and Other Essays*. Edited and translated by Justin O'Brien. Vintage Books, 1991.

A Clockwork Orange. 1971. Directed by Stanley Kubrick, performances by Malcolm McDowell, Patrick Magee, Warner Home Video, 2001.

Cottingham, Chris. "Nirvana Unplugged: Suicide Note or Just a Good Gig?" *The Guardian*, 14 Nov. 2007, www.theguardian.com/music/musicblog/2007/nov/14/nirvanaunplugged.

Crowley, Martin. "Bernard Stiegler Goes Seal-Hunting with Joseph Beuys." *Forum for Modern Language Studies* 49.1 (Jan 2013): 45–59. doi.org/10.1093/fmls/cqs063.

David Bowie and the Story of Ziggy Stardust. Directed by James Hale, performances by Jarvis Cocker, David Bowie, Marc Almond, BBC Cymru Wales, 2012.

Dumbadze, Alexander. *Bas Jan Ader: Death Is Elsewhere*. U of Chicago P, 2013.

Easy Rider. 1969. Directed by Dennis Hopper, performances by Peter Fonda, Dennis Hopper, Columbia, 1999.

Eriksen, Neil. "Popular Culture and Revolutionary Theory: Understanding Punk Rock." *Theoretical Review* 18 (September–October 1980): 13–35. Republished, *Encyclopedia of Anti-Revisionism On-Line*, www.marxists.org/history/erol/ncm-6/punk.htm.

Espai 13. "When Lines Are Time: Rosana Antolí." Press Release. *Fundació Joan Miró*, 2016, www.fmirobcn.org/media/upload/pdf/rosana-antoli-ndp-eng_NOTA_EN_1467222246.pdf. Accessed 8 Dec. 2018.

Feldman, Melissa. "Blood Relations: Jose Bedia, Joseph Beuys, David Hammons, and Ana Mendieta." *Reclaiming the Spiritual in Art: Contemporary Cross-Cultural Perspectives*, edited by Dawn Perlmutter and Debra Koppman, SUNY Press, 1999, 105–17.

Fox, Charlie. "An Avant-Garde Falling." *Performance Research* 18.4 (2013): 63–8. doi.org/10.1080/13528165.2013.814335.

García, Santiago. *La novela gráfica*. Astiberri: 2014.

"Ghost Rider." *Suicide*, Red Star Records, 1977, reissued, Mute US, 2000. www.youtube.com/watch?v=Dn7SBQ6X5HU.

Labrador Méndez, Germán. "The Cannibal Wave: The Cultural Logic of Spain's Temporality of Crisis (Revolution, Biopolitics, Hunger and Memory)." *Journal of Spanish Cultural Studies* 15.1–2 (2014): 241–71. doi.org/10.1080/14636204.2014.935013.

– "Las vidas subprime: La circulación de historias de vida como tecnología de imaginación política en la crisis española (2007–2012)." *Hispanic Review* 80.4 (Fall 2012): 557–81. doi.org/10.1353/hir.2012.0041.

Labyrinth. 1986. Directed by Jim Henson, performances by David Bowie, Jennifer Connelly, SONY Pictures, 1999.

Lefèvre, Pascal. "The Construction of Space in Comics." *A Comics Studies Reader*, edited by Jeet Heer and Kent Worcester, UP of Mississippi, 157–62.

Loy, David R. "The Lack of Self: A Western Buddhist Psychology." *Buddhist Theology: Critical Reflections by Contemporary Buddhist Scholars*, edited by Roger Jackson and John Makransky, Routledge, 2000, 155–72.

Mariani, Nicola. "My Animal Dance. Entrevista a Rosana Antolí." *Nicola Mariani Arte y Sociedad*, 25 Sept. 2012, nicolamariani.es/2012/09/25/my-animal-dance-entrevista-a-rosana-antoli/.

McCloud, Scott, *Reinventing Comics*. Paradox Press, 2000.

– *Understanding Comics: The Invisible Art*. Harper Perennial, 1993.

Mesch, Claudia. "'What Makes Indians Laugh': Surrealism, Ritual, and Return in Steven Yazzie and Joseph Beuys." *Journal of Surrealism and the Americas* 6:1 (2012): 39–60.

Peeters, Benoit. "Four Conceptions of the Page" Translated by Jesse Cohn from *Case, planche, recit: Lire la bande dessinee*, Casterman, 1998, 41–60. *ImageTexT: Interdisciplinary Comics Studies* 3.3 (2007), Department of English, University of Florida, 1 Oct 2017, www.english.ufl.edu/imagetext/archives/v3_3/peeters/.

Reynolds, Simon. *Rip It Up and Start Again: Postpunk 1978–1984*. Penguin, 2005.

Schoell, William. *The Horror Comics: Fiends, Freaks and Fantastic Creatures, 1940s–1980s*. McFarland, 2014.

Scorpio Rising. 1964. Directed by Kenneth Anger. *The Films of Kenneth Anger*, Fantoma Films, 2010.

Tate Modern. "Joseph Beuys: Actions, Vitrines, Environments." *Tate*, 2005, www.tate.org.uk/whats-on/tate-modern/exhibition/joseph-beuys-actions-vitrines-environments. Accessed 15 June 2016.

Tumlir, Jan. "Bas Jan Ader: Artist and Time Traveler." *Bas Jan Ader*, edited by Brad Spence, The Art Gallery, University of California, Irvine, 1999.

Waldrep, Shelton. *Future Nostalgia: Performing David Bowie*. Bloomsbury, 2015.

Watts, Alan. *This Is It*. Random House, 1973.

– *The Way of Zen*. Pantheon, 1957.

Witek, Joseph. "Comics Modes: Caricature and Illustration in the Crumb Family's Dirty Laundry." *Critical Approaches to Comics: Theories and Methods*, edited by Matthew Smith and Randy Duncan, Routledge, 2011, 27–42.

Contributors

Samuel Amago teaches courses on modern and contemporary Spanish literary history, cinema, comics, and culture at the University of Virginia, where he is a professor of Spanish. He is the author of *Spanish Cinema in the Global Context: Film on Film* (Routledge, 2013) and *True Lies: Narrative Self-Consciousness in the Contemporary Spanish Novel* (Bucknell UP, 2006).

Xavier Dapena specializes in visual culture and political imagination, and his dissertation explores forms of politicization in graphic novels in contemporary Spain. Having received an MA in Spanish and Spanish American literature from the University of Colorado at Boulder (2014) and an MA in film and media production from the University of A Coruña (2009), he is currently a PhD candidate in the Department of Hispanic and Portuguese Studies at the University of Pennsylvania. Dapena's publications on Spanish graphic novels have appeared in several scholarly journals and edited volumes, and he is a member of the Plataforma Académica sobre el Cómic en Español (PACE), Asociación de Críticos y Divulgadores de Cómic (ACDCómic). He also contributes to several comics publishing journals and websites.

Emily DiFilippo is an assistant professor of Spanish at Loras College in Dubuque, Iowa. She earned her PhD in Spanish literature and culture from the University of Illinois at Urbana-Champaign. Her research is focused on the intersection of disability, gender, and sexuality in contemporary Spanish culture. In a forthcoming article in the *Bulletin of Contemporary Hispanic Studies*, she discusses the literary figure of the disabled female detective in the context of the Spanish housing crisis.

Ana Galvañ is an illustrator and a comic creator from Murcia, a town in the south of Spain. After her time studying at the Faculty of Fine Arts in

Valencia, she moved to Madrid, where she worked as an independent art director. Later she left advertising to pursue comics and illustration full time. Her work has appeared in publications coordinated by Fantagraphics, Nobrow, Ultrarradio, Vertigo DC, Off Life, Autsáider, Apa-Apa, and Fosfatina. Recently, her book *Pulse enter para continuar,* a compilation of five stories that travel between science fiction and fantasy, was published by Apa-Apa Cómics.

Eduardo Ledesma is an associate professor of Spanish at the University of Illinois at Urbana-Champaign, where he teaches Hispanic and Lusophone literature, film, and new media. He is the author of *Radical Poetry: Aesthetics, Politics, Technology, and the Ibero-American Avant-Gardes, 1900–2015* (SUNY Press, 2016). His articles on film, new media, and digital culture have appeared in *Studies in Spanish and Latin American Cinemas, Arizona Journal of Hispanic Cultural Studies, Revista Iberoamericana, Revista Hispánica Moderna,* and the *Revista de Estudios Hispánicos.* He is currently completing a book titled *Cinemas of Marginality: Experimental, Avant-Garde and Documentary Film in Ibero-America* (under contract with SUNY Press). He is also working on a manuscript about blind and visually impaired filmmakers.

Matthew J. Marr is an associate professor of Spanish at the Pennsylvania State University, where he specializes in contemporary Spanish film, literature, comics, and popular culture. His most recent book is *The Politics of Age and Disability in Contemporary Spanish Film: Plus Ultra Pluralism* (Routledge Advances in Film Studies, 2013).

Christine M. Martínez is a PhD candidate in the Department of Spanish and Portuguese Languages and Literatures at New York University. Her research interests include the comics form, visual media, ecological theory, and critiques of neoliberal development in Spain and Southern Europe.

Pedro Pérez del Solar received his PhD from Princeton University (2000). He has published articles on Spanish and Latin American comics in journals such as the *International Journal of Comic Arts, IJOCA, Iberoamericana* (Germany, Spain), and *Revista Iberoamericana* (Pittsburgh). He contributed to the volume *Toward a Cultural Archive of La Movida* (edited by William J. Nichols and H. Rosi Song, Farleigh Dickinson UP). He is currently a professor in the Humanities Department of the Universidad del Pacífico, in Lima, Perú. His book *Imágenes del desencanto: Historieta española 1980–1986* [*Images of disenchantment: Spanish comics 1980–1986*] was published in 2013 by Vervuert/Iberoamericana.

Index

TORONTO IBERIC

1 Anthony J. Cascardi, *Cervantes, Literature, and the Discourse of Politics*
2 Jessica A. Boon, *The Mystical Science of the Soul: Medieval Cognition in Bernardino de Laredo's Recollection Method*
3 Susan Byrne, *Law and History in Cervantes'* Don Quixote
4 Mary E. Barnard and Frederick A. de Armas (editors), *Objects of Culture in the Literature of Imperial Spain*
5 Nil Santiáñez, *Topographies of Fascism: Habitus, Space, and Writing in Twentieth-Century Spain*
6 Nelson R. Orringer, *Lorca in Tune with Falla: Literary and Musical Interludes*
7 Ana M. Gómez-Bravo, *Textual Agency: Writing Culture and Social Networks in Fifteenth-Century Spain*
8 Javier Irigoyen-García, *The Spanish Arcadia: Sheep Herding, Pastoral Discourse, and Ethnicity in Early Modern Spain*
9 Stephanie Sieburth, *Survival Songs: Conchita Piquer's* Coplas *and Franco's Regime of Terror*
10 Christine Arkinstall, *Spanish Female Writers and the Freethinking Press, 1879–1926*
11 Margaret E. Boyle, *Unruly Women: Performance, Penitence, and Punishment in Early Modern Spain*
12 Evelina Gužauskytė, *Christopher Columbus's Naming in the* diarios *of the Four Voyages (1492–1504): A Discourse of Negotiation*
13 Mary E. Barnard, *Garcilaso de la Vega and the Material Culture of Renaissance Europe*
14 William Viestenz, *By the Grace of God: Francoist Spain and the Sacred Roots of Political Imagination*
15 Michael Scham and Lector Ludens, *The Representation of Games and Play in Cervantes*
16 Stephen Rupp, *Heroic Forms: Cervantes and the Literature of War*
17 Enrique Fernández, *Anxieties of Interiority and Dissection in Early Modern Spain*

18 Susan Byrne, *Ficino in Spain*
19 Patricia M. Keller, *Ghostly Landscapes: Film, Photography, and the Aesthetics of Haunting in Contemporary Spanish Culture*
20 Carolyn A. Nadeau, *Food Matters: Alonso Quijano's Diet and the Discourse of Food in Early Modern Spain*
21 Cristian Berco, *From Body to Community: Venereal Disease and Society in Baroque Spain*
22 Elizabeth R. Wright, *The Epic of Juan Latino: Dilemmas of Race and Religion in Renaissance Spain*
23 Ryan D. Giles, *Inscribed Power: Amulets and Magic in Early Spanish Literature*
24 Jorge Pérez, *Confessional Cinema: Religion, Film, and Modernity in Spain's Development Years, 1960–1975*
25 Joan Ramon Resina, *Josep Pla: Seeing the World in the Form of Articles*
26 Javier Irigoyen-García, *"Moors Dressed as Moors": Clothing, Social Distinction, and Ethnicity in Early Modern Iberia*
27 Jean Dangler, *Edging toward Iberia*
28 Ryan D. Giles and Steven Wagschal (editors), *Beyond Sight: Engaging the Senses in Iberian Literatures and Cultures, 1200–1750*
29 Silvia Bermúdez, *Rocking the Boat: Migration and Race in Contemporary Spanish Music*
30 Hilaire Kallendorf, *Ambiguous Antidotes: Virtue as Vaccine for Vice in Early Modern Spain*
31 Leslie J. Harkema, *Spanish Modernism and the Poetics of Youth: From Miguel de Unamuno to* La Joven Literatura
32 Benjamin Fraser, *Cognitive Disability Aesthetics: Visual Culture, Disability Representations, and the (In)Visibility of Cognitive Difference*
33 Robert Patrick Newcomb, *Iberianism and Crisis: Spain and Portugal at the Turn of the Twentieth Century*
34 Sara J. Brenneis, *Spaniards in Mauthausen: Representations of a Nazi Concentration Camp, 1940–2015*
35 Silvia Bermúdez and Roberta Johnson (editors), *A New History of Iberian Feminisms*
36 Steven Wagschal, *Minding Animals in the Old and New Worlds: A Cognitive Historical Analysis*
37 Heather Bamford, *Cultures of the Fragment: Uses of the Iberian Manuscript, 1100–1600*
38 Enrique García Santo-Tomás (editor), *Science on Stage in Early Modern Spain*
39 Marina S. Brownlee (editor), *Cervantes'* Persiles *and the Travails of Romance*

40 Sarah Thomas, *Inhabiting the In-Between: Childhood and Cinema in Spain's Long Transition*
41 David A. Wacks, *Medieval Iberian Crusade Fiction and the Mediterranean World*
42 Rosilie Hernández, *Immaculate Conceptions: The Power of the Religious Imagination in Early Modern Spain*
43 Mary Coffey and Margot Versteeg (editors), *Imagined Truths: Realism in Modern Spanish Literature and Culture*
44 Diana Aramburu, *Resisting Invisibility: Detecting the Female Body in Spanish Crime Fiction*
45 Samuel Amago and Matthew J. Marr (editors), *Consequential Art: Comics Culture in Contemporary Spain*

www.ingramcontent.com/pod-product-compliance
Lightning Source LLC
LaVergne TN
LVHW090155080826
844660LV00013B/812/J

* 9 7 8 1 4 8 7 5 0 5 0 3 5 *